Atlantic Challenge

by
Angus Matheson MacKinnon

P.O. Box 1878,
Sydney, NS ,Canada

ISBN 0-9698337-3-3

Canadian Cataloguing in Publication Data

MacKinnon, Angus
Atlantic challenge : epic solo voyage across the Atlantic

ISBN 0-9698337-3-3

1. MacKinnon, Angus—Journeys—Atlantic Ocean. 2. Research II (Sailing ship). 3. Sailing, Single-handed—Atlantic Ocean. 4. Voyages and travels. 5. North Atlantic Ocean. 1. Title.

G530.M32 1995 910'.9163'1 C95-950294-7

Working on foredeck with Mary, in Sydney

Launching

Foreword

Crossing solo over the Atlantic is never the same for everyone, man or woman. Each voyage is as different as the moods of the ocean, and as definitive as the weather, among many factors, dictates.

In this respect my voyage is no different from that of others. At the same time, because this is so, my voyage was unique to me.

Also, while I anticipated a straightforward crossing, which, logically you would expect in the middle of summer, it turned out to be something very different, and evolved into what was, as far as I know, an unprecedented challenge. I could have declined, and bowed to the negative events of Providence, and hailed a passing ship. But I did not do so.

That is what this book is about, namely accepting an unprecedented challenge. What made me do it? That's a good question. All I can say is that I could not resist it.

Angus Matheson MacKinnon

Arnish, October, 1995

Acknowledgements

To Doug of Dick's Marina, Sydney for all help, getting *Research II* ready.

To John, J.R. and Brad of Northeast Canvas and Sails, Halifax for getting my experimental sails and double rigging completed in time.

To the Canadian Coastguard Service in Halifax and Sydney for watching out for me.

To aircrew of Maritime Command for *farewell* pass on leaving Canadian waters.

To the Canadian Broadcasting Service and the Cape Breton Post for keeping my friends up to date on my doings at sea.

To coxswain Neil Collins and Damien Murphy of Irish warship *Le Eithne* for a Celtic welcome, and taking messages for my wife Mary.

To Captain Charles Buckle, for advice and help after arrival in England.

To all the members of the Swanage branch of the British Royal Lifeboat Institution for their kindness and help.

To motor yacht *Princess Amarant* and fishing boat *Catherine* for all kindness.

To Captain Neil M. Hardy, honourary secretary, Swanage branch R.N.L.I., for getting photos and information in time for publication.

To Mike, Martin, and Nick and Peter for looking after *Research II* after my arrival in Swanage.

To my wife Mary, for backing me prior to, and during the trip and afterwards proofreading this manuscript for publication.

To all the friends known and unknown to me, in Canada and in Scotland, who were praying for me, even though many of them did not think that I would be coming back.

To one and all, I say a big Thank you.

A.M.K.

CONTENTS

Saying Good-bye to friends in Sydney

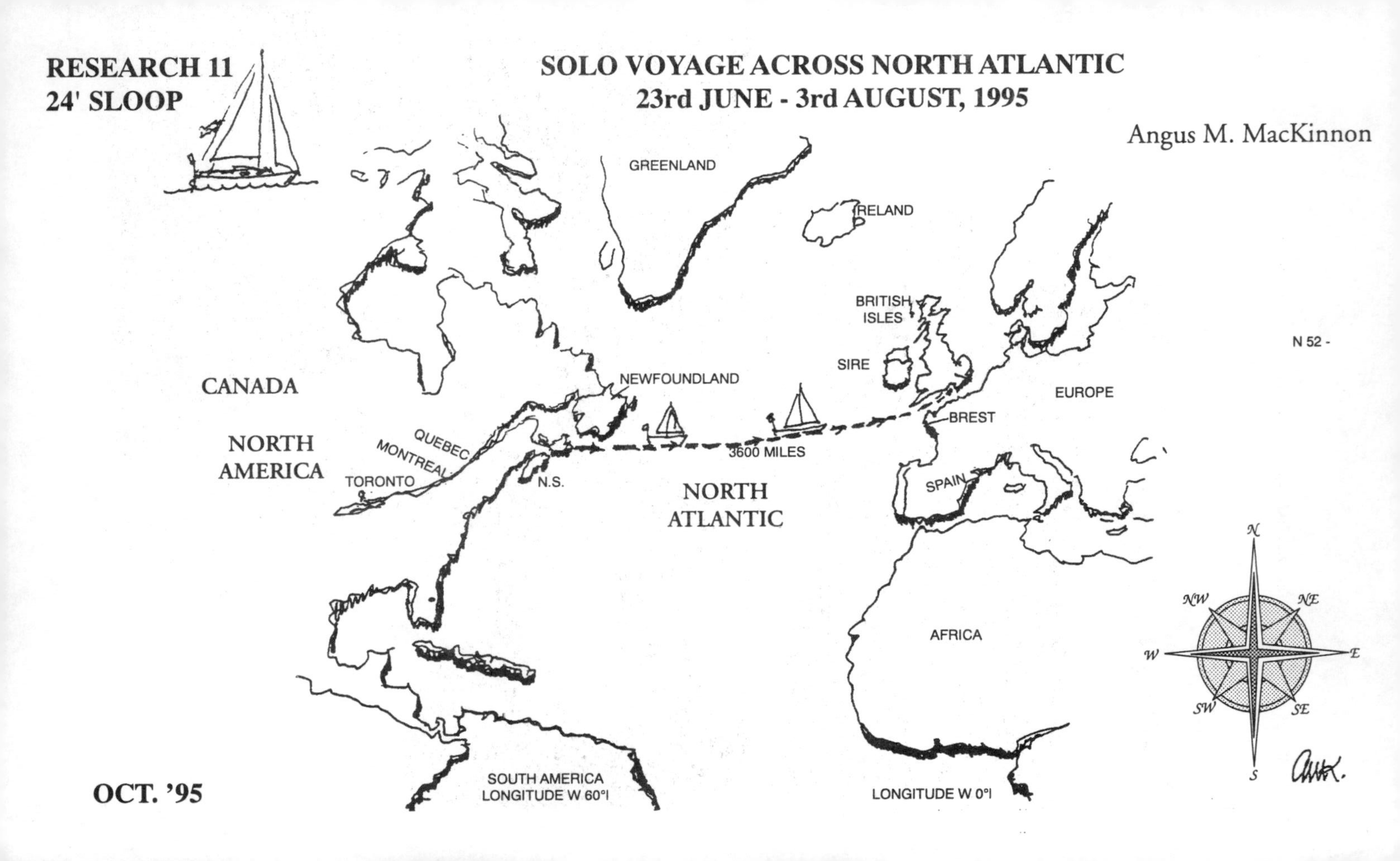
RESEARCH 11
24' SLOOP
SOLO VOYAGE ACROSS NORTH ATLANTIC
23rd JUNE - 3rd AUGUST, 1995
Angus M. MacKinnon
GREENLAND
IRELAND
BRITISH ISLES
N 52 -
SIRE
NEWFOUNDLAND
CANADA
EUROPE
BREST
NORTH AMERICA
QUEBEC
MONTREAL
TORONTO
N.S.
3600 MILES
NORTH ATLANTIC
SPAIN
N
NW
NE
W
E
SW
SE
S
AFRICA
SOUTH AMERICA
LONGITUDE W 60°
LONGITUDE W 0°
OCT. '95

PART 1

Getting Ready

CHAPTER 1

It's Time to Go

The worst of the Canadian winter was over; signs of spring were in the air. Among these was the relevant one for me, Hashem's Recycling, Sydney, was open. The snow had gone and trucks entered and left through the big gates, as they would do all summer. I stopped and went in to check if there was anything interesting. Over twenty years earlier, I had introduced myself to the proprietors, brothers, Paul, Abe and George and I was given a special permission to browse through the yard in order to salvage mechanical parts and metal for experimenting in my basement workshop, and fitting out boats.

This day in March, 1995 I found myself in my old habit, standing there in Hashem's Yard. The adrenaline was coursing through my veins as it had in the past whenever I saw something good. There before me in the middle of discarded gearboxes, electric motors, typewriters, lawn mowers, was a feast for the eyes, the very mechanism I was seeking to make a proto-type self-steering unit for my boat. Years before I had conceived the idea of a Scull-Oar. It was based on my experience fifty years earlier, when as a boy, I used to scull the small family boat across the bay in the idyllic waters of Lochewe, in front of my home in Aultbea, in the North West Highlands of Scotland, now the twilight zone of the Gaelic language and culture. As I stared in front of me, I could hardly believe my eyes. There was the mechanism, exactly what I required, comprising the best modern engineering and mechanical parts exactly identical to rough drawings which I had made of the projected proto-type in my study.

That was a crucial moment. Would I, now, not really very well, over the hill in many ways, having put too many years on the clock of life to consider any arduous physical adventure - would I turn away and satisfy myself with wistful dreams of what might have been, or would I pick up this 'find' for a few dollars, thus taking a step forward towards fulfilment of a long cherished goal, before it was too late? I tell you as it happened. As I stood there, a voice said inside me, 'Angus, you have to take it. This is it. You'll never get this again.' I bent down, picked up the mechanism. That was a decisive action. Within a few months, the Scull-Oar, of which this mechanism was to be an integral part, was to be the key factor in an ocean adventure, and arguably, the deciding factor between success and failure.

There was something else. I had just finished a manuscript on a new book of devotional thoughts on the Psalms, a work which I loved, but which inevitably involved subjective thinking and left me very tired. I had to do something completely different to restore my equilibrium and buoyancy.

On my regular visit to my family physician, I mentioned rather casually that I needed to make a little trip in the boat by myself.

He paused, then looked at me quizzically, and said, 'What's this nonsense about a trip?'

'I've always had it in mind, since I came to Glace Bay.' I replied.

He didn't say anything, but looked towards me. I think there was a kind of sparkle in his eye. I reflected in my mind as I thought of this. I wonder is Dr. Nicholson, who has spent nearly sixty years in this general practice and is a household word in the community, I wonder is he related to the veteran sailor yacht designer, Charles A. Nicholson, a founding partner in the famous yacht building company in Britain, Camper and Nicholson; or is he related to Ian Nicholson, ocean voyager and yacht designer?

Anyway, the doctor said no more, and I therefore took this as a reluctant acquiescence. He knew my health. He knew that I was no longer young. He knew that I had a disability, with generic blood-pressure problems, strange clotting of my blood with a bruise.

At home I told my wife Mary and my son Norman that the time had come, that my long-cherished solo-trip was the therapy I needed to counter the destructive effects of my broken heart, which followed a family sorrow. Furthermore, here I was, with a second volume of my books completed. I could not simply start another without a break. I had to do something completely different.

I had long before this subscribed to the doctrine of thought/action. By this, dynamic energy is not wasted by mulling over what one is going to do. Rather a person goes ahead to create or carry out what is conceived in the mind, or simply to do at once what is decided in the mind. This doctrine of thought /action produces dynamic results, even at every level of daily living as well as in the great endeavours of life.

'Go for it, Dad.'

That was Norman's reaction. Mary agreed, albeit with some degree of resignation. The question was, when would I go and was it to be the real thing, not just a little solo trip to St. Pierre and Miquelon, but the long haul right across the North Atlantic?

I really needed, as we all do, to let my heart wounds heal. I had to stop all reflective thinking over a family loss and leave the Lord, my Saviour, the Great Physician to bind up the wounds with his healing love. What a glorious God who reigns over the universe and yet has time for little people, to heal their sorrows! That is why believers through the ages praise him and live, looking to Him in life. Hear a poet king:

He counts the number of the stars;
he names them every one.
Great is our Lord, and of great power;
his wisdom search can none.

And in the verse before this in Psalm 147,

Those that are broken in their heart,
and grieved in their minds,
He healeth, and their painful wounds
he tenderly upbinds.

Breakfast Announcement

I shared my decision with the family. At breakfast I announced that I was going across the Atlantic. I would test my self-steering gear and once and for all try out the latest version of my invention the Auto-sail. Thirty-five years earlier, I had built a Heron sailing dinghy in the biggest and best guest bedroom in the Free Church manse in Strathpeffer, where I was minister. I made my special sails exactly to the dimensions of the standard one for that boat. On test in the sea, the sails worked. You could open or close them for sailing, by pulling a cord, in a moment. That first one was like a Venetian blind. I improved on it with the Mark II version. Now there was the Mark III on the drawing board and before I discarded it, I wanted to make a proto-type and test it once and for all. I knew this was the final one, for better or worse. I commissioned Northeast Canvas and Sails, in conjunction with Doyle Sails of Marblehead, to make the eight panels or sails, which would comprise the sail area of jib and main. I, meantime having had much of the material before hand, got down to it making the hardware, required for the novel rig.

There is no shame in failure. Shame is in not trying, or not doing our best. Thus, accepting the fact that the sails might well not prove viable - especially in light of the improved and simple developments of furling fore and aft in recent years, I resolved to test my ideas once and for all, even just as an experiment. Here was the opportunity, while at the same time testing my self-steering invention, in a trip across the Atlantic.

As you see, the motivation was there. Time was slipping by; years followed one another in quick succession. Soon it would be physically too late for me. "Time to go," said my understanding and beautiful wife, Mary, who knew there could be no healing for me without a complete change and this would achieve the double purpose of giving me time to heal and getting this sail business out of my system once and for all.

Health trip

And something more. This was a real health trip. I was but following the advice of Mr. G. Peabody Gardner, longtime director of the General Electric Company of the United States: in Boston, US. He was a great yachtsman, who wrote several books on his love affair with the sea and boats. He tells in one of his books about his vacations spent cruising in the Maritimes and especially in Bras-d'Or, how he once reflected on the considerable cost incurred, maintaining his fifty-foot yawl and commissioning it, each year. He posed the question, should he stop this indulgence and financial waste, as so many people including friends and relatives, viewed it? Then he looked at the other side of the coin, the health dividends these active physical demanding trips meant for him. As he put it, the money expended on owning and keeping a yacht in commission, was less than he would otherwise spend on physicians, were he was living an easier life of comfort and inaction. And who could put a monetary price on the ameliorative effect on health, which invariably is the accompaniment of an active holiday on land or sea!

I also saw this long ago. Boats in isolation may seem an egotistical indulgence of vanity and waste. But they comprise a vital factor as do most hobbies what ever they are, within our means. In fact spiritual thinking is often linked to the sea and the Bible and boats are not at variance with each other. Rather the therapy of the spiritual has a physical counterpart in the love man and woman have for boats. Of course the spiritual is greater, but there is something mystical and pure about the sea which does not exclude the essence of altruism nor the definitive forms of nobility that link our existence to the non-transient. Taken in the consensus perspective of all who have answered the elusive call, the sea and boats comprise the closest analogy in creation, to the spiritual voyage across the longitudes of time. It is not difficult to identify with the sea captain who became England's poet Laureate, John Masefield:

I must down go to the seas again,
To the call of the running tide;
'tis a wild call and a clear call,
Which may not be denied.

We are not all the same

Mark you, I do not claim that all should think as I do, and I respect, if I do not admire people like the Apostle John who wrote the Book of Revelation, when he moaned that in heaven, in contrast to his house arrest on the island of Patmos, there would be 'no more sea'. I think this really reflected his frustration at not having a boat.

For me, heaven is like a great harbour, like that of San Francisco, a vast estuary, where the tide is full in, where the waters cover every shore with their unbecoming waste and formless mud banks. I think of it with thousands and tens of thousands of boats, a continual activity as they pull into the dockside, in different generations of human life, in all the varied craft from ancient triremes to the latest fishing craft. I see ships like Asian junks, crowded with refugees, many battered and damaged as they limp in to journey's end and fulfillment of hopes. No one tying up at the quay of heaven is ever disappointed, who has followed the Way of Life. I can see them now as I reflect in my mind, sailing ships, and steamships, all crowded with human beings, and now and then a canoe or a little boat with a single soul. All, in the diversity of human conjecture, who have both heard and responded positively to the call of the Jew from the despised Highland province of Galilee, to follow him. They read the sign and were ready when they knew, that for them the call had come. It was **time to go**, and they launched out on the human journey that has an immortal climax and a dimension that is none other than life eternal.

The Challenge to Go

Time to go is an imperative. When the signal comes to you and me, we should be ready. That is the challenge. We are challenged to GO, be it a journey, a job to do, a sacrifice to make, an obligation to fulfil. The clock of time and of destiny ticks on. For we believe everyone of us, the humblest to the greatest, is created for a purpose, a role to play, an individual and distinctive pattern of life, which while giving glory to God, also serves to make our lives an experience of joy and fulfilment. These times of decision, are like the tide. When the tide is full, then we can launch the boat, not at low water. As Shakespeare put it:

There is a tide in the affairs of men,
Which, taken at the flood, leads on to fortune;
Omitted, all the voyage of their life
Is bound in shallows and in miseries.
On such a full sea are we now afloat;
And we must take the current when it serves,
Or lose our ventures.

'Time to go' says the sergeant, and the company go over the top.

'Time to go,' and the sprinter springs from the starter blocks.

'Time to go,' says the instructor, and the young boy or girl leans forward into a dive, for the first time from the heady heights of the platform in the swimming pool.

'Time to go,' as the final year student responds to a calling of service to manking and God.

'Go fo it, Dad'

I did.

Leaving Point Edward

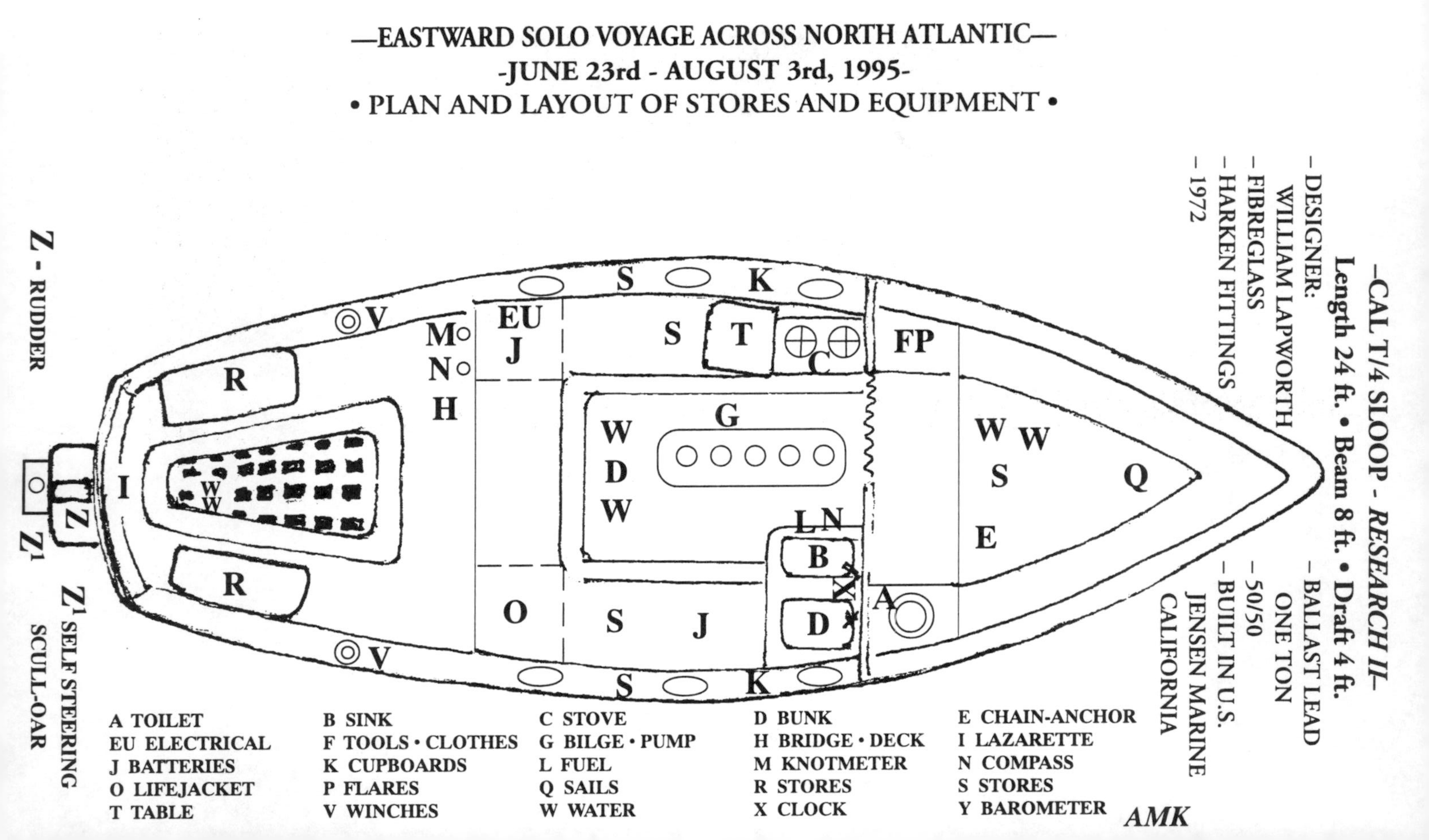
—EASTWARD SOLO VOYAGE ACROSS NORTH ATLANTIC—
-JUNE 23rd - AUGUST 3rd, 1995-
• PLAN AND LAYOUT OF STORES AND EQUIPMENT •
–CAL T/4 SLOOP - RESEARCH II–
Length 24 ft. • Beam 8 ft. • Draft 4 ft.
– DESIGNER:
WILLIAM LAPWORTH
– FIBREGLASS
– HARKEN FITTINGS
– 1972
– BALLAST LEAD
ONE TON
– 50/50
– BUILT IN U.S.
JENSEN MARINE
CALIFORNIA
A TOILET
EU ELECTRICAL
J BATTERIES
O LIFEJACKET
T TABLE
B SINK
F TOOLS · CLOTHES
K CUPBOARDS
P FLARES
V WINCHES
C STOVE
G BILGE · PUMP
L FUEL
Q SAILS
W WATER
D BUNK
H BRIDGE · DECK
M KNOTMETER
R STORES
X CLOCK
E CHAIN-ANCHOR
I LAZARETTE
N COMPASS
S STORES
Y BAROMETER
AMK
Z - RUDDER
Z1 SELF STEERING
SCULL-OAR

CHAPTER 2

Count-Down

The middle of June was my projected time of departure. I needed the three months at least since my final decision, for preparation of boat and gear. To friends I could only say that I was going on a trip, and I did speak of St. Pierre and Miquelon, the French islands off the south coast of Newfoundland, as a possible destination, but I also added that my trip was really in that direction. This was a relentlessly busy time of preparation.

Stores

I made an inventory of the needs of the voyage,which I reviewed with Mary, who after thirty-three years of marriage knew my likes and dislikes, and all my eccentricities.

For me, especially in the restrictive circumstances, alone on a little boat without refrigeration, it had to be a very basic, curtailed range of nutritious food. I reverted to the traditional Highland staple food of oatmeal brose, or in Gaelic *brochan.* This brose, -it could also be made with barley - was the food of young and old in the Highlands of Scotland through the centuries. Even until as recent as the Second World War, most children ate a bowl of brose in the morning before going to school, and very often ate a bowl of porridge a milder dish, before going to bed.

Brose was the secret weapon of Highlanders. The clan life came to an end with its distinctive symbol, the kilt being proscribed by a foreign English government, after the 1745 Jacobite assertion of Scottish Independence. Highlanders were recruited in their thousands by the shrewd William Pitt, the elder, prime minister of Britain, during the Seven Years War. That included campaigns against the French in

Canada, involving the fortress of Louisbourg, the gateway to the St. Lawrence and watchdog of the Maritime coast. Also thousands of Highlanders were part of the historic and honourable military duel between generals Montcalm and Wolfe, on the Heights of Abraham in Quebec. The corollary of this is in evidence in Quebec today where there are numerous clan names like Mackenzie and MacNab. After serving as soldiers in the British army, it was customary for men to be given a grant of land, where they built a home, married and settled down on their little farm with the security of a small army pension from the British government. Pitt recognized the unique value of Highlanders as unbeatable infantrymen, hardy and swift as the deer. He proved them all over the empire from Canada to India. Highlanders could march for days, could run in a charge, between the horses of the cavalry in battle, all on the strength of their traditional brose.

The Power of Brose

This would be made within moments in four ways. First, by pouring hot water over a handful of meal, in a pan. Second, by pouring cold water over the meal in a deerskin pouch. Third, by drawing blood from a sheep, cow or a slain deer and mixing this with the meal. Fourth, and this was for special occasions, especially in anticipation of battle, a favoured vocation of the Celtic peoples, whiskey was poured over the meal. This became a very potent food, a food that fired Highlander in body and also in spirit so that he became almost invincible in ferocity. No wonder *'uisge-beath'*, when used with discretion, was looked upon with a kind of reverence. It then was called *brochan-teine*, or *fire-brose*. Highland spirits in their more direct form are still considered to be the only foolproof protection against the deadly damp and cold of the hills and the glens.

You can imagine how the sight of Highlanders, in their various tartans according to clan, engendered fear in the hearts of the enemy. MacDonalds, MacKinnons, MacPhersons, Stewarts, Grants, MacRaes, MacLeods, MacKenzies, Munros and all the subsidiary clans, all lean and fit - it was a punishable crime to be overweight-

made them a ferocious antagonist, raring for the excitement of battle, supercharged with this unique fiery diet inside their stomachs, making the blood race through their veins.

The centrality of brose or porridge is institutionalized in a Gaelic *port-a beul,* a song that is a blend of music and words and is therefore called mouth music.

Brochan lom, brochan lom,
Brochan lom a suithean.
Thugaibh aran do na gillean
Leis a brochan suthean.
Brochan lom, tana lom,
Brochan lom a suithean.

But enough, I just cannot over emphasize the importance of brose in the psyche of the Highlander. I could not go wrong with a bowl of brose in my stomach and this was therefore the chosen basic part of my staple regular diet for most days at sea. Many lone voyagers have relied on Scottish oatmeal or rice as basic food at sea. Another guarantee of health was in the choice of two bags of potatoes and two bags of onions. Mary bought these selectively, and all the other foods, mostly in tins. These were packed in plastic bags, so many of each. The idea was to prevent the labels from deteriorating. When that occurs, there is no identity. You literally do not know what you have until the tin is opened. This results in a kind of speculative gambling. You do not know what you are going to eat for a meal, but you can tell afterwards what you had.

The urge to experiment

Some people are happy with things as they are, whether the status quo is efficient or inefficient. Others, and I am one of them, just cannot help wondering whether there is a better way than that which is currently accepted as standard. This urge to experiment was a real factor behind my trip. I wanted to test my idea of what I long ago called the Auto-sail and this trip was the perfect opportunity to put a prototype through its paces in all kinds of conditions. This would be the last version and I could not rest without giving it a chance. If it turned out to be successful, good and well; if not there was the satisfaction that it had been tried. John and Brad of the firm of Northeast Canvas & Sails in Halifax, in conjunction with Doyle Sails of Marblehead, Massachusetts agreed to make the sail panels, four for the fore boom and four for the main boom. I had much of the material for making the hardware, like the two special booms with goosenecks which swivelled from the mast. These were a foot lower than the boat's designed rig, an arrangement which on the passage had nearly fatal consequences for the ship's crew. There was a lot of work in making all the extra rope work. There was a headboard for jib and for the main with sheaves so that there was the option of hoisting each sail panel separately on its own halyard. I had a system of quick release connectors to master sheets on either side of the mast leading back to jam cleats in the cockpit. As it turned out on test, several of these items simply fell apart. Ocean sailing conditions just cannot be compared to local coastal or inland conditions. It is beyond description, to try and describe the power that is generated at sea. Only the strongest and simplest fittings of sail and gear can stand up for any length of time, when you sail day and night in ever changing conditions, from calm to storm. Even the calm can wear sails and attendant gear, when the boat is rocking without the steadying effect produced when the sail is pressed by the wind.

Self-Steering

I worked every weekday morning from March 23rd making my Scull-Oar. This is arguably the most important item for a single handed sailing. I had the advantage of getting first class engineering parts from the discarded mechanisms in Hashem's Scrapyard. Nevertheless, I myself had to make vital parts which synchronized together. This meant trial and error, making and remaking parts with much intensive and exacting care, cutting and shaping in stainless steel.

About my concept of the Scull-oar, I had learned from studying other units on the market, so that my own ideas were not something in a vacuum. We all are debtors to one another in life. All units embody principles by which the wind vane corrects deviation of a boat from its course, either directly by activating its own rudder or indirectly by counter action on the boat's own rudder. My unit is uniquely related to the principle of sculling, embodying a singular distinctive vital mechanical feature, never before introduced in the making of any other model. Furthermore it is a third of the weight of any on the market. It is completely portable. It has variable adjustment for height of the unit above the water, so that the blade can be lowered for depth in the water according to different conditions. Its reverse role as rudder in its own right, a role which mine would be called to fulfill, gives a dual value, a kind of insurance that contributes to peace of mind and added safety for the solo mariner.

Apprenticeship of the sea

I was tutored by my father and brother Ian, an engineer, in the basic art of seamanship, as a boy in Aultbea. Just think of my situation. I would wake up in the early morning, listen to the sound of the sea, hear the salmon jump upwards in the silence of the morning calm, or hear the distinctive sound of a shoal of mackerel as they somersaulted together a few yards from the shore. How easy to roll out of bed, say a wee prayer on my knees in thanksgiving to our Heavenly Father and add a request for a good catch of fish in the net. I used to ask God to keep out the dogfish. Then I'd pull on my trousers and soon would be rowing out to look at the trammel net. The trammel net is like three nets together. The centre net is usually one and a half inches square, - salmon mesh. On each side there is a net with a large mesh of six inches. In practice, the net catches all kinds of fish. They pass through the outer mesh, hit the centre one, panic and push this finely made one through the other large outer mesh on the other side. The effect is, a pocket is created from which they just cannot get out. One drawback is that often it is difficult to extricate a catch. I think of several times when we had difficulty in doing so without tearing the net. This would be true when a powerful conger eel, four feet long was coiled inside. Remember such a beast is one of the most menacing creatures in the sea and very difficult to handle. While in the net, it is restricted. When you eventually slipped him out of the net, he made life difficult in the boat, to say the least. It was then a gladiatorial contest right there between him and me. Would he get his teeth into my rubber boot before I could incapacitate him! I think back to these days of simple and pure happiness. What a contrast to the restraints and limitations of school when I would come home on vacation throughout my teen-age years? I would dream all term of home and the joyous activity of boat and water. How utterly satisfying to look at the net as it came in over the stern, to free the lovely cod, *bodach ruadh* or *trosg*.

What joy to bring in a lovely plaice a *leupag*. And to crown a good catch, there was the odd salmon, *bradan* safely snooked in the all-purpose trammel net, with its scales freshly falling out, and covering your hand as you extricated it from the mesh of the net, a six, a ten, a sixteen pounder. Why, this was the life of a king. Our home table would be full and several needy neighbours would share in our provision. Then I would row over to my half dozen lobster creels, and invariably take home a goodly number of the metallic blue crustaceans, lobsters *giomaich*.

Boats

The *Cal T/4* was in many ways the ideal for a person of limited means. I had many boats before this, the plywood Heron which I built in Strathpeffer, a Harley Mead built gaff sloop the *Mascot,* which I acquired from the MacKenzies of Dalmore, Alness. Then I had a beautiful Shetland double- ender, built in the island of Unst. *Faoileag* like the traditional *sixreen,* generically the same as the Norse longboat. I had several other boats including the *Seal*, a beautiful thirty foot centre-cockpit sloop once belonging to the Wills estate, the Cigarette people who own the estates of Applecross, Wester Ross. It had a Thornycroft Handibilly engine, which I replaced with a Kelvin poppet valve. When I got the boat it was old and damaged. With much labour I rebuilt it in an endeavor like many others of limited means, to create my dream boat. I also acquired a forty nine foot Zulu fishing boat, the *Gift* and recommissioned her with a Gardner 5LW engine. Up until the 1960's, most fishing boats in Scotland on the West coast had Kelvin engines, most boats on the East coast had Gardiner engines. The same engines powered the double decker buses in all the big cities of Britain. The *Gift* was a real boat, and what a beautiful engine which I bought for very little from Wiliamson's Salvage, Inverness! It was nearly new and came out of a big road tractor which had jack-knifed on a corner - a common happening on the narrow twisting roads round villages in Britain. When the age of the motor car arrived towards the end of the 19th century, there was a clash of interests between those who had large estates and the public for whom roads had to be built. In Britain, the powerful families who owned most of the rural areas didn't like common highways to go through their private grounds. The common good was second to the interests of the historically established and legally entrenched. The result is a legacy of twisting roads meandering round these estates with high walls built at public expense. The worst effect, is a long list of fatal accidents directly attributable to the capitulation of public authorities to the will of the rich landowners. This has no counterpart in America and Canada, where you can cross the continent, motoring on long stretches of highway that take precedence over private interests, for the greater good of the public and national interest. The sad thing is that the general population accepted this cancerous moral evil with the resignation of religious predestination, a residual by-product of the Divine Rights of 17th Century kings in Britain and the carnage goes on. Most of the fatal accidents on the roads in the annual statistical records, are directly linked to this policy, begun in the 19th century and a grim legacy still embraced without challenge as we approach the third millennium. Check this on the coastal roads South of Greenock, on the sides of Loch Ness, in Ross-shire near Dingwall, in Sutherland between Dornoch and Helmsdale to name but a few locations of recurring road accidents. Visiting Britain recently, I saw there is some change in that the new motorways skirt the towns, and provide an alternative at least for through traffic.

Learning from old seamen

My apprenticeship for the sea was also gained in an informal way through seasoned advice from ex mariners, like John Bethune. My rowing companion and life-long friend, Kenneth MacLeod, who grew up to be a captain of a submarine service ship, rendezvousing with NATO submarines in mid Atlantic, spent many evenings listening to John Bethune's tales of the sea at the turn of the century, when he as a ship's carpenter and sailmaker, crewed the tea clippers commuting between China and Britain. These aimed to be first with the latest cargo of tea for the Exchange in the London market. These *greyhounds* of the sea like the *Thermopylae* and the *Cutty Sark*, also struggled, as all sailing ships in Europe and America especially, in a last valiant attempt to maintain sail against the inroads of steam power. Add to this the influence of many retired mariners in the Aultbea area, and living in the biggest war-time naval base in the Northwest of Britain, my acquaintance with boats and water was in a modest if only amateur way, not inconsiderable. You could say that this self preparation was the secret of self preservation, a necessary prerequisite in most cases of hazardous endeavor.

Specification and lay-out of boat

My *Cal T/4* had been built in California twenty-three years previously, to the design of William Lapworth junior. She had a beam of eight feet with a ton of lead right at the foot of a central orthodox airo-dynamically shaped keel. She had integrally built-up sides to form the cabin similar to many of England's Maurice Griffiths' designs like *Lone Gull* and its successors in Britain. But unlike his family designed boats, the *Cal T/4* was low and was essentially a small ocean racer. Apart from the shell of the hull there was added strength in the way that she was honeycombed with compartments up to about sixteen inches from the floor. There were no large bare areas of hull skin without corrugation of some formed construction. This is the key to strength, as used every day in sheets off metal and other materials in the building industry. The Chinese realized this long ago. They built one category of large junk, making the whole interior right up to the deck level, a honeycomb of compartments, so that the ship was not only immensely strong, but also practically unsinkable, as damage to the hull would confine incoming water to a limited area. In the case of my boat these compartments were also constructed as an integral part of the hull. And even below this in the formation of the reverse curve forming the keel and the transverse sections fore and aft, strength was built into her. She was fibreglass and showed little or no sign of her age. There were two reasons. One, the dryness of the climate and the natural heat where she was built made her fibreglass construction as hard as steel. Also she had been taken to Lake Ontario, sailed there but stored for years without use, while her owner a Dutchman was abroad.

Forward was a vee bunk, with storage below in four compartments. Next to it between the two bulkheads, were the head to starboard and a clothes hanging area to port. Inside the main cabin there was a sink unit and ice box to starboard. To port was room for the stove with pots and pans stored below. I had a small table hinged out from the top of the stove unit. Behind this was bunk or sitting spacc. On each side were slotted cupboards with an inset shelf on top just below the port lights. This feature which I had built into the yacht was of great value for deep-sea sailing as many vital stores and goods like navigation tools and books would not get wet. That has to be qualified by the effects of knockdowns. But even when these occurred, strangely no water came up from the floor. Only when water spewed in through the hatch directly, would there be wetting. Thousands of boats are still being built to the same design.

The *Cal T/4* was perfectly balanced with a large powerful rudder outboard of the stern and a long tiller. That last feature had its negative side. I think this was given to it so that a person could steer the boat from inside the companionway. This I actually did, at one point on my trip, by necessity. Besides the self-baling cockpit, there was access through a hinged seat to the inside. Also there was a removable vertical hatch, closed throughout my trip. This gave access to the inside of the transom so that you could check stern fittings. I had installed a stainless steel box around the rudderpost to hold the Self-

Steering unit. Two struts rose from this to each side of the stern guard rail. Staunchions and lifelines extended forward to the bow pulpit. I put new lifelines on for the trip and also an extra staunchion on each side just behind the pulpit. It seems to me that this is a treacherous area for anyone to be working on deck in any kind of sea, especially as is often the case, the lifeline is attached near the bottom of the pulpit staunchions. If ever I felt danger and fear of imminent loss of my life, it was while working there far out at sea on the foredeck. An extra set of navigation lights were put on the mast head. My knotmeter was not a log so that I relied on DR and Longitude bearings. The depth meter was used only out of curiosity even in the English Channel as I was not sailing near land. There was a clock and the vital barometer, with pleasant cabin lights. All this would require considerable electrical power. In practice only one or two items were in use at any one time. As I had left the outboard behind, I had to have an alternate source. This was a flexible Siemens Solar unit which I had on the cabin top or on the top of the dodger, when this was up. I had two heavy duty twelve volt marine batteries. I kept one fully charged and ready to replace the other if necessary. Navigation lights were always on during the night as a vital necessity. This would be in absolute terms, as *Research II* crossed the ocean into the busy Approaches to the English Channel, the largest concourse of ships in the world. An ordinary multi-wave receiver including short wave and VHF with independent batteries was my regular link with the world, especially through the BBC and CBC short wave transmissions. I took out the water tank. I chose to carry water in flexible plastic carriers. Should one fail or some microbe spoil the contents, then I had the rest all safe and sound. In the conditions of the ocean I, for my part, like the control and flexibility of using the portable five gallon carrier, with its own tap. I carried seven containers. One great advantage was that they could be placed in different parts of the boat. As the voyage progressed, you can imagine that the weight of thirty-five gallons would decrease. For sailing purposes all disposition of weight is important, especially in a small boat. For my trip it turned out that the disposition of weight by shifting stores and equipment would be a key factor in overcoming what might be termed adversity. From the day I set eyes on the Cal T/4, I knew she was perfect for an ocean passage.

Extra Equipment

I had a two-burner alcohol stove for cooking. It was in gimbals which I had made in stainless steel years earlier. There was a depthfinder, knotmeter and two short-wave radio transmitters. I had six extra circuits put in the electrical system. I had a barometer and besides the compass in the cockpit, there was another in the cabin which was handy to read, when indoors. I had a radar reflector near the cross-trees, which after a few days was transferred to the stern. Sadly, the location of the battery low down in the boat would make all my electrics the victim of incoming water as the boat was thrown about by the seas of gale and of storm.

My son Norman gave a good coat of anti-fouling to the bottom; a few other small jobs were done and *Research II* was launched and waited at the quayside at Dick's marina in Sydney, very convenient for final preparation and victualling. All necessary goods were loaded aboard, including tools, like hacksaw, files, adjustable spanners, large and small vice grips, and numerous shackles and extra fittings, and fuses. The mast was stepped, all shrouds and stays attached. All hardware relating to the experimental Auto-sail Mark III was shipped, including the two special booms which I had made with all the special fittings for the sails. These fitted into slides bolted to the mast to take the goosenecks. The foreboom swiveled at the tack on the mast, not at the bow. The boat's own boom was taken off from the mast and stowed on deck. The new booms fitted about one foot length below the original. This was to make allowance for the increased length of the headboard, also made in aluminum, at the top of the mast. At the time I failed to realize that the main boom, being a foot lower, meant the potential danger of being hit in a jibe when in the cockpit.

Charts / Navigation

Day after day, I ticked off items as they were attended to. Charts ordered in Sydney Ship Supply arrived, to cover the Atlantic West and East and the approaches to the English Channel. I also ordered one to cover the Azores and the Bay of Biscay, to be prepared if I was driven south. Sails at last arrived from Halifax, and shopping for numerous bolts and blocks for special fittings was over. I had a large coil of nylon rope. This would serve for extra sheets and numerous needs including replacement through wear and tear, an inevitable concomitant of any ocean voyage. I had Reeds Almanac, the Nautical Almanac, Sailing Directions for the North Atlantic, Shipping Routes, Course Protractor and parallel ruler. I had two sextants, but kept the better one at home.

I had also purchased a Garmin 24 Global Positioning System. I familiarized myself with this new wonder calculator weeks before I left. Released by the United States Military after the adventurous and exciting episode of the Gulf War, it has transformed all navigation, bringing it into the super- high tech age. I had only the basic unit without computerized charts and other accessories. Nevertheless, as long as I had dry batteries and reasonable skill, my position on the curvature of the earth's surface could, as a rule, be ascertained in minutes, by the computerized synchronization of satellite reception. Thus, when switched on the instrument gathered information from the satellites at that time passing overhead. Where three and preferably four were actively responsive, my longitude and latitude could register, as well as the course I was taking and my speed. Nevertheless, there were times, even two days at a time, when no satellite reading could be received. One should also remember that such negative times usually would coincide with bad weather when the sun also would not be visible for a sextant shot. Everything in this world has its limitations and life must be lived with adaptability within the given parameters. Thus the GPS complemented orthodox or traditional celestial navigation. It should be remembered that there are other areas of advancement. Ascertaining one's position through Dead Reckoning is made easier and more accurate for the ordinary mariner because of the instruments available today, without dragging a log. Accurate calculation of your position by DR is a very reassuring and satisfying activity, especially when you find that you can compare favorably with a GPS. Further, there are no 'black' days when correlation of satellites is impossible.

Doing one's best

Whenever the individual leaves the crowd by some endeavor, he puts himself on the line. For every doer, there are a thousand lookers on. For every person who sails the seas, there are a thousand armchair sailors. These last are the analysts, the dissectors, who make a study of the mission. They carry out a post-mortem; they give a gratuitous autopsy. They catalogue the data and with the precision instrument of the human brain, unoccupied itself with any dynamic purpose, they claim the liberty of making judgment on the individual who had the temerity to leave them, the armchair sailors, reading the magazines on shore. They imagine that somehow they are indicted and exposed in their paralysis of fear and inaction. But that is an aberration of facts. We all are different in our constitution. I recall, when living as minister/schoolmaster in Out-Skerries to the North of Scotland, some young men, brought up with the sea at their door, turned from a fishing life. One left to work in farming on the mainland; another left to become a fireman in London. The fact is that we all may be very much fulfilled in some other endeavor which is achieved without public notice or acknowledgment. As Milton put it: '*They also serve who only stand and wait.*' Failure is relative. To survive a voyage is ultimate triumph, irrespective of failure of gear or error of judgment. We are not masters of the sea. The sea humbles the mariner and after all calculation, there is still the x factor of Providence, the permissive will of the Creator who has the whole world in his hands, irrespective of what little man thinks or plans within the limited parameters of his finite knowledge at any one time of existence. *Man proposes, God disposes.*

The true meaning of 'failure'

The definition of failure with its attendant corollary of shame is in 'not doing our best'. Further, though we cannot always help failure in part, we can react positively to the visitation of misfortune and our doing so can mitigate the failure being dominant, thus turning failure into triumph. Then you have the sweet word of 'overcoming' where our life is linked to our partnership with our Maker and Redeemer.

Then our life is a record of victories, of overcoming, of being knocked down but rising up; of losing battles, but coming back again to try again and winning. This means that wh*en we do our best, God will do the rest,* a proven formula endorsed and proven by countless travelers to Zion over the centuries of time. Thus I approached my coming voyage. I knew only that when we have given an enterprise our best shot, God our Heavenly Father will see where we come short or failed, because we are fallible.. But the glory of it which makes us lift our voices in praise to heaven even above the wail of the storm, is this, that He who is mighty, is already in the cockpit, to keep our little boat afloat. He is there in the cabin in the dark where the mariner is thrown around, and He gives that special strength to go on bailing the hundredth bucket of water when the lone human being is closed in by the wildness of the elements and the claustrophobic pessimism induced by the night. It is He who then brings an end to the turmoil of the seas and smiles in the coming morning, with a clear sky, to lift up our spirits, a steady breeze and the warmth of the sun, to dry out all our soggy clothes.

Thus I prepared for my trip, stroking off items as they were dealt with, and carrying over as in an account book those still to be done, to the next day in my notebook. As the weeks went by and D-Day approached, the list grew less and less. Sadly we are human and fallible. Therefore there were omissions at the beginning and this, coupled with the limitations of memory and the stress of immediate concerns, had their own consequences. It is also true that I was older, my memory not being as good as it could be. Also the very reliance on visual lists in my notebook - an expedient used everyday as a minister in a busy parish congregation, had in it the potential for omission.

Sample of daily schedule from my note-book

Tuesday 13th June, 1995

Morning 5.30 a.m.

1. Bore top of Self-Steering rudder stock for control lies swivel
2. Clench tangs on booms. Must finish
3. Attach fitting for vangs on each boom-self threading screws

In Sydney

4. Collect sails from bus station
5. Shop Canadian Tire for oilskins
   water carriers
   Alcohol - two gallons at Home Hardware plus brass release clips
   Kerosene- one gallon
6. Get brass lamp from steel boat
7. Sydney Ships Supply. Charts, Reeds Almanac

At boat

1. Fix bracket on stern for self steering
2. Radar reflector
3. Fix Toilet valves
4. Fix on stern name
5. Fix control lines to tiller

Evening at home

Headboards for sails each with its own halyard - must complete tonight.

This is one random sample of the Count-down process preparation, six days a week between March 23rd and Take-off June 23rd. Each day began as usual at 5:00 am as a rule, unless I was not well. I had a short worship, singing a few verses of a psalm, read a few verses from the Word and a short prayer. Then it was orderly and systematic work until the evening. Only special visits to hospitals and homes broke this pattern and some of this I did on Sundays. Bit by bit, most if not all items were dealt with and humanly speaking I was ready. Count-down would call a halt to all preparation when it reached zero.

Research II would shortly leave Dick's marina in the sheltered waters at Sydney River, and exchange them for the undulating motion of the unpredictable Atlantic.

For the most part, D-Day (day of departure) approached with a slight degree of excitement, but also for me, an intensified effort to have all preparation complete. Once at sea, little or nothing could be done, compared to the pre-voyage time on land with tools in your own workshop.

CHAPTER 3

Taking leave of friends

The days passed in quick succession until the middle of June. I had to say Good-bye to many friends, especially those whom I knew I would not see again on earth. One special friend was William MacLeod. He had been in our home at Arnish some three months earlier with his wife Sadie, Stanley and Elsie MacRury, and Mrs. 'Billie' MacVicar. In some way these and others in St. Paul's, especially the Gaelic-speaking remnant, had a place for me as the equivalent of a 'minister without portfolio.' I recall their visit to our home at Arnish that Sunday and as we closed our fellowship singing a Gaelic Psalm, tears could be seen welling up in the eyes of the gentle Highlander, William MacLeod. There is no shame in shedding a tear when we think of God's everlasting love. Could it be that William felt within him, that it would soon be time for him to leave us for his everlasting home!

Shortly after that William felt unwell and dizzy. He was diagnosed in Halifax as having an inoperable brain tumour, giving him two months to live. My last visit to him was on Monday of the week of my departure. I gathered with the family in the General Hospital in Glace Bay, praying in Gaelic, the language of our fathers. I quoted then the universal and immortal hope of all who look to God in believing faith and live by His grace in the fraternal family of His church on earth, from Psalm 23:

Is e Dia fein as buachaill dhomh,
cha bhi mi ann an dith.
Bheir e fainear gu'n luidhinn sios
air cluainibh glas' le sith:

Tha'g aisig m'anam dhomh air ais:
'sa treorachadh mo cheum
Air slighibh glan na fireantachd,
air sgath 'dheagh ainme fein.

Seadh fos ged ghluaisinn eadhon trid
ghlinn dorcha sgail' a' bhais,
Aon olc no urchuid a theachd orm
ni h-eagal leam 's ni' cas;

English

The Lord's my shepherd, I'll not want
He makes me down to lie
In pastures green: he leadeth me
the quiet waters by.

My soul He doth restore again;
and me to walk doth make
Within the paths of righteousness,
even for His own name's sake.

Yea, though I walk in death's dark vale,
Yet will I fear none ill:
For Thou art with me; and Thy rod
and staff me comfort still.

My hand was on Bill's shoulder. His eyes looked out dimly as consciousness wavered between light and darkness, for he would be soon leaving on a journey for which he was ready, prepared with the shoes of the Gospel of peace through Jesus Christ and His Finished Work on the Cross. All else was now in the background, before him a road opened, a glorious road. He knew this, his dear wife Sadie, his children Sandy and Marlena and their children knew too, that it was time to go. For him it was time to go to his eternal home, to a God whom he had faithfully honoured and to a Redeemer whose shed blood cleanseth from all sin, of whom John the Baptist long ago, said when he saw Jesus on earth:

'Behold the Lamb of God,
that taketh away the sin of the world'.
(Gospel of John 1:29)

I took leave of my friend, as those who must part ways for a season. It was count-down for both of us. Within three days count-down would be down to zero, Bill to that land of eternal joy, I to the horizon of a new experience, which in the most pragmatic moments of thinking, I could not possibly anticipate. Thus in a sense we were both starting on a journey into the unknown. For all knowledge of eternal things or of voyaging across the ocean, must ultimately be learned in the consciousness when we experience it and that infers the prelude to each is based on the knowledge of faith. For both the billows of the spiritual Jordan or of the Atlantic would rise to shake our small craft. For both, it was our souls or spirits which were really on test, to triumph or be defeated. But more, for both it was the same Lord and Redeemer, Jesus the Christ, who would take us to the other side.

I parted from my friend, that faithful elder William MacLeod. He was not unique, for the world has many unsung heroes in Christ's service, humble people living a life of outgoing kindness to others and following their Lord. Of such is the kingdom of heaven.

There was one other visit I had to make. The retired matron of the Cove Guest Home had requested, through her cousins Charlotte and Kay in Glace Bay, that I visit her in Sydney. For years, I had known her in her professional capacity as matron. But that is not what stays in my memory. I remembered Anne MacAskill in a last vigil in the night hours, waiting for those under her care to pass from mortal sight. One of these was a Gaelic - speaking woman, a member of St. Paul's, a real untiring worker to the end of her strength. On that specific occasion I made a Gaelic prayer and quoted John 14:1-2.

> *Na bitheath bhur cridhe fo thrioblaid: tha sibh a creidsinn ann an Dia, creidibh annam-sa mar an ceudna.*
> *Ann an tigh m'Athair-sa tha iomadh aite-comhnuidh: mur bitheadh e mar sin, dh-innsinn-sa dhuibh. Tha mi'dol a dh'ullachadh aite dhuibh.*

English

> *Let not your heart be troubled: ye believe in God, believe also in me.*
> *In my Father's house are many mansions: if it were not so, I would have told you. I go to prepare a place for you.*

As Mary G. passed peacefully from earthly sight, the seasoned matron who had witnessed scores of old folks reaching the end, was weeping, not at defeat - but at victory. For there was an overwhelming sense of victory in the room that night. Now nearly twenty years later, Anne MacAskill herself was near the end. When I saw her, her mind was clear as a bell and her voice strong. She was not even lying down. She greeted me warmly and told me that the last call was near. I knew that she was ready for that last call. Her life was a long proof of walking in the paths of righteousness and obedience to her Master. I shared with her some thoughts of our Lord and his all-sufficiency and spoke of the glorious things that she often had heard about and believed in. The fact is that when we go through deep waters of pain and suffering as she was doing, with constant physical pain, the spirit flags, and weariness makes us forget the dynamic positives. I told her I was going on a trip on my boat. We parted, sharing a love to our Lord which made us love each other and believing that we would meet again in God's will in the place, the *house of many mansions,* which He has prepared for us.

Parting from friends, especially those like Anne MacAskill and William MacLeod, whom I would not see on earth again, had a peculiar wistfulness and poignancy, which could not exclude deep emotion. We cannot help it for we are made like this. In the bonds of Christian family throughout history and coextensive with the four quarters of the globe, partings are for a season only. Whether on the sea or in the spirit, Time to Go and Count-down at last comes to zero, but this is not a negative, but a calendar day in the chronology of life's journey. It is not the end of the road, but as the old Scot's woman whispered on her deathbed, 'It is only a bend in the road'. Our tomorrows are in God's hands, and we shall meet again in heaven.

Another William MacLeod, a contemporary of my father, whom I assisted at a communion weekend in Dornoch, in Sutherland in the sixties, spoke of his experience as a chaplain during the Great War, especially just before one battle, when a division comprising English and Scottish battalions were on the eve of leaving the trenches. The guns behind them had opened up a tremendous barrage, the usual prelude for 'going over the top'. With him was another chaplain, an Anglican. The latter came over to him and said:

"My friend, it's time to go.'

He paused, and went on:

'If I don't come back, we will meet up there.'

That Anglican chaplain did not come back. The other chaplain Rev. William MacLeod, my host, had a long life of distinguished service in the church and the community, before leaving earth's scene to join the company of the Redeemed. What a thought for all in the diversity of Christian discipleship and service, who comprise Christ's church on earth! What an immortal crown and full triumphant life is offered to young people as they stand on the threshold of adulthood! How our souls rejoice that all sorrows will be left behind, all pain, all failure, all darkness, all sin, - all because Christ our Lord has purchased a piece of real estate in glory for us, and makes us ready with the purity of righteousness. That is not a dream. That is a reality, which though hidden from our finite vision, will become visible in the immediacy of heaven, when we come into our spiritual inheritance. Hear John, as he beheld glimpses of glory, when he was banished to life on the island of Patmos.

> *'After this I beheld, and lo, a great multitude, which no man could number, of all nations, and kindreds, and people, and tongues, stood before the throne, and before the Lamb, clothed with white robes, and palms in their hands'.*
> *And cried with a loud voice, saying,*
> *Salvation to our God, which sitteth upon the throne, and unto the Lamb.'*
>
> (Revelation 7:9 - 10)

Lord, give us all such a passing, when the last call comes to us. So that the day of our death may be turned into one of rejoicing.

CHAPTER 4

Going Public

The phone rang on the pier. It kept ringing. At last I stepped off the boat and lifted the phone. It was George Garland of the CBC. I was brusque and off-putting in my reply to him. But grudgingly, I consented that he come and interview me. At least, I thought to myself, he had the courtesy of asking my permission, a little like the English executioner, who nervously offered an apology to Mary, Queen of Scots, with the dubious reason that the Scottish Queen had to be rubbed out to remove the threat to Queen Bess, who was at the time sitting on the English throne.

Sharing hopes with other people

You could not sail the Atlantic without going public. And when I think on it, there would be, as someone said, something anti-social and unnatural in doing so. Further there were practical considerations to think about. When speaking to the authorities about my intention, Wally MacLeod, a member of the Coastguard, and himself a boat owner, told me that I would be expected to inform them of my trip and destination. And on arrival, that I was expected to let them know that I had reached the end of my voyage safely. One is also answerable to Customs, but apparently only when you reach the proximity of the other side of the ocean. That for me turned out to be rather unsatisfactory.

Put your best foot forward

Once I knew the Press were onto me, I resigned myself to it. 'Well', I thought, 'if the Press is coming, so be it. Angus, you are a bit tired, on the go all day without your usual afternoon rest (*norag*). You have to smarten up. You are a terrible sight for the camera. You just cannot go on as you are and let your wife down. She would be quite within her rights to disown you.'

I took my own advice - there was no one else around at the time to offer any other wisdom.

I foraged in the suitcase in the boat and found a clean shirt and put it on, after a quick and summary wash in the questionable sea water of Sydney Harbour. With my best Cape Breton cap, I went off to the Shopping Centre and had a good meal. On my return to the marina, there was the semblance of a crowd beginning to gather near my boat. Mary, my wife was there and Fiona Jane, my daughter, with her Finnish friend Mina. Also there were reporters: George Garland from the CBC and Dan MacGillvary from the Cape Breton Post. With these were their photographers, and camera teams, led by Vaughan Merchant for the Post and Gary Embrett for the CBC. Vaughan Merchant was an immigrant Englishman who thawed me out of my suspicious frostiness, by his seeming enthusiasm for my trip.

You'll never see him again

Some of my closest friends and many people whom I did not know personally, did not entertain an optimism with regard to my immediate future. It was easy to imagine when they heard of my departure, that they shook their heads in sorrow, resigning themselves to a press report with negative bulletins after an appropriate and discreet interval. I could imagine hearing: 'Scots Canadian sailor succumbs to storm', 'Minister goes to Valhala'; 'The demise of the ancient mariner'; 'One way ticket for solo voyager'; 'Clergyman makes supper for sharks'. Fortunately all such prognostications were just imagined and are far from reality.

No going back

I was committed to going now beyond any question. In a way, the final decision was made for me. The Press were the heralds who were given the license to proclaim my departure. Skepticism might colour their views, but it was their business to boldly break the news in newspaper and radio and television. It was left to me to give substance to all the fanfare.

In effect, the media pulled the trigger on the starting gun for me. I was like the runner, still with my feet in the starting-blocks, making last minute adjustments. Suddenly, the CBC TV and ASN in the Maritimes and the Cape Breton Post, fired the starting gun. For me, the poor lonely soul had no option but literally to take off.

With the cameras on me and amid expression of best wishes, I backed out from the quay, calling to everyone to behave themselves when I was away and telling them to make sure to be in church on Sunday. The thought did occur to me, that I might appear a bit hypocritical, as I would be absent from pew or pulpit for the immediate future. The wind sprung up and darkness was not far away, as I sailed off into the evening, down stream through the estuary, past Sydney on the starboard with its glittering glass government buildings, contrasting with the grim pillars of the languishing SYDCO steel plant, now sold to China. To port, was the residential area of Westmount, the West end of the city with the Dobson Yacht club, where the stern of Martin Brennan's *Sorca* could be seen jutting out from the quay.

Engine or no engine?

After some thought, the decision was made to leave my Evinrude outboard at Point Edward. I did not like the thought of having a gas container inside the boat with the potential of its obnoxious smell, when there would be the heavy rolling movement in bad weather. Also, considering the extra weight, it did not seem sensible to drag the engine across the ocean, just for a few miles manoeuvring, in the English Channel. That reasoning, though plausible to me at the time, had its negative consequences, and in retrospect, the decision was the wrong one, and one I would regret. But we act true to character, and Norman, my son, has repeatedly observed that Dad seems to like the 'hard way' as opposed to an easier way, when it comes to boats. My own self-analysis leads me to think that I am irreparably tholed to my early upbringing of hard labour when the Highland boat the s*goth* and the Shetland *sixreen* had a simple tanned lug sail. Then apart from use of the sail rowing was a daily task, six miles being a regular chore with my friend Kenneth MacLeod, and sometimes twenty miles, when we would return from *Sgeir an Araig* and *Fura,* the location of the haddock bank at the mouth of Loch Ewe by going right around Isle Ewe.

At Point Edward I spent the night tied up to the quay, not far from an Italian warship which was visiting Canada. All next day I spent preparing the boat, especially the experimental sails, for the Atlantic. As I worked I thought about my trip, and the conviction came to me that I was doing this trip vicariously, just a bit like the minister or priest for the congregation. A whole lot of people looked to me to live out the experience, and though they did not feel called to do it themselves, they joined with me in spirit, in the doing of it. Mary, faithful Mary, had taken home items which I wanted to leave. Thursday morning she was there again with the camera to record last minute scenes of my departure. There was a swift tidal current right in front of the quay which pulled any craft into the channel. With this and the fitful and uncertain wind, I just could not get *Research II* back to the quay to take my leave with a final embrace of my wife before I left. Also she had a Hayward safety harness and a camera for me. I called to her to throw the safety harness to me as the boat passed as near as possible. Alas, it fell short and went to the bottom. There again, it seemed I would have to do it 'the hard way'. I would have to do without the camera as well. I had enough, I swung *Research II* around. That current was determined that I'd never get back to the quay.

I'm off, Mary, my darling, I'm off,'

'Mo ghaoil ort. Tha mo cridhe briste ga'd fhagail'

(I love you. My heart is broken, leaving you)

I heard myself calling out these sentiments over that seemingly unbridgeable gulf between *Research II* and the quay. The thought that we would never meet again, did pass through my mind, like the shadow of a cloud silhouetted across the sun-bright field on a summer day. But the thought did not stay, rather it moved off like the cloud crossing the field, chased by the wind.

As I looked back to Mary, the clock of time turned back and images of the past when first we met at a Free Church Youth Conference at St. Andrews, came vividly to my mind in quick succession, Mary Stewart, the *clever* scholar of the prestigious Nicholson Institute of Stornoway in the Hebrides, the university student, young, beautiful and full of laughter and fun, whom I fell in love with; seeing her stepping off the train at the platform of the windswept Waverly station in Edinburgh on our first date; the beautiful bride whose wedding pictures were displayed an inordinately long time in Patterson's, the photographer in Inverness. Then the images passed into a blur from those of joyfulness to those of sadness, of hopes and disappointments, of fulfillment and loss, of prosperity and adversity, the thick catalogue of life's experiences together with our family, over the years. And always, there was Mary, the centre, the anchor of the family, and sharing with me a faith in Christ that bonded us together in the covenant of God's redemptive love with his people for time and for eternity.

Then, words of prayer passed my lips in a whisper,

'Lord, keep Mary and bring me back to her again from all the challenges of the seas, from fog and storm, from the darkness of the night and the hidden dangers of the ocean, which are all known only to Thee.'

Thus we parted. I turned *Research II* so that her bow reached for the estuary. On shore, Mary recorded my departure as I headed out of the Sydneys. The wind was uncertain and capricious, still one minute, and then blowing in little puffs. After a while, to my frustration, it strengthened from the northeast. With her usual rig that wouldn't matter, but I had my Auto-sails up. They clearly did not have windward efficiency, in a relatively narrow channel, and against a strong incoming tide. After some considerable time, and many tacks, I cleared the headland of Point Edward. By this time the day was wearing on, the sails were obviously not tuned enough for a boat to face the ocean. It's true that I could visualize them operating successfully, but only after several modifications, trial and error; in other words, further experiment and fine tuning. It is the same with all proto-types. Cars, however well designed, have to have all their bugs ferreted out by years of testing by the makers, before they are finally ready for public use. At this point, I knew that it needed a moderate steady breeze even for an initial testing. Instead there was this fresh to strong northeasterly flow, which kept *Research II* from getting away from the starting-blocks. Also, I would have to change the halyard arrangement whereby each panel of sail had its own independent of the others. The luffs would not synchronize with the nylon rope, even though I had the boom vangs which kept a steady downward pressure on the booms. All I could say at this point was that the sail panel attached to the forestay and the sail panel attached to the mast were a success. But the free standing panels just could not keep a straight luff. There was an added reason for this. Because they were all long and narrow, being vertical, the sail-makers felt that they should omit embodying the usual curvature in sails. It was believed that if this had been done, the sails would be flapping and unmanageable.

With just a hint of disappointment, I considered it wise to change over to the ordinary proven sails, and reserve the option of using the Auto-sail in different combinations, all or parts of them, during the voyage. I tied up at the Northern Yacht club in North Sydney and spent the evening on deck work. I still kept my new main boom in place and lashed the regular one to the deck. Later on it will be seen that this would be something I would regret, and which would have near fatal consequences. The foreboom was left in place with the gooseneck at the mast opposite that of the main boom. The taps of two water containers were not shut off properly, with the result that they were half empty. I topped these up, so that I was starting off with the seven full ones. The containers were distributed fore, aft and in the middle under the companionway compartments, low down. This was one great advantage later on. I could use the weight of the containers, which was considerable, along with other weights like the anchor and chains, as well as stores, to trim the boat. A sailing boat is essentially like a see-saw or an old fashioned scale. There is a point of balance near the centre of its length, but not at the centre. The shape of the hull and displacement decide this. If weight is kept close to the centre, the sailboat is lively and responsive. If the weight is concentrated at either end, the boat will have a different motion. The bow will lift slowly to the waves. Again it depends upon the shape of the boat, what is the right deployment of weight. I speak of this here, because the trim of the boat was to be a vital element in the progress of *Research II* and meeting the challenges that lay ahead of her. Throughout the evening I went over everything I could think of. Every turnbuckle was checked for wiring and every locknut and clevis pin. I was more conscious of the rigging than the boat. I had good reason.

Some years previously I had a nasty experience one morning, leaving the Sydneys to take *Research II* round to Catalone in Mira Bay. That morning, conditions seemed ideal. The wind was on my quarter from the North West, moderate and steady so that I had the big genoa set. By the time I had reached close to Low Point Lighthouse near New Waterford, the wind had increased so that *Research II* was flying along. I regretted having the genoa up and was just going to get it down, when there was a crack. In a moment I saw what happened. The backstay holding up the mast had broken, the dread of every sailor. Worse still, the break was at the masthead, so that there was no way that it could be repaired. The ensuing minutes became a crisis of considerable proportions. There was I, alone, the wind increasing by the minute, a large sail area set, the mast wobbling so that my eyes were fascinated with its movement as it bent forward, held only by the mainsheet attached to the boom. At stake was the value of the mast, possibly the sails, and worse still the cabin top, which could be ripped out if nothing could be done.

Instinct led me into action without delay. I relate the sequence that followed as best I can remember, for there was no time to sit down and make decisions; as we are so prone to do in the protracted sessions of committees, a favourite past-time at all levels of society. There, projected decisions are mulled over, and decisions are seasoned and modified so that the outcome is matured by time and the wisdom of many. A crisis will not wait for a committee. Consider me at this point. There was no time and there was no one else to consult. Yet it was the hour for action without delay. A dismasting is a mini-disaster and an economic loss where there is no insurance cover, as it was in my case.

I jumped up and grabbed the end of the boom, adding my weight to the pull of the mainsheet on the horse. I hung on as *Research II* heeled, presenting a figure of a man dangling one minute over the water, then back over the cockpit. Here the long tiller became my salvation. I found it with the toe of my shoe as it swung uncontrolled below me. I pushed it to starboard and held it over. True to its character, *Research II* responded and the bow turned in a half circle still at speed. She now was turning back to Point Edward and Sydney. As she came around into the wind, the pressure slackened on the sails and therefore on the mast. I leapt down and pulled the starting cord of the Evinrude. The engine sprang to life; I pushed it down in the slot and into forward gear. Then throttle, and we were in business. I grabbed the tiller and all in a few moments, I had *Research II* head to the wind, without giving her time to stall. If so, she would have fallen away to race again down wind and to potential calamity.

When the boat was going on a steady course, I had time to figure out a temporary answer to bring us back to port. There was only one solution. I would no longer be using the foresail, as I wanted the sails down as soon as possible. Very quickly I left the tiller, loosened the halyard and pulled the genoa down inside the lifelines. I disconnected the halyard from the sail, led it aft and tied it to the backrail. Now I had a substitute for the backstay and all was safe. The mainsail stayed up until I approached the lee shelter of Point Edward, then I took it down. As I motored back into Sydney, it was with a great sense of thankfulness. I looked at my watch and saw that the whole traumatic experience took two hours until it was over. But the moments at the crisis point were crucial. The long tiller enabled me to bring the boat around into the wind to take the deadly pressure off the mast. Secondly, the outboard did not fail me.

Had it done so, the outcome would have been diametrically different. If there was a topping-lift, that is a stay from the masthead to the end of the boom, this could have been used as an emergency backstay. As it was, all the pressure was acting through the leech of the mainsail and at any moment the sail or the sheet could tear or pull out of the horse below fixed to the bridge deck.

That experience made a deep impression upon me. From there on, I resolved that there would be two backstays. The cost, although considerable, did not come into it; I had all the rigging doubled. It was one of those imperatives which must be complied with for my very life. Now I examined every item of the rigging for the second time in case I missed something, so that all turnbuckles were tightly wired, all locknuts tightened, and all clevis pins safely secured. I had learned my lesson the hard way.

It seemed to me that I had looked after everything vital for the trip. By nine p.m. I relaxed. I went ashore and phoned Arnish to ask Mary to bring over the camera and the new suit of sails, main and jib. I just could not get through on the phone, and after trying several times, some weariness came over me, coupled with pain in my left leg from standing still. In short, I put the phone down and did not try again. I had had a long day, since I woke at 5 a.m. I was quite weak and had no nap, as I was used to having during the day. When I lay down, I fell instantly asleep.

RESEARCH II - SOLO VOYAGE - CANADA TO ENGLAND

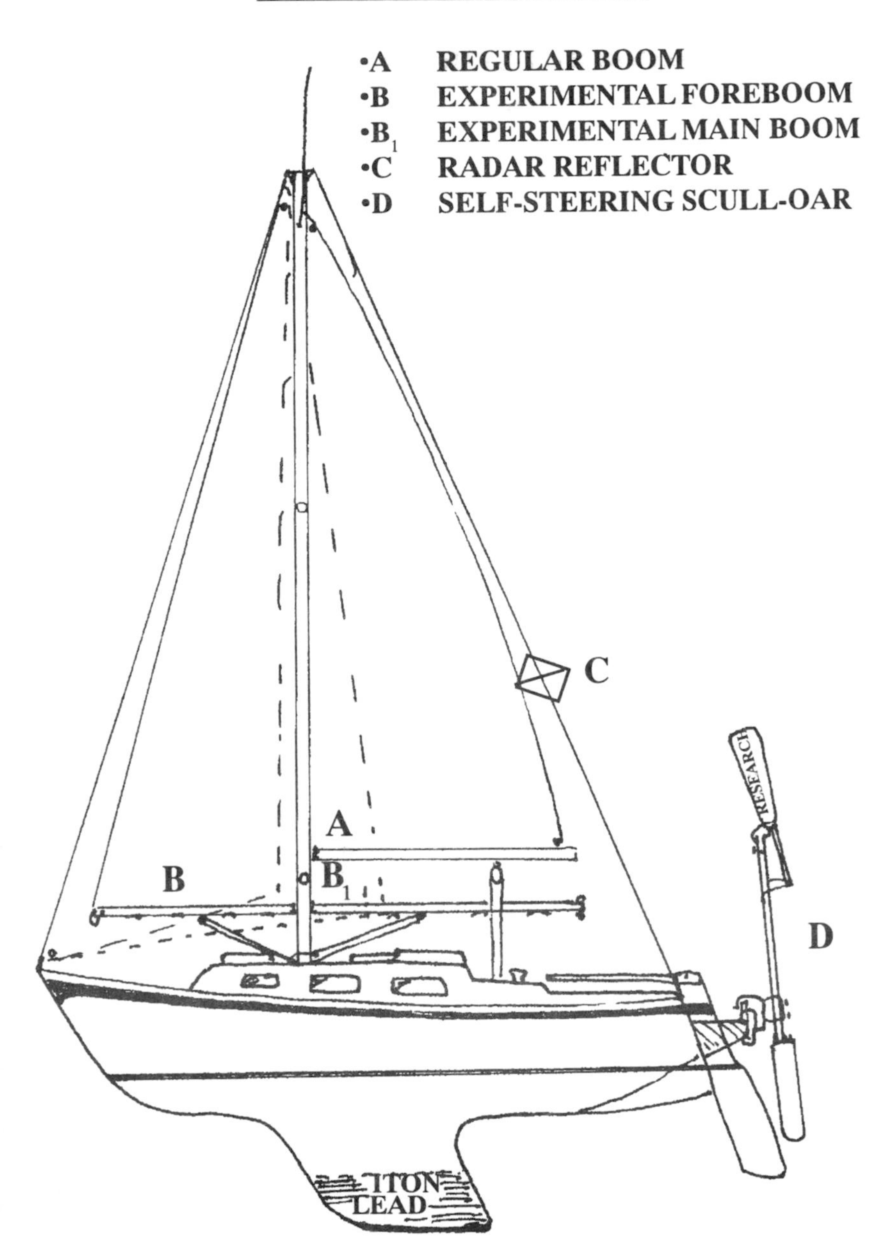

OCT./95

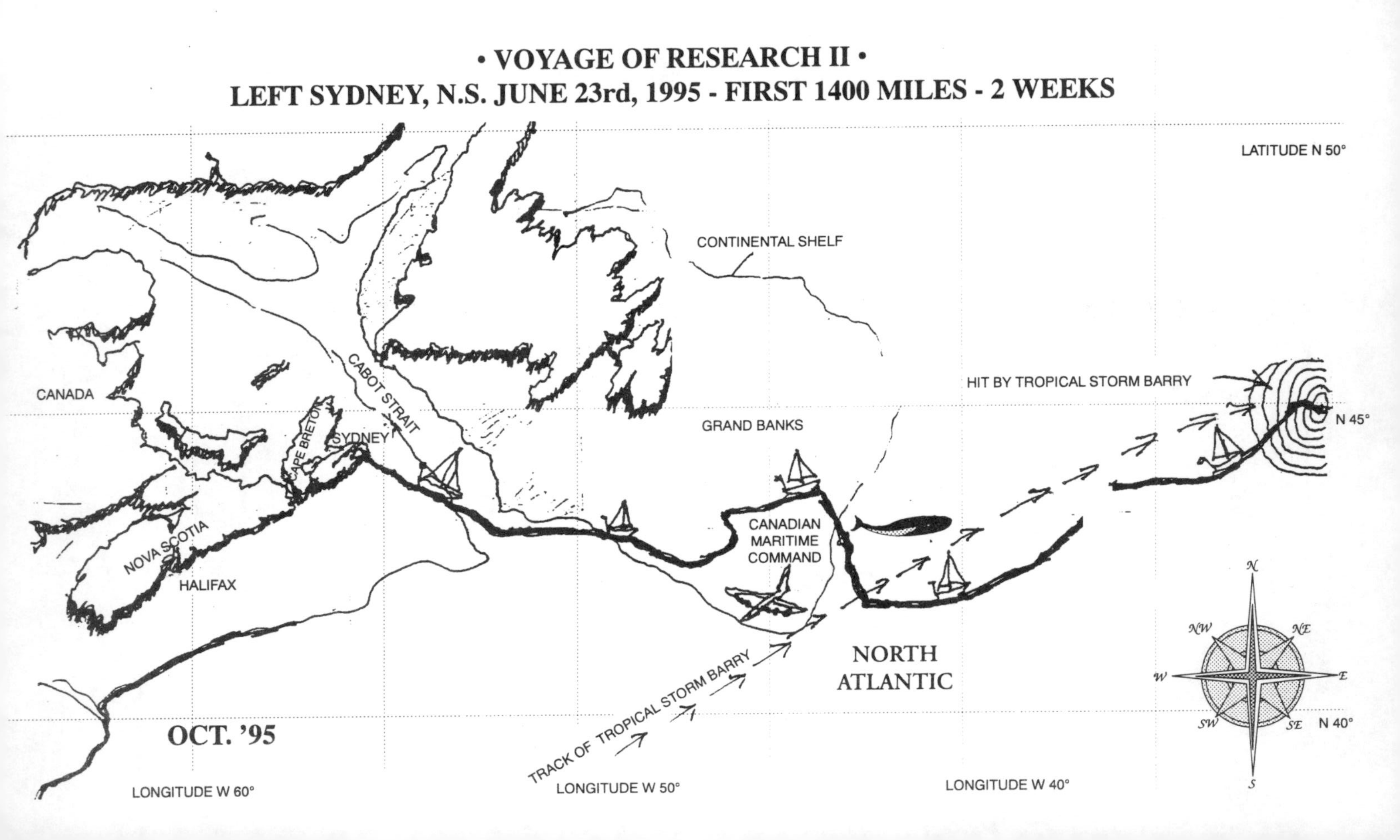
• VOYAGE OF RESEARCH II •
LEFT SYDNEY, N.S. JUNE 23rd, 1995 - FIRST 1400 MILES - 2 WEEKS
LATITUDE N 50°
CONTINENTAL SHELF
CANADA
CABOT STRAIT
CAPE BRETON
SYDNEY
GRAND BANKS
HIT BY TROPICAL STORM BARRY
N 45°
CANADIAN
MARITIME
COMMAND
NOVA SCOTIA
HALIFAX
NORTH
ATLANTIC
TRACK OF TROPICAL STORM BARRY
N
NW
NE
W
E
SW
SE
S
N 40°
OCT. '95
LONGITUDE W 60°
LONGITUDE W 50°
LONGITUDE W 40°

PART II

The North Atlantic -The American Side

CHAPTER 5

Departure

On Friday morning at 0700 hours, *Research II* slipped away from the Northern Yacht Club. It would be the last contact with North America. Now she headed out before a southwesterly early breeze. It was a glorious morning. As we passed North Sydney and drew near Low Point Light, the big Ferry backed out from the pier and then turned to sail for Port au Basque in Newfoundland. Thoughts came to me linking the past with the present, as the huge ship thundered past me. Here I was in my little boat going off to Scotland and this ship going off to Newfoundland. The clock turned back to the beginning of the century in my mind, as I thought of my father who as a young Highlander came out to Canada, until he returned to fight for his king and country in the Great War of 1914-18. I identify him with Newfoundland as he did at least one trip on a fishing schooner, working on the Grand Banks. Subsequent to this, he fished on a big schooner in the Hudson Bay. He used to tell us, as children, how a feud arose among the crew which comprised Portuguese, Norwegians and also Japanese. Tension at last reached a crisis and a deadly fight broke out on deck. He recalled the fisticuffs and men falling down. Then, he saw the sun glinting on a knife in the hand of a fallen crew member. In a moment there was blood spilt and several men severely injured. It stopped when the skipper fired a shot and at the same time the burly mate lifted two men by the neck, bringing their heads together with such a crack that they collapsed at his feet. That was enough. The rest scattered, licking their wounds. I recall my father relating this, as he sat in the armchair on a winter night with my mother beside him and us, all eight of us, round about the open peat fire in the family room of the manse. My mother was darning socks, which in those times were all of wool and lasted only days before holes came on the heels. There was no end to darning.

Two girls were also working with wool and needles; another was sewing some bit of material for a dress, with the help of her mother to guide her; the rest were doing their homework. I as an exception, with a reading book on my lap, was intently gazing into my father's face as the vivid picture drawn by his words registered forever on the screen of my young mind. There was no need of television to fire the imagination. Good story telling and the stillness of attentive, drama-hungry children made time fly. Backwards into the past of memory, or forward to the uncharted future in speculative predictive possibilities, what did it matter? It all filled an evening with productive delight. The clock of time is always to me a local expedient; like the marks on a ruler or a measuring tape for easy reference and convenience to separate and store our different human experiences in this finite world. Each life is made up of past, present and future, but the mind can bring all these into the immediate consciousness. It is as if time is the servant of reality and, as such, is secondary as an expedient, as opposed to generic human experience.

Research II passed Low Point making her way slowly, for the wind was light, avoiding the many buoys of lobster pots. These and fishing markers were everywhere with scores of lobster boats and prawn or scallop draggers, going about, doing their business. The lobster season in this area began on the 15th of May and would not finish until the 15th of July. The boats came from the coastal towns in the immediate area, many of which I recognized. Fishermen took time to give me a wave. Some I knew personally, from Glace Bay, New Waterford, Lingan, Port Morien, Main-a Dieu. They knew that my little boat was not on a little coastal cruise. They would read the signs. She was low in the water as she was loaded with stores; and at the stern was the Wind Steering Vane which is the hall-mark of a yacht making an ocean passage, especially where the skipper is also the crew, the cook and the mate.

Goodwill

I felt that I had the goodwill of Cape Breton. It's true that many friends would not like me to go on this trip. But they would not be offended as I did so. Besides the therapy that I expected to gain in the experience, there was an inner compulsion, which just could not be denied. As I was born by the sea, with the changing music of wind and wave wafting through the window of my bedroom with its enchanting call, brought up as it were, with a fatal love affair for boats, I felt that even in a humble way, I had to follow the immortal loners; like Slocum, Gerbault, Tommy Drake, Dumas Pidgeon or Chichester and many others who follow them, finding the experience of life alone on the ocean not necessarily a substitute, but at least a complementary and enriching experience as part of our life experience. Aloneness, hardship, the violence that only the sea can show, deprivation of sleep, the absence of all comfort, the imminence of death by the risk of storm or being run down by ships in fog, or the boat sunk by a waterlogged timber, or as the case was graphically told in Dugald Robertson's book and film, 'The Savage Sea', where the boat's two inch oak planking was splintered to matchwood by a whale, - it's truly strange how all these cannot cancel the call to launch out and head for new horizons, on the one road that connects all people on earth, the sea with all its hypnotic moods.

Motivation

Surely no one motivation completely fits all who go off alone to sea in small boats. Some do so as a recoil action to rejection on land; some because of failure to fit in to the many changing pressures that demand conformity and uniformity and that look upon individuality with something near hostility. Some go to sea alone, in order to 'find themselves;' some go in order to analyze life and sift truth in their consciousness, to find its essence. Some go to find spiritual affinity unimpeded by the distraction of noise and people and all the concomitants of our modern day, like a scientist who seeks out the isolation of the laboratory and carries out his tests in a vacuum, free from impurities and contamination. Some go in order to experiment and prove an idea. The reasons are many and various. But there has to be a bottom line, a kind of basic common factor shared by all. And by definition this can only be translated as a compulsion. In spite of all negatives, no lone voyager would have missed the experience.

I sailed along the coast with its rugged storm-eroded cliffs, passing in turn all the townships; New Victoria, New Waterford, Dominion, New Aberdeen. I came to Glace Bay with the landmarks of hospitals, churches and the power station. Even as I write, the fate of all three is in question in a climate of economic change. As I crossed the wide opening of the 'Bay', *Research II* made slow progress as she faced the contrary tide that flowed north between Flint Island and Schooner Pond. Eventually I got through, crossed the bay at Port Morien and closed in to South Head, at the extremity of the north west arm of Mira Bay. The day was now far spent and the evening was drawing near. The sky had lost its friendliness and clouds, strange and dark, formed hostile patterns in the north-west. I came close in to South Head. Immediately I passed it, Mira Bay came into view. This was the moment of truth, the last opportunity to go or not to go. Yet though I analyze it in these terms now, the thought did not occur to me to turn back.

Last look at home

As I rounded the point, the wind hit the sails. It came from the southwest at the head of the bay. *Research II* heeled over to port, tugging like a dog on a leash, willing me to let her have her head in the ocean element for which she was designed. My eyes scanned the long bay and reached up towards Catalone and Arnish, our lovely Cape Breton home. Dimly in the fading light, even with the binoculars, it came into my view. Shortly I would leave it, its idyllic setting and its beauty, and exchange this for the volatile and contrary motions of the North Atlantic.

I thought of my beloved Mary, and daughter Jane who would probably now be settled down for the evening reading a book. All kinds of thoughts met like the swirling eddies of the tide coming in to meet a river stream. But there was no turning back. My dream of long ago in Glace Bay now unfolded. I enacted it as the headland receded, and even the freshening wind urged me on, 'It's time to go;

its time to go.' 'That's the headland you saw in your dream long ago in Glace Bay, South Head.'

Yes, I was just passing it as I saw in my dream. All the voices seemed to agree, and within me the will assented, as white foam rose over the gunwale.

I was off, I slacked the sheets and turned east. On a broad reach, the sails filled away, *Research II* seemed eager to share in my destiny, to reach out, to launch into the deep, to try, and somehow whether attended with success or failure, ultimately to prove the triumph of the spirit. I steered a compass course to clear the East Scaterie light, blinking spasmodically on the outer extremity of the island, which geologically is a continuation northeast of Main-a-Dieu, and is separated from the mainland there by a narrow strait. Scaterie island is about nine miles long and was once a thriving and prosperous fishing settlement. It was evacuated some fifty years ago. At least one neighbour at Catalone, Jack Steele, lived there as a child, before all the families left. He told me of the simple life as the families of early settlers adjusted to that relatively hostile environment, the resourcefulness of the people in gathering the rich harvest of the sea during the summer, and the many ways in which they adapted to the long hard winter. All his memories of these childhood days hadn't a hint of boredom, but were crowded with reflection of excitement and action. Following the usual pattern of people being sucked into the vortex of expanding cities with often the shattered hopes of a better life, Scaterie, like a thousand geographically isolated communities, has now no human inhabitants. Visitors go there in the summer. The past is like a book they read, where the names of those who lived and died there are registered on the gravestones in the churchyard, the silent witness to the lost riches of a once thriving and contented people.

The Cormoranderie rocks

Darkness was not far away as I sailed past the island extremity. I could see the white Lighthouse buildings, until recently, occupied by families and latterly by the keepers on their tour of duty. What an impression of menace and danger presented, as I looked out from about a mile distant! The seas here were a turbulent confluence of wind and tide. *Research II* cut through this seething mass of conflicting waters, driving on to the east. Brought up to fear the sea and especially rocks, a chill passed through me, pervading my body right into my stomach, as I witnessed the scene between me and the Lighthouse. Stretching towards me was a long line of half hidden rocks. These jutted out into the Atlantic like the jaws of a crocodile, inspiring in one the same menace and fear. Who could tell the dark nights of the past when ships met their end in helpless capitulation to nature's ferocity? Was I not looking at a cemetery of ships and human beings - who could separate them- a cemetery of a hundred wrecks over the centuries of sailing and steam ships which were devoured by the insatiable appetite of these jagged and hungry rocks, smothered, as I watched, in a cauldron of boiling contradictory currents and seas?

Like Joshua Slocum, as he and the *Spray* turned away from Nova Scotia into the Atlantic and weighed up the pros and cons of his projected enterprise of sailing alone round the world and wondered what was before him, so I also on a much lesser scale reflected on what might be waiting for me. One thing was certain, I would soon find out. It was a relief to get past that last landmark of the continent, excepting Newfoundland, which in more ways than the geographical has a uniqueness of its own. I set my novel and self-designed self-steering gear. This was potentially worth two crew members but that potential had to be proved in practice. There was a kind of spice and excitement in contemplating the test. In the case of the auto-sail, I was going through the motions in testing it. I felt that I owed it to myself to give the idea, so long entertained, one last chance. But in the case of the Scull-oar, it was quite different. I was certain in myself that it was a winner, but subjective views and opinions do not cut ice in the world of reality. It had to be shown to be successful. There was nothing like an ocean voyage to prove it.

A car has to stop at a filling station to refuel, a horse has to get a rest and be fed; that is the rule of life. And I, who had been on the move all day since the early hours before dawn, now also felt the need to refuel. I checked out my stores and opened a large tin of Irish Stew, spooned it into a pan and heated it up on the gimbaled stove. Within ten minutes, it was ready and all went down the hatch, the whole panful, with the satisfying relish of healthy hunger, followed by a large cup of hot black coffee.

As I emerged from the cabin, I looked round about me in the fast disappearing light. Darkness rose from the horizon in the east, reminding me, as would be evident throughout the voyage, that night covered Europe, when day obtained in America as the earth turned on its axis counter-clockwise, opposite to the apparent movement of the sun westwards across the sky. The arc of darkness closing in the sky was like the retractable roof being closed over the stadium in the Skydome in Toronto. To the north, the waning moon was on its back, a pale and impotent disc, itself an indication of unsettled weather. Already the inordinate heat on the continent this summer of 1995 was causing a reaction on the sea, of cold and hostile air currents, sucked from the Arctic regions of north and east. Though I had bought an expensive Log book, I decided that my record of the voyage would be a combination of log and journal, where both instrument readings and calculations would be written inclusively with narrative and comment. In this way the record would not comprise two separate parts; how could they really be separate anyway? At first this log journal appears stilted and factual, but soon I loosened up and decided to expand by discoursing on themes as they occupied my attention. These may seem trivial to the landlubber, but they are of amplified importance to the lone mariner, where his habitat is limited to the dimensions of his little boat.

The log/journal for Friday 23rd June 1995: Sailed from North Sydney 7 am Eastern Time. Lovely morning. Fair west wind.

Forecast: Southwest wind 35 knots.

Traveling 'Companions'

Strictly speaking, I was not going solo. A lone cockroach showed up shortly after leaving port. He may have felt that, since *Research II* had said 'Good-bye' to Canada, he could safely come out without being returned and taken into custody for a misdemeanour. For my part, I felt that he might have friends aboard. It would never do to be soft in this respect. We are all influenced by past experience. Forty-five years earlier, when I was a recruit stationed in R.A.F. Bridgenorth, there was a plague of cockroaches in the mess. Young airmen lined up to have their plates filled at the heated stainless steel counters, with the white dressed cooks serving behind. It was a fascinating sight to watch cockroaches appear from every corner and face the hazard of trying to cross the counter. It was not uncommon for a cook to scoop up a crisp cooked cockroach along with the bacon and dump it into your plate - a kind of bonus. It was not the time to protest or go on hunger strike. That would only land you in the guardroom anyway, to face a daily routine of rigorous drill from an intimidating sergeant and a round of fatigues, doing the most unpleasant tasks reserved for miscreants on the camp.

Visions of these days came vividly to my mind, like freshly painted scenes on an artist's canvas, and persuaded me to take a negative approach. I had to steel myself and rationalize my ruthlessness in this. Was I cruel to God's creatures? Was I indicted as an enemy of life, rather than a friend of my fellow creatures? Would I be haunted, like the ancient mariner and *Research II* be visited with grave misfortune? He had shot the albatross as his ship sailed the ocean, and there followed the awesome consequences, told so graphically to the wedding guest in Coleridge's poem, "The Ancient Mariner." But we have to keep things in perspective. Surely a cockroach could not compare with a huge ocean bird like the albatross! Furthermore, I wouldn't mind one cockroach, but would it stop there? How many others were aboard? They multiply at a fantastic rate, and traditionally love ships. My artist friend and fellow Scot, Donald Shearer, told a story of cockroaches that I had never forgotten. Donald, then an art teacher, helped with supervisory duties when I was resident house master at Balmacara House School. Balmacara House School was, at one time, one of the mansion houses of the Matheson brothers who made their fortune along with William MacKinnon in the Pacific and Orient shipping Line, still flourishing today. All three brothers, associated with their castles and estates in Stornoway, Lewis,

Duncraig and Balmacara in Lochalsh, along with William MacKinnon, were knighted by Queen Victoria. The story related to Donald's return with other soldiers from the Far East after the War in 1945. Several thousand troops were jammed into the troopship like sardines. Suffering from heat, especially crossing the Indian Ocean, and with nothing for the soldiers to do, some sharp entrepreneurs organised a gambling business on the lowest deck. In the absence of horses and greyhounds, cockroaches were the chosen runners. Each soldier had his stable, if you like of cockroaches, which were kept in matchboxes. These they fed and molly-coddled with every kind of comfort and privilege. The cockroaches were quite tame and usually responded well to training for the races. It all was good fun, until spoilers came on the scene, as it often does in all human activity, especially when there is betting and gambling. Some cockroaches were starved almost to death before races, to make them run faster after the bit of fried bacon pulled by a string, like the hare before the greyhounds on a normal race track. Some winners had won by such a wide margin that an inquiry was made, revealing that they were given alcohol or tobacco by inhalation before the race. By heating the tobacco or the spirits, the usually quiescent cockroaches, it was found, left the matchbox when the lid was lifted at the starting line, as if they were propelled by a rocket. One great advantage of the cockroach racing on board ship, according to Donald Shearer, was that the troops were so pre-occupied with this diversion that the long voyage from Singapore to Southampton, round the Cape of Good Hope, filled up their time without any serious, deviant, anti-social behaviour.

Now, it was out of the question for me to contemplate cockroach racing. But false kindness on my part could lead to a take-over, should these creatures be given a chance to multiply. Why, in our democratic age of human rights and animal rights and instant protests and suppression of free opinions by the majority, there could be a take-over, a protest demonstration right on the deck of the *Research II,* with all the usual symbols of democracy, lists of grievances, claims to universal liberty, assertions of primary privilege. And in all this, a swelling number of militant and hungry protesters, propagating as fast as nature would allow, down below in every corner of my humble cabin. Can you not hear them, 'Have we all equal rights, humans and animals?' Dare anyone suggest any hierarchy of class in a proud claim of superior ethnic origin from exclusively bred chimpanzee; dare any human being claim priority over any other form of life? These are real issues and real questions that rise and pile in bundles of confusion in our wonderfully enlightened day, and there are no trite or easy clear answers. The conclusion I hurriedly came to was that I could easily be faced with large numbers of creatures, equal and sacred as living brothers and sisters, who could collectively vote to turf me out. And hey, presto! My fate would be similar to Captain Bligh, master of the English frigate the Bounty, who was forced by mutiny to leave his ship with a few loyal friends, to take his chance of survival in a long-boat. How readily sincerely and tenaciously held views can lead from the sublime to the ridiculous.

Some might think that I am making too much of the presence of an insignificant cockroach. But after what I told you of past experiences, I hope all who read this will agree that I was justified at least to some extent, as I closed my eyes and flipped Cuthbert cockroach over the side, and hoped at the same time that he had no other friends or relatives aboard with him.

CHAPTER 6

The Choice of Route

The question asked of me often before setting out from Nova Scotia, was, 'What route are you taking?' Or, 'Are you taking the northerly route or the southerly route?' I was always hesitant about committing myself to either. My guiding principle being that I would head south for part of the way. Then, turn northeast and sail as close to the 50th parallel of Latitude as was feasible, this being roughly the latitude of the English Channel to which I was heading. You cannot be dogmatic about direction when sailing. My intention was pragmatic. I wanted to avoid the cold and the fog and the turbulence of sea associated with the Grand Banks of Newfoundland. I could take practically a straight course following the 50th Latitude, sailing past Pierre and St. Miquelon, on past St. John right across to the Fastnet at the southern tip of Erie and on to England. This would approximate to a Great Circle course. But then there was the cold. I am not one for too much heat, but cold is a weakening factor at sea and reduces alertness and lowers efficiency. When life depends on alacrity and calls are made for dynamic bursts of energy in the darkness of night, when the boat is lashed by mountainous seas and precludes any indulgence in the normal necessities like food and sleep for a protracted time, cold is enemy number one.

Icebergs

If there is a rival to this title, it could be the danger of an encounter with residual ice flows, and migratory icebergs. These are still a possible enemy in the month of June. Though the more northerly option was the shorter, more direct route, I had a vivid recollection of sailing to Canada in June of 1960, on the Canadian Pacific liner, the newly launched *Empress of Canada*. Not too long before we reached the Longitude of Newfoundland, sailing south of it, roughly on the 48th Latitude, the liner slowed down. I watched on deck at night and in the morning. A dozen of the white monsters stood out of the sea like ghosts. Remembering that each iceberg is about eight times the volume of that which is visible above the water, it was easy to realize that they constituted a deadly menace, that could humble the greatest human claimant to invincibility, or mastery of nature. This was proved in the case of the *Titanic* in April 1912 when the largest ship in the world at the time, and claimed by its captain to be unsinkable by God himself, was slit open by nature's frozen blade, with the ease of a tin-opener. No, I would not take the northerly course. These were cogent reasons for avoiding it. I am more convinced than ever that icebergs are a potent menace and a justifiably decisive factor in choosing a more southerly route after receiving a letter from that courageous sailor and grandmother Mary H.J. Harper of Gwynnedd, PA, USA. She is an inspiration to many thousands of retired folk who think life is over for them, by sailing alone in her yacht, *KUAN YIN II*, last year from Newfoundland to Ireland. I quote from her letter,

'I was fortunate with no hurricanes, my closest call was sailing between two large icebergs.'

To me, the thought of waking up to find oneself in this situation makes me shudder. I must bear south to avoid a repeat experience in my venture.

'The Grand Banks'

In the Sailing Directions of the North Atlantic, and in every reference to this area, we are told of the predominantly cold weather and disturbed sea patterns. The sight of large seaworthy ships on television, their bows rising upwards out of the seas and then disappearing downwards in a pitching movement, discouraged me from crossing the famous fishing ground. The danger of being rammed and sunk by heavy steel trawlers or factory ships was a significant and relevant one. I intended to go south east to skirt the famous 'tail of the bank.' Up until the early spring of 1995 it was well known that there were forty to fifty large fishing boats and factory ships of various national registrations, from the Iberian peninsula to the South American continent, plowing back and fore. It is notoriously true that the weather-hardened masters of these ocean tractors give little time or thought to surveillance for small craft. How sad but true. The Grand Banks, the source of fish for Europe since the Middle Ages, and the very lifeblood of the Maritime economy of Canada and specifically of Newfoundland, to which that province owed its origins as a permanent fishing settlement, was almost played out. Through the arrogant abuse and unlicensed greed of men, coupled with the unbalanced application of technology to nature's resources, in its historic role as the rich larder of the sea for millions of people, the Grand Banks, associated with reasonable and viable harvesting of the sea, was overrun with massive dredgers of the seafloor. Canada has taken a stand against the deep-sea poachers. It has asserted its authority and responsibility as steward of this famous food source of history. In doing so, after an international duel in which Canada won 'on points' against the European Economic Union, Canada as a nation has 'come of age.' Now the Grand Banks would predictably be a safer place for small boats to travel even in the inevitable fog. An international conference held at Dartmouth, Nova Scotia this fall, has confirmed a protracted moratorium on the indiscriminate fishing on the Banks. For the foreseeable future the quotas of cod and other fish, like halibut, are drastically reduced. In the short term this means hardship, especially for Canada's Maritime provinces and the traditional fishing countries of Spain and Portugal. But wisdom and realism has prevailed, even though Canada had to go to the inordinate lengths of maritime 'cowboy' tactics and is even being taken to the international court at the Hague, for international piracy.

In its duel over fishing responsibly, Canada has 'come of age.' Brian Tobin, Fisheries minister, has put Canada on the map, giving it a kind of colorful flair, which hitherto seemed out of character with the prosaic, polite, inoffensive 'also ran' image, attributed to it as an ex-colony and child of the now defunct British Empire. Go to Britain and speak with fishermen in the Channel ports and others who followed the Battle of the Grand Banks and you will find there is a new respect for the victor. Further it is seen now that all combatants are winners. Canada has emerged as a nation to be reckoned with, not as an egotistical grabber of the harvest of the sea, but as a responsible steward and watchman, for the good of all nations. The result is that hopefully fish stocks will recover, so that they will be preserved as a controlled and on-going provision for the needs of this and coming generations.

Meantime, the threat of being run down by one of the huge fleet of fishing trawlers and factory ships on the Grand Banks, was greatly diminished if not eradicated. But it is hard to adjust one's thinking to exclude its possibility.

Fog

The northerly route is also the more direct route, but has one more characteristic; and that is fog. Fog has no connotations of good for sailing in a small boat. It is linked to negatives and even though disaster may be avoided, its presence could potentially change a happy dream into a disorientating nightmare. An authoritative description of the area is given by a specialist in oceanic science. It was enough for me. I quote:

> *In the region of the Grand Banks, the Westerly airstream... encounters alternatively, the warm waters of the Sargasso Sea on one side of the Gulf Stream and the cold waters of the Labrador Current on the other.*
>
> *These sudden and drastic changes in temperature produce the notorious fog banks of Newfoundland - a hazard made even more treacherous, by the icebergs swept down from West Greenland by the Labrador Current. It was precisely this combination of surface wind currents and resultant fog which caused the tragic loss of the prestigious liner, Titanic in 1912.*

(from Atlas of the Oceans)

You can understand that for me, the Grand Banks and the seas to the northeast of it presented a hostile barrier for me to cross, as a landsman would view a desert, and as hazardous as a pedestrian would contemplate crossing a busy motor way.

I resolved to head south east to Latitude 43 degrees, thus crossing the southern end of the Grand Banks. At the same time this would obviate crossing several shipping routes of the big merchant ships which ply their trade back and fore between Britain and America. My intention also was to sail south of the sea junction beyond the Grand Bank where trans-ocean ships rendezvous to make their change of course for the ports inland via the Cabot Strait, the ports of Halifax and St. John and those of the eastern United States, chiefly New York.

The mountains under the ocean

If you cut through the Atlantic as you would a cake, you would have a section showing how the contour of the sea bottom varies from Nova Scotia to Britain's Land's End. On each side of the Atlantic the sea floor extends outwards for a considerable distance. This is known as the Continental Shelf. Then it drops down to the ocean depth. In the North Atlantic the sea floor rises at the centre to a height of approximately two thousand feet, or about half way up to the mean level of the ocean. This mountain range is called the Mid-Atlantic Ridge. The top has a ridge on either side with a hollow in between. That hollow is really a rift valley, similar to the rift valley in Scotland, running southwest from Inverness to Fort William. The Scottish rift valley is filled in with the string of lochs, including Loch Ness which is credited with harbouring a family of early maritime mammals.

Proof of Nessie

Is there really a Loch Ness monster? There is one bit of evidence that I personally cannot get out of my mind. I have never heard it made public, in spite of all the digging by journalists and monsterologists, and let's face it, there are many of them, seeking to prove or disprove the presence of 'Nessie.' Let me tell you of this hitherto unpublicised fact. About forty years ago as a Divinity student, I was preaching in the Free Church congregation of Glen Urquhart. The old church at *Cul-na kirk* has since then been replaced by a new one. Between services I was invited to have a meal in the home of an elderly woman, whose house was situated near the north side of Loch Ness and not far from Castle Urquhart. A short time earlier, John Cobb was killed when he was practising for a world water speed record. You can see a monument raised to his memory beside the loch. The house was old then and very likely no longer stands. My hostess gave me a very good dinner of fresh Scottish lamb. Afterwards, we had a long conversation which, in spite of it being the Sabbath, at last turned to the question of Nessie. I was intrigued, to say the least of it, when she made it very clear, that it was real. Brought up on the croft, adjacent to the loch, she told me that since a child she believed in its presence. Moreover, it was her conviction that there was a family. She sensed my skepticism and I saw that her face clouded as with an affront or challenge to her credibility. She rose up from her chair and paused. Looking to me directly, she said, 'I have something to show you, if I can find it. No one has seen this as far as I know since it was washed up on the shore a very long time ago.' With that, she disappeared and could be heard making the sound of someone moving furniture or boxes. The light in the little cottage was getting dim as the sun passed on its way to the west. After something like twenty minutes, the old lady came back. 'Here it is. Make of it what you will,' she said, passing to me with both her hands, the object of her search. My recollection of it is still clear as if I am holding it in my hands before me. It was obviously the foot of some very strange creature, except that this was hollow like a man's boot. There the likeness stopped. The foot comprised a large pad with long fingers or toes extending forward. It was not unlike a hen's foot, but roughly about sixteen to eighteen inches long, and about twelve inches in height. It was made of tough leathery skin, yellowed with age and dried and withered as something left untouched for a long time. I recall, gasping with astonishment and, in spite of myself, feeling a growing sense that this could indeed be none other than the cast foot of 'Nessie'. Suddenly the old lady took the 'foot' fossil from my hands and disappeared from the room with it. No word about it was exchanged thereafter. It was as if she had closed a book, unwilling that any other should glimpse a scene from the sacred past, and question her integrity.

Forgive me for the digression, but I thought this an opportune time to relate this, so that at least the fact of the presence of this 'fossil' be recorded for posterity, whatever the 'experts' may make of it. Now back to the Atlantic.

This rift valley extending southwards along the longitudinal spine of the Mid Atlantic Ridge is unstable, as the meeting point of the two continents American and European. Within it is the area of igneous or volcanic activity. In 1963 the igneous activity became so marked that the lava erupted from the ocean, forming a new island. The Icelanders call it Surtsey. You can understand that all this irregular sea bottom has a determinative effect upon the weather. Especially is this the case as the temperature over the Rift Valley is affected by the volcanic nature of the rocks below it, and the spasmodic evidence, as seen in Iceland, of continued activity. The seas are whipped up into giant masses of water, especially as a storm reaches the slope on one side or the other of the Mid Atlantic mountain range. For a boat it is a bit like a car traveling over a very bumpy road which has hollows and ridges, instead of a smooth level surface. Clearly, crossing the ocean involves being prepared for this, and accepting that it would be no Sunday picnic. It is also true that the temperature varies according to the friction of the sides of the Rift Valley under the earth pressure of the two continents east and west, along with internal movement of underlying rocks under pressure which is causal to volcanic activity.

The Farady Fracture

While the Mid Atlantic Ridge runs north and south between the continents, there are breaks every so often through this mountain range. These run east and west. But since the Ridge itself has a twist like a snake at the juncture between the northern and the southern part, following the relationship of North America to South America, the Pass or Fracture is also twisted like the isthmus of Panama. Since I was crossing between the 43rd and 50th latitude, my track would take me through the Faraday Fracture. This break in the mountain range was like the Pass of Killiecrankie in Scotland, made famous by the battle in 1789, won by the Jacobites whose leader, John Graham of Claverhouse, was killed. Thousands of cars and buses carrying tourists stop at this historic site and beauty spot every summer.

The Faraday Ridge, as the name suggests, is called after the great 18th century English scientist, 'father of modern magnetism and electricity' Sir Michael Faraday. I must say that I felt a privileged affinity to the great scientist but humble Christian, whose name is registered on this underwater contour of the ocean. Inevitably, this underwater feature of the sea bottom would also be a formative factor in the pattern of the sea. All irregular features of the sea bottom contributed to less than ideal sea conditions.

If the Atlantic were dried up

If the Atlantic were dried up and you crossed the ocean floor instead of the water mass above it, your journey would be something like this. You would leave Nova Scotia and descend at a slight angle to the edge of the Continental Shelf. There you would drop suddenly, like going over a cliff. When you picked yourself up, you would start climbing a mountain. You would have to clamber over huge masses of rocks and sedimentary gravel. As you went forward, this would give way to hard glittering volcanic rocks. Your climb would take you two thousand feet up, which is half the depth of the Atlantic Ocean as we know it today. For thirty miles you would dip down into the rift valley, which is geologically unstable. Then up to the ridge on the other side, and down the mountain on the European side. Somehow you'd climb up onto the continental shelf there and possibly hail a taxi to take you to London, just like the thirty stowaway immigrants from Sri Lanka who came ashore in Nova Scotia and asked for a taxi to take them to Toronto. Now, if you followed the route that *Research II* was taking, you would not have to climb to the top of the Ridge. Instead you would pass through the Faraday Fracture, or Pass from west to east. Your trans-Atlantic journey would take you down the other side, the east end of the Ridge, until you came to the Continental Shelf about the Longitude of Ireland. There you would have to climb onto the Shelf and in the shallower waters round the coasts, make your way towards the dry land of Europe or The British Isles today.

I have, as you see, taken pains to give as graphic a picture as I can, of the underwater contour of the sea floor. Why? Yes, because apart from the power of the wind to create the waves, the sea bottom is also a major factor. I am convinced that all the factors together, of weather and underwater mountains and valleys, ridges and defiles, create in a storm something so unique, so animated, so powerful, so interactive as a seething confluence of vast conflicting volumes of sea, that there is nothing on the earth's surface that can compare with it. And should a large ship like the British liner *Queen Mary*, be nearly torn apart, as happened to her once on passage across the North Atlantic in a storm, how much more vulnerable would a little sailing boat like my *Research II*, as it set out across the Atlantic, should it encounter a storm. I have to add that even as I write at this time in September, 1995, the liner *Queen Elizabeth II* was hit by a freak wave in her passage off Newfoundland to the north of my course. That large queen of the British shipping fleet suffered damage, though nothing too serious.

The Gulf Stream

I was now on my way, with approximately thirty-six thousand miles to go. I would endeavor to keep to the projected course, but it would not be a straight line. Wind and weather would play their part and to a considerable extent dictate my progress. There was also something else. The Gulf Stream current passes in a northeasterly route towards the British Isles. By my choice of the more southerly course, *Research II* would have the full benefit of this strong current. On the other hand, I calculated that when I reached the Approaches to the English Channel, I would have to be wary of being swept north through the gap between Wales and Ireland. I was nervously conscious that a southwest storm could do this, as history is a record of scores of sailing ships which missed the Channel or came to grief on the Needles, the awful rocky devouring teeth of the Scilly Isles. In view of this, it was my intention as I will later advert to, to sail closer to the French side of the Channel. All this 'planning' of my course was premised on the assumption of predominantly southwest winds throughout the voyage. This was a reasonable assumption as you will agree. 1995 with its record temperatures in Europe and America would prove to be the exception to history.

I was warned by several friends, including one who had served in the Merchant Service, that I would have indifferent weather, to say the least, when *Research II* reached the Approaches to the English Channel. It would be a good many weeks before that became an issue. Meantime, I would sample what the Atlantic could do, and in the experience, learn when put to the test what my little boat could take. Also this would be a learning experience of my own resources and a proving of a working faith in the living God, who hitherto had never let me down.

CHAPTER 7

Daily life at sea

Life at sea in a small boat is quite different from life on land. For one thing you are restricted to the confines of a small space. You cannot go for walks. Instead, you go for 'crawls,' like a cat clawing your way forward, always on the alert against going overboard by slithering across the sloping deck, a movement made easy by a deep green sea that chooses to give an unasked-for boat wash to your already spanking clean deck.

Down below, there are three key positions in the cabin. They form an equilateral triangle whose sides are each three feet long. One is the kitchen area where you sit beside the sink and icebox, at the table for a meal. You know where all food items are stored, so that you reach behind you to the cupboards, and feel for your oatmeal, marmalade or milk powder. You are in a strategic position to reach for all requirements with minimum movement. You lean forward to your store of tins - all heavy items are kept low down in the boat - or reach for your Rye-Vita or biscuits in the cupboards opposite. Second, is the two-burner stove opposite. You kneel down on the floor to attend to this. All pouring of hot food is done by filling your bowl or cup placed on the floor so that it does not move. The third point is the area under the hatch. Here, for the most part, I slept athwartships. As the boat usually sails at some angle of heel, I sleep with my feet at the lower end. This is very useful because if the boat goes off course, by jibing or being suddenly thrown sideways by a large sea, I wake up as my position is reversed by gravity. I roll over onto the floor so that I am then kneeling at my humble bed and in a moment I am out in the cockpit with my torch to deal with the situation. If this system fails, progress is impeded. If I wake up without an emergency, I do the same, namely roll out of bed so that I kneel down at my bunk and then I pray to our Heavenly Father, giving him thanks for bringing me safely along my way. Much of this is part of life ashore. It would be hard to stop this habit of a lifetime and, in any case, why would one do so? For the whole voyage this routine is followed; I speak of the three point triangle of sink, stove and sleeping quarters. I sit at the kitchen table; I kneel at the stove; I sleep under the hatch.

'The spirit is willing but the flesh is weak'

On one occasion, either through complacency or exhaustion, I slept through the night, dreaming vividly of sailing along fast and well. At daybreak I woke. True enough, *Research II* was sailing along at 5 knots. But something was far wrong. The sun was peeping over the horizon behind the stern. You see, *Research II* was hurrying back to Canada, on a compass course that would bring her into St. John's, Newfoundland. It made me wonder if I should have called in at St. John's. If I had done so there is little doubt that I would have thoroughly checked every bit of gear and the boat fittings. Then, any observed weakness could have been dealt with before going on. Or was it just the proverbial hospitality of Newfoundland that in a mystical way affected the boat so that she wanted to take me there? There may be something in that. But the hard truth is that I failed to get up because of human frailty.

As a rule I rarely sat out in the cockpit during the day. I did at night if there was a ship in the vicinity, or if sailing demanded my attention. The beauty of sleeping under the open hatch was that I could watch the stars and know if I was on course, on nights when the sky was clear. The Plough would be visible to the northwest, but turned upside down by the morning. But it always pointed to the Pole star, which stayed constant to the north. The planets, especially Jupiter, made an appearance in the southern hemisphere. In practice, you could know you were on course, that is, sailing east, by watching the stars. But you had to treat the planets and stars differently because unlike the Pole or the North star, which retains its approximate northerly bearing, their position in the sky changed throughout the duration of the night.

Log: Day 2, Saturday, 24th June, 1995

Self Steering worked all night. Had sleep for three hours till 5 am. Gale-force winds, heavy following seas. Dawn overcast. Sun came out, very cold. Put out my patent drogue over the stern. Slowed her down but still doing 5 knots. By Dead Reckoning sailed 144 miles over the past 24 hours. Speed at night 6-7 knots. Compass course SE 120'-130' Bad weather, hard to make adjustments to Stanley, the Self-Steering Unit. Big waves sometimes break aboard into the cockpit and into the companionway. Problem with water in battery area. Pumped out several buckets full.

My feathered friends

At sea there are no humans when you travel by yourself. But you have your companions. On land we are not very aware of our friends in nature. Their presence is only academic or economic as they are pushed into the background of reckoning unless they can make money for us in some way. That is why our environment is no place for birds. It's all rather difficult. Pigeons, by depositing their excrement, literally destroy buildings - look at Glasgow or London. And in Canada, the national pet, the Canada Goose has become so prolific and demanding, that traffic has to stop when a mother and her brood, along with cousins, uncles, aunts and hangers-on, decides to cross over the busy road. Furthermore, the lovely looking geese form the equivalent of an ice-rink. So that it is only the inbred skill of skating that often enables a pedestrian to keep his footing, where the geese have gone before. Maybe they should be trained to have a paper bag and use it when nature calls. That would be a worthy project to challenge the environmentalists. The trick is to strike a balance. To stop the traffic as a mother goose and her kids make the crossing is alright. But when forty or fifty other geese follow suit, you have a potential traffic problem.

We all need to slow down

And yet, when you think of it, maybe that is what we all, in our up-tight urban hectic life, need to slow us down and make us reflect. At sea and in the context of a vast ocean all round you, one solitary bird is the object of your attention. Thus you peer out over the sea and as you spot a bird, you welcome it as a fellow creature of the God and Creator of all. For all his creatures are part of the pattern of creation, each giving texture and colour in its unique contribution in the great tapestry of unfolding life. We in our human consciousness, are given the privilege of evaluating and appreciating the whole picture; the enriching animated graphics, the music of nature's songs and the beauty of its diversity of colour, and the wonder of its form.

At sea, I look for signs of life. Black and white sea swallows or terns dive at the stern, plunging into the boat's wake. Clearly they are fishing. These birds appear just before dawn and then again in the twilight. I welcome them, as if they are saying 'Good morning' to me and at the end of the day in the *gloaming,* wishing me 'Good night.' Large gulls swoop down to survey *Research II.* These are seasoned inhabitants of the ocean. Storm or calm, they are in their element. When the weather is bad and the sky is overcast, there is little sign of bird life. Then when good weather comes, the birds return. The exception is the sea-swallows. Very often they are there when I awake in the dawn before sunrise, fishing at the boat's wake or again just after sunset. What a gift God has given to us! How much we should appreciate the lovely little creatures on land or sea. I think of the chickadees, the blue jays and my favorites, the little finches, which stay with us all the year round at Arnish, feeding in front of our window at the bird feeders. How matchless the beauty of the little males dressed in their courting summer coat of pure yellow. But now out on the open sea, even the sight of a big black-backed gull is also precious. And then there are these fat birds, the guillemots, podgy compact creatures that defy the waves even in a storm. They are all my friends, I say to myself, and aloud, I call to them and praise God for them. For they represent life and share with me the habitat of the sea in all its contrasts.

Log: Saturday 2200 hrs.

Position: N 45' 18'' W 57'32"

Course: 120-130 SE

Speed: 4 plus knots

Tried to get weather but cannot. Tried calling Halifax on Channel 16. No luck. Something far wrong with wiring. I think wires are crossed from instruments. My barometer fell off the wall, not working. This is big calamity. Regret left new suit of sails. Could be serious consequences. The ocean is feeling out everything, boat and gear and also myself, for weaknesses. Fog, fog, fog. Visibility a hundred yards. Night closes in, a dark grey oblivion, and the boat speeds on. Pray the Lord will sustain me. Steady roar of wind.

Contrasts

We are used to sameness and uniformity in our lives on land. This leads to boredom. And that leads to our being vulnerable or susceptible to promotional advertisements. Some may lead to good diversions or activities, other may lead us astray. On board *Research II* every day is different. Life is full of contrasts. Life is full of surprises. This is built in as the infrastructure of everyday life. It is the basic pattern and not the exception. The exception would be if there was sameness and uniformity. Take the wind for instance. The *Research II* and I - I'm going to use the first person plural, WE after this - we were not in the Trade winds. This meant that although the prevailing wind might well be from the southwest, there would also be changes of wind from other directions.

The weather continually changes. Since leaving the east light of Scaterie, I had two days of gales. Now on Sunday morning the gales abated and the seas subsided. I took in the drogue. The southwest wind still blew, giving me a speed of 5 knots. I considered it tranquil after the heavy seas of the gale. But all this is relative, the waves were not exactly baby waves and the ocean swell had long undulations. But this was a great contrast to the gale, especially after the night. I quote from my journal and its scribbled notes;

Log: Day 3, Sunday, 25th June, 6:30 am, 1995

The Lord be praised, He kept me safe through the dark watches of the night, when the waves chased *Research II* onwards to the roar of the wind in the rigging. For the best part of the last two days the cold was penetrating and the fog cast a grey blanket over sky and sea. Now as we crossed the southern part of the Grand banks, and kept heading southeast, the sun was trying its best to get through. Even to see the faint outline of the sun was reassuring, and contrasting with the opaque faceless uniformity of the grey sky.

Log/Journal

6:30 am: Set compass course SE by E. Wind SW 4-5. Speed 5-6 knots on knotmeter. Sun trying to break through to the East .

Time: 4:30 pm: Pleasant sailing. Position N 44' 48", W 55' 58" speed 4.5 knots. Worked at Stanley the Scull-Oar. Solved problem. Had lines too tight. 1. Should be gently slack using shockcord. 2. Cut out spreader pulleys. Crossed lines to tiller.

You can see that each day was different with varied sailing conditions of sea and weather. There was a routine, as a rule, for every day, which I kept to out of habit. This was to a large extent very similar to that which I followed on land, whenever possible. This was especially true of my sleeping habits. I retired at 10 p.m. and got up at 5 a.m. as usual on land. And in the afternoon I had my nap. At night, however, my built-in alarm clock would make me stir every hour or hour and a half. I would reach for my torch and check that all was well, and especially that we were sailing on the right course. I am fortunate that I can sleep at any time day or night, just like my father.

The use of Cat-naps

I recall when my father took me south to get my eyes tested by an optician. This was before the British National Health Service. I'll tell you the sequence from the Sunday morning before we left, as it also illustrates the demands of a minister's life and how he met them.

He conducted four services that day, beginning with an English service in the Naval Base where he was wartime chaplain; one at the regular hour in Aultbea in Gaelic; an English one in Poolewe at three o'clock in the afternoon; and the last in the evening at Inverasdale in a hall packed to capacity with everyone from little children to the not so young in the village, and also every able-bodied person who could walk from the adjoining villages of Cove and Naast some four miles away. I tell more about this in another book on his life. Meantime I write to illustrate his endurance and capacity to sleep at any time. I accompanied my father on his tours of duty, whenever I was free. We got home about 10 p.m. On Monday we left in the car at 4 pm, parked the car at the home of Provost (mayor) MacRae's house in Dingwall, boarded the train at 7 pm for Inverness, changed to the overnight train for Glasgow. Arrived in Buchannan Street Station Glasgow 6 am; walked to Duncan's hotel, Union Street. Wash, shave and breakfast and read Glasgow Herald. 9 am, took me to Lizaar's the optician, checked my eyes for glasses. Visit to Aunt Annie. Train to Waverley Station, Edinburgh. Church Committee meetings at the Mound. Train back to Glasgow. Collect new glasses from the optician. Shop for half an hour for gifts. Dinner at Duncan's Hotel. Board night train for Inverness, thence to Dingwall, jump in car at 7 a.m. Home to Aultbea - I was out for the count and Dad wakened me in the garage. Then Prayer-meeting and baptism at Laide in the school that evening. The fact is that my father was exceedingly strong. And one gift he had was that he could sleep at the proverbial drop of a hat. I was fortunate that I could do this too. It was just what I needed as I set out over the North Atlantic.

Reading the sky

The sky is a book that we can read. When the sky is clear, the stars, planets, constellations, and every impulse of energy are transmitted to us as visible light even when the source has burned up millions of years ago. They all bring excitement and animation to our consciousness. How can we not wonder at the local phenomenon of our little moon, and marvel how it causes the seas to go out and come in with the tide, to provide the daily feeding ground for the sea birds and provide the means for sea creatures to hatch their young in the sands! The sun itself we can think about, though we cannot look at it directly. It triggers off our thinking about God, and his visible projection on the screen of time in sharing our humanity; Jesus Christ, the Sun of Righteousness, the one and only superstar of our spiritual solar system. When the sun's rays rise over the horizon in the morning, how can we not be moved to think of Christ? And, in the metaphor of the physical, realize that it is ourselves, like the tilting earth, that have to turn receptively to Christ the Light of the world in believing faith and unqualified love.

Who can adhere to a doctrine of creational chance, or what 'educated' person can espouse a philosophy of human sovereignty as we look up to wonder at the seemingly homogeneous mass of stars that comprise the Milky Way? How can any balanced human being, thinking multi-dimensionally, claim strategic control over matter and life, when each of us are on the stage of life for a split second of time and collectively for not much longer as a species of life? Looking at the night sky brings coherence and order to our thinking, and makes us differentiate between the stellar bodies, the planets of our solar system, our local world, and the vast background of the worlds of other solar systems that, comparatively speaking, are permanent in relation to us. In short, we are humbled as we look out from our little boat and contemplate the environment about us. You will notice that when you are in a city or an urban lighted community, it is hard - even impossible - to see the stars of the sky. Go out of the city into the dark countryside. Then you see the stars vividly clear. At sea there are no crowds, no city lights, no distracting sky-scrapers or high-rise buildings to blot out the book of the stars with all its pages of wonder.

David, the King of Judah, often slept in the open beneath the night sky when he spent over a decade as a guerrilla leader, pushed into that role by the jealousy of King Saul. You can imagine him lying there with his hands folded under his head and reading the night sky. He tells himself how this stimulated his thinking and led him to be full of wonder at the might and wisdom of God. And more than that, he realizes how humble we should be that God has endowed us with such gifts and delegates to us the stewardship of his world. Listen to the shepherd poet,

When I look up unto the heavens,
which thine on fingers framed,
Unto the moon, and to the stars,
which thine own fingers framed.

Then say I, What is man, that he
remembered is by thee?
Or, what the son of man, that thou
so kind to him should be?

For thou a little lower hast,
him than the angels made;
With glory and with dignity
thou crowned hast his head.

(Psalm 8 Scottish Psalter)

We are not suggesting that we all have to go to sea alone in little boats in order to get a spiritual perspective. David was in the desert when he first realized that there before him was the book of the stars. But he lived long after that and still saw in his mind's eye the vivid pictures with their didactic message. That's the wonder of our being, namely that we have a built-in memory and recall system in the computer of our minds. We have a great capacity so that our experience of sense and spirit can still be with us in all the inspiration and dynamic joy of God's presence and his grace, even when the days of our life are overcast, and the years bring the lines of suffering to our face. Even our aloneness is only relative. David had his loyal soldiers sleeping all around him. Ultimately, the metaphors of nature, even in the pragmatic wonders of the universe, are just triggers which start us thinking and nudge us into the spiritual dimension, as an automobile changes into a higher gear ratio, where the soul is awakened to the new or renewed world of communion with the Spirit of God. And this is surely mirrored metaphorically as an integral part of this completeness of life, in the astronomical setting of our terrestrial habitat.

Reading the book of the sea

Apart from the sky, the sea changes continually. This is especially so in the North Atlantic. I have already adverted to the influence of the sea floor, the continental shelf on either side of the ocean, and the wonder of the under-sea mountain range known as the Mid-Atlantic Ridge, along with the defiles or mountain passes, the Gibb Fracture or the Faraday fracture - the equivalent of the Khyber Pass in Afghanistan, or the Pass of Killiecrankie in the Scottish Highlands. You do not see these influences that contribute to the changing conditions of the sea, but you study the sea itself. Much of your free time is spent trying to get the messages that indicate what kind of weather is brewing, or just looking out and marvelling at the patterns, which are really like scenes of geographic locations we might record on the camera and browse over after our vacation, on a winter's night. The contrast is that the sea is mobile, volatile, moving all the time. The trees may bend to a storm on land, but the land itself is not moved. The sea, on the other hand, is always moving under the keel. It is hard to describe the delectable peace of looking out over a quiet sea where the carpet of water is covered with a million ripples of a steady breeze, and the wake of the boat is left astern as the bow cuts a steady furrow ahead. It could be said that, on average, three-quarters of a voyage is pleasure, comprising a variety of experiences of nature's joys that can be experienced solely and exclusively by the lone traveler on his little boat. It's not that company of other human beings is negative. But when I am by myself, my consciousness is not distracted by that of another. Therefore, I am pervaded with awareness of the sea, and totally receptive to its visual energy emissions. It is therefore like the pages of a book, where words convey messages to our minds.

The flat calm has its beauty, but speaks many negatives in the ocean. It heralds a day of tortuous wallowing of the boat from side to side and the flapping and flogging of lifeless sails, and of course no progress. If it is accompanied by a hot sun in a cloudless sky, you cannot help thinking of a contrasting gale being on the way for the next day. Sometimes the sea is a sheen of silvery light, a glorious mirror of solar luminosity; at other times when the wind is strong, a thousand whitecaps or breaking crests dot the surface, so that all resembles a parlour, as the sun's rays shining through the window, highlight the pattern of the carpet on the floor. The sea is also as changeable as the moods of a human being.

The sea is living

It is equally animated, a living mass of multitudes of cells or molecules. Water forms shapes which are many and various. I read this book of the sea and distinguish between friend and foe. The friends are the gentle waves with their white collars which push *Research II* along at a good speed. But then there is the other kind, the kind that are formed as a storm builds up. They are antagonists that seek you out to destroy you. They roam the ocean looking for victims. They call you to marshal the greatest resources of fortitude, and only if these are matched by equal virtues of your boat will you survive. Their naked purpose is to destroy; their sight within your vision or even their proximity unseen in the darkness of the night, warrants their awesome appellation as *messengers of doom.* Before they appear, the sea is activated in a process of incubation as a child is formed in the mother's womb. After birth it grows, becomes an adolescent, and reaches maturity. Oceanographers have calculated that some of these waves contain up to 30,000 tons of water. Unseen forces change the level of the ocean into a heaving pattern, rising like a wall against the grey, spume-filled sky. If it is night, you are conscious that the sea moves below you as if a giant is shaking the earth underneath. The surface takes on a folding movement, as if it simulated the geological folding of the mountains that form our mother earth. The horizon disappears behind the ridges of the wave troughs. Below your keel, there is a moving force that one minute lifts you up to the crest of a hill and then brings you down into a deep trough. That is just the broad picture. It is tolerable to live with. If there is a ship to be seen, every so often you get a good view of it as *Research II* rises on the convex arch of the sea hill. If it is night-time, you have the same effect except that the ship presents an intermittent light on the horizon.

The harbingers of doom

Every so often the tolerable violence of a storm causes the sea to reach unimaginable terror in the special emissaries of destruction, the 'messengers of doom.' I speak now of the liquid creatures, the animated deadly creations, that are born in this pregnant condition of the storm. There is a clear distinction between a gale and a storm. A gale, even a vicious one, is local, lasting for possibly twenty-four hours. But it is superficial, something on the surface. It is true several may comprise a continuous sequence, and then the consequent wave mass and configuration can give birth to rogue waves from changing wind and cross-seas similar to those linked to a storm. Then the distinction between gale and storm is academic. But the gale is generically different from a storm. A storm, though it is caused by the atmosphere, in its effect is a stirring of the ocean right to the bottom, as you would stir a pot of porridge on the stove. Its effect upon the surface of the ocean is the equivalent of an earthquake on land, except that this is protracted by the continual upheaval of the sea in increasing volumes and lasts for days.

Sir Edward Shackleton

The distinguished geographer-explorer made a relief 800 mile voyage from Eliphant Isle in the Antarctic to the whaling station in South Georgia in a 20 foot lifeboat, the *James Caird.* He describes that voyage with its continuous gales and the meeting of an extra special one of these rogue waves:

A hard north-westerly gale came up on the eleventh day (May 5th) and shifted to southwest in the afternoon. The sky was overcast and occasional snow squalls added to the discomfort produced by a tremendous cross-sea - the worst, I thought, that we had experienced. At midnight I was at the tiller and suddenly noticed a line of clear sky between the south and the southwest. I called to the other men that the sky was clearing, and then a moment later, I realized that what I had seen was not a rift in the clouds but the white crest of an enormous wave. During twenty-six years' experience of the ocean in all its moods I had not encountered a wave so gigantic. It was a mighty upheaval of the ocean, a thing quite apart from the big white-capped seas that had been our tireless enemies for days. I shouted, 'For God's sake, hold on! It's got us!' Then came a moment of suspense that seemed drawn out into hours. White surged the foam of the breaking sea around us. We felt our boat lifted and flung forward like a cork in breaking surf. We were in a seething chaos of tortured water; but somehow the boat lived through it, half-full of water, sagging to the dead weight and shuddering under the blow...

This kind of wave never is still enough for you to catch a definitive shape. It is a monster, that has continual movement in itself. You see it some distance away and tense yourself as you surmise will it see you. It is huge, towering up before you against the grey, spume-filled sky. It moves like an angry mountain that has broken apart, driven by forces deep down within it. Its crest is like the white collar or the lace of a woman's dress. As you look at it, the foaming white is turned into a misty brightness so that it appears like a patch of the sky itself. A flash of optimism makes you think that it represents a break of light in the steel-colored shroud that closes you in, in the storm. It has seen you. You know it. It is coming after you. It is now running towards you, a roar emitting from its mouth like the laughter of a demon as its spots its prey. What do you do then?

The captain on the 'bridge'

What a God we have, the creator of the world and yet the personal God who knows the little sparrow before it falls to the ground, and controls the dynamics of the universe! Those who worship him, live by his mercy and rely upon his grace, walking in the 'paths of righteousness' so that they can commune with his Spirit, just cannot fail. They overcome. **No power can separate them from the love of God in Christ Jesus.** They are winners. They hit the jackpot every day. Their investments grow with compound interest in the stock-exchange of spiritual values. They have chosen the grace-units of the international Trust, which we see imperfectly as the struggling Church. Some have consigned it to oblivion, to the archives of history. They have given it up for lost like many of my dear friends who thought that I was lost and resting in Valhalla. But the Church of Christ is the Ark of the Covenant, It is invincible. It is built of the seasoned planks of God's righteousness. Its timbers are the statutes of Heaven's laws and these are fastened together by the everlasting nails of crucified love, **the love of Christ that passeth knowledge**. It is powered by the breath of the Almighty and it is so large that there is room for all, *who-so-ever-will*, the poor, the broken, the fallen, the weak, the helpless, those who use their wealth as privileged stewards to serve all, the public leaders in high places, who like Daniel, and the 'men of the covenant' in 17th century Scotland, whose fealty was first and foremost to God.

There is room for all who stoop low at the door of Christ as the King of kings and Lord of lords, in humble contrition of spirit, so that they get aboard. And because the Ark is promised victory, even in the midst of the storms of life you can hear singing to the praise of God. Listen to the matchless words of a believer long ago in a song bequeathed to the church for all ages.

Who go to sea in ships, and in
great waters trading be,
Within the deep these men God's works
and his great wonders see.

For he commands, and forth in haste,
the stormy tempest flies,
Which makes the sea with rolling waves
aloft to swell and rise.

They mount to heaven, then to the depth
they do go down again;
Their soul doth faint and melt away
with trouble and with pain.

They reel and stagger like one drunk,
at their wit's end they be:
Then they to God in trouble cry,
who them from straits set free:
O that men to the Lord would give

praise for his goodness then,
And for his works of wonder done
unto the sons of men.

(Scottish Psalter Psalm 107)

The hidden world below

I go on reading the book of the sea. Remember the sea is three-dimensional. I look over the side and see down through the water. The Atlantic is about four thousand metres deep, and in parts rising half-way to the surface, in the irregular terrain of ridges and ocean - floor hills. I think of the rock formation, the gravel covered slopes and in the ridge sides, the caves and hollows. There is a world of life right under the boat. Ground fish of every exotic variety swim below, many never seen by man. All kinds of creatures of life, soft and spiky, make a living for their life span; shellfish, with their solid protective shield, like lobster and crab, spend their days in the crevices of the rocks, the equivalent of our urban high-rise structures. Maybe, sometimes they share the same problems of overcrowding, housing scarcity, and certainly health problems which we do on land. The new movement of ecological awareness and environmental guardianship against the encroaching economic industrial giants of supposed Utopian enlightenment is praiseworthy. But visually, the pages of the sea can be read too. Just below the surface porpoises and dolphins play around the boat. The porpoises roll over, often three behind each other. I watch them and I think there is a reason. After many hours watching them, it seems to me that the foremost one churns up the water and the two behind eat the plankton food. The order changes continually, as the second goes forward and the first one goes around to the back. Thus each one has its turn at the front to churn up the waters and everyone gets a meal. Porpoises, which vary from about three feet to ten feet long, are traditionally associated in coastal areas with the coming of bad weather. But that is not a cast-iron rule. They follow a shoal of mackerel right in close to the shore. Then their presence, rolling along, is a good sign to the fisherman. The fact is that when the ocean is relatively quiet, you can see the creatures very clearly. As you watch the porpoises diving under the keel, shooting alongside from stem to stern, or gathered in a circle, in numbers up to twenty or more, imitating the whales as they corner a congregating mass of plankton, you simply enjoy them being with you. It is company. They are alive and as you are conscious of them as God's creatures, it is hard not to believe that they also have some kind of communion with us. The other surface creature, the dolphin, is distinct from the porpoise. As the porpoise rolls over, the dolphin appears to hold its head up so that its body takes a concave arc like the bent shape of the pole when an athlete makes his jump over the bar. How can I describe to you my relationship to the dolphins? I see them a few feet from the side of the cockpit. They are so friendly and playful, jumping sometimes completely out of the water like a salmon. The difference is that they open their mouths - they have long beak-like snouts. Then you hear them audibly calling out. I speak to them, saying, 'Hello, how are you? Wonderful to see you,' just as a minister does when visiting a home in his parish. And just as I was always welcome at every door, irrespective of ecclesiastical label or no label at all, it seemed to me that the dolphins make me feel part of the family. They, in effect, befriend me and 'take me in.' Their antics around the boat seem full of joy and their high-pitched sounds are like the bursts of laughter of happy children. I look for them and call them. If they are not there, I miss them and long for them. For in some way they communicate their joy to me, especially when I feel sadness within my heart.

Life at sea is full of contrasts. There are crises to be sure, when life itself is in peril. But if you were in my place on *Research II* you would know wonderful times, days of intense joy and spiritual peace. You would share with me meetings with the largest creatures of the sea and commune with them in a mutual harmony that defies language to express in full.

Life at sea alone in a little boat brings you to the critical point, the threshold of life itself, where you live or die, and for a moment hang over the precipice of time and stare into the depths of eternity. Through faith in a living Christ who stands on the other side standing in His risen power, you know that you also will overcome as He has overcome. And if it is His will that you join Him there, His *arm is not shortened that it cannot save* but is stretched out for you to grasp. And who cares, if all your finite strength is gone, He reaches out with *His everlasting arms* and carries you over the chasm, Himself, in His redeeming power. And if you live through the moments of crisis, you are enriched beyond measure.

When all is well with me

Join me on many a day as I awake after a good night's sleep. I roll over and kneel in a short prayer to my Heavenly Father in thanksgiving for the rest of the night. I peer out of the companionway. *Research II* is sailing on a close reach. I check her compass course, 95' east. All is well, 4 to 5 knots. I look back to Stanley the Scull-Oar. He is there standing like a sentinel on duty keeping *Research II* on course. I am full of wonder at his efficiency. I listen to him, *Clickity-click, clickity-click, clickity-click,* as the Vane rocks gently back and fore like a metronome. Then a pause which coincides with a wave, pushing *Research II* off course a few degrees. Stanley responds. The vane corrects. Then after thirty seconds, Stanley resumes equilibrium, *Clickity-click, clickity-click, clickity-click.* What music it is to my ears. And I cannot help feeling a wave of pride, may the Lord forgive me, in that Stanley, the robot, was made my myself.

The dawn lightens and waits for the morning sun to appear in the east. I read the sky. It heralds peace and a good day with a healthy wind. Clouds above are quiet and still, without the dark ragged frowns of nature's anger. I stretch as I stand in the companionway, surveying the world about me as the sky dome rests on the circular disc of the ocean. No ship is in sight, no intrusion of any kind breaks the natural setting of the aqua-highway that joins every continent across the world. There are literally no demands on me. I pause and reflect with a feast of satisfaction as *Research II* sails on her way reaching out across the sea, with gurgling laughter from her bow as it merrily cuts through the water. Almost reluctantly,

I recede in to the cabin and kneel down at the stove to boil up a kettle of water for morning tea. What a life, I think effortlessly within me, as I raise myself again through the open hatch and turn to greet the sun, while I sip my thermos mug of tea. Who would want to be anywhere better than here to drink in this *spiritual* experience in an effortless absorption of passive reception, as the pen of nature imprints on mind and heart its unique and overpowering imagery?

CHAPTER EIGHT

Knock out in the Cockpit

It's amazing how quickly we forget bad times. The sea encourages this. You suffer tribulations, reaching into yourself to find the strength to face days of bad weather with every kind of problem and danger. Then it is all over, the sun comes out, the seas subside and on you go, revelling in the joy of sailing. But we must get back to the records. I quote,

Log: Day 5, Tuesday, 27th June, 1995

Northeast gale since last night 10 p.m. Big seas. Phosphorescence lights up the darkness. Very cold. S'Brd tack. All changed in cabin. Bedding, clothes soaking wet. Very difficult to move. Blows, blows, blows. Bad night. Self steering held her SE Wind stayed NE.

I recall that night as *Research II* heeled on a reach, the seas hissing at the stern as the boat raced through the darkness. The night was pitch dark. I felt enclosed in a world of my own. I stood there for a while holding on to the raised coaming of the weather side as Research plunged on at 45'. On the lee, the rail would disappear as a white phosphorescent mass of water raked the length of the boat to leave the stern into oblivion. I was standing at the same angle, my eyes watching Stanley the Scull-oar. The vane was not moving and the blade was locked under pressure of the sea. Theoretically the vane is not efficient when this is the case. It is supposed to be rocking like a pendulum. But here it was, the boat sticking to its course and the Self-Steering blade steady at an angle to the sea. And we were traveling fast. I watched the knotmeter register 6-8 knots. And in surges of the sea, the speed rose to 9 knots. I was an onlooker. Forces were controlling me. Nature's power was harnessed to man's ingenuity. There was nothing more that I could do. I felt detached. To look forward was futile. What was there but inky darkness and the wild seas? What a miracle, a frail human being in a little boat cutting swiftly through the seas, the wind shrieking through the rigging and the foaming phosphorescence lighting up the stern in a patch of brightness. The seas themselves emitted a hissing sound as they whipped past the stern. I felt, as I said, detached, almost superfluous. By midnight, it seemed to me that there would be no change all night. I had been there scrutinizing the behaviour of the boat and especially the performance of the Scull-oar. The rhythmic motion of the boat, as it sped on its way, never changed. I went below and closed the hatch. I slept like a log till daybreak. Then breakfast - Corn Flakes, Vienna sausage, beans and hot tea.

Wear and tear

All the rope work and adjustment to rigging brought cuts and bruises to my hands. Add to this salt water and you have a problem. This was magnified because no plaster would stay on my hands, unless of course I took a few days off duty. That you cannot do on a solo voyage and would not be tolerated even though you had a crew. My thumbs both had an open red cut like a furrow in a ploughed field. I filled the red sores with Ozonal. Knuckles were red and skinned. Bruises and abrasions appeared on the back of my hands, but I had no recollection of how and when they happened. I thought for a time that my hands would be permanently marked and disfigured. But amazingly, they toughened up with new thick skin and the cuts receded into history. Repeatedly the northeasterly turned clockwise with the sun to east. The result was that I was often pushed southeast. I had to get used to this tendency to be pushed south-east. Meantime *Research II* sailed on between 4 and 6 knots.

A broken tiller

Stanley was not working efficiently. The cause was in the tiller. It was sagging down. It was obviously broken between the cheeks. I examined it there and saw that it still hinged on one crossbolt. The trouble was that the tiller was too tightly set on the head of the rudderstock. In the dark I had fallen over the end of the tiller so that it broke. That was the potential negative of the tiller being so long that you could steer from the companionway. And now the negative was a reality. I cut the tiller along half its length. I then spliced it on to the remaining half, whipping it all so that it was very strong. It still was just as efficient, as the control lines from Stanley never were forward of the middle of the tiller anyway.

The radar reflector fails

I had a big radar reflector under the port spreader on the mast. As I surveyed the rigging, I realized that it was gone. The brass swivel fitting gave way during the night and the reflector fell. It was providential that no ship was coming in my direction as it would not have known my presence. The masthead navigation lights would hardly be seen at any distance. Fortunately we were heeled to starboard. If we were heeled to port the reflector would have dropped into the sea. As it was, it fell on deck. I had a twelve foot long aluminum pole. I slit one of the vanes on the reflector and attached the latter to the end of the pole. I then secured the pole to the port backstay. I extra-tightened the stay and secured it against loosening with new wire round the turnbuckle. Now the reflector was secure. And also the threat of it tearing the mainsail was eliminated. I was proud of my work. I surveyed my repairs with satisfaction. It occurred to me that in both cases, I actually had improved efficiency. The long tiller had been an annoyance for years and the location of the radar reflector on the spreader was obviously a potential menace to the sails. I had worked throughout the day as Research sailed on to the east. Now it was evening. The sun had crossed the sky and shone from the port quarter astern. It still set in the northern hemisphere as it also rose in the morning. In the course of the voyage, bit by bit, sunrise and sunset would every day be more southerly, as we had passed the longest day on the 22nd of June now more than a month before. It was a glorious evening, with the sun astern. She was doing 4 to 5 knots on jib alone. Tiredness came over me, as there was little or no rest for the past 48 hours. It would soon be dark and if I put up the main, I might well have to get out and reef or pull it down again. I crawled forward and tended the sails on the foreboom. I had the jib outhauled so that the tack was controlled as with a spinnaker, the foreboom swivelling on its gooseneck at the mast. I reflected on the night that was past and the speed of nine knots. We still were doing up to six knots with the jib. Why be caught out with too much canvas? The fact is that my boat was very fast and the hull shape offered no opposition to the oncoming sea.

Getting into hot water

Down below for the night, I prepared a good hot meal. Irish stew along with my boiled potatoes and onions. I liked tea after food. I use powdered milk. For the first few days, I had mixed the milk and put it in a bottle. But since we were no longer on land, on the sea it quickly turned into curds, shaken like a churn with the motion of the rocking boat. Now my revised method was to make the milk in my cup each time I needed it. We are always learning, aren't we? Also until this point in time I reached to the stove by crouching on my feet and then sitting back and pouring the kettle into my thermos cup on the floor at my feet. That might be alright in the calm of a harbour. But I learned the hard way that I was doing things the wrong way out in the North Atlantic. I had put a big spoon of milk powder in the cup along with a tea bag. The thermos cup itself sat on a cloth so that it would not skid across to lee and spill. I then crouched and leaned forward to the stove and took the kettle of boiling water in my hand. Gravity did the rest. The boat gave an extra heel and I fell back to my seat. The kettle spilled its contents onto my foot and over my right hand. There was no time to waste. Burns, I knew from past experience, could incapacitate me and the pain of the scalding water was coming right up like a thousand jabs of needles to my heart. I whipped off my sandal and sock. Reaching behind me I grabbed a packet of baking soda and hastily mixed this with cold water and covered my ankle. My hand was also red and three or four big blisters were already forming. I covered my hand with the white muddy solution. I kept doing this for an hour so that no air could get at the burns. I added more paste so that all the time the ankle and hand were continually cooled like an engine with the water in the radiator, or more like the limbs of someone wallowing in a therapeutic mud bath. It worked. The process of huge expanded liquid-filled incapacitating burns was neutralized. Thankfully, after a week and continual plastering with the therapeutic paste I could pretend they didn't exist. After two weeks, I had to look at my hand and the curious red patches to recall the pain. New skin was already replacing the old under the withered white blistering. The only change in the formula was in that I replaced cold water with cold tea. Somehow I thought that tea would add an extra healing touch.

Driving a lesson 'home'

There is always an advantage which we can gain from a calamity. Thus, the calamity is converted into a learning process. And if there is pain attendant on learning, the lesson will never be forgotten. James, the son of Mary Stewart, Queen of Scotland, was educated in Scotland as a boy before he became monarch of the United Kingdom at the Union of the Crowns in 1603. He had a private tutor named George Buchannan. The Scottish man of learning was of the traditional school of teaching. You were taught the lesson in the three-fold manner:

1. The lesson was presented to you;
2. It was analyzed and explained to you with examples;
3. You were grilled orally with relevant questions to answer orally or answer on slate or paper.

If you failed to respond positively at the third stage, several strokes of the leather strap or flexible willow cane were administered to drive the lesson home. The principle was clear. The Latin declension or verb conjugation had missed your thick head, like a nail driven through two boards, which missed the one below. The answer was simple except that the schoolmaster used the belt or the cane to drive the noun or the verb into the pupil's memory. There was a lifetime guarantee with this method of teaching. King James's experience in school gave him a knowledge of Latin and Greek, of which he subsequently was proud.

Voices

It is well known that voices are heard in boats. I leave it to the reader to come to his or her own conclusion, whether this is a subjective impression, or has some acoustic significance relating to the boat. For me, both are responsible. The solo sailor is so because he represents a store of life experiences. He is a walking bank of received input from all associations throughout his life. Even though he is not consciously listening to music or some conversation or speech, these impinge upon his receptive faculties without effort. And, like all energy, even sound, they leave their own permanent photo imprints on the disc of his memory. No computer disc or CD could match the human being for its millions of 'memory.'

From the Journal: Yesterday it was music which I think I traced to the rocking of the gimbaled stove. What a relief to find a rational explanation! But listen. There again there are the sweet strains of the violin. I was convinced there was a rational explanation. And I found it. The music came from the electrical wire leading down from the solar generator as it rubbed back and forth against the cabin wall. Next day: Today, whatever I did, there was no explanation. I could hear a steady sound of voices, as of a man and a woman, speaking in turn. This was identifiable as a broadcast program you might hear on the radio or on television. I checked all three radios, but No. The voices continued as clearly as you could wish. When I tried to identify them, they assumed a strange ring about them as if they were coming from a long distance away. I leave the subject at this point. The fact is that throughout the voyage I had this phenomenon continually, whenever there was relative quiet of weather conditions. This phenomenon was quite distinct from the voices of individual people to which I shall advert later.

The explosion

We were now passing over the south part of the fog bound fishing banks, south of Newfoundland. Just east of this one day, I was quite alarmed. Weather conditions were quiet at the time and *Research II* was sailing close to an east - the desired direction. Suddenly there was the most violent explosion. The whole atmosphere was affected. Reverberations continued for some considerable number of seconds before the sound died down. What could it be? My mind thought of three possibilities:

1. A plane - possibly the Concorde was passing and the sound was from it breaking the sound barrier.
2. The Americans were putting up a space rocket. I heard all this from the radio, and that the launching had been delayed until this point because of bad weather.
3. I recalled seeing something on the chart which made me uneasy.

I now perused the chart of the Atlantic west. There, just north of my present position was an area with a warning mark for shipping - **FIRING AREA - ALL SHIPS KEEP OUT**. My reaction was almost instantaneous. All at once I had visions of very unpleasant happenings. Pictures of war scenes came vividly to mind, Enemy bombers droning overhead, whistling sounds of sticks of bombs dropping down from the skies, and then detonation. Huge plumes of water and spray as bombs plunged into the sea, with some turning the decks of ships into red bonfires. It all gave one nasty sensation that chilled the stomach and brought goose flesh to the back of my neck. Just think of it, the US lobbing test missiles into the Atlantic and one of them, even the shell casing, coming down on my little boat. Think of the damage! And further, I did not have insurance cover. And even if I had, I realized that it was unlikely that I would be around to collect it. It occurred to me at this point that I appeared selfish, as my wife Mary would also not be able to collect any compensation. If you look at my position at this point, at North Latitude 44' 18"; West Longitude 52' 19", you will see *Research II* did a big turn south. The Log reading records Course SE 150-165 Speed 5.7 knots (av. 4). That tells the story. I was running south for my life, before an empty rocket or any other missile fragment had a chance to sink my boat.

It's worth it

A glorious day now followed the gales and high sea. The weather had quieted last evening and now the angry look of the sea gave way to a smile. I raised the mainsail. I had to put down the dodger. I found that it was quite unsafe to go forward on deck with the dodger up. It was treacherous to stand up. My method was to crawl forward on my knees. That itself, along with the necessity of crawling in the cabin, had a very painful effect on my knees. Both developed calluses like the hard leathery sole of the foot. Sometimes this pain was excruciating and I would push myself forward sometimes instead, in a sitting position with my legs stretched in front of me. It is still very hard for me to understand the extreme pain of crawling on deck. Clearly knee pads are the answer, like those used by construction workers, on asphalt roofs. For my purpose and that of other sailors on small sailing craft on the ocean, the pads would have to grip the deck like the sole of the shoe or sandal.

The years take their toll

Apart from the chronic hazard of tender knees, there was the undeniable fact that I was not young. Thirty or forty years earlier, I could spring forward like a cat and do all kinds of chores with ease. Memories of these days came back to me, of running to the road from the peatbank in the hills above our home in Aultbea in the Scottish Highlands, carrying a large bag of new peats. I thought nothing of running, springing from one firm spot to another, avoiding the marshes. A vivid experience came back to my mind, of being in the water for half an hour in Loch Alsh, near the Isle of Skye, in the wild days of the month of March. I had on thick clothes and heavy leather boots with rows of steel tackets and steel heel and toe plates. The latter were a handicap as every time I kicked down to tread water, the weight on my feet, simply pulled me down further. Yet I was none the worse for the experience, and when ashore, I continued for hours, though soaking wet, to look after the boat, the beautiful Mascot, built in the Isle of Wight by Harley Mead. She was being towed at the time, without her ballast keel. Excessive speed by the pulling motorboat capsized her so that I, the sole occupant at the tiller, had to take to the water. Now, forty years later, and with the wear and tear of life, the *earthen vessel of the flesh* had a hard task to match the will of the spirit. But never mind. The spirit of man is immortal and invincible.

Log: Day 6, Wednesday, 28th June, 1995

The morning was perfect like the sunset. The sea was a glittering disc of placid joy. Sea birds called to say 'Hello, How are you doing, Angus?' Porpoises rose and turned over beside the gunwale. A flying fish took to the air for a morning flight, but not in my direction. Otherwise I might have had him for breakfast.

When I had first wakened, the sun peeped up over the stern, a red orb in the northeastern sky. Something was far wrong. *Research II* had turned around and was sailing back NW to St. John's. I am sure *Research II* wanted me to call there. I quickly turned her round and headed NE by E and trimmed my valuable crew member Stanley the Scull-Oar. What a crew member! Just think of it, he makes no demands on me as long as he is adjusted to the course; he doesn't eat or sleep; he doesn't complain or protest. No, he doesn't ask much; just a little tender loving care. A drop of oil, a shot of grease, a little adjustment to his collar, a slight rake of the vane to keep his head from bobbing forward in heavy seas, like a boy nodding off to sleep in a church pew when the minister preaches too long. Everyone needs some attention. How a patient loves a nurse to come to the bedside to care for him! A car owner cares for his car. For me, Stanley was my baby. I did not consider it tedious to spend time, even five hours, coming to know its foibles, its capabilities, its potential, its idiosyncrasies. Tender loving care pays. Stanley responded by giving me carefree sailing, days and nights without a hand at the tiller. The sea presents a new species of choices, a refreshing change from land life. For me, it seemed at this point that these choices were, in part, made for me and not altogether by me. What would you want? A gale with jib up and reaching a speed of 9 knots, or the contrast of a relative calm, with full sail and the boat heading back?

I was always conscious of course changes and their relation to the distance travelled eastwards towards the UK. As I mentioned, the distance travelled by the boat on its zig-zag line, dictated by weather and wind, would be greater than the actual distance eastwards. I calculated my distance travelled by the boat through the water by taking the mean speed per hour and allowing for an estimate of currents - the Gulf Stream in the mid ocean.

Day 6: SW fresh Last 24 hours 103 miles. DR. to date from N Sydney 693 miles.

Log: Day 7, Thursday, 29th June, 1995

Weather fair but sky grey. Steady wind SW fresh. Sailed NE by E compass course. Stanley keeps us on course. I slept from 9:00 pm until 7.30 am. Very tired. Twice looked out. Cold, made cup of tea. 4 -5 knots steady Jib only SS good.

Glorious day. Passed 50' West Longitude. Slight cloud. Cold even in sun.

Is someone speaking to me?

Repairs. Jib not setting. Go forward. Turnbuckle on forestay has broken. The fork has snapped. Tremendous pressure on jib in the gales now past. Spent time on transfer of jib tack to other stay. Secured broken forestay to pulpit.

Day good. Spent much of day on maintenance. This was a daily routine. I did some maintenance task as a rule for part of every day. Today, there were many left over from the gale days. These had to be attended to. If you saw *Research II* at this time you would see that she had the usual sails, but I had kept on her the new booms with their goosenecks on the mast, which were rigged for the Auto-Sail. I kept the aft boom on as I could use it either for my Auto-Sail or for the orthodox mainsail. You would notice that this boom was attached to the mast about a foot lower than the conventional boom. I stress this point as a lower boom brings in a risk factor which can be serious.

During the day, I had the main up. As the wind had freshened in the afternoon, I had reefed it down. There was a good SW wind so that the mainsheet was full out with the boom practically at right angles to the boat's course. Every so often, we would veer to right or left because the jib would become blanked out by the mainsail. This was a full maintenance day. I was engrossed in this mechanical side of the voyage and only when it was necessary, gave thought to the sails. That was the great thing about having Stanley the Scull-Oar. But every so often Stanley showed his limitations, which he shares with us all.

I was working in the cockpit at the time and had just straightened up and turned round from a chore, fixing the drogue so that it would be ready to use in an instant. Suddenly I heard a crack like a gun. It is hard to explain, but it took a moment or two to realize that the crack came from the side of my head. The boom had jibed. It swung over in the usual total silence, but with the speed of a rocket. The boom wasn't heavy. But the blow was like a Karate chop. Manually, I corrected the situation and *Research II* was back on course. I could hardly believe it as I felt a huge lump on the side of my head. I recall saying to myself - there was no one else around to speak to, "I'll have to watch out for that boom, or it will kill me."

The wind continued to freshen. An hour later I was still at my chores and specifically absorbed in an adjustment to Stanley the Self-Steering Scull-Oar. Without paying attention to the continued veering of the boat from side to side in the rising wind, I did not think of the increasing pressure downwards on the boom which followed. This was acerbated by the absence of a topping lift which serves to keep the boom horizontal. Also, the boom was pressed down to a large extent by the vang from the base of the mast.

I finished the adjustment to Stanley, and had just turned around, when the boom jibed. The boom struck me again in the same place. It sounds strange, but I did not feel a thing. The lump already there, along with the woollen bonnet on my head, cushioned the impact.

The evening had come and the seas had grown sharply so that *Research II* was liable to broach to. I resolved that the main had to come down so that the jib would be free to pull *Research II* along through the night without any worry. Just as I was about to clamber up to the mast, to lower the main, without any warning, the end of the boom hit me again. I have the distinct recollection of my knees buckling under me, and then darkness.

A past experience

I recall once as scrum-half in an inter-House rugby game at Keil School, Dunbarton, watching the ball bouncing towards me along the ground with a wild crowd of big forwards charging after it. The obligation on the scrum-half was mandatory. According to the *blue book* his duty was simple and explicit. He had to stop the advance, by falling on the ball. He then would roll himself around it and the scrumload of husky forwards of both sides would kick him with their feet from every angle to release the ball and get it back to the wing players. Obediently on that occasion, I bent my head. A huge forward, who played for the West of Scotland, at that moment reached me. His massive knee met my head. The memory is still clear after nearly fifty years. My head jerked back and I had the sensation that it was being pushed into my shoulder blades.

I rose from darkness to see faces all around me. I was in a hut. A man's mouth was moving as he looked at me. Faintly I heard, "MacKinnon, Do you hear me?" I struggled to coordinate my mind and my sight. Of course that is Mr. Wilkinson, the Latin master and referee, and I'm in the pavilion, and these are the faces of the teams, all crowding around me and staring at me. I emitted a whispered sound, "Yes."

"Good, that's topping", said Mr. Wilkinson decisively, "Alright, back on the field, chaps." With that, all vanished. The referee turned at the door, "Come back when you feel ready. We need you. MacKinnon House is down." And with that, he was off. I knew exactly what was expected of me. Ten minutes later I was back in the game. It was all in the day's work. Keil was for boys, and it made men of them.

Forgive the digression, but here I was in the middle of the Atlantic, nearly fifty years later, now rather battered by many storms of life, and running into this familiar experience. My knees buckled, then darkness. My next recollection is that of sitting cross-legged on ropes, and a bucket in front of me on the cockpit floor. Everything was moving around me, and now and then water splashed over the gunwale. A gurgling sound came from below me as the water exited from the self draining floor. The boat was parallel with the waves, going like a train with white horses lifting her weather side so that I was continually being thrown forward against the bridge deck. Arrows were piercing my head. I could not see on my right side. I pulled my bonnet up so that I could see. My hand stuck. The tight hem of the bonnet would hardly clear the side of my head. Vaguely, I wondered. Then I realized that the bonnet was stuck because the lump on my head was now huge. I had a curious sensation as I felt its shape through the wool. I pulled the bonnet off from the other side. But still I could not see. I felt with my hand and realized that my right eye was hidden in a lump of swollen flesh. Without thinking or any conscious effort, I tumbled into the cabin through the companionway. I couldn't see anything but instinctively I knew where everything was. My hand reached up to the Aspirin and Tylenol on the top shelf to my right. Scarcely seeing them in front of me, I took two of each kind out of the bottles and swallowed them, with a drink of water. This was the time for pills. I had a tremendous headache. I had to order my legs to move. It was action stations. Wounded or not, the main had to be handed and the boat brought under control and back on course, before the twilight passed into the darkness with its amplified dangers and imagined terrors. With great effort, I clambered out, and pulled down the main and lashed the boom. I recall, saying to myself - again as there was no one else to speak to - "I'll have to be more careful, I'll have to be more careful." But was that the real message?

Now that the main was down, I reset *Research II* on course to the east. I have no recollection of doing this but I must have done it. All I do remember is waking up in the early hours. Then the real message hit me like a brain wave. A voice came clear and loud speaking to my thick head, 'Take that menace of a boom off. It is too low. Put back the boat's own boom, and all will be sunshine.'

I quote from my journal notes: 'And that is what I did today, Friday, all morning. And lo, all is well and the boom is now far away from my thick head.'

A chat with a passer-by

Friday morning. 30th July: I slept all night. Maybe the crack on my head had an effect upon me. I dreamed of Mary, *mo nighean donn bhoidheach,* my beautiful dark-haired maiden. Thoughts came to me. Was I fair to her? How much did I hurt her in life and deceive her? Did I expect too much of her? But I loved her and always will.

I dreamed long of Bill MacLeod, whom I had last seen on his deathbed, with his wife Sadie and family. I could not get him out of my mind. In my dream he was speaking to me and telling me that I was on the wrong tack and heading for South America. I kept putting this into perspective and, even in sleep, dismissed his injunction to me as frivolous and irrelevant. But I got up anyway and, sure enough, the jib sheet had got caught on the gooseneck fitting on the mast - the slide I had attached to the mast. The result was that *Research II* was heading for Buenos Aires.

This Friday morning was very calm. I hadn't seen it like this before. Bird life was prolific. Gulls and terns and sea pigeons were all out and about, making the most of it. There was little or no wind as I worked on the main boom change so that there would not be a repeat of yesterday's irritation. A whale came along and stayed with me until I finished it. I think we are all in it together out here. Possibly I am being taken as one of the family. A strange but wonderful feeling came over me. We are never alone. Look at the company all around me. We had a conversation, which went something like this:

Whale: 'How are you making out, Rev Angus? You're from Nova Scotia. I see your boat has CBBC on the transom. Is that the Cape Breton Boat Club?'

Captain: 'No,' I answered, 'These letters stand for The Catalone Bay Boat Club, not too far from the mouth of the Mira River.'

Whale: 'Are there many in it?'

Captain: 'Enough. We cannot take any more members at this time. We are kind of exclusive. Expert mackerel fishers. There's Edward, George, Roddie and Gordon; Arthur, J.J., Wayne, Harvey, Sam, Malcolm, Danny, Charlie. Also John, Lewis, and Tommy and Malky. Malky has the flag boat of the fleet, a boat specially built, beamy with a little cabin and a nice little shelter forward, ideal for Malky and his friend Tommy. The two of them can be seen on any good summer evening jigging for mackerel in the Bay, just for the fun of it. Malky had the boat built in Guysborough and paid for it by working late in the Glace Bay Water Department. I should add, also, when he was not racing his horse at the Sydney Race track. You can see the boat. You can't miss it. It is called OVER-TIME.'

To my surprise, the whale leaned over sideways and his eye looked at me as he said,

Whale: 'You don't need to tell me. I know, I know.'

Captain.: 'How do you know?'

Whale: Who doesn't know Allistar MacGillivray's Song of the Mira? I spend time each year in the Mira Bay, just hoping to hear it.'

This exchange with a seasoned traveler of the ocean 'made my day', just as a visit from a minister can make the day of a house bound soul in his community.

I have been told, by old folk especially, that a visit from a clergyman, minister or priest of any ecclesiastical regiment, as well as of their own, had been a ray of sunshine. And most have said to me, when I next saw them, 'He made my day.'

We all like company. We need it. Beggars can't be choosers.

Almost any of God's creatures, with of course a few definite exceptions, of humans as well as other animals, would be welcome out there for me on the ocean.

I continued with the tasks at hand. Whenever conditions were favorable, it was essential to get maintenance done, especially to vital items relating to safety and function of the sailing machine. This was the time you closely examined every turnbuckle and clevis pin and studied the tension of the shrouds. What always concerned me was if there was a change, a visible one. But apart from the second forestay, which I spoke about already, failing at the fork in the turnbuckle, there was no sign of any other failure. I am certain that I would have a very different story to tell, had I not doubled the rigging and, in fact, increased its strength as I used 3/16th stainless steel wire throughout.

Later I was occupied at the delicate task of tuning Stanley the SS Vane to head *Research II* due east compass course 120', with a 2-3 knot breeze, when my new friend the whale rolled alongside. As I worked, one minute he would be on the port side and then appear close to the boat on the starboard side. I could see his body close to the boat on the lee side. He was big. I could feel *Research II* reacting to his movements as his body moved. He must have displaced at least twenty tons.

It seemed that we were accepted, I and him. There was also Stanley the crew member standing erect at the stern, nodding his head, the wind vane, back and fore. It is not improbable that the whale thought Stanley was my companion on the trip. Anyway we were one together with the wind and the sea, Wilmot and me, two of God's creatures.

It was natural for me to wonder why he was there, staying so long with *Research II*. I came to the conclusion that he was checking me out to see that all was well. I could feel his friendly compassion, he, the master of the ocean, his natural habitat, I, the traveler alone in that frail little boat. He had a paternal, friendly, helpful interest, a kind of brotherly concern, for my well-being. Maybe he was God's messenger, reassuring me as he was directed by our common Maker, to keep an eye on me.

Anyway, when all seemed well and ship-shape, the compass steady, without a hand on the tiller, my good friend left me. I know that he'll be back to keep an eye on me.

How strange, I mused, on this little planet where about 6 billion people live, that I travel 800 miles without the sight of a ship or any human being!

Log: Day 8, Friday, 30th June, 1995

1700 hrs.

Position: N 40'22" W 48' 58"

Speed: 3.6 knots.

Wind variable SW-W 1-2. Little progress last 24 hours. Fog closing in afternoon. Time for a sleep. SS temperamental in light winds.

Log: Day 9, Saturday, 1st July, 1995

Weather: Clearing fog. Very cold. Becalmed for 24 hours.

Breeze rose about 1300 hours. Trimmed sails and SS. Tried boomed out foresail, Trade wind goosewing style, but reverted to fore and aft rig.

Two whales stopped by to say hello. I' m sure one of them was our friend whom we met yesterday, the one who knew Mira Bay, and the Song of the Mira. Possibly the other was his good wife whom he took along with him to show her this visitor to the middle of the Atlantic.

The breeze stiffened and gave *Research II* 4 knots. There was little of wave, but an undulating uniformity as the boat sped on her way with the following light wind. The sea was beautiful and calm. All was in marked contrast with earlier days. The difference between 'difficult' conditions and this delight was like the difference of night from day.

Running short of alcohol

Every so often at sea, we are faced with the consequences of some omission or mistake before we began the voyage. That is one major difference between coastal cruising and ocean voyaging. In the case of the former, you can always pull in to some port on the way to obtain whatever you need. In the case of the latter, you are stuck with your mistake and that's that. You just have to make the best of it. For instance, I meant to take two cans of Methyl Hydrate for the stove, and one can of Kerosene for the storm lantern which I used as a heater as well as a light in the cabin. Instead I bought two cans of Kerosene and only one of alcohol. The alcohol was the vital requirement for hot food on the two burner alcohol stove. The Kerosene was for heating, only as required, and in part for cabin light. This was to economize on electrical power as much as possible in saving the cabin lights. Now as I looked at the amount of fuel left, it was plain that I would run out of alcohol before *Research II* was half-way across. The thought of cold food was not a happy one. It would have a very negative impact upon my disposition. Hot meals were a vital condition of good humour and contributed to a readiness to tackle anything when called upon, as the going got tough.

I resolved that I had no option but to follow the discipline of rationing, as in wartime. I would have only one hot cup of tea or coffee every morning and one hot meal in the evening- I had a mental vision of my lovely potatoes and onions which seemed of very good quality, steamed and cooked to perfection, as an absolute necessity. As it turned out, I could steam the potatoes and onions together and they were cooked faster than in a Microwave oven. This I decided I would demonstrate on land when I returned to mother earth, if challenged, and if in Providence, I was still around.

To this point, although we were in the middle of the hottest summer on record in Europe and in America, there was no need of a freezer for food. The butter remains rock hard, and my hands, in spite of all the work, are perpetually cold. They are hacked with open cuts and no plaster will stay on them. The egg on the side of my head has gone down somewhat. That is, relatively speaking.

Everything has some use. It is a guarantee that my bonnet will stay on my head. The whole area is discolored and bruised and very tender to touch. I find it hard to see my image in the mirror as the latter faces the door. All I can make out is the face of a man who is unshaven and whose face has two contrasting sides, the one with the egg appearing much darker than the other. Skin has peeled off my little finger and blood will not stop pouring out while I am working. It is more trouble than it is worth to try and keep plasters on my cuts.

Buckets

No boat is complete without a bucket. I had two of the plastic variety in commission throughout the voyage. One was a general purpose bucket for cleaning purposes. I never got around to putting a rope on this one in order to make it easy to pull in a half bucketful of water for washing. I use sea water for all of this, including washing the dishes. I had another which was identical except that it was a different colour. I had a good rope with a spliced loop for the hand, so that it would not be accidentally lost by the force of the sea pulling it out of the hand. Using this was very efficient. This, I used instead of the ship's head. Before setting out, I had closed the valves so that the head was out of commission. In any case, there was a fair amount of equipment stored forward and usually this spilled out of the fo'c'sle into the head area. I therefore used the bucket for nature's needs. This wasn't the place for holding a shroud with one hand and surveying the horizon, while having a leisurely slash. There was one complication arising from using the two buckets. In the dark at night, it was not easy to see the right bucket. I must say it didn't worry me if I used the wrong one now and then. I could visualize that this laxity, associated with bachelor indifference, would not be tolerated had there been feminine company. Meanwhile no one ever complained or checked. In these harmonious uncomplicated circumstances, life went on very smoothly for captain and crew in the boat's household activities.

Garbage

I could be wrong, but I had the impression that there was very little garbage on the ocean. It is true that visually this did not mean much as much garbage does not float. Therefore you could see on the ocean only that which stayed on the surface. There was some plastic, mostly parts of foam boxes. Also some small containers and glass or plastic bottles. It is well known that bottles cross oceans and it is reasonable to assume that a great deal if not all of floating garbage from America comes ashore on the west coast of Britain and Ireland.

Inside the boat, I flattened tins and threw them overboard. Being metal, the acid nature of the sea would soon reduce them to nothing. I had very little else except plastic bags. These I kept on the boat as they took up very little space. Any leftovers of food, and there was practically nothing of this, I flung out for the birds who quickly gobbled it up.

Log: Day 9

Fog closed in about mid-day. Then a sound. It was unmistakably the fog horn of a ship. I peered through the fog, to no avail. But there it was again, now louder. It kept on, getting louder until I thought that I was hearing also the sound of engines. But I could see nothing. It occurred to me that this must be also true of the ship. Here it was pounding through the ocean and in no way could it possibly see me. I went below and pulled out my own fog-horn, a small but powerful compression model. This I used, giving a succession of short penetrating blasts, after the successive acoustic overtures from the unseen but approaching ship. Here we were out on the ocean, exchanging trumpet-like notes. We kept up this slow duet with blasts alternating, his big deep one and my sharp high penetrating one. The ship must have come abreast of mine and then passed me as the sound of the horn grew weaker and eventually ceased. We were close to the shipping route between New York and the Clyde industrial area of Scotland. How strange that we had this exchange, though we never saw each other! It was reassuring to think that *Research II* must have been picked up on the ship's radar screen, though visually unseen. Also one felt that observation by the duty officer over a period of time would give my track, and therefore course or direction, and also speed, to which the ship could respond by giving me a wide berth. There would then be no sudden emergency, in which the ship would not be able to avoid me.

The magic of the sea

An hour later the fog cleared and the sun shone in its fullness. What a vista, I thought, as I surveyed my aquatic habitat! There was a calm sea with the welcome ripples of a light breeze. I could hear the music of the bow, cutting inexorably through the water. Above and around me, sea birds were busily going about their daily chores, and looking hopefully for some scraps. It seemed to me as if they were picking up habits associated with human society, lining up like a queue for their turn. (I pause. I see the knuckle on my left little finger is bare. I'll just have to put a plaster on it.)

We have now moved East about a fifth of the distance. Sydney, my starting point, was approximately on Longitude West 60'. And my destination near the Solent in the English Channel was close to zero, on the Greenwich meridian, where West Longitude stopped and East Longitude began. The actual distance I traveled, according to Dead Reckoning and position calculation, was over 900 miles, but the distance Eastwards was 800 miles. This works out at roughly the average of all loners on the ocean, a hundred miles made good over the ground per day. It will be noted that on some days up to 150 miles were covered in 24 hours. On the other hand there were days when we were becalmed and made little or no progress except through advantage of the Gulf Stream.

Log: Day 9

Position N 43' 49"; W 48' 22". Compass heading 120' SE

Speed 2.8 knots. Hope this situation continues with an increase of wind.

What did I eat on my trip? Certainly there was not bacon and eggs, toast and tea. The fact is that I was very happy with my diet and did not miss any of the extravagance that we are pressured into eating on land. Furthermore, returning to the simple life had a profoundly good effect upon my health. There is an open question, which is not settled. Is it the nature of the Spartan diet followed at sea, or the continual movement of the body, induced by the motion of the boat, that is responsible for losing weight? There are arguments on both sides. But the answer must remain only an opinion and not a verifiable fact, because both conditions are true of life at sea alone in a small boat.

For the record, here is a food list for a day's eating.

Rise at usual time of 5 a.m.

Tea or coffee

Regular: Breakfast 8 - 9 a.m.

Oatmeal Brose

Cornflakes/milk, Rye Vita, butter, marmalade.

Large thermos mug of hot tea.

Lunch 12 - 1:00 p.m.

Sardines/salmon biscuits and cheese; Blueberry jam

Or, Bowl of hot soup, Cream of Chicken or Beef/vegetable, with tin of beans in it.- Very acceptable.

Siesta

Main meal 5:00 - 6:00 p.m.

Staple diet . Steamed potatoes and onions - equal portions, with ham, corned beef, meatballs/gravy, Ravioli, carrots/peas,

Irish stew.

Coffee -two cups a day, Snacks while bars last and coke or orange drink once a day.

Retire to bed 9:00 - 10:00

This is the norm, if conditions permit. To some extent this was followed throughout the greater part of the voyage. Exceptions precluded eating for up to 48 hours.

Coastal Command checks out

I had just submerged into the dreamy oblivion of my regular afternoon siesta - a life-long habit following Winston Churchill's lifestyle - when I was awakened by the drone of an aircraft. I struggled up and, looking out of the companionway, I was in time to see the four engine camouflaged bomber make a pass overhead. I surmised that this was an aircraft of the Canadian Maritime Coastal Command. It passed fairly low and seemed to head west towards Halifax.

Rather excited by human contact, after nine days at sea, I waited in the cockpit instead of going below to salvage what remained of my sleep. But the drama seemed over and disappointment made me feel sad, so that I turned to climb down into the companionway. So that's it, I thought. They didn't bother to take a second look. Here I was, taking the Canadian Flag, the Maple Leaf, across the ocean, and it all means nothing to them. Just as I stepped into the cabin, there was a roar. I looked up. There was nothing in sight. I looked ahead to starboard and there, a sight met me that lifted my heart with joy. It came back, approaching very, very low over the sea, Canada's Coastal Guardian, friend of fisherman and sailor. Here it was taking notice of me a lone Scots/Canadian in my little 23 year old boat. As it came nearer and nearer, emotion welled up in me, a kind of pride, that this was proof that Canada meant something, that there was a human face in the institutions and here it was a demonstrated fact. Closer and closer she came, still low, very low across the sea, like a big bird with its outstretched wings. Suddenly she was there, passing my bow. I waved and waved, unashamedly happy that they had noticed me and come back, as it were, to say: 'Hello, take courage, keep going. God be with you.' The pulsating red light seemed to say *Au revoir,* as the aircraft roared off, and banked, turning westwards back to Canada and its base.

This was something to think about, to chew over and digest. This was a big moment for me. You cannot grasp how important it was, - contact with human beings. We take it for granted, as we meet people every day in life. And even though we are by ourselves, we are surrounded by human activity and as a car passes, we can wave to the occupants even if we do not know them. And often as not, we get a wave back. Go out to the roadside and try it and you will see what I mean. It is a carry over from our pedestrian ambulations, where we greet a passer-by on foot, with a 'Good day' and traditionally get an acknowledgment of good wishes.

This visit of Coastal Command made my day. There was not one day since leaving Nova Scotia when they could have spotted me as visibility was practically nil, except for a few openings of sunshine, when the sun beat the fog for an hour or two. This was also a watershed for me, a moment of truth for the voyage. We were passing the outer extremity of Canada, now well beyond the outer end of Newfoundland to the north. I could not expect any further visits from aircraft on coastal surveillance. We were now leaving the Continental Shelf, and plunging as it were into the depths of the ocean, the unknown mystery habitat of the leviathans of the deep and a world below where in the variety of fish and crustacean inhabitants, fact indeed is stranger than fiction.

Communication

It was my hope that somehow or other, word might get to Mary that all was well, before she set off with Jane for Paris.

Repeatedly I tried to get some life from my radio, but no joy. The primary concern was for some weather reports. But in actual practice, deprivation of this is not the end of the world. Consider it. The weather report warns you of coming gales or storms. But that's it. You hear of trouble coming your way. But there is no help in this, to get through what is ahead of you. It does help in that you can prepare for it, reef or hand sails, make all as ready as possible for bad weather. On the other hand, when you get warning of coming trouble, you may get nervous and become agitated beyond justification. Also, all around you, you have the sky and the sea which as we said before, are like textbooks. We read the sky and study the sea and with the alertness of our senses, we become aware of coming changes. If these are for the good, like lovely sunny weather and favorable winds, good and well. Let them come as a pleasant surprise. If the changes are for the worse, there is more than a grain of relevance in the proverb:

'Don't trouble trouble till trouble troubles you.'

When you are by yourself, you have to be on the alert all the time. Your self-reliance is linked to your life and a sixth sense gives you added awareness of danger and the need to be prepared for it, to the utmost of your ability. Sequences are rehearsed in your mind long before you ever leave the starting point of your voyage. There are many and simple action sequences like this which are automatically followed. Down with the dodger; out all hands; tend jib, reef main; or change jib, down main. Your mind is preprogrammed for different situations, just as a computer is loaded and programmed with set procedures to function as we want. You also know your boat, and if not, you should not be out on the ocean with it. It is part of you, something living and loving, like the horse is to the rider, or the big modern ship of the road, the tractor trailer, is to the driver.

At this stage I look back and reflect over the journey thus far. I know that the Great Pilot is with me and I am humbled. During the gale, for ten hours of darkness in which *Research II* reached 9 knots, as I slept a sound sleep in the cabin below, with the jib only, pulling her along, I consider that I was fortunate. In my helplessness, I knew that there was literally nothing I could do in the situation. I very calmly had left the cockpit, trusting the Master Pilot of the universe, and *the friend that sticketh closer than a brother,* to keep all safe. I stretched out my exhausted body in my sleeping bag below and fell instantly into a sound sleep until the morning, when the force of the gale had abated. And what if my mortal journey was over! So what! For me, there was the serene and complete conviction that I would awake to the morning of an eternal day, in a world where the sun never goes down because Jesus Christ is that everlasting star, the permanent sun of the spiritual solar system of the new creation, and the power source that spells out life eternal, to as many as receive him.

Yes, when I think of *Research II*, going like a train, through that night of grey fog, howling wind, cresting waves and inky darkness, with me sound asleep, exhausted, down below in the cabin, I praise God for his loving care. And I do not forget the designer William Lapworth. That night, *Research II* never yawed with the consequent dangerous condition of 'broaching to'. The balanced hull, the deep heavy aerodynamic keel, the powerful far out big rudder on the stern, all lent themselves to the performance of a miniature ocean cruiser at its best.

Back to the present. After all that excitement of the visit of Coastal Command, I returned to finish my siesta below, later to wake to a beautiful evening, sailing East at 2-3 knots. It's time to put the potatoes and onions on. Out.

Log: Day 10, Sunday, 2nd July, 1995

Last evening as darkness fell, I saw a ship's light on the starboard quarter. I watched as it bore away in a northwesterly direction, possibly heading for Halifax or the Cabot Strait. There is always a continuous stream of ships passing through the Cabot Strait between Nova Scotia and Newfoundland, as this is the entrance to the St. Lawrence Seaway leading to the great seaports in Canada and the US.

The wind increased with the coming of night. With a following strong southwesterly, speed increased to a steady 6-7 knots all night. Seas were rough and wild. I stayed up in the cockpit and dozed now and then for *norags.* About 8:00 a.m. the wind moderated and backed south. *Research II* continued on a broad reach eastwards towards Europe. Fog mingles with warmth of the sun. I took off both sweaters. Porpoises played all around, familiar friends of childhood. I felt 'at home' among them, as they brought back the happy recollections of long ago, and the glorious days, 'out in the boat' with my life-long friend Kenny MacLeod, now a retired captain of a naval auxiliary vessel and part of NATO's submarine surveillance.

Sunday, almost automatically, brings me to reflect upon the things that belong to the spirit. Thoughts of family, of my wife Mary, and Norman and Jane come home to me. I pray that God would bless them. Thoughts of our lost son Donald, evoke great sadness and sorrow, so that my heart is broken. Then I remember that God binds up our broken hearts. He comforts me, touching me with his tender love. I feel a hand upon me, gently lifting me up and turning my face to look to him. I see Christ and the face of his suffering on the Cross, as he called out, 'Father forgive them for they know not what they do.' Then I see a picture of Him risen at the right hand of the Father, a triumphant image of victory. And I hear a voice saying, 'I have overcome the world. He that overcometh, I will grant to sit with me on my throne, even as I also overcame, and am set down with my Father in his throne.' I know that the Lord has "chastised me sore" for all my sins and provocations. But his love is enduring and suffering in the context of love has a purifying or sanctifying effect upon the soul.

My independent Short Wave radio receiver is very good. I hear the BBC World Service. There is a spot on questions of faith every day and on Sunday there are services broadcast. In the service today, the speaker tells of being at the opening of the Cathedral in Manchester when the mayor took a child up on the dais beside him. He used this to illustrate the prophetic message of Isaiah, 'a little child shall lead them,' as the promise fulfilled in the Kingdom of God through Jesus Christ in the New Testament.

The speaker went on. Power traditionally persecutes the weak. The powerful are entrenched and institutionalize the weak and the have-nots as a permanent factor in the infrastructure of society. The reason why there is so much opposition to a real take-over by Christ as the Lord and dynamic leader of community life, is that the weak are kept out of positions of authority. Jesus displaces the power seekers when unworthy.

It is a great privilege to identify with other human beings in worship in God's house and learn together from His Word. Sometimes we cannot be present physically in the house of worship on the Lord's Day. But in our day of wonderful communication, just think of it, here I am in the middle of the Atlantic and I can share in a service of worship and daily spiritual thoughts with millions of other people, wherever they are in the world.

Log: Day 11, Monday, 3rd July, 1995

We are now well past the Grand banks. The depths there was roughly about 60 fathoms. Just think of the difference. The depth now has plunged to over two miles. We have literally dropped off the edge of the Continent of North America. You can surmise how the surface of the sea changes. There is now a very perceptible increase in the wave pattern. There are long undulations, round heaving masses of water commonly called a swell. This becomes the base. As the wind does its work, there is plenty room to develop really big waves. Even big ocean ships are lifted seventy feet high to plunge down into a trough. That is my recollection of the Empress of Canada. I was in the forward cabin. Sleeping was a marvellous experience of feeling one minute, very heavy, and next as you went up up up, you came to the point of coming down again, when you felt you weighed nothing at all. It seemed an excellent formula for putting one to sleep.

Now, my ship was rather smaller, but she still had to weather the same seas and she rose to the wave tops and plunged into the troughs the same as the big ships, even the Q.E.2, which took a battering from a rogue wave, not far from my course, a few weeks later.

Waypoint	9	
Position:	N 43.53"	W 46' 37"
Course:	75'E	
Time:	1600 hours	

We were now at our lowest point of Latitude, and I turned *Research II* northeast as I felt I should get up nearer the 50th parallel. I could do this only when the wind was to the west. This was clearly the exception so far, a very alarming realization. As a rule, the westerly wind and particularly the southwesterlies blew for 90 percent of the time in normal years. Here, there was a radical departure from the accepted pattern. We had cold northerlies already. This would evolve into almost consistent northeasterlies for the greater part of my journey ahead. As I said before, maybe it is not so good to know what is before you, or you would be discouraged.

Monday, 3rd continued

Fog blots out all. Eventually sun burns its off. Distinctly warmer. There is a heat haze. I take out all bedding and clothes for drying and airing in the cockpit. Morning spent at electrical chores. The searchlight has somehow shorted whole circuit. Had to cut it off.

I make assessment. The primary need of battery power is:

1. For Navigation lights at masthead.
2. Cabin lights - used sparingly.
3. If possible for Radio.

This latter equipment is malfunctioning. I cannot get it off the transmitting for receiving. It is all very galling, knowing that I have the best and most beautiful set.

This is a good day. I look overhead to the speckled sky. Today Mary and Jane leave for Paris. They will pass over me about midnight. We are used to seeing airliners and their vapour trails in the sky at our home in Arnish, Cape Breton. The planes are either descending or ascending on their Trans-Atlantic flights. Now in mid-Atlantic, to my great disappointment, it is almost impossible to see any track of a plane overhead. There is no sound of jets and no sight of planes. They are too high up in the arc of flight they make between the continents.

Last evening I heard a ship's foghorn. But there was no sight of the ship. *Research II* sails on. She's very independent.

CHAPTER 9

The Phantom Ship

Sailing by oneself on the ocean is viewed by many people as a time of introspection, when the solitude accentuates our frailty and when stripped of all the cozy wrappings of our comfortable life, we become vulnerable to negative reflections. Many would eschew such isolation, either on the ocean or on land, and choose the option of being surrounded by crowds and be insulated from preoccupying introspective thinking, by a continual variety of activities. One should note that there is significance in the fact that most secondary activities come under the appellation of 'diversions.'

It is easy to classify sport, games, and all participation beyond the primary call of our collective life, in this category. This is not to make a value judgment upon them. We can be used to help somebody through meeting the person in some out-going activity. But if activities can be interpreted as diversions, it is logical to assume that we are in some way being diverted or side-tracked from the main road of life, or to a greater or lesser extent, distracted from giving thought or attention to something more important.

There are many people whoseem happy as they pitch in to every activity. It is their way of living a full life, without giving themselves any time for reflection and taking stock. Probably we all subscribe in part, to the view that this is the formula for a full life. And it has its merits. It is surely arguable that if we are thinking about ourselves, we are guilty of some form of egotism, even if it is in the religious context. Thus, there is a kind of continual pressure in our conformist selves to 'go with the crowd' and 'keep with the pack.' It spells out safety in numbers and absolves us from thinking for ourselves, and instead, cultivating 'popularity,' 'being with it,' 'following the crowd,' 'doing the in thing,' 'political correctness,' 'yuppie group' mentality, modern 'herd psychology.' These all seem harmless as reasonable facets of collective society, and carry with them, in a vague but persuasive way, a kind of moral imperative of collective participation.

But wait. These are the diversionary roads, the recruiting tactics for the regimentation of society, the secondary roads that potentially lead our world astray. All of these, even masked by innocuous sport or dressed in intellectual respectability, or emotional fulfillment, can lead to exploitation and manipulation of people. Our emancipated age, of which the 20th century is the apex, has the odious distinction of being top of the list when it comes to mass murder of our fellow human beings. Selective groupings should not be automatically assumed to be good, even though they fill the legal requirements of being moral.

Take nationalism for example. Nationalism is, by definition, the antithesis of a world family under the rule of righteousness and love. For nationalism is the medieval type erection of insular walls of separation along ethnic, religious, privileged, and historically contrived lines of distinction. This is not only true in the secular field. It is also true in the religious context, Christian or otherwise. Then we speak of denomi- nationalism, which is the same in substance as nationalism, except that different names can obtain within the structure of the latter.

At sea, ordinary thinking stops

At sea, by yourself, the converse is true of the situation on the land. All the pressures to conform to, to join in, to follow the fashion, to be in the crowd, are absent. You might think that this would lead to inverted thinking and our being wrapped up in introspective negative reflection. This is the interesting thing. The exact opposite is the case. What happens is that you stop all your ordinary thinking. Most of our ordinary thinking arises from the pressures of our busy society and all the bombardment of missile-like commercials that are hurled at us every day, through the 'media' and every visual and auditory advertisement. And that includes the peer pressure of community or exclusive separatist group, religious and secular to which we subscribe or are exposed to. Those who refuse to join any separatist group have some justification.

A veteran soldier who had fought in Europe with the Allies in the Second World War, would not become a member of any group in the church, though he contributed to the church and was, in practice, part of the family. His explanation to me was frank, and his wife agreed with him. He spoke of his experience during the War and concluded that all the fighting was due to the fact that everyone belonged to some group, national or religious, and that this was the simple reason for all the bloodshed. Of course the answer is not that simple, because the historical evolution of society is many-sided. But there is a great deal of truth in what this veteran Canadian soldier believed.

The emptiness of partisan separatism

A German immigrant to Canada told me that during the Second World War, his father found himself fighting with the Russians, at the beginning, when Russia invaded Finland. He himself, fought on the opposite side against the Russians as the latter became identified with the Allies. There can be nothing justifiably moral in this *Sohrab and Rustum* style alignment. It is a contradiction, in terms, that members of a family are justified in killing one another. The basic concept of our humanity is that of belonging to one family, one of great variety, but one family where the law of love gives expression to our renewed humanity. Neither secular nor religious definition in terms of creed or culture is alone able to embrace this cohesive and determinative essence. For its nature is generically neither secular nor religious but is spiritual.

The spiritual answer

As I write, a crisis confrontation between native North American Indians and other Canadians was, until a few days ago, heading for a violent conclusion, the tragic route followed so often in the United States. But one man, a spiritual elder in a small Indian community in Manitoba, defused the situation. His formula was spiritual and when he used it, a new spirit dissolved the differences, basically differences of perspective. That kind of spirituality has no religious or secular counterpart, and in many ways is the antithesis of both. It supplants both by absorbing them and transforming them. Adherents then have a new dynamic that is brought to every kind of human problem and makes every one of these capable of amicable solution.

Then killing your fellow members of the human family, in the name of your country or your religion, your law or your own perceived preservation could become obsolete. Technologically it is feasible to incapacitate, rather than to kill. Yet some police in Canada are trained to shoot to kill another human being, with out any mention of training to incapacitate. Killing is the exercise of absolute power, a usurping of the authority of God. No individual should do this as a general exercise of authority in the name of citizens. We all are implicated and share in corporate guilt. Its only sanction is defense of self or immediate family. Remember the sixth commandment, *Thou shalt not kill.*

It is the shameful indictment on our intellectuals that their discoveries are applied primarily to the weaponry of destruction. We all know that *isms,* especially the big ones of our age, like Communism and Fascism and Nazism are out, demoted, disgraced, abandoned. Their badges are worn only in secret societies, as symbols of nostalgic adherence to their past short-lived glory. Yet if you examine the alternatives in the supposed free world, there are many *isms*, national and political, cultural and religious, which make our human family in the world, a honeycomb of separatism and elitism, along racial, ethnic and ideological lines. As I listen out here on the Atlantic to the events unfolding in former Yugoslavia, that beautiful country and wonderful brave people, whose partisans under Marshal Tito kept the lamp of liberty alight in Eastern Europe during the Second World War, the conviction grows that all *isms* are snares to exploit human sincerity and to distort moral judgment. The effect is to perpetuate spiritual blindness.

No Vacuum

There is no vacuum - hopefully - in our heads. When ordinary thinking stops, as it did for me at sea, new thinking took its place. This new thinking was effortless, a kind of corollary of my solitude. I did not even read my Bible as a daily rule. I was not occupied with inverted thinking. Rather I was stimulated from without. The environment around me was refreshingly different. In all its three dimensional variety of sky, sea and life, there were no pressures upon my own autonomy, my own *persona.* Instead of being squeezed into shape by 'normal' pressures of our society, I was allowed as it were to expand to my own natural shape. In many ways, I was alowed to shrink to my proper size, seeing myself not in the dubious ratings accorded to me in the community, but a small speck on the earth's circumference - known and precious only to God my Maker.

What is important

What impinges on me as important is the fact that this led to a quiet, orderly and synchronized view of life, like the focusing of binoculars, when at last all seems so wonderfully clear. God on his throne and God in created life, had no contradiction. Nature, in its different manifestations, comprised a pattern of order. Life, both human and animal, was the wonderful work of the Master creator. It's not that struggle, even violence, suffering, or conflict ceased. But given the right view and entertaining the right spirit of the universal law of love, the divine dynamic derivative, made manifest to mankind using the Hebrew people as the means, and their religious rituals as a shadow of the real, the consequent prevailing disposition was one of completeness and calm.

Some thirty years ago I was shown a book in the wheel house of a Russian ship in the North Sea. It was the Poetical Works of Robert Burns the Scottish poet. In the explosively humanist age which was labelled the *age of enlightenment,* that of the 18th century, Burns did not find the answers to life. And as with most people who do not find inner peace, he sought refuge in the company of others. Yet

Burns encapsulates the most universal longings for a better world, the wistful hopes that arise within the most cynical. Thus it was reasonable for communists in their partial enlightenment to adopt his poems as expressive of the goals of the common man.

When the 'books' are examined and we are faced with the inescapable fact that 'we are found wanting', and even the best of us is guilty of 'coming short of the mark,' Burns strikes a deeper note than communism ever acknowledges as valid in the nature of man. Hear him in his *Prayer in the prospect of death:*

Where human weakness has come short,
Or frailty stept aside,
Do thou All Good! for such thou art,
In shades of darkness hide.

Where with intention I have erred,
No other plea I have,
But, Thou art good; and goodness still
Delighteth to forgive.

Stimulus of the sea environment

I now turn to the environment of the sea about me and its effect upon me. Inevitably the mind assimilates the data and interprets. I speak only for myself and as faithfully as I can, record my subjective impressions. What I see, I make no apology for, as such were always observed visually or audibly in a calm ordinary situation without any stressful pressures. Indeed, that is exactly what I believe is demonstrated, namely, that when the ordinary 'pressures' of our land life are absent, we are exposed then to real basics in our environment, of the natural world and of the experience of human society.

Time itself appears like a local expedient, a monitor to differentiate experiences in the human consciousness. After all, our consciousness at the moment that we reflect upon some experience, our own or that of others, is put in a labelled bracket of time or measured for length by time, like using a ruler or marking dates in the calendar. But the experiences are there even when they are past ones. Time records the moments of the present, but usually shuts out the experiences in the past so that they are hidden from us. The same cannot be said of the future, for these experiences have not taken place until they are realized, as human events. The past ones are subject to recall, but those of the future cannot be recalled, for they have not yet become a reality. Prophecy is in a different category from recall. And prediction relates to given data and the element of probability and reason, again, in a different category. You could say that the future is like the building lots marked out in a housing area, on which houses are yet to be built.

The party

At dusk I was treated to a party. I look over the side of the boat. There is continual activity of jumping fish. There are porpoises, a good number of them racing and rolling under and around the boat. There is quite a commotion, visible and audible. I can see right into the water and there are fish similar to dogfish. Of course dogfish are not, as a rule, found near the sea surface. These are possibly small sharks. The porpoises, at least a dozen of them, are rolling incessantly at the bow and the stern. Dolphins jump out right beside me, and make a call from their open mouths, so curiously like humans, with their long snouts raised out of the water. I have a stainless steel jigger in the boat. It would be simple to catch a fish. But I could not bring myself to think of this. I accept that it would be very different if the larder were empty.

Utopian harmony

Meanwhile there is a wonderful atmosphere of harmony, the calling greetings of the jumping dolphins, the splashing of the porpoises and the turbulence of the little sharks right up against the side of the boat. This put me in mind of the articulate churchman who spoke of Isaiah's prophecy of hunted and hunter- *the wolf lying down with the lamb*. One thing is certain, the impression upon me was very positive, even the sharks, playing close to the boat, were full of joy. The spirit rubbed off on the skipper of the *Research II*.

'Join in,' the ocean children seemed to say.

'Look at me, see what I can do,' was the message of their carefree antics, as all played together and joined in the closest semblance of a Utopian concert of peace and goodwill that you could find within the limits of the sea.

Voices

I mentioned that I stopped 'thinking'. I became passive. My mind slowed down and you could say that I was in 'neutral', that effortless state of taking things as they come, instead of working out *thinking construction patterns* for each day and each part of it. Isn't that what we are doing in our ordinary busy life? We have to put our mind to so many different things that our minds are continually constructing or building bridges of thought, and edifices of our own interpretation of the events and materials of our day. We are putting our construction on things, the imprint and influence of our way of thinking. It is not that this is a bad thing, but then again, in so doing, we are aware only of the present and the audible sounds and messages they convey to us. It is all like a busy marketplace, where the noise and continual activity is at its peak. In contrast, when all is silent and people have gone away, you can linger there among the stalls, and the air itself is pregnant with a thousand voices and sounds, just outside the threshold of the human ear.

For me, by myself as *Research II* moved along, voices spoke continually in a variety of programs, the voices of men and women. My mind was as it were in neutral. I was passive. I was not 'thinking,' imposing my own construction upon the evolving day. The sound of my own voice or the sound of my own thinking could not be heard in my consciousness. There is no vacuum. Just as there was no distraction of our collective environment impinging upon my senses, and therefore giving me to be conscious of the very different messages from the external entities, the animate and the inanimate, round about me, so there was no distraction within me from my own mental activity.

In this situation, all kinds of messages which had come to me over years of living, came to my consciousness. This was not active memory. We can recall many experiences in the course of ordinary life. But here by myself on the open sea, radio programs from long ago, especially from the BBC, some with conversations and then cheering after a speech, kept being heard. It was always in the cabin. It appeared as if the cabin acted like a large sound box, where my subjective stores of long forgotten sounds, now emancipated, escaped from the past. Now they bounced back to my auditory senses and consciousness in a totally effortless recall process, on my part.

I am certain, that if conditions were ideal, without the imperfect continual motion and the external sound of wind and wave, that all the sounds and voices would relate to past hearing on my part. We know, as a fact, that the energy of sound is like the ocean wave. The wave travels thousands of miles. Similarly, we speak of the acoustic wave, illustrated in radio transmission, of long, short or medium, or very high frequency. You could say that the air about us is crowded with millions of these sound waves. Possibly in our day the air is overcrowded. We all hear a very limited amount. Probably, there is automatic selection, by each of us too, according to our tastes and inclinations and knowledge. Thus one listener hears one point in a sermon while another does not. But the latter remembers some other point, which the first could not recall hearing.

It is easy and reasonable to understand that in the sea environment of the little boat, and my passive receptive situation of non-thinking, sounds relating to past times, which still are there in the air if you like, became audible as I suggested. I cannot give another explanation. I could hear these voices speaking just as if a radio was on. I checked and double-checked a score of times to make sure no radio receiver was switched on, but it never was.

Normal logical phenomena

Several points appear conclusive and are linked to this phenomena as a rational effect:

1. The air is full of a million sound patterns, call them voices or messages or programs. That, as we suggested, is a known fact.

2. Every species apart from the different receptive inclinations of humans, hears differently. Animals and birds and creatures of all kinds have different thresholds of hearing and hear on different frequencies or pitches or wave lengths.
3. When conditions allow sounds to escape, as it were from the past, which relate to our personal hearing, cavities like the cabin of my boat (or it could be a cave on land or an empty auditorium or sports stadium) become the acoustic similar to that in a musical instrument.
4. Acoustically, as the sound is magnified, our sensory reception is activated too, to hear what normally is beyond the threshold of our hearing, but is there all the time around us.

Sharks and sharks

I tried to picture the concert of harmony all around the boat that day. Alas, like so many situations in life, the picture seemed to be flawed. The peaceful scene of inter-species' amity and concord appeared at least potentially precarious. On the outside perimeter, I saw something like a submarine periscope. This was big. Little sharks three feet long might play beside the boat, but here was a sinister intruder, a dark stranger. It was not alone. Another followed behind. They were clearly a law unto themselves, the *Mafia* of the sea, the deadly predators of normal peaceful life, the ocean counterpart of all spoilers of our human society. The presence of these sinister visitors seemed to have a chilling, if not a dampening effect, upon the disposition of other creatures. It seemed that the rest cleared the way about the boat as the fins could be seen turning and coming towards me. The two came straight towards the boat very boldly. They took over where the others left off. I was amazed. In length they were about fifteen feet long with the dorsal fin cutting the water, so that the shape of the shark could easily be seen. The nose was pointed, looking from my position, and the mouth underneath appeared big enough to be threatening. An eye looked unblinkingly sideways, it seemed, in a baleful appraisal of this curious synthetic pod, with an odd human peering out of the cockpit. I looked back at him, but obviously, he was master in this situation within limits and he was not going to over-reach himself. Like the lion in the wilds to whom fear is unknown, so is this embodiment of power in its compact created perfection. The two ocean bandits circled the boat, looking it over. They took over from the lesser actors in this aquatic show. Then, both left. I felt as if the leader had inspected *Research II,* like a marine surveyor and his assistant would do, and gave his approval. It would not surprise me if I received a certificate of seaworthiness from my visitors.

Brinkmanship!

There were not many birds around in mid-ocean. Now and then some species of gull appeared, as a rule, just one or two at a time. They would fly low over the waves and sometimes swoop so that they were hidden in a trough between waves. One flew around the bow from the 'blind side' as a scrumhalf would do around the blind side of a rugby scrum. This gull could not have seen the sharks until the last moment. As it swooped it almost touched a fin, banked steeply and wheeled away. It seemed startled, taken by surprise. But then maybe some gulls, like humans, enjoy a bit of brinkmanship, just for the thrill of it. Others, like humans make mistakes.

Log/Journal: Weather good. Southwest steady. The sea is beautiful, a living carpet of light and dark; the primal soup of created life forms, yet itself the creation of the Creator, the Living God. I must accept delay. Lost two whole days and most of a third in calm and contrary winds. Hope this continues 3-4 knots during the day; 4-5 knots at night and reaching to 6 at times.

Position: N 44'18"; W 44' 10".
Distance: 110 miles.
We are now right in the Gulf Stream current.

Log: Day 12, Tuesday, 4th July, 1995

Some homework. Last day's distance 150 miles. 180 miles to reach Longitude 40'. This will be more than a third of distance across.

Note on direction. Exactly in line over the self-steering vane, I see two jet vapour streams, presumably from London. I must be going in the right direction. After all, this leisurely sailing is literally an alternative means of transport.

Log Reading: GPS 7 pm, Waypoint 11

Position: N 45'24"; W 42' 05"

Not far from Longitude 40'. Beautiful day. The sea is like a silver saucer of glittering harmony, sea birds, sharks, porpoises untroubled by man.

Stanley, the helmsman

It would be out of the question to sail by oneself without a self-steering device. I speak of course for myself. Without this extra crew member, the voyage would be a nightmare of endurance and continual deprivation of rest and sleep. Sir Francis Chichester had a bad experience down in the savage lower southern latitudes, the 'Roaring Forties' on his world trip, when his self-steering gear would not function properly. His Laurent Giles designed *Gypsy Moth IV* needed modification to her keel, carried out in Australia when he reached there. But no one can imagine what it took out of this inveterate pioneer flyer and sailor, to keep his boat going, without the relief of a self-steering gear. Only a man of iron will and single-minded purpose could have done this.

For me, I was obsessed with Stanley, my Scull-Oar. I designed it. I made it, albeit using some engineering parts from modern manufactured appliances. But for three months, prior to setting out, I spent 4-6 hours every weekday making and remaking all the parts for this wonder machine. Then, there was the tuning and fine tuning for weeks, with Stanley stuck in the bench vice, with his hat off (the Vane, while the rocking mechanism was tested to swing flawlessly as a pendulum and transmitting its movement in a converted applied form to the oar.)

As I look at Stanley standing there outside the transom, I marvel at the miracle. Here I am day after day, night after night, sailing along and Stanley keeping *Research II* on course. I reflect on the steps that were necessary for this almost unbelievable leisure.

1. Finding the right type and one that was right for the voyage. Research is a beautifully balanced boat, finger light on the tiller when sails are properly trimmed fore and aft. For me, even if I could afford to buy the different self-steering units on the market, or if I incorporated their design in a unit made by myself, none of these would be suitable for *Research II* without compromising her performance. All units, at present, on the market are at least 45 lbs. in weight. There may be an exception but I am not aware of any and I apologize if mistaken. That would seriously affect my boat, the *Cal T/4*. Stanley, my self-steering unit weighs about 15 lbs. That is about a third of the lightest on the market. There is no compromise in strength. That is reinforced and guaranteed by incorporating parts from modern first class engineering. These use light alloys, but are immensely strong for their weight.

2. I had the task of coordinating the technical movements, so that Stanley could do the job. I found the necessary parts in Hashem's Recycling Yard, in Sydney, a veritable gold mine for an experimenter. Add my own exacting bench work incorporating my ideas, and there you have it. Before Stanley leaves the workshop I test each part for function. When a part is seen to malfunction, or is considered inadequate for strength or coordination, then I face the inescapable necessity of making another. In my case, stainless steel parts like quadrant and gear wheel were each made three times before satisfaction. Then who can measure the utter gratification as Stanley functions perfectly right there in the basement. I would go down three or four times a day, even in the middle of the night, to set it swinging there in the vice, just for the sheer pleasure it gave me to see it functioning flawlessly.

3. Test Stanley in the real world. Stanley started his life as a means to an end, the emancipation of the skipper from all

labour. There was now a change. Stanley, in many ways, was now the central figure, the more important. The voyage was in this perspective, a means to an end, serving to prove Stanley, to try out his capabilities and to vindicate its creator, and the supreme confidence he had in his creation, that it was a 'winner.' During the trip, Stanley himself would need attention, as a nurse has to give attention to a patient after his operation, or a mechanic gives attention to a car, to keep it running well. For me, even though the creator, I had also the role to play, of finding out its capabilities and to tune Stanley so that the Scull-Oar would function at its maximum efficiency. That is not just a simple lesson. Every self-steering gear requires different settings in different wind conditions. Not only has it to be reset when the wind changes, but there is a wealth of knowledge to be learned with regard to its performance in different wind conditions. When this is known, there is an understanding between skipper and crew. It is no discredit to Stanley or disparagement of his capability, when the skipper takes over the helm for a season - a season of nature's wrath that makes demands of pre-emptive measures and instant reaction to the treacherous wiles of wicked waves.

There is also the by-product of learning in the field, in this case the sea, namely that there is always room for adjustment and improvement. Thus the rope pattern to the tiller was modified and the second arrangement of pulleys proved to be better. Another instance related again to the connecting ropes from the scull-oar. I had them attached to a six inch long bolt which swiveled on the head of the oar. These swept downwards on each side. In certain conditions of steep seas, I lowered the stock of Stanley -adjustable height was a valuable added feature - so that the blade would not be lifted out of the seas thus rendering the unit sporadically to malfunction. In practice in that situation, the blade coming out of the water as pressure was released on it, tended to pull the bolt out of the head of the oar. It never did so completely, but I was apprehensive that this might happen and, in conditions of weather, that would be critical. Therefore I changed matters by inserting a cross bolt like the top of a capstan, to which the connecting ropes were now secured. I could do this as I took a selection of tools including a hand drill, for repair and maintenance. This modification served well for the rest of the voyage. By carrying out the work in favorable weather, I did this without taking Stanley aboard, itself a simple matter, but necessarily requiring it to be out of commission completely. The fruit of all this labour is the immeasurable satisfaction of watching the self-steering unit operating, all on its own. Just think of me, rising in the morning at dawn after a good night's sleep, stretching myself, rolling out and standing there in the companionway. The compass points east, the knotmeter reads 4 knots, and Stanley waits for acknowledgment. Clickity click, clickity click, clickity click, he keeps saying, and nodding his head with the wind vane on it, from side to side in rhythmic rest, inducing harmony. A sudden jolt by a wave turns the boat a few degrees off course. Stanley stops clicking. His head holds still, pushed by the wind sideways. The boat returns to her compass course. Stanley waits until this is complete. Then he relaxes again, resuming his leisurely vigil. Clickity click, clickity click, clickity click.

Bad Weather

I write from my journal notes at the time: meantime, just as I finished this task and felt so gratified that all was shown to function well, even should I have to lower Stanley further to keep the blade underwater, sunset overtook me. The good day was over. A change was in the air. It was sunset, but you could not see the sun go to rest on the horizon. The northern sky had darkened. Thick black clouds manoeuvred into strategic positions, each loaded with its own battery of missiles. The night was about to fall over this segment of the planet earth as an enemy and not a friend.

As I lifted my eyes to read the sky, the sea was already beginning to receive another shaking. I think it was so used to it that it was resigned to the effect of the wind. The sea itself would react in due course and become an angry animate enemy with which we had to contend and come to terms with, if we were to live. As I looked up, the sky was quickly darkening, without the reassuring lights of friendly stars or nearer planets. As it did so, it brought a chill which made me shiver with just something more than the cold. For this night would contrast with the idyllic day, I was sure, and I anticipated its imminent and inexorable approach, with ominous but undisclosed intent. I must make myself ready and charge up with fuel to meet what ever was ahead of me. I went below and cooked up my evening meal.

Action stations

I had just got hold of the pan with my potatoes, onions and Irish Stew, when *Research II* went over far. It was that sudden. Everything below that could move, did so, and water poured in the fore skylight, and from the wash of the cockpit, many gallons rushed below. With the pan still in my hand, I struggled out of the companionway. Holding the tiller, I assured myself of some stability - domestic order down below could wait. But whatever was to be done, I would not lose that meal of piping hot stew and onions. In haste, with one eye on the boat, I ate the whole panful of Irish Stew, made by the Scots people from the Fraser Valley, with the potatoes from Prince Edward Island. This would be an insurance of vital energy that would stand me in good stead, before the night and its black violence was over. I threw the pan towards the open hatch way, into the cabin. The chaos already there could wait. Sadly my favorite spoon, one of a set given as a wedding present by my uncle John and aunt Joan in Dumbarton thirty-three years earlier, disappeared from then on. I searched everywhere and resigned myself to the likelihood that it was already on its journey downwards into the mile long depth of the ocean floor.

At war with the elements.

The inky blackness of the night indicated that the sky had a lot of anger quite different from a transient mood. It was just too bad that we were in the path of its wrath. Rain poured out of it and dropped down in sheets. The wind had increased, as quickly as you would change into high gear in a car. The cross-seas became treacherous and the motion of the boat under me, increasingly unpredictable. We were right in the centre of a wind change from the steady delightful cooperative southwest that had been pushing us along so comfortably, to a northerly. This was a cold-blooded blast that quickly grasped the sea and turned it into vicious lumps of curling energy. The darkness now complete, only helped to generate phosphorescent light on breaking wave crests and closed me in, in my little boat.

In historical long-term perspective, my demise was truly insignificant, and I was well aware of this. Objectively, here was a capsule of human life and a few fragments of technological know-how, the clues which could place me as a migrant being of late 20th century history. The possibility inherent in the situation could lead to a future study of planet earth and the findings from the Mid-Atlantic Basin, of such fragments, which could be, along with the remains of a thousand other craft, a feast for marine archaeologists.

I had to man the tiller as Stanley, the Scull-Oar, was confused by the fitful gusts and contradictory winds. Sometimes I would reset him but that was out of the question now. I peered at the knotmeter and read, 6,7,8,9 knots in the gusts. This could not continue. The starboard rail was awash with foaming white water. It streamed along to the cockpit and made a curious wall as it passed along the gunwale, the speed of the boat keeping the water from flowing in. What had to be done was clear. The main had to come off. How easy to say that.

As I rehearsed every move in the vital sequence of doing this, I crushed the negatives that screamed their logical opposition to my resolve. Let the sheets of cold rain lash the heaving deck; let all the phantom fears marshal against me as they rose in my dry throat to protest my futility. Duty calls. The mind sees the opportunity, the split-second pause, as wind and wave change their grip. The will commands; I spring like a cat forward to the mast; I have already downed the dodger, which lies flat over the hatch; I unloose the halyard and rise to my feet, with the halyard end, easing it out with my left hand and pulling the main hand over hand down to the boom. This is no time for frills. I clamp the boom inside the lee rail. The main is off; *Research II* still plunges forward, but now she's on an even keel as the jib pulls her onwards, still going like a rocket. All this is a sequence with each movement a vital one, not only to deal with the requirements of the moment, but in such a way that gear would be ready to use again without trouble. For instance, I mentioned that even in the stress of the moment, I took care to control the main halyard. If not, the loose rope, flailing about the mast could get tangled in the rigging and cross trees, so that I would have a major problem when raising the sail again. And so it was, even after securing the main and lashing the boom, *Research II* still *whispered* along at 8 knots.

A night's work

Possibly two hours passed - I never took my watch out of the cabin. I manned the tiller, until it seemed to me that the seas had fully responded to the change of wind from southwest to the north, north-westerly, and then to north. I found that I could not stay awake. Up until this point in time, I had worn my big warm anorak. Now it was, for the first time, soaked through by the heavy rain. It was a dead weight of total clammy wet, closing round my body like a wet poultice, and draining all the warmth and goodness out of me. Sleep was an imperative, a call that could no longer be denied. I cajoled Stanley into commission. Obediently, he took over to keep us roughly going east. I pulled myself over the bridge deck into the cabin, struggled into my sleeping bag and with the torch at my hand on the floor, fell instantly asleep.

Four times I was up because *Research II* jibed. Tiredness flowed like a liquid through my body, crying out against every physical demand. I believed in the boat. That belief was now being tested. I could not see the configuration of the seas, but every now and then she was violently shaken. Always this brought on the red light of real concern for the keelbolts. In the morning from 3:00 a.m., the motion was grim. *Research II* would be deadly quiet, then shudder from stem to stern. Then she did a remarkable performance. How shall I describe it? Yes, like this. It was a cross between the upper-body antics of the English comedian Frankie Howard, and the lower body gyrations of America's singer Elvis Presley.

The wind moderated at this point - my notes are hard to decipher. But the lumpy seas created a confluence of conflicting water masses. The sporadic bursts of violence, to which *Research II* was subjected, called for some action. I got out and hoisted the mainsail. This stabilized the boat and, like a bicycle, she now went forward.

Below, I pumped out 10 buckets of water, that is 200 strokes of the pump, from the bilge and from floor compartments, where water rose on the lee side. It was enough to make me pause and reflect. I indeed had much food for thought. A voice within me spoke with urgency,

'Angus, don't push her; don't push her. You are a thousand miles out in the Atlantic. You have heard but not seen the sight of another ship. This is day 13. Just think on it.'

Encouragement

I had to put some order on the domestic scene, after the rather disturbed nocturnal conditions. I did not approach this task with any great relish, but it had to be done. It's amazing how our spirits can get a lift, if we simply get stuck into the tasks at hand. I first decided to check my water supply. Earlier the tap on two 5 gallon containers had moved somewhat from 'closed' position, obviously being knocked by something or someone. Half the contents of each had spilled out before I spotted them in the morning, stored under canvas at the stern. Now as I checked, I found that I had actually put aboard an extra 5 gallon container which was stored with others under my utility bed. The result was a pleasing count of 4 full containers, that is 20 gallons. Also, you remember that I had come away with half the alcohol needed for the voyage. Now when checking the water supply in the compartment under my bed, what did I find but a container from the previous season, which was three quarters full.

Now there would be no waste, but there would be no rationing either. I could have a cup of tea or coffee when I pleased. Nevertheless, I made careful calculations for use of water daily, and also for alcohol, making allowance for a protracted stay at sea beyond the projected estimate of 35 days. This discovery had a marked effect upon me. It was just what I needed. It lifted my spirits, which had been literally and metaphorically dampened, over the previous twelve hours. I set to,with renewed energy, to restore order and make everything ship-shape, during the rest of the day.

I managed to have a complete clothing change - in spite of the flood through the fore hatch, which soaked much of the clothing stored in the fo'c'sle.

Praise the Lord, I thought, lifting my heart to my Maker for a moment of remembrance. The rule is clear. *Do what you have to, the essentials, and the rest can wait till later.*

Log/Journal: Stanley liked the new northerly force 4. And *Research II* seemed to be in agreement, judging by the gurgling sound of satisfaction coming from her forefoot. This left me free for chores and rest, the latter which I had much need of, as there was little the night before. As I entered the cabin, I just glanced at the dials. We were on a course northeast by east, just perfect, I thought, and doing 4-5 knots steady on a close reach.

Passed the 40th west Longitude

Position: N 45' 42 W 40' 11"

Time: 1900 hours. E. time (Given 2 hours till 7 p.m).

Given that the distance from Sydney to the Solent was 3600 miles, that is 60 degrees of ongitude, we were now a third of the distance across the Atlantic. We were keeping to the average of most small boats, namely 100 miles a 24 hour day. We had come 1200 miles. You can understand that if you took into account all the zig zags and even backtracking, *Research 11* actually sailed approximately 200 miles more. If you also took into account the days in which we were becalmed and did not get ahead at all, you can see that our daily average of actual sailing was considerably higher than 100 miles.

But now I rejoiced that we had made the 40th west longitude. I think I can safely say that we have made it, twelve and a half days out of North Sydney. A grey bleak day. In spite of this, I was greatly encouraged that we had reached this goal. And the discovery of the extra water container and the can of alcohol gave me a great sense of optimism.

In thankfulness, again at the close of the day, I lifted my heart in prayer to my Heavenly Father, and praised him for his faithfulness. The psalm of David, the Hebrew poet who loved the Lord and the paths of righteousness, came to me, and I sang this softly as an offering to the Lord, in the language of my fathers,

Bhi tabhairt buidheachais do Dhia,
'sni sar-mhaith maiseach e;
Bhi tabhairt cliu, O Thi as aird',
do d'ainm-sa feadh gach re:

Do chaoimhneas-graidh 's a' mhaduinn mhoich,
gach lath bhi cur an ceil;
'Sair d'fhirinn ta neo-mhearachdach,
gach oidhch' bhi deanamh sgeil.

English:

To render thanks unto the Lord,
it is a comely thing.
And to thy name, O thou most High,
due praise aloud to sing.

Thy loving-kindness to shew forth,
when shines the morning light;
And to declare thy faithfulness
with pleasure every night.

(Scottish Psalter Psalm 92: verses 1 and 2)

Log: Day 14, Thursday, 6th July, 1995

GPS Reading:	Track 96' E 4'5 knots
Position:	N 46' 07" W 38' 19"
Time:	1800 hours

The wind went down and remained light from the northeast for the rest of the day. Last night I stayed awake until 2 a.m. I had reasons.

I watched the jets cross the sky. They were just silent dots of light pulsating high above me. But it made me think. They were on a parallel course with *Research II*. Just think of it. They take about 4 - 6 hours to cross the ocean, and I take 4 - 6 weeks to cover the same distance.

Apart from this, there seems something incongruous. Here is the great wide ocean, geographically a considerable part of the earth's surface. But there is neither sight nor sound of any ship or sign of another human being. That strikes me as very odd. The earth's population is growing with Malthusian rapidity, giving many thinkers an uneasy feeling that change is imminent on a cosmic scale, just around the corner, as it were, as we approach the third millennium.

Just as I write, I hear on a news cast on the CBC, that the Chernobyl nuclear accident in the Ukraine affected Belarus to the north, so that now the birth rate in that country of the former Soviet Union, is down by 50 percent. It could well be that the technologically developed sectors of world population may become sterile deserts, traceable to blind, bigoted, self-important scientists and politicians, in ignoring consequences of exploitation without conservation.

Sea colonies

1. It is foreseeable that living on land will have to be abandoned, because of the contamination and pollution of the traditional habitat. In place of this there would be sea colonies. There is no need for esoteric fantasies of humans, living on the sea-floor. Practical evolutionary development would be more like

an extension of the maritime life in junks on the Yangste river in China and boat dwellers in the islands of the Indonesian archipelago or the colonies of river inhabitants and marinas, traditional and novel, that are already a common feature in many western countries where the climate is acceptable and weather conditions good. In many cases thousands of retired people make their homes on boats and floating caravans and trailers already. It is easy to visualize an extension of this, which may ultimately revolutionize the face of the earth itself. These could well be the embryonic beginnings of a maritime habitat, where large land areas like Europe, parts of China, countries round about Iran, and parts of the Americas, will have to be abandoned.

2. I sat in the cockpit as the shadows of the evening replaced the sun, now hidden by the north-west horizon. The lights of a ship appeared to starboard. I shone my torch on the sails and watched her as she passed along westwards, possibly some six miles off. Time went by, the night was pleasant, the sky starlit and the wind favorable. It was my rule not to retire below, if a ship's light was visible. I waited therefore in the cockpit and watched as the ship made her way to the north-west. I watched, but it kept in view as the night was very clear and visibility was unhindered by any fog or mist right to the far-off horizon. When the ship's light would disappear, I mused, then I'll go below and curl up in my sleeping bag until morning.

3. I had gone below to get out my oilskin top, which I now wore instead of the anorak, when, to my amazement, suddenly a large ship, ablaze with lights appeared some mile or so at my stern. My immediate reaction was almost panic. We are used to the danger of a ship ramming us from the direction of our course. But here was the danger of a ship coming at speed up to our stern and sending us to Valhalla. This impinged strongly upon my mind, as the navigation lights on the mast head of my boat could be seen only from the bow, and I did not keep

the stern light on. It was rather ineffectual anyway as it was right on the transom. It could hardly be seen also because of the steering gear. I reached for my binoculars as all kinds of thoughts raced through my mind. I would try and ascertain from her navigation lights what her course was and if she would avoid me. Bobby Sheink gave terrible warnings in his book, *The Complete Yachtsman* to beware of ocean ships, traveling at up to 30 knots, steered by the automatic helmsman, and no human on watch or at the wheel.

The Phantom Ship

I watched through my glasses but, to my relief, surmised that her stern was facing me and not her bow. She was high with rows of lights on different decks. It looked like a passenger ship, a really big one with dark silhouettes of funnels. I was puzzled. How on earth could she have passed me without my seeing her? Here she was on the same course line as *Research II* but going in the opposite direction. But then I had been looking to port, following the progress of the other ship far off on the horizon. She must be a cruise liner, I thought, and then wondered, 'there can't be many of these old ones left.' I watched her for at least ten minutes. It was a vivid picture in the clear night and the relatively calm sea. It was like a great hotel with all the windows flooded with light. Then it occurred to me that the ship had come to a standstill, also the question kept persisting in my mind, that the ship's appearance had been sudden as if it sprang up out of nowhere. All was not well, it became apparent, on this ocean cruiser, with probably over two thousand souls aboard.

Then I heard it. There was a deep rumbling noise echoing over the sea. It was like a great explosion, that kept reverberating for several seconds. I immediately thought of the jets which I had seen shortly before, snaking through the stars far above me. The noise continued. It occurred to me that there was something very far wrong. The jets in mid-Atlantic, I had come to assume, could be seen, but not heard. This was so, not only because of their height some six to eight miles above, but because of the speed and the distance they traveled, before the sound could reach me.

Then without warning, with the noise distracting me for a moment, the ship, one moment a blaze of lights, next moment disappeared. I recall staggering back against the cabin. What did all this mean? The rumbling noise had ceased. All about me was tranquil, yet the air was pregnant with a silence that was just over the threshold of hearing, as if voices were speaking, a great many voices, but their sound was just beyond my auditory senses to comprehend. Could a bank of fog mysteriously have intervened to block my vision, I thought, anxious to find a reasonable solution? Then the answer to that question became clearly negative. As I looked out beyond the stern, and beyond the location of the vanishing cruise ship, there on the horizon, I could distinctly see the lights of the ship which had earlier passed me to starboard on its way westwards.

I was as calm as the sea around me, and without excitement or any emotion, I knew that my sensory perception had in some way seen through time. The uni-planetary vision by which our perception is circumscribed by the immediate, was suddenly given three-dimensional vision. It is as if I suddenly could sec back beyond the horizon to Canada and Arnish my home, in my vision nestling snugly at the head of Mira Bay. The phantom ship, was it a mirage, a distortion of visible phenomenon of nature? No, there was nothing there in the darkness. Was it a figment of my imagination, projected on the screen of the night? That would resemble a magician pulling a rabbit out of his top hat. That theory just would not hold.

To me there could be only one explanation. I was in the vicinity of the tragic accident that happened to the largest ship of its day, the Cunard trans - Atlantic liner, *Titanic* on its maiden voyage to New York. To me, the pages of the book of time, the intervening years since 1912, were turned back to that calm night in April, when captain, officers and passengers were occupied in their social extravagances, completely oblivious to the danger of icebergs that was about to confront them. I saw a replay of the scene, a 10 minute excerpt from the sequence of events in that fatal exposure of man's ill-placed over - confidence in himself. Was this not the last scene but one, the pen-ultimate moment of unparalleled maritime drama, as the pride of man's creation, or the creation of man's pride, the optimum in advanced technology in its day, the unmatched limits of opulence, custom made for the exclusive rich, was ripped open as with a tin-opener, by a mere handful of frozen water crystals, commonly called an iceberg.

Loneliness

We must go on. For the first time a strong feeling affects me. No doubt it is induced by the ocean's vastness and the thoughts of loved ones. Such a feeling is negative. I counter these with deliberate thoughts of God who is so good to us. The Hebrew refrain in worship is one of glorious redemptive love from the Most High.

Praise ye the Lord, *for his mercy endureth forever.* And in another, Praise the Lord *for he is good.* Thus I have great defense against negative feelings of loneliness. Also, when the immediate environment emits messages, real and imagined which register on my perceptive faculties in the vacuum like situation of being by myself without the crowding overtures so gratuitously bombarding the senses, then God's voice speaks, using his word, reinforcing my faith and conviction that his Presence is with me, and that I am part of that Covenant of mercy that gives peace to the soul and therefore the derivative of calm and confidence to the disposition. I rehearse in my mind the words of Scripture: *Thou wilt keep him in perfect peace whose mind is stayed on thee.* It was evening, the wind was light; *Research 11* ghosted on, in a seemingly effortless impulse at 3 knots.

Company

I relaxed after my evening meal, warm inside me and now completely clothed right up to the chin in sweaters and oilskins, bonnet and hood. My sight on my right eye was as good as ever, although the lump on the side of my head was still a dark globule of bruised flesh.

I cast my eye out to starboard. There was a noise out there. I looked. Yes, there were 4, 6, no, 12, creatures all rushing towards me. Porpoises, dolphins, splashing, jumping. They surrounded the boat so that you could feel their antics affecting the boat. Now they were at the stern, then at the bow, some at the bow, others at the stern. They had me on my feet, peering now to one side, then to the other as a swarthy porpoise rolled alongside or a dolphin jumped with its snout out of the water and emitted a cooing cry of friendly greeting.

There was communion, one with another. I felt that they accepted me; that they welcomed me and that they were showing this acceptance.

This continued for quite some time and my friends swam along with me, diving under the keel and coming up the other side, as if laughing and playing with joy. I was filled with a sense of the spiritual and sang to them a Gaelic psalm. I just hummed it gently, the cadences rising and falling like the benediction of heaven on the scene of our meeting here in the middle of the ocean, so often an angry mountain of troubled waters, now for a pause, an idyllic calm, ruffled only by a benign and gentle breeze.

Thus I sang:

'Se Dia as tearmunn duinn gu beachd,
ar spionnadh e 's ar treis:
An aimsir carraid agus teinn,
ar cobhar e ro-dheas.

English

God is our refuge and our strength
in straits a present aid;
Therefore although the earth remove,
we will not be afraid

(Scottish Psalter Psalm 46)

Here God visited me with friends of the earth, the companions of the sea. They cheered me up in a remarkable way, with their performance for about 10-12 minutes. Then with a final fling, they all turned and sped away, leaving a silence a kind of vacuum, which made me miss them and hope that they would be back again. As they left, I couldn't help letting them know how much I appreciated their company. Thus, I found myself calling out gently to them,

'Come back; come back,' I called. 'Come back again tomorrow evening, any time. You will be welcome always to do your act. I'll be waiting for you as the sun goes down.'

And forgive me if I imagine I heard a reply, just faintly, as one of the dolphins turned round and looked at me. It was something like this,

'Sure Rev Angus, we'll be back again tomorrow evening if we can, God willing and if all is well with you and us.'

Somehow I felt that this was a watershed in my journey across the North Atlantic. Who would believe the variety of experiences to be lived in the ultra-immediacy of the ocean by oneself on a little boat, driven only by synchronizing the powers of nature to the receptive expedients of man's devices! Two weeks had gone past, each day with its own specific character. The evening sun dipped on the western horizon; I checked the compass course as a night wind added an extra push to the sails. All seemed ostensibly in order, with all the promise of a peaceful night. I went below, and laid myself down, committing myself to my Maker, and in perfect tranquillity, sleep came to me with its restorative genius, the healing work of mind, body and spirit, throughout the watches of the night. My eyes closed as I whispered to my Maker,

'I will both lay me down in peace, and sleep:
for thou, Lord, only makest me to dwell in safety.'

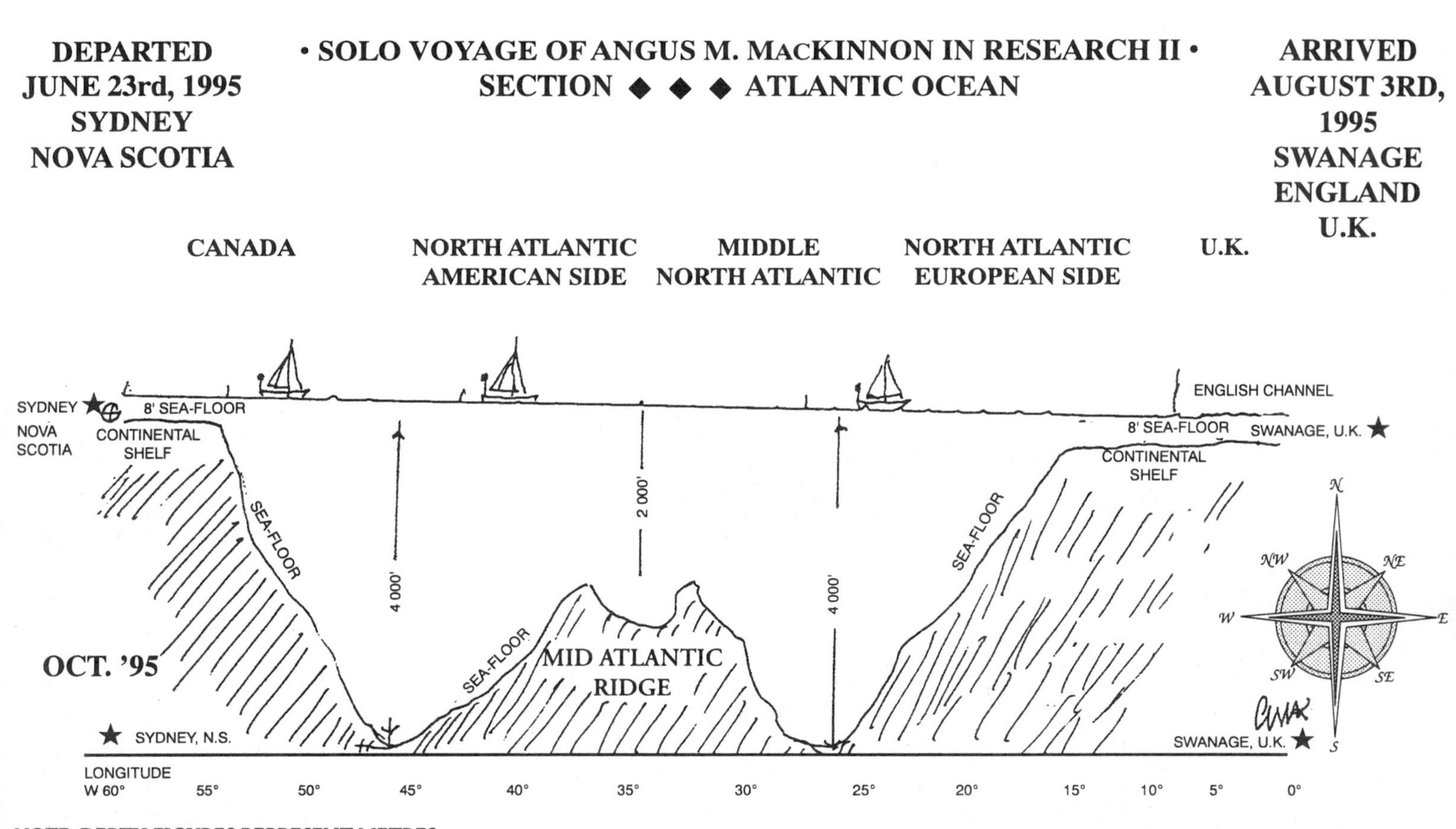

NOTE: DEPTH FIGURES REPRESENT METRES

Catalone Bay

PART III

Middle of the North Atlantic

JUNE 23 - AUGUST 3, 1995

SOLO VOYAGE

SYDNEY, NOVA SCOTIA TO SWANAGE, DORSET, U.K.

SLOOP CAL T/4 ◆◆ RESEARCH II ◆◆ ANGUS M. MACKINNON

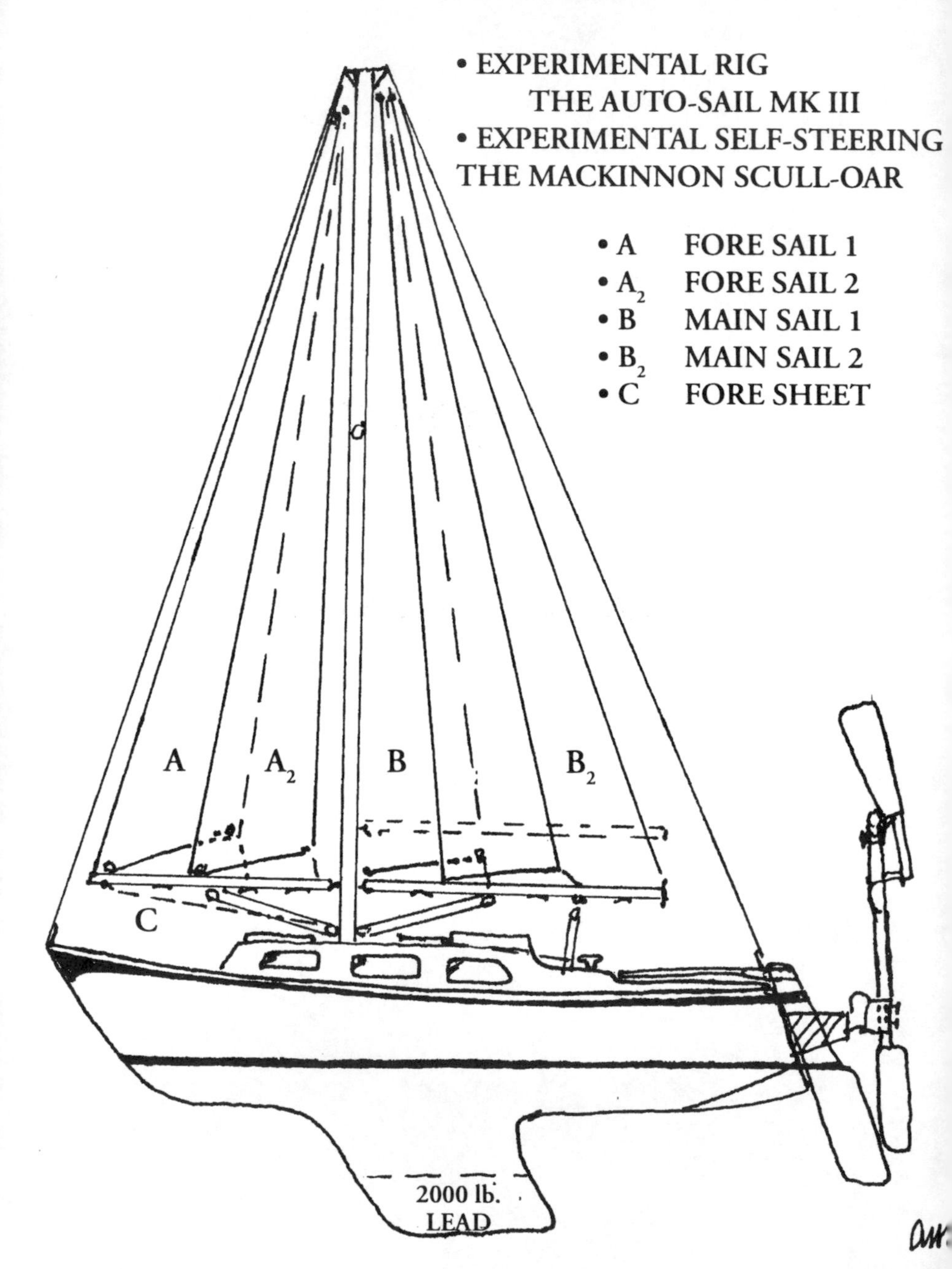

OCT./95

CHAPTER 10

The Storm

Log: Day 15, Friday, 7th July, 1995

This day began well, unsurpassed as a veritable reason for creation. A sparkling sun rose above the jib to make its apparent journey across the sky, lighted with ever changing deep animated colours that were, at the same time, too elusive and short-lived to describe. Overhead, the sky was a dome of blue, from which the power house of our planetary system poured out its solar energy, giving life to our half of mother earth, while the other half rested in the darkness of its own shadow. What an ingenious miracle of wisdom that challenges human cleverness to recreate in the micro plants of our nuclear age! At best man's capacity is limited and yet full of credit, when like the harnessing of the wind to the sailing ship, he harnesses the already existent power of creation, latent and manifest in his terrestrial habitat.

Special performance

In the evening there was a special concert of my friends, the porpoises and dolphins. They were joined by two whales, which I think were the two that knew the song of the Mira and had visited me before. There was a whole range of ocean life, including some gulls, and the black and white sea swallows. The sea creatures put on a good show, and the birds dived and swooped above them so that all appeared a harmony, a kind of benefit performance which, appreciatively, I accepted as a present for me. Maybe I was considered the guest of honour. Certainly there was no other about, and gratuitously I acted the role. In appreciation as the twilight closed the day, I decided to sing my thanks and so over the ocean wave, you could have heard the Skye Boat Song, which speaks of Bonnie Prince

Charlie:

Speed bonnie boat like a bird on the wing,
Onward the sailor's cry.
Carry the lad that is born to be king,
Over the sea to Skye.

Fighting against the storm

I paused; the night was near, and the performers had left the ocean stage. Nostalgia rose up in my throat and I joined in a moment of perfect stillness, as the sun's rays lifted off the sea, now eclipsed by the curve of the horizon. The reading on the Log is N 46' 87"; W 38' 19".

I could not help interpreting the evening's show, or at least dwelling upon the characters, especially the two whales. Questions called for answers. Was this visit a friendly farewell to a Canadian as he passed the outer perimeter of their Maritime Canadian territory? I liked to think that answer was the right one. But we were well past Canadian waters, even for a Brian Tobin and his National Canadian Pirates. But then another explanation kept thrusting itself to the forefront of my thinking and I just could not dismiss it, however hard I tried. Was this something else, a last performance before the lone sailor went into a mortal conflict, where he would face all the mighty forces of nature, already marshalled in regiments and divisions marching towards him, to make the rendezvous of battle in the coming night? A strange shiver made droplets of cold sweat drip down my spine. I just could not find the argument to refute this compelling interpretation and I felt an intuitive conviction that I had heard the swan song of my sea friends, who knew that nature's might was about to be unleashed upon me and my little boat.

Refuelling

Do not jump to conclusions. I did not think of myself as one condemned to the gallows. It would take more than a momentary wave of pessimism, to bury the buoyant optimism and confidence that was woven into the texture of my heritage and the dominant characteristic of my life. Something more. I, also like the creatures around me, was at home on the sea. I was in my element, as much as on land. I was part of that volatile environment, in mind and spirit as well as in the physical reality of my presence. And if I did not trust in the boat, I would not have left the Canadian shore. Intuitively, I knew by her looks, that she was born to be tried and that she could live in trouble, though she would not seek it out. The latent challenge of her excellence would be answered by nature's forces, before many hours had passed. I could not see the future. But I went below. I cooked my favorite meal. I knew it could be the last for a long while. Therefore I did not spare: potatoes and onions, a tin of beans and a whole tin of Irish Stew, all piping hot. I left nothing in the pan, but ate it all. My cheeks glowed with heat from the energy within me, and I felt that come what may, I was ready to give my best. I humbly lifted my heart to my God, in the confidence that he would do the rest.

I quote from the log/journal, written about this time:

Going well, the wind rising, coming now from the north west, as it backed from the northeast. I reefed the mainsail, and headed into the night. Sleep, somehow was out of the question, an irrelevance as it was to soldiers in the hour before battle. I was conscious, very conscious of all about me changing. The night sky closed in, at first a pale blue carpet of opaque nocturnal canvas. Then the planet Jupiter presented itself in the south-east. Then the constellations made an appearance. Why, things were not so bad! What was I worrying about, I thought! I drew confidence from my friend the Plough with the Big Dipper and the assuring presence of the Pole Star. That night, the performance of my ocean friends, was complemented by a full performance in the sky, a kind of rivaling exercise, given to me, the one judge, to make my choice.

I could not see the colour of the sea in the dark of the night that now was upon us, but the sea was changing underneath me. Forces were at work, twisting and wringing the very texture of the waters, deep in the foundation of the ocean. It came home upon me that here was not the shallow superficial makings of a gale, an irritation of the seas, which could be shrugged off in a day or a night. Something was happening to the very earth beneath me. The sea was rising in an increasing upheaval as if some giant was raising it up as he rose from the ocean floor.

The practical effect, never mind my subjective sensations, was increasingly clear. Stanley could not keep *Research II* on course. I am afraid that there were contradictions in my mind. One moment I faced the reality, the ominous reality that something was wrong, far wrong. Next minute, true to human optimism, in spite of the seas themselves that hurried this way and that, as if they themselves were frightened children running from some terror, I persuaded myself that there was nothing unusual. I outhauled the jib on the fore spinnaker boom. It gave stability and it still gave R*esearch 11* a speed of 5 knots steady.

About 1 a.m. I met a ship coming west from the Clyde/Belfast area. I was aware that we were at this point crossing the regular shipping lane to and from the United States. As I watched, she took a long time to reach me, and at several miles away I could just make out her silhouette, a big carrier with a high superstructure at the stern with many lights.

Coming of the dawn

In contrast to the cozy comfort of that ocean giant, there was little or no comfort for me. I stayed in the cockpit, feeling under me the heaving seas, which had not yet reached eruption on the surface. I nudged the rudder, now and then, trying to keep to northeast or as close as possible to east. Dawn appeared suddenly ahead of me. It kind of took me by surprise, as if I woke from a trance. There to the east was a red orb, rising out of the rim of the sea as the earth tilted towards the sun. I watched, fascinated. This was a movie, a real life one, of which I was a part as well as a spectator, and far from the cozy seat of a theatre or the relaxing easy-chair of the family sitting room. Within minutes, the blood-red sun was eclipsed totally by a dark octopus-like cloud that stretched its dark tentacles across the sun. It did so as one would stretch out the fingers of the human hand to shade the brightness of an electric light. Within minutes, a cold blight chilled the whole spectrum of the sea as the darkness, an unnatural blackness, clothed the whole northern sky. The wind was now increasing; its cry could be heard in the rigging. It was like a musician tuning his instrument, and just striking likely chords, to make sure all was ready for the big event. He was already on the stage. Now the preliminaries were over. There was a hush over his audience; he was ready to open the concert. It was just beginning, and it needed no interpreter, no sage, no prophet to tell that a storm of unknown magnitude was now imminent.

The big red ore carrier

My instincts were paramount at this juncture. Seasoned thinking had already programmed my mind so that reflexes obeyed the sensory commands in an orderly obedience of motor compliance. I literally found myself standing on the sloping cabin top, handling the main, and lashing the boom down inside the rail, clawing my way over the slanting deck, with the dodger down. I recall the scene as if I were an actor on the stage in a frightening drama of irreconcilable forces. I turned around at that moment, and there, coming over my stern to port, was a large, very large red ore carrier about half a mile away, en route to the Clyde/ Belfast area, I presumed. While I had struggled with the sails, she had slowed down, if not stopped. I could clearly see her wheelhouse. Lights glowed from its windows. I felt that I was under scrutiny, as if I was being watched and surveyed. Maybe, I thought that they were waiting to hear me on the radio. Maybe they were trying to call me themselves to make contact with my little boat. They could not know immediately or for certain that I was by myself. As the ship stayed there, it seemed to me, I imagined that the captain was debating within himself what he should do. They could see me clearly. They could see, that, whatever the present situation, the sails were under control, only a small jib, albeit unsteadily, hoisted at the *Research II's* bow.

The captain's dilemma

I felt that I could read the mind of the captain as the huge ship lingered in the near distance. Its presence was rather overpowering, but I was loathe to wave or give any sign that could be interpreted as a negative. After all, I was captain of my ship, cook and crew and also mate. My word was law, and no voice questioned me. I thought of the conflicting thoughts that must face the captain of that massive edifice of steel. He knew that something was coming, a taste of which was feeling out the seas and the air already since the evening past. And here, not far from him, visible on top of the seas, then hidden in the bottom of the hollow troughs, was a tiny yacht flying a Canadian flag, a sister to the United States. Would he also guess that only one man, whom he saw in his yellow oilskins, clawing down the mainsail, was also the full ship's complement! I felt a concern for the captain's dilemma. He of all people knew the forecast. Tropical Storm Barry, which had threatened the Caribbean, and balefully speculated on destroying the Florida coast, had already turned away, in a northeastern track. From the radio I gathered it was centered 400 miles east of Halifax. Now it had come north and east, in a great arc of violence, whose perimeter closed in every living thing and every floating vessel of man, in the compass of its power.

What should the captain do? He got no response on radio from this lone little yacht, now about to be devoured in the tempest. He could see its captain, but from him got no plea for aid or sign of distress. I think I could read the captain' s mind. He knew that I was not caught out on a Sunday afternoon picnic on an inland lake. He knew the gales that had already met me on my way. I knew that he had come to a decision.

I watched his ship head off to the northeast, just a bit to the left of my course. I mused, it was 26 hours since I awoke and came on duty the morning before. And I was still here in the cockpit at the tiller. It was a strange sensation indeed, as the big red ship grew smaller on the horizon. It seemed to me that I was in a corridor, left behind, while the ore carrier steamed off at speed to safety in the eerie atmosphere of the early dawn. You could tell that the atmosphere was charged with pressure. As *Research 11* made its tentative way, weaving along in an unsteady course, rising up to respond to the wind, falling down into the false calm of the hollows, I looked out over the weather side.

The orange life raft

There was something in the water, something different. No, it was not a log. No, it was not a creature of the ocean. There in the track of the disappearing ore carrier, now bearing down in the direction of my little boat, was a yellow cylinder. At once I saw it, and recognized it as an emergency life raft, like those carried on ships and fishing boats. I had thought about taking one with me before leaving. In fact I had examined one at the home of a friend, Donald Matheson, in Little Narrows. He had it on his tug, which he used for his construction and ship servicing business in Bras d'Or, especially in connection with the Nova Scotia power plant built right on the coast near Point Aconi. The tugboat was not in commission, and I had the option of taking the raft. But I decided at the time that it was too heavy to stow on *Research II*, especially as it would have to be on the cabin top. That four man raft looked similar to the one in the sea, right there in the track of the ship, except that this one was orange colored. It was about fifty feet out, as we came abreast of it. The conviction came home to me that the captain, in a moment of reflection, ordered this to be dropped overboard, so that I could have it, should the elements prove too much for my little craft. I could be wrong. But don't you think it more than a coincidence that this life raft appeared in the wake of his disappearing ship, and right in my path, just as all nature was breaking loose all around me ?

As this thought mingled with others, either through unwillingness to turn from my course to lay claim to this 'find' or from some other dogged perversity akin to my stubborn make-up not to beg, I passed on and did not glance back to see the life raft, that would have ensured my survival. What thrawn, stubborn natures we have, especially those that are woven in the texture of Celtic pride! Pride, defiance, almost recklessness, count more than capitulation or any appearance of weakness.

The long hours followed each other; the seas grew bigger, the hollows deeper, the crests higher. Hour after hour, like a machine, I gauged the seas and steered my little boat, before the chasing storm. The storm was now getting a grip of the seas, and the air, lifting the spray into flying and blinding spume. I pulled the hood of my oilskin down to my eyelids and peered out through the slits of my eyes, trying to anticipate the motion of the seas. The morning gave way to noon, I surmised, and looked at the knotmeter registering at times 8 knots, and never less than 6.

Breaking crests heralded a lot to come, more than I could possibly imagine. The hours slowly went by and I became conscious that it was not possible for things to continue as they were. Every hour was worse than the last. Special waves, the elite commandos of the ocean forces were now approaching, every so often like mountains from behind me as if they had been traveling and growing stronger and bigger for many days, which indeed they had been. I struggled grimly to the task of fending these off, and coping with them. It's true they were few, but they made me continually alert for their attack. For they were live monsters, messengers of doom, agents of total merciless violence. On each occasion both in the night and day, *Research 11* was locked in combat with the evil weaponry of their power, turned over like a scone on a kitchen griddle and given an equal roasting, but of the ocean variety.

When the *demon* spotted me

I'll tell you only what I did during the day on one of the four special encounters, during *the storm*. I will leave the night experience to your imagination, as words just could not describe it. I pulled the hatch closed over my head as I ducked into the companionway below. There was a silence, like the silence of the count-down to zero at a construction site, as workmen wait for the blasting charges to go off. Then zero. A loud hissing sound; a man hits the side of the boat with a sledge hammer. The blow shakes *Research II* like the linen sheets shaking on a clothes-line behind your house. The boat rises below me so that I'm pressed onto the seat; we go up and up. Then we start coming down. Levitation brings my head to the ceiling. But I do not come straight down. Now I pitch forward so that my forehead jams against the porthole opposite and my whole body is a helpless heap of soaking flesh in a mess of everything moveable that can fly out of a cupboard or shelf.

My eyes open and I see pure white foaming, frothing water on the outside of the glass. *Research 11* is right over on its side. It all is so graphically clear. I'm passive in the hands of Providence. *Research 11* comes down and straightens up. As it does so there is a vicious jerking as if it is gripped like a rat in the teeth of an angry dog. Water has spewed in through the closed hatch soaking me like the spray from a firemen's hose. The sea has filled the cockpit so that it forces itself down below through the hinged cover on the thwart. I am thrown backwards to the other side of the cabin in a reflex action. I stare at the water pouring along the lee, running over the piled-up sleeping bag and clothes and over the battery compartment. Water sweeps over my feet as the bilge overflows. But all that is superficial. I can deal with it.

What follows in the next ten seconds, makes me lift my thoughts to heaven and a cry leaves my lips as I call on God to keep the boat together. The whole boat is pounded so that it shakes from side to side and fore and aft. It is squeezed by enormous pressures from incalculable volumes of water pressing against the sides and above. As the cabin threatens to burst and the whole boat shudders, I hold my breath and grit my teeth as my lovely boat is crucified to protect me. Will the keel bolts snap, even one of them? If so, that is *finis, 'lights out'*. If one bolt goes, there is no doubt the rest will follow suit in turn. Then *Research 11* would turn belly-up and be transformed into the sea-coffin of its whole crew. But all holds. There is the sound of rushing waters outside. She shakes herself, like a dog coming ashore shakes the sea water off its coat. We rise up. We're still here. We are still alive.

'Lord, you saved me once again until next time.' I am not fit to sing a hymn of thanksgiving. At that moment I *am still and know that He is God.* He has spoken. He has shown with an irrefutable certainty that he is greater than the storm and that its demon waves can do their worst, but *Research II* will rise again. We will rise again, my little boat and I. We will rise again and overcome, for God who loves us will never let us down. Do hear that, you who are faced with trouble that threatens to overwhelm you. Praise the Lord in the day of prosperity, and he will be with you in the day of trouble.

Apart from these memorable gladiatorial bouts, through which *Research 11* struggled to get back to an even keel, there was the continual sparring that all the time occupied my strength and depleted my energies.

You will excuse me, if I write at this point in retrospect. Journal notes are not available. The time was not propitious for taking notes. There was little basis for believing that anyone would ever get the opportunity to read them anyway. No pen could write what followed over the next twenty-four hours. What I record for you and any others who may read this, will never, never match the living, roaring avalanche that tried its best to overwhelm us. This was nature's masterpiece, a mature storm with all the room of the ocean to swing its mighty muscled arms of wind and wave in a composite arsenal of seething contradiction, where lateral direction gives way to the vertical eruption of the waters of the ocean. There was no horizon to see, only the peaks of the mountainous waves and the hollow of the valleys. Think with me and imagine if you were looking out of an upstairs window of your home and casting your eye down into a valley some two hundred feet across. On the other side there is a wall of water which is broken in a jagged mixture of seething foam with a cloud of spray shooting up from the other side. There is a rumbling deep sound that makes you wonder. Then you turn and see a curling wave sneaking in from the side and throwing your boat on her beam-ends. You go down into the relative calm of the valley, then you are lifted up, up, up, and jostled by contradictory waves that wash your boat whiter than any washing machine.

Lord, remember how frail I am, and how great the storm. Thou art greater than all the forces that threaten me. Come so that I will see your power. Come with your grace and calm the waters that we may survive.

Thus I prayed to the God who never let me down before.

I am moved to weeping with emotion as I recall the long hours, and the continual battle of fighting against defeat and countering all the overpowering forces with my depleted strength.

You may remember that I had, to this point, still got the jib up. But it was already tearing at the luff. I could not let it tear any further, and in any case as the day wore on, it was clear that it would cause greater problems, should I miscalculate, and the boat broach to. Furthermore, the shortened tiller was now often heavy in my hand to turn. Uneasiness filled me within. I knew that I had to fight for my life. As breaking crests now boldly hit my back and split, to hide the cabin in their spray, I loosed the sheets, at the same time jumped forward and crawled along the heaving deck.

I recall how easy it was as I passed forward of the mast. It was easy because the stern had lifted up and now I was thrown forward in a heap, caught in the pulpit and covered with green water. The bow rose as the wave arched its back below me. I clawed my way back to the mast, loosing the halyard and, by habit holding the end, I went forward again, to pull the jib down hand over hand, to make it fast along with the loosened sheets. I should say at this point that the jib was not fully down but still presented a reduced area. When the boat went over on its side, somehow the top of the halyard got jammed, so that the sail could not fully come down. This was small, but sufficient for the boat to keep course and at times to reach surfing speed over the top of the waves. In all this, I was thankful that I had the foreboom, part of the extra gear for my Auto-sail. When I had lashed it down tightly, kept down with the purchase of the vang below it, and secured at the tack to the deck, it acted as a central security system to which I could hold for my safety.

Time ceased to count, as I negotiated every evil challenge from the following seas. Even with the jib nearly down, we raced along, and every hour, the seas developed secondary waves, rising suddenly from every direction.

I was always strong. I was born that way. Since I was young, I liked to exercise my strength, often without reaching my limits, as far as I could recollect. It gave me great satisfaction to lift the heaviest stone and raise it on the dyke, as we built up the stone perimeter of the glebe land of the manse, in far-off Aultbea, every spring to keep the sheep out. It is also true that once I succeeded in lifting a log over a dyke, like a Highland *caber*. I passed out and came to on the ground. I had done it. I was so pleased. But my wrist had broken in doing so. After that it became my hobby to do things alone, but requiring the use of purchase with block and tackle and moving burdens like boats, with rollers and levers. Now, I was in a conflict with a difference. It was a combat of survival and my antagonist, this storm called Barry, though just passing through on his journey, had patience to wait around long enough to overwhelm me. In this context strength would be measured, not only physically but primarily, in will. And will could only be as strong as the spiritual sinews of my faith, in God, in myself and in my little boat. If any one of the three should fail, I knew in the background of my mind that there would be no human record of my oblivion.

Something had to be done

The day wore on. I could not sit in the stern to steer. The tiller was too short for me to steer from near the cabin. I took the oak boat hook and with black rubber ties I lashed it to the tiller, as an extension. The beautifully made boat hook had a whipped rope handle. It represented the skilled workmanship of the 'old school' of navy apprentices. And that it was, the gift received from an exiled Englishman, Peter Oxley, who now lives near me in Mira Bay. For an hour or two, I continued to keep the waves at bay as they chased after us. I cannot say exactly how long. I was now standing in the companionway with the perspex vertical shutter in its slides. Sometimes the seas would cover the cockpit, and I knew that water was sloshing about on the cabin floor. How shall I describe it? Think of me swaying there, holding the tiller extension, using it to hold *Research II* from broaching to, as every now and then, the wicked waves came at her. There was no reprieve, no respite. Time became a vague anguish of consciousness. There was no horizon, only rising mountains. We were lifted up and up and then sped down a slope. It was never a smooth slope, but a rough conglomerate of swirling waters with its own variety of trouble. In this, *Research II* would buck and stall, so that as her head came up, her stern again was vulnerable. I tensed time after time and swung the tiller to the side to counter the force of the sea.

There are limits

I had to face it. This could not continue. What was going to happen on the second night? Twenty-four hours on one chocolate bar and a Coke. No rest or sleep for thirty- eight hours. In that time, continual stress and constant concentration, punctuated with deck work. I was enclosed in a world of wildness. Air and sea mingled together in spray and spume. The aspect of the sea was dark and foreboding. The night was not far away. Time and again I pitched forward, as sleep involuntarily overcame me. I would jerk awake and reorientate myself, repeatedly trying to shake off the inevitable sleep that must ultimately win. Though I could live on catnaps, I always was one for sleeping, without the prolonged deprivation now at hand. As a young boy, sitting in the hard pew of the church hall in Inverasdale, at the fourth service my father the minister was conducting on the evening of the Sabbath, I would capitulate to nature's remedy for tiredness. Just think of it, a little boy sitting it out in a long Gaelic service, with the hall packed with people and hot with condensation running down the inside of the windows as the kerosene lamps shed their yellow light over all. Do you wonder that I would sway and fall forward almost to the floor, sitting there in front of the pulpit!

I never forget the mortification, when once I nearly reached the floor, my father paused in his sermon and asked an elder nearby to keep an eye on me. From there on, I would sit beside him. I felt rather proud of myself, kind of well-favored, almost important, me little fat, apple-cheeked, Angus, now given special place right there beside an elder, a real elder. I could not come to any harm even if sleep came over me, for the great big hand of Roddie MacDonald, was like an anchor weight, that kept me securely on my seat.

Now far out in the Atlantic, I gave one more repeat performance as sleep overcame me and I pitched forward. The perspex shutter gave way in front of me as the teak slide split, and I followed, sprawling over the bridge deck, pulling the tiller to the floor.

Hove to

That woke me up. I shook my head. Looking out over the stern, there was no horizon, just a wall of black water, and it was all around me, moving continually up and down. I forced my consciousness to keep command. How easy it seemed, to let everything go, and curl up and capitulate to nature's powers. I had to take control, or the storm would control me. Necessity made me down the jib completely, lashing it around the forestay, so that *Research II* now lost way.

In the cockpit, there was a coil of rope and attached to it was a sea anchor, an experimental one, which I made and brought along to be tested. You will understand that you could not really test this except in a *real* storm. Now I let it out over the quarter. I would have liked to put it out over the bow. But frankly, I just could not make it again, over the heaving deck, swept repeatedly by waves. I could see the orange sea anchor caught in the seas. I pulled but it would not come in. Instead, I was gratified to see *Research II* turn obliquely to the seas and lie now in relative peace. I watched her for a while, before I was sure that all was well. We were coming to terms with the storm. The storm dictated the terms, certainly, but *Research 11* had the ability to respond.

With that, I closed shop, as it were for the day, and went below. I could not face the task of cooking a full big meal. Besides, conditions were not ideal, although it was imperative that I eat something. I lighted the stove and heated up a tin of mushroom soup. I somehow secured the perspex shutter with a cord from the hasp, so that even as a wave might hit the shutter, water would not pour in. I pulled the hatch completely over my head, stretched out athwartships below it and sleep claimed my limp body as weariness won. All night *Research 11* was hove to. I was fortunate indeed that she could look after herself, while I slept. You can see the point. There was no choice. I went below about 7:00 p.m. I had had no rest or sleep for 38 hours, since 5:00 a.m. the previous day. I simply could not stay awake.

Though sleep came, I was troubled. Sleep was fitful and shallow. My mind would not stop. In spirit I was out there as darkness masked the angry work of the storm. The boat was pounded with hammer like waves, so that the motion was constantly changing. Three or four times during the night and the following day, *Research 11* was thrown on her beam-ends. The sequence of that experience, that murderous attempt to annihilate us, was almost book-perfect. You were hit with a sledgehammer; you went up, up, up. When you reached the top, over you went on your side so that the horizontal became the vertical even a bit past the vertical. It occurred to me that it might be the point of no return. Then as she righted herself, down *Research 11* came in a reverse action, levitation almost leaving you clawing to the offside cupboards. Then a sense of enormous pressures of water on the sides and from above, with water spewing round the cabin with a refined nozzle like force of a fire hose. And to round it off, there was the *finale. Research II* got up like a boxer after being knocked down, stirs back to consciousness and picks himself up to take some more punishment. So my little tough boat would not stay down, but would rise again, shuddering from stem to stern. At that point, I, thrown backwards would hold on with my hand locked on the top shelf and my teeth clamped together in tight-lipped suspense, willing the keel bolts not to snap under the stress.

Signs of trouble to come

From my position below, there was a growling sound from the rudder area. I was used to this. The stainless steel bracket around the rudder stock to which the self-steering gear was attached, caused, I thought, a gurgling turbulence as the stern rose and fell. I tried to interpret this noise and assured myself that though louder, it was nothing new. I struggled out several times and shone the torch on the stern. I relashed the rudder makeshift extension. But I knew that the rudder was only partly held secure. But what could I do! Seas broke on the weather side jerking the boat up on its side. Then quite often a sea would hit the boat from the official lee and a sheet of water would cover the gunwale, filling the floor of the cockpit.

As the second dawn of the storm broke, I looked out. There were intermittent groans coming from the rudder area. I looked more closely and noticed that the tiller was distorted, and arched upwards at the top of the rudder. I concluded that this was due to the stretching of the rubber tangs, used to bind the extension to the shortened tiller. After another hour, I came out again. The sound was different.

The tiller breaks off

One look told me the tiller had parted from the rudder stock. It lay in the cockpit, useless. The stock of the rudder had nothing more than a ragged black remnant of wood, stuck in the cheeks. Something was far wrong. The seas hit the rudder so that its blade banged from side to side. Freed from the restraints of the tiller, it yawed violently sideways, so that the blade pressed like a lever against the transom. The rounded aerodynamic shape now gave strong purchase so that the rudder was being levered away from the stern, and bending the gudgeon pin. There was a twist in the two foot long gudgeon rod and it had lifted almost out from the rudder slot. I grabbed my large vice grips and clamped the top under the remnant of tiller. The waves repeatedly banged the rudder from side to side. One moment we were high and dry, next the stern was submerged in foaming water. The rudder was uncontrollable. I held the vice grips closed over the top of the gudgeon pin. Then it happened. The gudgeon pin broke. I was left holding two inches of it. The effect was almost immediate. The rudder, now free, worked back and fore, at the mercy of the power of the waves. I tried to grasp the rod below, but lost it.

Trying to bring the rudder inboard

The rudder was now alive, a living thing, all seven foot of it with its eighteen inch wide blade. I was determined to save it. The bracket round it was only 10 inches from the transom as the stock was only 8 inches. My aim was to lift the rudder right up out of the water. Only then could there be some respite and peace. My hands reached down, trying to raise the rudder out. I looked down at my hands. There had been many cuts. That was normal, even though some were still raw and open as they did not have a chance to heal. Now I saw my salt washed fingers and wondered with a kind of detached dispassionate curiosity at my own limbs. The knuckles were nearly all peeled of skin to the flesh. They were like large red spots painted on my fingers. On the palm of my right hand the skin had folded over from the pad so that it was something like a sausage-roll, with red flesh under it. There was no sensation of pain. Repeatedly my hands and fingers had tried to grasp the moving rudder as it banged and gyrated inside the stainless steel bracket. Needless to say the stainless steel edge of the bracket did its work on my flesh. I should be thankful that my hands were not injured or my fingers sliced off.

One more try

I paused.

'I must get that rudder up,' I said to myself.

'I am not going to lose it. It's a beauty and part of my boat.'

Once more, I clung to the stock as the boat heaved underneath and the rudder threatened to slip away through the bracket. Then down came the stern and both stern and I plunged under the sea. I angled the rudder sideways just right this time and the blade came shooting up. It was now quiescent, free from the battering of waves. Holding it, I saw that it could stay jammed in the bracket right there raised high above the transom. With rope, I lashed it to the stern guardrail so that it was strongly secure.

When I made all safe and secure, I returned to the cabin and cooked breakfast. What I would do in response to this adversity, I deferred until later.

This was the time for real food. I must refuel. Whatever was before me would demand my renewed strength. There was no doubt what that was, Scots Brose, double rations, hot tea and Rye Vita, my substitute for fresh home made bread. If you visited me over the next half hour, you would find me on my knees with one hand gripping the cupboard shelf, the other holding the kettle of water on top of the stove. In the storm, with the alternating elevation and plunging of the boat, the kettle would not wait on the stove. As it was with every sway of the boat, the flames, which always like to remain vertical just like mass affected by gravity, would peep out alternatively from one side or the other of the base of the kettle. I had to be on my guard that my hand would not get burned.

The strange contradiction

Contrary to all logic, I suddenly felt great, absolutely on top of the world. Let no one take away this hour from me, I thought within myself. I felt the sides of my mouth crack open with a wide grin, as well-being and a renewed zest percolated through my whole being. What strange contradictions make up a human being! Here I was in the middle of an Atlantic storm, in a rudderless boat, being thrown at times so that the mast was hidden in the sea, and I was as buoyant as a schoolboy who has just pulled a trout from the country stream on his way home from school. This is my thing, I thought. This is for me. I'm going to savor the mental feast. One of the main factors in the equation is now missing, namely *the rudde*r. A rudder is considered an essential even though you invent a thousand mechanical devices to operate it. You need it on a boat as necessary as on a jetliner. But this only increases the challenge to turn what could be called by many, a routine little trip, already made by scores of hardy loners, men and women, into a voyage, where the handicap in the view of many knowledgeable people, could be construed as the guarantee of failure.

Two thousand, five hundred miles to go

I suppose, if a surveyor assessed the situation at this point, I would be written off as an insurance loss. 2500 miles to go and no rudder in the North Atlantic. And to cap it all, this in a year that made history, in that the southwest wind was on holiday and in its place a cold northerly worked its way east with the sun, for most days of this summer. But I had not taken out insurance. I had a policy nevertheless. There was no guarantee with it but it had this motto written on the parchment which was given to me long ago by my father. It read, 'If you do your best, God will do the rest.' It was as simple as that. Foolproof, a certainty. Nothing could revoke it, nothing could disprove it. With this you could do anything in life that had the sanction of God's will, and even the pursuit of a personal goal, as long as it did not conflict with His law. This was no time for recriminations, and certainly not for a condemnatory assault on one's self. What good would it do even to nail the culprit, far less select a scapegoat, especially if the finger pointed back like a boomerang to myself! Nevertheless, I had much to think about and I wanted to clear the decks, as it were in my mind, so that I would be free from there to reconstruct a positive course of action. I therefore reviewed the situation with regard to the rudder and its sudden obsolescence. What led to this?

1. A year earlier, the rudder had been damaged. I had it repaired. Also, I had replaced the stainless steel gudgeon pin with a copper one, the only one available at the time. The gudgeon pin broke off where there was a holding pin of 3/32 of an inch. That clevis pin sheered off.

2. The lateral strain pulling and pushing the rudder back and fore in the storm took its toll.

3. The broken tiller, when I fell over it over the bridge deck caused the rudder to swing completely sideways, and the construction of the composite stock helped to induce a powerful leverage, acting outwards on the rudder pintles.

4. Because of my preoccupation with Stanley the self-steering

gear, so vital for the voyage and made by myself with the deadline start in mid June, I failed to deal adequately with the rudder situation.

5. A simple omission of putting the rudder question on my list of tasks to be dealt with, led finally to the oversight.

6. Had I remembered, I would not only have acquired a new stainless steel pin, but I would also have taken the old one along as a spare.

But the rudder was aboard and not lost. We should never give up. With that one last try, turning the blade at an angle and using the timing of the waves, I managed to pull the rudder up through the bracket opening of the self-steering unit. I had poured out at least an hour of mighty effort, and persistent will before I succeeded. But no one could take this moment away from me. I did it. The beautiful rudder was now safe aboard, and there it was at the stern, rising high above the guardrail, lashed to the latter securely. I resolved to leave it there, out of the way, rather than tie it down on the cabin top. I also left the shattered remnant of the tiller, still in the cheeks at the rudder head, a perpetual reminder that laminates and beautiful varnish can hide dark treacherous rot unseen and unsuspected.

Another look at my hands, as sharp pain stabbed at my nerves, caused me to think of the absence of any pain when I was working so long in the suspense of the emergency. It seems, pain is irrelevant when overcoming. If it intrudes, you brush it aside, as an irritation. Overcoming is stamped on your will and will not accept anything less than victory, in spite of every argument or persuasion of logic that is flung against it. And what is the result? Overcoming, and that means, broadly speaking overcoming adversity, contrary winds and visitations of Providence, as these meet us all at one time or another in the voyage of our life here, this process of overcoming, breeds its own species of joyous victory. The result is that the original calamity is countered and reinterpreted as **opportunity.**

Being tested and proved

We are on this planet, not as fickle creatures of chance but products of design. We are, as human beings, the most wonderful products in the world, animate or inanimate, capable of incomparable good, but also of unimaginable evil, as history even of this century is proof. We are here to be tested, to be proved, to see the stuff we are made of and whether or not we live up to our designer's expectations, and fulfill his will. To succeed is possible, but not given to all. But to try is for all and to entertain the possibility of success. To him that has faith, all things are possible. But they are not all probable. To be probable, is to add to faith something more. It means adding our resources, our efforts, our dedication. Then these together with our faith are translated into the composite instrument of dynamic living and achievement of specific purpose. Each contributes, like the members of a sports team or a structured work group, exercising our different talents or skills in the corporate endeavor of noble humanity where trying, working, enduring, waiting, persevering, and rising up after falling, lead to **overcoming.**

Opportunity

It is truly strange how life takes different turns. Here I was being given an opportunity:

(a) to test my auto-sail. It seemed clear to me at the time that the conventional sails could not possibly work on a boat without a rudder. On the other hand, it was just the perfect opportunity to prove the multiple sails of the rig I designed. How strange that I was resigned to leaving them out of the picture, at the start of the voyage, because of perceived limitations in the preliminary test. Now, it was forced upon me to get them out as my salvation.

(b) My self-steering unit Stanley, as I call him, would have a greater and vital role to play because now it was the only means of keeping Res*earch II* on her course, so that the captain mate, cook and crew could have their sleep and do all the necessary duties of each day.

(c) This would also be a test of myself, of my faith, of my will. If both of these held up, so would all the rest of me, in all my capacity to think, to contrive, to put together a solution, to improvise, to modify, to adapt - as R*esearch II* met varying conditions of wind and sea. And there was time to experiment, and room to make mistakes, yes, and to correct them, and to tune the solutions to perfection and at last hopefully, to sail up the English Channel, to cross the finishing-line, and justly but humbly claim victory.

I mentioned that we are full of contradictions. The moments of buoyant hope and dogged confidence were sometimes fleeting and short-lived. They were interspersed with other thoughts that also claimed a hearing in my mind, thoughts that had only too accurately, a basis in reality. Thus I had to struggle against these. Age had taken agility from me. The young lad who leapt over sinking Highland peatbogs with ease carrying a big bag of peats on his back, now needed every ounce of strength of arm and leg to drag his body over the wet heaving deck. Already I had several spasms of bursting fiery pain which doubled me up on the floor of the cabin. Fortunately, I had taken the prescription pills for this contingency. My legs were strong, but when I thought on it, - and thought for such negatives was rationed and only forced upon my consciousness, - numbness made my left leg like a piece of wood, so that I was curiously unaware of its presence. I would then collapse and fall when it was needed.

But enough. I was always as strong as an ox and though our strength wanes over the years, if we do God's will, he gives strength also to do those extras of our will, that do not conflict with his. These may even be linked to personal fulfillment, unique to each one of us, and by interpretation, be a proven test of our faith. Better, I think, that I slip into the deep with the friends of the sea as witness to my demise, than sit it out on land in the comfort of a home, with unfulfilled goals and dreams of what I might have done.

Log: Day 17, Sunday, 9th July, 1995

Log/Journal Notes: *Research 11* hove to in tropical storm Barry. Impossible to work on deck. Wait below, most of time listening to Radio Canada. Also worship service from St. Anne's and St. Agnes church in London, on the BBC. Jazz service.

Beautiful rendering of Amazing Grace, the hymn composed by John Newton, ex-captain of an English trader in the slave export business to America.

Minister defines JAZZ in the terms of the story of the widow's son from Nain.

Contrasts life and death. Heart of the Gospel. Jesus king, crucified but not criminal.

Jesus presented life in Contrasts, and not in uniformity. JAZZ folk lived to express contrasts and not life in uniformity. Uniformity kills life, Contrasts make life dynamic.

Waypoint 14

Log Position:	N 46'29"	W 35' 29"
Time:	13.47 ET	

Evening sun breaks through, but seas impossible.

A bit down in spirits.

Focus thoughts hard. Knocked about continually. Blows. Cannot cook, stove jams, as boat keeps rocking too far over. Tried but pan lifts up as boat drops. Cannot hold it without spilling. Motion too violent. Knees are in agony. Too much on my knees, hard to believe it. Bailed out every so often. Sixty buckets, I think, since Friday. Try hose into cockpit when possible. Twenty strokes of pump fill a bucket. I am fairly tired at this point.

Must focus thoughts. When the storm is past, must have strategy to sail without a rudder. This is the big challenge.

Aim to use my own new sails with added challenge of steering, both SS and sail balance fore and aft.

This comprises:

1. Purpose
2. Definition
3. Direction of energies

This is test of self-steering - of sails - of human endeavor
Pray God will give success!

Bailed out 100 strokes, 5 buckets. Extremely difficult to move or do anything below. Motion violent all the time, day and night.

Fears are a reality, JAZZ minister said. Many different kinds. Need to identify our own. Mine is to fail to do my best. Not to lose, but not to do my best. To lose is irrelevant, not my business. It doesn't come into the equation. There is no shame in losing, but there is no reason to entertain the idea.

On the other hand, hope is persistent in human beings, said the JAZZ minister and Jesus Christ represents this.

And this hope I hold on to, within the definable limitations of worthiness attendant on my little journey. I have limits in my self and the boat has limits. I am 63 years young and the boat is 23 years old and much gear is original.

Looked out. Saw one little black and white sea-swallow. Not another sign of life since Friday evening concert. Trust Monday will be back to normality.

DETAILS OF SAIL DEPLOYMENT TO SUIT WIND

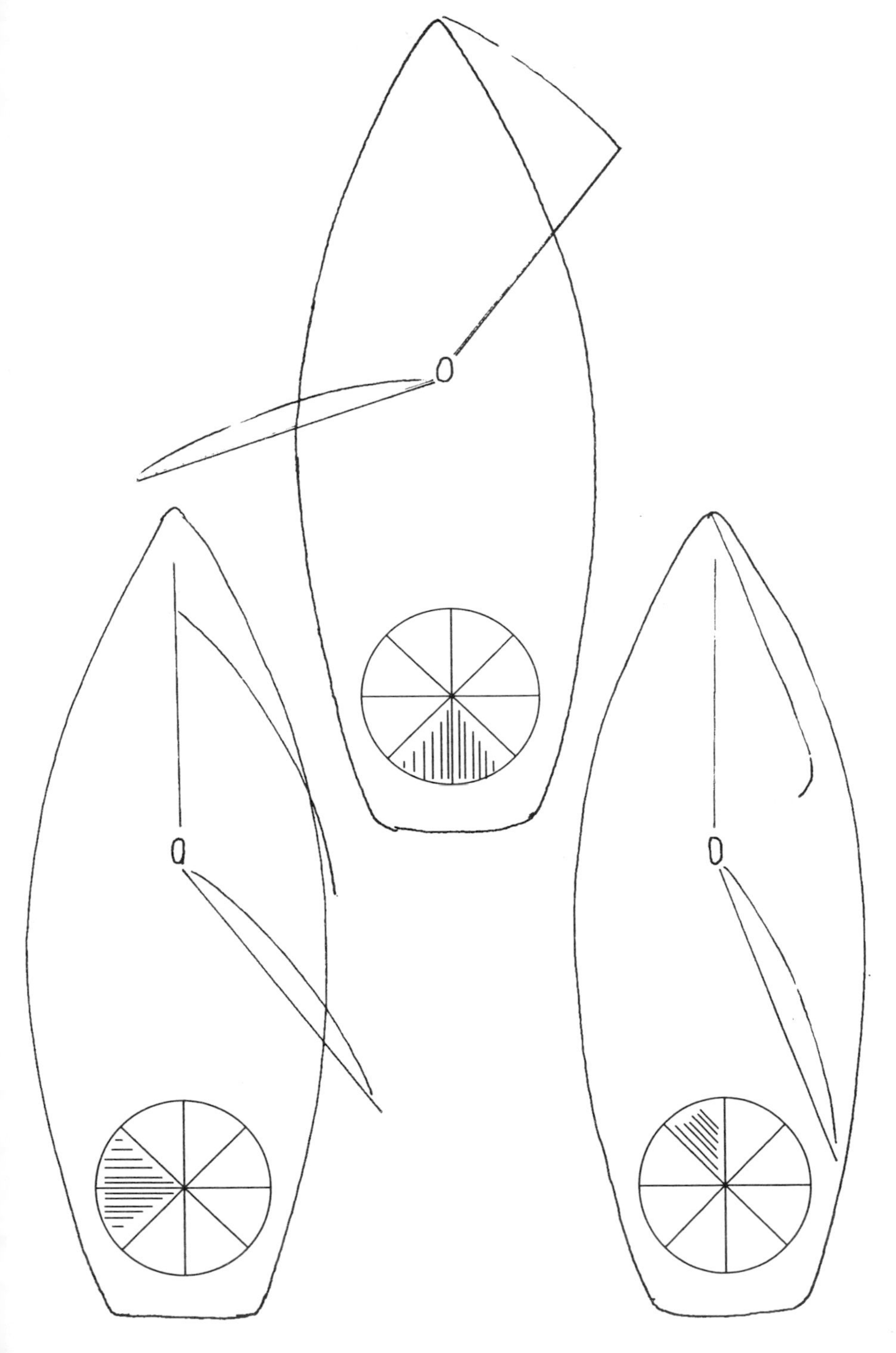

CHAPTER 11

A Curl in the Clew

Log: Day 18, Monday, 10th July, 1995

Woke to end of tropical storm Barry. Hope so. 5 a.m. My usual time. Wind now fair. Seas way down. One glance at compass was enough. If *Research II* was moving, it was back to Canada. What happened was that the storm wind had made a wide arc and now in a reduced velocity, the wind blew from the north with some east in it.

I gulped down a big mug of black coffee. I knew I had a job to do. My mind was clear. The storm had done its worst. It tried to break me, to smash the boat. Without the double rigging, mast and all would be a formless mess and hope of going on would have no substance.

My ship was wounded, but on analysis, superficially. We were in a new phase. The storm had dug deep and dug up a challenge, a challenge of great magnitude, that now I resolved to meet and **OVERCOME.** In a way, it was good that I was by myself. I am not one to entertain negatives. They pile up at the door, knocking impatiently to get in. They pack the waiting room of my mind, like the ailing patients in a doctor's surgery, but with me, these negatives will have to wait so long that they eventually get up and go. Why? Yes, because I keep positive thoughts right there at the centre of my thinking and however small they may be, I fire them up like a ship's boiler, and soon they are full of steam and dynamic purpose.

Log note: Action intense, insistent, continuous. Never give up - this is a critical day.

I had given God his Sabbath, albeit in my mind - he forgives me - the steps of action were already as clearly decided as taking the lines of a boat.

5:30 a.m. saw me on deck. I threw off oilskins and anorak and bonnet. I cranked my gammy leg. Somehow I was as fit as a fiddle and raring to go. I had a purpose. Excitement to fulfill it, confidence that I could do it, deriving from the necessity not to fail, - all these made me ready for the day's work.

Day's syllabus

Raise my own sails fore and aft. I spare the details. But after 6 hours I was back in the cabin for a breakfast of Scottish oatmeal brose, my staple meal, made in three minutes with hot water and meal, a taste of salt and a spoon of sugar melted in on top. Just leave this for an extra two minutes with a saucer or some cover on top and ask a blessing. You would be surprised how utterly delicious it tastes with creamy evaporated milk. Then it was tea and Rye Vita with marmalade. Truly this was a delectable treat after three days without food except a tin of soup. Then to work again.

I had dressed the foreboom with four of my panel sails. The wind now from the N'NE made it very unmanageable. I had put all up on the same halyard, a revision of my original intention of four separate halyards for each panel both on fore and main boom. This was ruggedly simple, but it just would not work. The luff of the sails would not all be straight. This method was clearly a failure. *Research II* had to sail east and that meant close to the wind. The four sails together were just not competent to do this. And at this point we were heading backwards. There was no chance at all that it would work, sailing east.

Now I decided to try two of the panels sails. This I did. I deployed my swinging foreboom and tried to get *Research II* to turn around. But try as I might, I could not get her to budge. She kept going west, on a steady lope back to Canada.

You cannot know how much it pained me to hear the gurgle at the bow as *Research II* backpedaled. This had a devastating effect upon me, with all the connotations of failure banging and screaming at the door of my mind, wanting in, to take me over and drown me in pessimism and impotence. Just think of my reception, if I had to be pulled out of my predicament by some passing ship and dumped unceremoniously on the quay at Halifax, New York or even Sydney! What a queue of pundits who would echo the refrain, 'I told you so,' even many of my close friends who, in this respect, have a radically different approach to life.

'Blast them all,' I said aloud, as the thoughts came near me. 'They'll not have me as carcass meat to confirm their own timidity and safe, smug security. But reality showed a definite bleakness. Remember the bottom line. I had no rudder and 2500 miles to go. And at that moment, after eight hours work on deck, *Research II* was making her way - I thought darkly as I looked at her - yes, I must say it, I think she was doing it deliberately, sneaking back home, trying to get out of the difficulty, taking the easy way out. My eyes caught the symbol of my calamity, the broken down rudder, raised now at the stern like a useless totem pole, an ugly injured victim of the storm and its devastating power. And protruding from its head, the jagged remains of the tiller whose rotten core was masked by the beautiful appearance of the varnished laminates.

The Philosophy of Thought/Action

But there are two sides to every story. In contrast to all the pointers to pessimism, there was my chosen philosophy of Thought/Action. Think what to do, and do it. For me at this time, the foresails were only half of what had to be done. They were patently unhappy at this point. As I marshalled my energies to apply myself to the main, I could not bear to leave the foresails up as they were aiding and abetting *Research II* in her crafty scheme to hurry back to Canada and peace. The brass snap shackles for the mast-track were very stiff and even after loosening them with WD-40 and working them free with vice grips, it was with a struggle that I completed the work. Before this I stripped her of the mainsail and conventional jib, stowing these for good, as I thought at the time, in their bags down below. I now had two thirds of the conventional mainsail area on the main boom, and setting well in the fair wind. Alas, we were heading in the wrong direction. But there it was. Now, I put all my mind and energy to face the moment of truth, to try and grasp with one final effort the ultimate crowning prize of the day's work. At the same time, that day was fast waning and close to evening; for the captain, weariness cried out, to turn in, curl up and go to sleep.

I shook myself, and strengthened my resolve within myself. I can do it; I know I can do it; *I can do all things through Christ who strengtheneth me.*

Going beyond the limits

A long time ago, I drove a Dodge 10 ton truck with a six cylinder Perkins engine, three times a night on the round trip from Beauly Quarries to the construction site of Cluanie Hydro-electric dam in Ross-shire, Scotland. This was a student job all that summer. The truck was in new condition and kept by Logan's, perfectly maintained by his own garage, to run 24 hours a day on two twelve hour shifts. The engine literally did not stop. I jumped into the cab at 7 p.m. as the regular driver finished for the day. For me, the engine governor, which kicked in to prevent the vehicle doing more than 60 miles an hour, was an irritation, especially on the return trip, the lorry being empty. I therefore would disconnect the governor, so that I could go faster. Now forty years later, in mid-Atlantic, I was tempted, yea almost compelled to do something similar. Before I did so, I would exhaust all other avenues. Then, that last alternative, the forbidden one, would stand alone as the last resort.

The expulsion of all incompatible thinking

To see a goal, to reach out for a prize, to believe that it is really there, is not enough. As I tried with every resource of mind and trick of the physical, all my efforts to turn *Research II* around to sail east to Britain, failed. Yes, they failed one after the other. I set Stanley and reset Stanley, I worked the sheets more and less, but *Research II* hurried steadily backwards. I had been on my feet since the early morning, climbing up and down, working with ropes and blocks, raising and lowering halyards, handing sails. Tiredness and hunger suggested to me that I call it a day. Then the thought of the boat getting her own way and sailing back threw every negative out, like Britain's prime minister Margaret Thatcher throwing her Cabinet minister, Sir Iain Laird and his cohorts, out the side door of 10 Downing Street, so that there was not one of the original Cabinet left to accompany her on her own departure from office.

Elimination

Thus in my mind there was nothing left but to adopt the 'final solution.' I would pit my own self against the wind in a 'do or die contest' that would decide in finality who was the winner. To do this, I raked the figure of Stanley forward, so that the blade was lifted out of the water. I prepared myself physically for the next move, noting that the seas were still considerable and the wind brisk, even as we sailed before it. Whenever you sail with the wind, you underestimate the wind strength, because your apparent speed masks the true wind speed. Then with a mighty resolution of will, fighting against fatigue, and the continual pain of my chapped knees from crawling over the deck, I raised the two foresails with the tack of each on the foreboom. I led separate sheets from the tack back through the fair leads to the side winches and cleats. All looked well. The four sails filled nicely out hauled on the foreboom and synchronized with the main on the other side. We were goosewinged, a wonderful delight in theTrade winds, but anathema for me in the North Atlantic at this point of time, for we were going in the wrong direction.

Now I sat back in the cockpit. With both sets of sheets, repeatedly I sought to get her bow to come around, but to no avail. The sun was declining in the west, as *Research II* happily sped back to Canada at a rate of knots. I just could not bear to look at the knotmeter. This was a crisis, no question about it. This could be the moment of truth. I still had that one last alternative but it was not ingenuity. Rather, it was a composite of spiritual faith and physical strength. It was not a combination, but a composite. In this, spiritual power was induced by faith into the physical. In the first you have a mechanical faith, in the second you have a chemical reaction. The Spirit of God acts like a catalyst so that faith and the physical merge together and become a dynamic force. You can call this anything you like but it can not be undone. This is not automatic in action, nor will it operate on any form of presumption, even by the greatest saint. I was reluctant to use it as once it had nearly cost me my life. But I knew the reason why I had failed. I had not prepared myself sufficiently for the moment of action. But now I was ready. I had the decks as it were cleared. My mind and heart were brushed and swept like the kitchen floor of all that would hinder. My soul was alive, dynamically believing in the power of heaven, and the promise of God that his power is made perfect in weakness. My will was trained already to obey my soul's commands. My will read the instructions on the screen of my mind as the latter computed the factors in the equation. I saw in my mind the sequence of what I had to do. That was my best. I could do no more than that. It was now or never.

The last resort

With the self steering gear taken out of commission, both fore and aft sails were full as the north wind filled them from the quarter; *Research II* rocked amicably from side to side, going at a good rate. I slacked the foresheet and I pulled the mainsheet in as fast as possible until the boom was above me and the wind spilled from the sails. Letting the sheet go free, I jumped up on the cabin top and, bending at the knees, bowed my head and put my shoulder to the boom. With a stubborn resolution of mind and will, I pushed the boom against the wind to try and bring it over to the other side. For a moment or two, it looked as if I would succeed. I pushed further, and further, straightening my legs under me.

Then a sudden gust of wind, a sudden wicked lurch of the boat, and the sail and boom came back at me. I let go in time and tumbled backwards into the cockpit. I picked myself up and remember saying to myself, 'I'm not going to let go; I'll not give up.'

Pulling the mainsheet in once more, I jumped up again on the cabin top, bowed my head and bent my back against the gusts of wind with all my might as Sampson of old. I pushed on and on until the boom rested on the opposite shrouds. I locked my knees as would a horse, my lungs almost bursting, and a speckled haze dimming my vision. I could do no more; I had given it all I had. That was my best. Timc passed in microseconds. Then the other factor kicked in. I believed that God was with me. And at many times before in my life, he had never let me down. How could he let me down now? Man's extremity is God's opportunity.

Prayer, urgent prayer

I could not raise my head. My voice was muffled in my gasping throat. Yet the feeble cry rose to heaven, a bleep on the screen of omnipotence, an SOS from an old irascible believer, right in the middle of the Atlantic. I made that special call to Heaven's Gates, whispering it in the Gaelic tongue,

'O Thigherna mo Dhia, cruithfhear an cuan; dean trocair orm, thig 's cuidich mi. Dean aithnichte do chumhachd agus do ghloir.'

('O Lord my God, Creator of the ocean; have mercy on me, come and help me. Make manifest thy power and thy glory.')

Seconds passed, my eyes were glued to the bow, seeing all in a kind of misty haze, like watching the spoke of a clock to see if it would move. One moment the bow thrust onwards and westwards. Then I saw the bow stop. Was it just a pause? Would it begin again? I watched, my eye glued to the stem. It had started moving back. I held on grimly, my knees now almost, but not quite, buckling underneath me. Yes, the bow was moving. Yes, *Research II* was coming around, first to southwest, then to south. My body trembled, my lungs were filled as with poison of spent air. She continued to turn, southeast, then east. The pressure of the boom against me was off, as the sails now filled with the wind above me. Letting the mainsheet slip through my hand, I pulled myself back over the lifeline and the grey black water underneath me. I fell back over the bridgedeck into the cockpit and gasped for air. My head cleared. I stayed there and watched. The wind now hit my face. *Research II* had turned around 180 degrees and now set off eastwards for Great Britain.

Worshipping and working

What can I say? How can words describe the miracle? Once again the formula worked. *Do your best and God will do the rest,* although it's true God who loves me, gave me a hard time. How I praised the Lord, right there, slumped on the cabin top. I sang a psalm in English Psalm 95:

To him the spacious sea belongs,
for He the same did make;
The dry land also from His hands
its form at first did take.

O come, and let us worship him,
let us bow down withal,
And on our knees before the Lord,
our Maker let us fall.

(From the Scottish Psalter)

Quickly, even as I sang, I rose and trimmed the booms and sheeted the sails - they were each separate on the booms. Then I jumped up on the transom and set Stanley, studied the sails, and jumped down to check the compass. I kept spectacles and watch inside the cabin. Then up I went again, to adjust the wind vane.

The next Challenge

I now had overcome one challenge before me. There were 2500 miles to go. But I was able to get my boat to sail on the chosen course. This was a glorious victory. From now on I would be able to repeat that victory every time *Research II* went astray. And that brings us to the next challenge. I had to get the boat to stay on the course. There could be no rest, at best only a pause in the day or in the night, until this was achieved.

How long it would take to deal with this I could not know. Optimism prompted me to believe that I could succeed within the next twenty-four hours. Indeed we are so constituted, that when we believe in ourselves and this is reinforced by a past victory, it appears that the next victory is just round the corner. That was the situation for me, as I now faced this second challenge.

The Self-Steering unit no longer could function as it was designed to do, namely to activate the powerful blade of the boat's rudder. Now it was reduced in efficiency, to react in a reverse capacity using the force of its own rather puny thin oar blade directly. It became clear to me that Stanley just could not do the job alone. I had to work the sails and the sheets to find the rest of the formula for success.

To sail before the wind

Broadly speaking, there were two aspects to this further challenge. The first was to succeed in sailing before a wind. That meant any wind from the west, either northwest or southwest. If the wind came from any point on the west arc of the compass, clearly, wind power would automatically act upon the sails, if the latter were trimmed to take advantage of them. Differences of angle will determine sail settings so that it is easy to visualize the yacht moving forward with the wind somewhere on the compass behind it. Success here requires having the main balanced against the jib. If pressure on the main is excessive, the boat will wheel around. If the wind is strong, the main can be taken down. Now the boat will be pulled along by the jib. But there can only be success if the wind is directly behind. If, from the various points to north or south, on the quarter, the bow will react by bearing off to the lee. I found that it was impossible to maintain the boat in such conditions, by using the sheets.

What I did was move the tack of the jib aft. I had my own foreboom. I could put the jib on this or as I did until the halyard jammed, put my own multiple sails up. These I moved along the boom track until I had balance. So that the main and jib were efficient. Coordinating the fore and main sheets became a challenge of skill. This I learned to use in the day or the night. This is not just technical.

It relates to having the feel of the ship and the sea. We are born with certain aptitudes. For me, synchronizing sail and wind was a natural employment. I cannot say that it was easy. I find emotion welling up in me, as I think of the many times that a wave or a gust undid all my work and *Research II* took off to some unwanted destination.

Once I had the boat going in an easterly direction, I would jump up and reset Stanley, the Scull-Oar. The trouble was that there was a gap, a time span of possibly thirty seconds. That may seem nothing but with one person on board, it was a major factor. Consider, I had to finish fine-tuning the sheets, check compass course, jump up to the guardrail, declutch the head, turn vane edge to wind, look up at the Canadian flag on the shroud and/or my own mini wind vane on top of Stanley's Vane. Then I had to reset the vane, engage the clutch, and jump down to peer at the compass. I cannot tell you how often I did this in the day or in the night before, at last, joy and victory came. Our life here is not one big drag through the years. It really is made up of alternating grind and little victories. One little victory can fill us with overflowing joy. Nothing can spoil that moment. We can savor it. I can tell you, that when I had tried for six hours to get *Research II* to obey my will and then, when I was at breaking point, managed to win, I was overcome by a sense of positive triumph.

I would look with wonder as the boat seemed to say, 'Alright, you win.' And away she flew. I should also say that it was imperative that both sheets from the foresail had to be made fast. There could be no play. Efficiency related to the final tuning. Even with this the boat would yaw as the wind lessened or freshened. The Scull-Oar could not steer a boat on to a course. But it could and did keep my boat on course. I could envisage a scenario where there were two or more aboard. Then one could work the sheets to synchronize the sails, and the other actually use the Steering Oar to put the boat on course. For a loner, both actions had to be undertaken, one after the other. I should add that where the wind was more or less directly behind, I sailed goose-winged, and the Scull-Oar kept us on course. If the wind reached gale force, I used my auto-sail on the main with my auto sails on the foreboom or the conventional jib. The foreboom was sheeted out opposite to the main and high speed was maintained.

Usually I let her run like this, the knotmeter registering 7 to 8 knots and sometimes right over 9 knots. The fact is that the distance made good eastwards was often complemented by a considerable extra distance sailed. On several occasions, *Research II* sailed back sixty miles in twenty-four hours before I succeeded in getting her back on course. Do you wonder, that these occasions of overcoming, remain with me as watersheds of my life experience? No wonder that at the time of triumph I would sink to my knees in reaction and tumble into my little dark cabin that was my ocean home. And there I would release my pent up emotions, as my whole being filled with wonder at the goodness and the mercy of the Lord.

To sail against the wind

The second scenario or aspect of the challenge appeared formidable. Human optimism is a big bag with a hole in it. Immediately after the great crisis of the storm, during which I lost the rudder, this challenge faced me. From the Monday evening when I succeeded, as the storm abated and the wind was now blowing from the north and east, I was faced with keeping *Research II* on course.

Exulting in a triumph was always short-lived. It is not enough to score a victory and get the boat on course. She has to stay there. And just remember, I had no tiller or steering wheel. The fact is that I was on duty continuously from that Monday night. For over a week, I snatched only moments of sleep. When in the cabin, preparing a meal, my eye was always on the cabin compass. I had little rest. If I fell asleep with tiredness, for an hour, I would find *Research II* off course again. And there followed the labour of getting her back. But slowly my skills in this were sharpened and my time improved right down to the single figures, but in minutes.

The challenge was to keep the boat on course with the wind ahead of the beam. Let me explain why the Scull-Oar alone could not do this, however efficient it was, when the boat rudder was not in commission. There were several reasons: 1. The blade could not compare in area with the conventional boat rudder. 2. Because we were going against the wind; the actual wind strength was greater, and thus the wind's deflective action was considerably more powerful when acting on the bow. 3. The Scull-Oar, like most wind operated self-steering units, is not an initiatory force but a reactive one. The Scull-Oar is passive, the blade is in line with the keel, when the boat is on course. When the boat is deflected off course to port or starboard, the Vane reacts to the lateral pressure of the wind, transmitting this to the blade, twisting it, so that it swings outwards. The fact is that there is a delay in the reaction. It takes time for the self steering unit to complete its counter action. During that time, maybe ten seconds, or only four seconds, depending on the wind, the boat continues to veer off course. If the boat has a rudder, this delay is inconsequential. Normally the power of the rudder will bring the boat around. But for me, without a rudder, the onus was split between Stanley and my ability to trim the sails. Even at the best of times, when I would try and sleep down below in the cabin, my mind was on deck with Stanley and the sails. I knew that she went off course when the sail started to flog. Or worse still, when she fell away. Then the angle of heel changed, and I knew this below in the cabin.

I could not alter Stanley, but there were many possibilities in manipulating the foresheets and the mainsheet.

I already adverted to the necessity of pulling the second sheet taut so that the clew would not move. You can see that this appeared superfluous on a close reach. We traditionally think that we must make the slot of the foresail and the main as narrow as possible in order to get efficiency. Hour after hour I tried this. I would take the foresheet from outside the shroud and lead it to the fairlead near the mast. But again and again *Research II* would luff up or fall away. Then I realized that I must practice compromise. I will keep the sheet outside of the shroud and let the boat bear away a few degrees, even to the southeast. That was a concession that I was reluctant to make. I tried it, but again this failed.

My days and nights were turned into a continuous experiment. I became as agile as a cat, my weight went down, as food became secondary. I became obsessed with this problem. I sat in the cockpit working the sheets, given a break for maybe ten minutes. Then off course the boat would go and though I had Stanley set behind me, he just could not do the job. My hands became grey-white, my fingernails almost disappeared. In the daylight or in the darkness of the night, I was continually there in the cockpit, loosing sheets, winching them in, slackening, tightening, a never-ending process, alternating with a pause, my eyes fixed on the sails. I found myself rocking with my old weakness, as sleep threatened to overcome me.

The Curl in the Clew

It is now Friday morning, almost a week since the storm. There is little mercy as the grey dawn breaks. As the north wind blew onto us with its unfriendly chill, I was still there, mechanically repeating the experiment, loosen one, tighten the other; pause. Let the mainsheet out, try again. The day wore on in a timeless tyranny of repetitive experiment. Suddenly something happened. I had missed out slackening the second foresheet. I was at a low ebb. All week, I ate very little. I was washed up, the wind was against me. I was losing and I would soon have to admit it.

Then I realized something was different. I had paused, to wait, until I mechanically faced the next time. But the next time was not coming. I looked to the bow and I saw *Research II* begin to luff up. Then, as if by magic, in the space of two seconds, she checked herself and though she lost a little speed, her bow fell away again and she picked up speed on her compass course. This was a miracle. I stood up; I leaned forward, my eye riveted on the sheets. They led me to the clew. At once I saw the answer. **There was a curl in the clew.** I will leave my readers to see the wonder of this. I will let lone sailors share my joy. The long grueling work was over. Again I had won. I had kept on, draining myself of all but residual resources, where the will could hardly pick a cupful of sustenance to activate my body to implement its orders. Then, it happened; God kicked in. *When I had done my best, God did the rest.*

And you know, my friend, I did not pray that morning. In a way I was past praying. Night and day, morning and evening were woven together by my concentrated obsession to find an answer. I was almost broken by the week that was now past since the storm called me to answer its challenge. My legs were wobbly so that I could not easily stand; my posterior was so sore that I could not comfortably sit. I had two thousand miles to go, and the sheets were fraying where they passed the shrouds. The jib was torn and I could not change it as the halyard was jammed at the top of the mast so that I could lower it only to a third. But I could not get hold of the peak to raise another sail.

My oilskins enclosed me in a wet clammy containment, with my leather hushpuppies whitened by the salt water. I know God, the living God, *who fainteth not nor is weary* was watching me. I was doing my thing. He had not told me to make this trip. This was a personal decision. God - He is so long-suffering with us - makes allowance for our varied propensities. In the covenant of his mercy, he gives us liberty and rein, as long as we fulfill our duties and as long as our schemes do not conflict with his will. Indeed God uses our individuality to test our faith. We become the experiment of his will, and as the covenant children whom he has redeemed through the shed blood of Christ the eternal Son, he kicks in with his saving power, just before we pass breaking point. Now the night was over, the morning had come. *Research II* reached forward, and time after time I watched with bated breath as she completed her sequence, always coming back to her course.

The sun broke through the grey sky before me. Its rays pierced the crisp cold air. I looked up and I thought of the Lord, the Sun of Righteousness, who had surely risen upon me with his healing and redeeming power.

I stumbled into the companionway, almost falling on my face. The long battle was over. It would take time for my weary mind to grasp the implications of this victory, this monumental discovery; **you must put a curl in the clew.**

I won, I won. I won the prize. The long day was over. Let the night come; let adversity come again; let nature pit against me every invention of weaponry in the arsenal of its unexplored genius, I have overcome. And if I can overcome, all who share with me a faith in the living and loving God, **will also overcome.**

Elation

I am greatly exhausted; I am hungry and spent. But I am almost paralyzed with elation. There was much yet to do and it would yet be done. But I did not want to break the spell. Was it ever known? No rudder, no tiller, no wheel, but *Research II* tripping along, heeling slightly to the northerly, on a close reach. No, all was not perfect, the secondary panels, the hindermost ones, fore and aft, were faulty. But we were sailing, not just before the wind - any rig could do this - but against the wind. And Stanley was keeping her there. Hopefully, the wind will change to the easy familiar southwest. Meanwhile we are thankful, as if we had a feast. I was out soon again to gaze at the wonder of my success. I looked at the miracle before me; the boat going forward on her own. My naturally strong body, pushed to its limits by the taskmaster of my will, now cried out for a break. My mind itself appeared to enter a trance -like dimension of sheer wonder. My eyes were fascinated by the sequence that kept continually being re-enacted as the boat sailed on, every so often veering to right or left, then checking herself before it would stall. And lo, she came back on course.

Demonstrated achievements

I now slumped down in the cockpit and let my mind dwell on it all, savoring every step in the sequence that led to this victory.

There were these two demonstrated achievements. The auto-sails proved themselves. And secondly, yet related to this, the Self-Steering Scull-Oar synchronized its function with the balancing sails. Here I was in the cockpit. There was no tiller to touch. It had crumbled into oak mush and its rotten stub stuck out in silhouette against the waning light. There was no rudder. Yet that slim oar blade of my invention at the stern used the wind to keep the boat on course. No doubt in the days to come, different wind conditions will yet make a further challenge. But if *round one* went to the storm, *round two* went to me. After wallowing in the storm-tossed seas, going nowhere, even heading backwards, Research II was now going forward, and the great thing was, it was sailing in the right direction.

A visitor

I told you that I thanked God. He vindicated my faith once again, so that I'll never let it go until the day I die. Then it will be unnecessary, like a crutch to a person with a broken leg who can walk again. But thanksgiving is not a spurious short-lived appreciation, a quick appearance in church, a cheque to the church hurriedly dispatched, nor even a prayer, beautifully worded and framed in the most exquisite music. Nor is it a sporadic cry to God, every time we get ourselves into trouble. It certainly is all of these, but it is more. Thanksgiving is a way of life, a direction of living, where all we do is done to the glory of God and each day we live is lived with a consciousness of his presence.

I went below. I lighted the stove. I heated up a tin of stew and a tin of beans altogether so that I had a panful of piping hot food. I was too weary to wait for extra potatoes and onions. In any case, all was a shambles in the forward area where the dry goods were stored. Everything, I say, was all turned upside down the result of the struggle with the storm. I made a big mug of black coffee. I finished my meal and, taking my big thermos mug of black coffee with me, I lifted myself up out of the companionway and sat down in the cockpit.

The day was far spent but still not over. The sun took a long time setting and in the continued happiness of my spirits, I sang softly in Gaelic some verses of one of the church's most favorite anthems. In it, God the Father, God the Son, God the Holy Spirit, the triune God is exalted on earth as he is in heaven. It is believed that David wrote the Psalm and the final three verses were added by his son Solomon, to close the second book in the anthology of praise which we call the Psalms of David. In Scotland, in the liturgy of the Celtic church, these verses are given a special place as the finale, in the closing of a season of worship, the *Orduighean*, (The Ordinances) or the Communion season. Chanted in Gaelic by an experienced precentor, leading the congregation on these special occasions, I say without qualification, there is nothing on earth like it, in its glory and sense of the eternal, as it rises in all the cadences of blending voices to the throne of heaven.

It was natural, therefore, for me to sing softly in Gaelic the words of that immortal psalm, to the old tune Torwood.

Bith 'ainm-san buan gu suthainn sior,
co-mhaireann ris a' ghrein;
Is anns an beannaichear gach slogh;
's beannaichear leo e fein.

Beannaicht' gu robh an Tighearn Dia,
Dia Israeil a ghnath,
An ti a mhain ni miorbhuile
le treis is neart a laimh.

Beannaicht' gu robh gu siorruidh buan
ainm glormhor uasal fein;
Lionadh a ghloir gach uile thir,
Amen, agus Amen.

English:

His name forever shall endure;
last like the sun it shall:
Men shall be blessed in him, and bless'd
all nations shall him call.

Now blessed be the Lord our God,
the God of Israel,
For he alone doth wondrous works,
in glory that excel.

And blessed be his glorious name
to all eternity:
The whole earth let his glory fill,
Amen, so let it be.

(Scottish Psalter)

I was revived by success and my strength replenished by a lovely hot meal. I surveyed the sea to the horizon, studying the disappearing shadows to the west. I was thankful beyond measure and lingered over the closing words of the psalm, savoring their import, almost reluctant to let them go.

Then suddenly I became aware of a commotion in the waters. The boat rocked visibly. A visitor was there beside me. He appeared, rising like an island out of a mudflat at low tide in an estuary, with the waters still clearly flowing from his back. He was between 10 and 20 feet from the side of the boat. Clearly this was a leviathan of the deep. I had plenty time to study him. In length above the water, he extended beyond the bow and beyond the stern. I estimated that above the water he was more than twice the length of the boat. I peered forward. A long shelf, a kind of corrugated stripes, could be seen where his head was just submerged in the water. I could not see the posterior, against the waning light to the west, but the disturbed waters made me estimate that the huge fin was almost at the boat. That meant that the full width of the tail fins, was between 20 and 30 feet. Should this tail, for any reason at all, be activated in a sudden and positive action, the result would be negative, to say the least, for me and my boat.

The whale moved ahead of me, and then crossed my bow. *Research II* bobbed up and down as the mass of water was displaced beneath it. The whale moved on and drew a wide arc, turning around and coming in again at the stern on my port side. There it took up position and there I watched it as it kept company with this new friend it found on the ocean. Whales react to noise. Lone sailors have been known to ring a bell every so often as they passed an area where there were whales present. Could it be that this chap heard the Gaelic psalm being sung and felt that it was his kind of music?

I was full of wonder at it all. Had not the day, yes, the last few days, shown me enough of nature's power? And here beside me, this giant creature, the largest extant on earth is marking time, keeping pace with me as we plodded along. I felt a real sense of communion with this leviathan. He knew more than any mariner or oceanologist. The experiences and adventures of his wanderings across the vastness of the oceans from South Georgia in Antarctica to Iceland in the Arctic north could fill the memory bank of a modern computer or all the pages of the largest encyclopedia. The fact that he was there beside me without a thought of turning away, convinced me that it was not by chance that he was in the vicinity, but by intention. He took to the psalm singing, but he had come along any way to see how I was getting along.

I called out to him, 'Hello Paul. So you came to see me after the storm! There was a noticeable movement of the water forward. I chose to think it was a nod of his head. Encouraged by this perceived response, I continued,

'Yes, we are now on our way again, by God's grace.'

Both of us exchanged thoughts, in a kind of primal empathy, a language of the spirit, where harmony is the governing principle and fear is absent. In this, there is no discord, but mutual communion, a shared experience of nature's riches, as the gift of God. We communed together for possibly fifteen minutes. Our conversation went something like this:

> Is your name Paul?'
>
> No. My name is Padruig, the Gaelic for Peter or Patrick as they say in Ireland.'
>
> Where are you from? I mean where were you born?'
>
> Actually, I don't know. It was somewhere in the ocean. But my folks never told me and I was too young to notice.'

He slowed down at this point or, if not, *Research II* got up a little more speed. His head was there under the water and an eye was hidden under a kind of shade. I wondered if I had in some way offended him or even embarrassed him. A monster like this could cause a very big calamity if he gave even one involuntary little shrug. Then to my shock and relief, he grunted and went on. It was not easy to make him out, but it was something like this:

> 'I know Loch Ewe where you used to fish as a young boy. I've often been there. I also know Stornoway. I have been in near the pier on the castle side during the night, and I've watched all the construction at Arnish point. I was watching when they launched the first oil rig.'

I was bowled over. This was incredible. You could feel the vibrations as the messages passed back and fore between us, like the fuel being piped from a naval auxiliary to a warship, or the counterpart in the air, or the lightening speed of a sailor tapping out a message by Morse. Padruig now moved forward again so close that his tail must have spread under my boat in the area of the Self-Steering Scull-Oar. I thought that there was a wobble in the vane pendulum.

I: 'It's great to have you alongside, *Padruig*, especially a chap with a Gaelic name like that as I am a fellow Celt. But please don't touch my little boat. I can tell you straight away, that it is definitely not another whale, although she is feminine, and a real lady with the lines and curves of a beauty-queen, as you already appreciate.'

He pulled away, almost imperceptibly. Maybe there was a hint of disappointment in the guttural reply, accompanied by a sigh of resignation. Meanwhile he was still there beside the boat and his movements, even the slightest, had a definite and corresponding effect on *Research II*. I felt that we might jibe, and the noise of blocks and ropes as the two booms jerked to the other side could cause the whale to give a startled movement of his enormous body, and especially that huge tail.

I: 'Padr*uig*', I continued, speaking very gently, 'You know the Americans and the Russians are rendezvousing in space just about this time. Don't take offense. But please use the same skill as these astronauts, one craft 200 tons in weight and both traveling beside each other at 3000 kilometers an hour, yet not touching each other.'

At that moment, the whale backed off somewhat. A slight sweat trickled down my neck under my oilskin. I hoped that I did not offend this nice big fellow. Maybe he was of the sensitive type, and construed my remarks as a hint to go. There was a pause. He had backed off, again, letting *Research II* go ahead. Now his head was right opposite the cockpit but under the water. The light was now poor, but I could see the bridge where his eye was below it and the corrugation of his external breathing apparatus was now dilating. My anxiety left me. Somehow I knew we were friends and that he was going to leave shortly. But I hoped that he would come back again.

Then the bombshell. He must have read my mind although I had said nothing. He made a guttural sound, a combination of phonetic glottal stops. I heard it distinctly, as clear as the voices in the cabin with which I was so familiar. Did I hear alright? Was I just imagining it? Could this possibly be true, a whale speaking in Gaelic? For the life of me, the sound was unmistakably the well worn Gaelic usage for taking leave of a friend, *"Bi mi g'a d'fhaicinn.'* That is the Gaelic for, 'I'll be seeing you.' I was dumbfounded. I couldn't say anything. *Padruig* slipped back and turned away, the vast expanse of his tail rising like a giant fan, raised between me and the sun now setting behind us. And you know, I think he was laughing.

I could only wave, as my new found friend disappeared. As the waters closed in behind his wake, I threw out a belated vocal thanks, *'Beannachd leat, beannachd leat, a charaid.* (God) Bless you,

'(God) Bless you, my friend.'

I trimmed the sheets and checked the Vane on Stanley to make sure it was in line with the direction of the northerly wind. Then I stood for a long time musing over the exciting events now past. What incomparable experiences I am having out here! Think of the company I have. I am surrounded by God' s living creatures, every one unique and perfectly designed for his habitat and manner of life. And now this. What food for thought before I go below for the night and close my eyes in sleep! What a tremendous experience, an encounter with a whale! What a happy exchange of thoughts, if not vocal as we know it in spoken language, yet just as valid in the invisible telepathy of mutual communication. And to crown it all, for him to sign himself off in Gaelic - well that was almost too much for me - but not quite. I smiled to myself and shook my head at the thought.

Down below, I had found time to clear up some of the mess,

relatively speaking. All was still soaking wet and clothes and gear of all kinds were in a soggy pile with tins of food mixed up. Underneath all this there was water sloshing over the floorboards in the head area, under the forehatch. When *Research II* was thrown over almost to the vertical, sea water spewed in through the skylight, even though the latter was clasped shut.

Once many years ago, while meeting heavy weather on the old Loch Seaforth on the Kyle/Stornoway run, the waves hit the upper observation room so that gallons of water sprayed on to the floor, with all the furniture sliding to the lee - passengers with them. Yet if you examined the windows, you would think that all the bolts every three inches apart would make that impossible. No wonder there was water in my little boat, but never did a drop come through the side portholes. I knew this for certain as items on the top shelves remained relatively dry - relatively, I say, because nothing was really dry on the boat while we were in mid-ocean.

Tragedy in France

Though I was out here in the Atlantic on my own, my thoughts were often on family and also continually concerned like, everyone else with the ongoing events of divided Yugoslavia. This evening there was also word on the BBC World Service news to which I listened continually, of 20 young people killed in a bus crash in France. What sudden, violent death is endemic in our sophisticated age! And for me, anything negative happening in France is of particular concern, as my wife Mary and daughter Jane are at this time in Paris. Meanwhile the night is near. I give one last look westward to study the sky. The sun has gone but there is still brightness in the sky; white light. I thought to myself, that I would have preferred to see red. But there it is. I would have hoped to have good favorable weather after surviving the storm. Instead, I knew that struggle was still the name of the game out here in the North Atlantic, a cruel inhospitable environment, which betrayed no feeling of mercy or allowance, in its mask of bleak grey sky and dark menacing seas. Even in this mid-summer July, a day at best when the sun shone, was clothed with a pale watery light without any real sense of friendliness for any living thing. That was my impression to date. It would need contrary evidence to convince me otherwise. I closed the hatch and switched on the cabin light, one only for economy to save electricity for the vital requirement of the masthead navigation lights. I made a hot cup of tea before I zipped myself into my sleeping bag. I lifted my heart in thanksgiving to my Maker, and prayed that as *Research II* plowed on through the unknown watches of the night, that He, the Master Pilot of the universe, would guide her and keep her on course.

The storm had come. It made its way northeast across the ocean, seeking out its contestants, or any that would challenge its power. It found me, a frail human on a little boat. But it had to concede defeat. We had won. My little boat shared the victory with me. But we won only because one greater than the storm was in our corner; our manager, our coach. *We are more than conquerors through Him that loved us.* There was also this. The battle with Barry left us wounded, but not mortally. We are judged by our reaction to trouble. This turns the equation of life on end, so that the negatives of life become positives, and the calamities of life become opportunities. Opportunities for what?, you ask. Yes, opportunities to prove our own untapped resourcefulness, to prove also that all things are possible when our faith is in the limitless power of the living God.

Hitherto the Lord has helped us. Tomorrow is another day. All tomorrows are really an illusion. The only reality is the present. The present will come when I awake and God will then, as always, be a very present help if it is a time of need. Until then, I will lay my weary body down. The storm has left me limp. Since its beginnings almost a week ago, time has stood still. It looked as if I was on the canvas for good. It tried literally to have me thrown over the side as I fought to get control. But I got up, and the bell went. I came back for one more try, like Sampson of old. But unlike Sampson, I first did my best. Then I called upon God. And that hidden power kicked in, the low gear that brought us around and gave me the victory. But mine is a double victory. Spurred on by the first, I believed I would gain the second. The days and nights fused together as one in my recollection of them. I was conscious only of the struggle to overcome. Now it was as if I bathed in the light of heaven's countenance. The day itself that began with the surly mood of an overcast sky, compounded by the cold from the north wind, now was more mellow and the sinking sun in the west spread a red glow through the *gloaming* (Evening sky). Traditionally this red sky was the herald of good weather to come.

What a way to end the day! What a sense of sheer satisfaction! What sense of achievement, of fulfillment percolated through my being! But above all, the total baffling sense of wonder, the overwhelming irrefutable conviction, that God the Creator of the universe, not only knows I am out here on the ocean, but that He heard my cry and He'kicked in' with His power - this defied thought to formulate or word to articulate. Equally no speech, no tongue can refute the immediacy of His dynamic presence.

With that sublime assurance, I fell instantly asleep.

CHAPTER 12

Fire in the Galley

Log: Day 19, Tuesday, 11th July, 1995

Unbelievably, another gale worked up during the night from the north. It is hard to accept the growing conviction that something is far wrong with the weather pattern this summer. Where is the steady southwest wind which traditionally blows for ninety per cent of the time, and takes a boat along for the ride from America to Britain? Not only so but the cold is unnatural. There is a harshness about the north wind that confirms prejudice and all the tales about the poor little robin from our childhood repertoire of poems:

The north wind doth blow
And we shall have snow,
And what will poor robin do then.

He'll sit in the barn
And keep himself warm,
And hide his head under his wing.

The difference is that the nursery rhyme was written about winter, and here we are in the middle of the summer. I was up in the night several times adjusting the auto sails. You can see in the photos how they looked. The only difference is that I took two of the sails off. That left two on the fore boom and two on the mainboom behind the mast. The forward one on each boom was fine, the luff being stiff and straight. The sail behind each was not responding to the north wind efficiently.

Log, Journal

Saw big ship from Britain in the night. Also one during the day. Heading NE by E slowly. Stanley doing the steering. Gale increases after 5:00 a.m. On deck working at sails, trying to get efficiency. Gale force wind now, surface breaking and spray coming aboard. She heels to lee, difficult to work on deck. Exasperated. New sails have not been strongly stitched. They are taking a punishing. One of them slips overboard. It disappears into the deep behind us, like an upturned giant skate. The other after sail is straining. The peak can be seen tearing. It just cannot take it. It is flogging back and fore with the crack of a rustler's whip, every so often. I take down all sail as we now have that gale from the north, a hard vicious beast. Wind veers to northwest and almost westerly. I raise fore and aft auto sails. All is peaceful. *Research 11* heads NE by E.

The ocean in a gale

The sun shines all day, so that relatively speaking you could say that here was a beautiful day. And it was, except that there were long mountainous seas. All day I worked to keep *Research 11* on course, that is, with her behind to the waves. A white-headed coamer just hit, making the boat stagger. It soaked me to the skin.

Must be philosophical. Here is the second gale in a week, one before and one after the storm, like two bodyguards, accompanying a very tough customer. The day wore on and evening arrived. Then night. I slept fitfully with the hatch open, enough to monitor the stars. The moon was full and shone into the cabin making it as bright as day.

Feel need of patience. 19th day out. Just half way. *Research 11* is struggling. Speed is elusive. Present sails performance not adequate. Lost 6 days sailing now, must discount the latest 2. However, must be thankful.

Trying the radio

I try the radio. It's exasperating. I just can't get reception on the Robertson. There is some control on the Transmitter that seems to have kicked in and I just cannot get anywhere with it. I'll keep on trying every day to see if I can solve it. Who knows, I might accidentally free it - isn't that the scientific method, discovery on the basis of chance or probability! I cannot help feeling deep disappointment.

Here is the best radio you could have, a Robertson/Shipmate, professional and with very few controls to confuse one. It is all so painful as reception and operation were so good before I left. Apart from a fuse, I cannot surmise what has happened. There may be some command which I do not know and I have no manual for the unit.

I took a GPS reading for the first time for four days.

Track Northeast 154'

Position: N 46' 95" W 33' 36"

Time: 19.86 Eastern

Speed 3.9 knots

Log, Journal notes

Am most uplifted. The Gulf Stream must be carrying us along so that we are getting a speed of 3-4 knots plus the current.

West 33'36" Longitude is far better than I hoped for since last Friday Longitude 35' 29".

Must have done well yesterday till 5:00 a.m. The self-steering is using the gale force and the current to push her forward.

Now for dinner: 6.30 p.m.

Potatoes, carrots and ravioli; fruit cocktail for afters. Then hopefully a restful night. Rain has soaked all in cockpit and all bedding and clothing below are soaked - need drying on good day. But who cares *Research 11* plows on and Stanley, my faithful crewman is at the helm.

What more could you want! There surely can be nothing so sweet on a journey, as the joy of the boat keeping on track and going forward. *Lord may it continue.*

Log: Day 20, Wednesday, 12th July, 1995

Semi-gale all night. Seas bad. Stayed below, no cares. Consolation that Gulf Stream was doing its bit.

All night I was aware that Mary was with me. Several times I had to get up and re-orientate myself to realize that she just could not be. What do you make of it? She was speaking to me, her voice as clear as a bell, calmly making conversation as she would do at home on land. And I kept up, putting my two cents in as well, vocally giving her a reply. Then realization, Mary just could not be here for she was in Paris with her sister Agnes and our daughter Jane. I wonder was she awake at this specific time, and her thoughts going out to her husband in mid-Atlantic?

The morning showed no abatement. The gale had evolved into a continuous process of viciousness. I had to force myself to get on deck. Life was miserable below. On deck it was worse, like slithering over a moving football. Being at sea on a test trip with several experiments - isn't that implied by the new name I gave her, *Research II* - demands continual monitoring and adjustment every day when conditions of sea and wind are variable. And when the given factors in the equation are changed, you have an ongoing crisis. And when the vital one of the rudder is removed, then you really have something to chew over.

The chosen option

The option I chose at this stage was to give my own autosail a chance. To some extent it worked. But we did not have speed. This was on the cozy side. There was not enough sail area to generate speed, except in a full blown gale or with a favorable following wind. The fact is the double sails fore and aft had not worked. The peak had already gone, tearing itself apart, and the other which replaced the lost one overboard, was also on the way out.

I set the auto mainsail, the one hanked to the track on the mast. It set well. Very good. Then for the jib. The hanks for the forestay were nearly all jammed. Also when I put the jib alone on the foreboom, it was impossible with wind and sea, to get a straight luff.

All this was exhausting. Age has proved that you can give a good day, but not without a rest. I went below and had lunch, Chicken Vegetable Soup and half a tin of cold ham.

That's what the doctor ordered

I got out again on deck and reviewed the situation. Now there were just the two autosails, one on the foreboom and one on the mainboom - the latter on the mast track. I could move the tack of the foresail back along the boom. I did this until there was a definite balance. Furthermore, there was not a large main to blanket out the wind from the jib. Also, because both booms hinged from the mast, I could swing both opposite each other to make a variety of wind directions workable for the boat. There was little or no yawing or luffing. Also Stanley could handle this, as the boat rig was so balanced that it took very little of the Scull-Oar action to correct, when the boat was knocked off course. As I looked over the ship I came to the conclusion that all looked propitious. My mood soared. The compass read Course NNE and a repeated glance at the knotmeter showed that we were doing a steady 4 to 5 knots.

Fire in the Kitchen

Now I come to the item mentioned at the beginning, one with ominous connotations which could have easily spelt out my epitaph, namely, The Fire.

As night came on I felt the need of a nightcap. Being continually dressed in clothes that were really soaking wet with the oilskins over them, day and night needed the internal heat of food and hot liquid to counteract it. I lighted the stove, but after filling the kettle with water,

I realized that the fuel was too low and had to be replenished. I refilled the stove burner containers with alcohol. Regrettably I spilled some fuel and failed to dry it up at once.

I then lighted the stove and put on the kettle, turning away to sit on the kitchen seat to get my Rye Vita and spreading cheese. The cabin suddenly seemed very bright, unnaturally bright. Looking up, I saw the glow of flames on the tray beneath the stove burners. That was enough to alarm me. Once, when much younger, I had a bad experience when a can of gasoline spilled on the garage floor, when cleaning clutch plates for my 1933 Austin 7. The memory of that incident with my overalls alight and the subsequent sequence of unconsciousness, leg burns and pain came all came vividly back to me.

Also there was the case of a transatlantic loner a few years earlier, when he was very badly burned, using an alcohol stove. Such thoughts rushed through my mind and did nothing to comfort me. There was one positive thought. Marine stoves may be diesel, kerosene, gas, or as I had, alcohol. From my reading, I concluded that alcohol had one very redeeming advantage. It alone responded to water to put fire out. The essential element in all crises is not to panic. If you panic you will not think clearly, and if you do not think clearly, you are liable to do the wrong thing or not do anything at all.

Believe me, all kinds of options came rushing to my mind, including the last and final option, which is to jump out of the boat as fast as you can before there is some kind of explosion.

I was up from my seat like a flash. I pulled the kettle from the stove. The flames rose up above the burner, and the evening dark of the cabin was changed into brightness as the flames glowed underneath the stove tank on the tray. I froze for a moment or two assessing the situation. Would the heat cause the stove tank to explode? What temperature did it require for this to happen in the case of alcohol? Vital seconds ticked away. The thought of the cabin turning into a conflagration was too much to contemplate. The time factor was important. Even the process of going out, getting the bucket, filling it and bringing it in - it all could be too late. Also there was one very cogent reason why I hesitated to open the hatch. In the previous situation when I had been badly burned, the fire was made much worse, because someone ran and opened the garage doors. Would not the same thing happen now if I repeated this move, so that extra oxygen would be sucked in to feed the fire? I seemed trapped in a dilemma. The flames meanwhile made a deadly glow on the cabin walls. Something had to be done, risk or no risk and that something had to be done at once, or it would be too late.

I turned towards the companionway, my hand reaching up to slide the hatch open. Just then it dawned on me, 'Angus you still have the kettle of water in your other hand.' I returned to the stove, and calmly poured the kettle water down into the burner. Within moments the fire was out.

My prayer of Thanksgiving to heaven was automatic. It was short, just a whisper, but it was for real. My God had done it again.

Who can measure the happiness I felt at that time, and taking my cup of tea a little while later! Life surely has many sides. There is nothing boring about life out here on the ocean. There are all kinds of experiences, challenging, dangerous, but stimulating.

Log Note: I'll call it a day, and leave the cares of us all and all whom we think of in need and distress, in God's hands.

Log: Day 21, Thursday, 13th July, 1995

Log Notes: Dead calm. *Research II* rocking, rolling, motion. I have been up since 3 a.m. No joy.

Did a few maintenance and repair jobs. Fixed retainer for perspex hatch slides.

GPS Reading: Course Northeast 75'
Position: N 47' 25" W 32' 02"
Time: 18.05
Speed 1.3 knots

Log: Day 22, Friday, 14th July, 1995

Yesterday was beautiful weather, but painful, so calm.

In the late afternoon, a slight breeze rose from the northeast. The effect was immediate. Around *Research II* turned, as the sails backed. Now she was heading for South America and I believe for Tierra Del Fuego. Visions of Joshua Slocum, 100 years ago having to keep off intruders by scattering tacks on the deck at night, was enough for me. I had a problem. There wasn't sufficient wind to generate enough speed to activate the Scull-Oar. Yet painfully, even slowly, *Research II* was backtracking, making a minus record of longitude for the day unless this was stopped.

For two hours I tried everything. *Research II* just would not turn. On, on, on, she went, with a mind of her own. She got it into her head that this was the way to go. Enough of this North Atlantic with its bleak grey skies, and battling against the cold north winds. Why suffer all this, when she could maybe drop in at some cozy harbour in the Caribbean and rest there at anchor in the warmth of lovely summer days?

Such thoughts came to me and I felt that my boat was being disloyal to me. The more I let my mind dwell on the situation, the more I distressed myself. If ever I had reached the point of almost panic, this was it.

The Miracle

Then, calming myself down, I called on my Heavenly Father, the Pilot of the universe, to hear me and see my little ship, a speck in the middle of the ocean. I pleaded with him to turn *Research II* around. What took place almost immediately can be seen in the records of Heaven. The breeze strengthened; the self-steering vane of Stanley bent over, activating the blade with a twisting action on the sea. I stared, holding my breath. Wonder of wonders, the bow was coming around. Would she come all the way around? I thought. I stood there desperately willing her, with the foresheet over the winch and in my hand.

She did. Around to the east, no, she steadied at southeast. The wind whistled now in the rigging and the main took up a business-like shape - my own little main, just a third of the usual one.

The joy of a little success

What joy, what joy to be on our way again. I had now entered a phase of continual and exacting attention to keep *Research II* going forward. Day and night became the same. I catnapped when I could. Whatever was before me, I had to keep every hour or two at least, adjusting, checking, changing the sails. If not, the alternative was to sit there in the ocean and become a helpless victim of the seas and the wind. I had to keep reinforcing my will and sense of purpose, barricading it up as with sandbags to keep out a flood from drawing me away from resolve. My body became a machine, that I ordered with my will as the latter got instructions from my mind. Open cuts decorated my fingers and hacks split my thumbs, which just would not heal. My left leg was numb all the way up from my knee and a deep pain made me feel that my lower abdomen was coming apart. But I was obsessed with experimenting. I could hardly wait to try something else, when the last method failed.

Now *Research II* settled down and was doing 3-5 knots. But I was uneasy. The wind was clearly freshening and the seas were now crashing over the cabin. I had my foresail winged out on the boom. I surmised, 'If I take it off the boom, I'll be able to sheet it home closer.'

The deck was heaving, the boat yawing from side to side, the foreboom veering forward and back.

But the Lord was with me. I secured the boom to the deck making it ultra tight with the vang to the mast. This was vital as I depended on my grip of the boom for safety. I also made the boom secure by making fast the foreboom sheets which I had rigged independent of the sheets from the clew of the traditional jib, now resting below. Now the foresail was free and sheeted hard. But *Research II* would not come further up to the east. She sailed on to the south-east, doing

5 and sometimes 6 knots on the knotmeter.

I sat back. I had done all I could. A calm came over me - a great calm - and an *assurance that the Lord was there with me.* I bowed and thanked him for his mercies and his great love to me. I didn't ask him for anything, just to keep me in his thoughts and remember me. What more could one want? Do you recall the psalm about remembering, a favorite with believers who are tempted to feel lonely and forgotten in the mad rush of this world? This Psalm also has a special tenderness for those who a*re broken in heart.* They do not need to specify what has crushed their spirits or makes them sad. God knows what they are going through and when they use the words of these verses, particularly as praise or prayer, all the riches of God's grace are opened up for them, and their needs are met by the abundance of his mercies.

Thus I sang softly in Gaelic to an old favorite Scottish psalm tune, Coleshill, knowing that the noise of the wind and the waves could not stop my God from hearing me,

(Gaelic)

Dhia, cuimhnich ormsa, leis a ghraidh
thug thu do d'phobuill fein;
O thig le d' shlainte sholasaich
gu m'fhiosrachadh am fheum.

Gu faic sinn maith do dhaoine taght,
's gun dean sinn aoibhneas mor
'nan aoibhneas sud; 's le t' oighreachd fein
gu'n dean sinn uaill 's gloir.

(English)

Remember me, Lord, with that love
which thou to thine dost bear;
With thy salvation, O my God,
to visit me draw near.

That I thy chosen's good may see,
and in their joy rejoice;
And may with thy inheritance
triumph with cheerful voice.

(From the Scottish Psalter: Psalm 106: 4 - 5)

I resolved to go below. Somehow I felt a great peace, as R*esearch II* plunged on through the wild darkness of the night, heading off course, down to the south-east. I wondered in myself how utterly calm and serene I was. I said to myself, 'I'll have to check on the Azores or maybe Gibraltar. We may be going there instead of the English Channel. Hopefully we will not be driven further south and have to worry like Slocum about the pirates of North Africa.'

Log: Day 23, Saturday, 15th July, 1995

Today was a perfect sailor's day. I had gone to rest in a fresh northerly gale, but serene in a calm confidence that all was well. And that seemed a contradiction as we were heading far off course. Yet I had slept well, especially after looking out and finding by midnight that *Research II* had herself swung up to the NNE. The fact was that the wind had backed through north to the northwest. I looked at the knotmeter - a steady 4 to 5 knots, and this continued all day.

I spent the morning just relaxing in the cockpit. It was glorious sailing. No other ship to be seen. I had seen two yesterday. One container ship going east was so packed with containers that you could hardly see the wheelhouse at the stern. That raised the question, Could she see me? She was a real monster.

Stanley gets a visit from the doctor

The Scull-Oar needed attention. Nothing serious, mind you, just the same attention that a mechanic has to give to the engine of your car to maintain it in good condition, or a nurse or a physician gives to a patient when he or she is feeling 'under the weather.' You could say that Stanley was not feeling too well and was literally in this condition, 'under the weather.' Stanley as you will gather from the photographs, had a long thin body - really a long tube of very hardened aluminum alloy. This long tube was held tightly in any height required by a stainless steel three-eighths of an inch in diameter stud, with a handle on the end to turn manually. Galvanic action had seized the stud so that Stanley could not be raised or lowered as required. The fact is that with the storm conditions and the resulting challenge of the sails, I had not seen the necessity to change the height of Stanley for nearly a week. In designing the unit, I calculated that the torque would be considerable, that is, the lateral forces acting on Stanley. As a precaution I had therefore drilled and threaded a second hole in the bracket and taken along an extra stud to use the two, if so required. The answer to electrolysis, which was the present trouble, would be to get the offending stud out and put grease on it. First I greased my spare stud and screwed it tightly into the second hole, thus assuring ourselves that Stanley would be kept in his place. Then I clamped on the big vice grips and applied pressure slowly back and forth. Slowly, there was a little give. Then a definite movement. At last, after about five minutes, I backed out the stainless steel stud, greased it liberally and screwed it tight again.

It all was very satisfying. The Scull-Oar can be raised or lowered now as required. And by using the two studs, there is no question of the torque twisting Stanley out of position. I was very thankful that I found the trouble in time. Had the stud been left much longer, it could well be that it would not come out without some metal breaking off. I cannot help thinking in myself, how alert and thorough I was in this respect, and at the same time failed to deal beforehand with the question of the rudder gudgeon pin. The fact is that I had forgotten to do this by not writing the work down on my job list, during the preparation before the trip. And during the trip I was not put in mind of the issue as the gudgeon pin was hidden under the tiller, which itself claimed my attention.

After failing to get any Satellite bearings in the morning, I tried again with the GPS in the afternoon.

Position : North 47' 51" West 29' 49"
Speed: 1.8 knots

Red - Letter Day

You will see by the position above that we have passed the West Longitude 30'. That makes this a very special day. We have covered half the distance across the Atlantic if we consider the Solent as our destination. That is 1800 miles. It would be easy to pop in at Falmouth or Plymouth or Dartmouth, but meantime we will keep thinking of the Solent as journey's end. Of course, it is out of the question for *Research II* to get through the Needles, the western entrance to the Solent, now that I have no rudder. I shall have to get a tow from the coastguards but we shall see. I did think of going up the Channel on the outside of the Isle of Wight and turning in to the Southampton Roads, past Portsmouth and then backtracking to Lymington, but I am not finally decided. We shall wait and see. Meanwhile every day is a continual challenge to keep going and we have not yet found a formula which will ensure progress, the vital progress necessary to complete the voyage at all, of a boat without a rudder and without another human being to give the skipper a rest. But never mind, this is truly a red-letter day, passing the half way mark, having come 1800 miles. Distance made good. Actual distance sailed by Dead Reckoning is 2150 miles.

Change to Atlantic Chart of Approaches to Great Britain

Now I take the chart of the West Atlantic, number 4013, off my chartboard, and fold it up to stow it in my chart case. Before I do so, I mark the course to date right to the side of the chart. Then out comes the twin chart Number 4012 for the Western Approaches to the British Isles. Two points about this chart are of significance. The scale is much bigger than that of the first. And also, while the other one covered the ocean down to the Latitude of Brazil, this new one only reaches down to 48th Latitude. This means that since *Research II* finished on the previous chart at 47' 51", our course starts on the new chart just below the margin on the left. On the other point of a larger scale, this is definitely an advantage in every way and makes it easier to project a course and generally to work out Dead Reckoning. The latter I do when I get leisure. Log reads: Still calm. Had good lunch. Soup, ham and biscuits.

Becalmed

As silent as a painted ship
upon a painted ocean

How true it was of the little yacht *Research II*, and with that visual incapacity, was the perpetual banging of sails and gear. What an irritating concert of various out of tune instruments, repeatedly creating a cacophony of tortured sound. Being subject to this all night is not good for boat or skipper. And to get this accompaniment all day as well is not exactly a treat, you can well understand. Apart from the irritation, the thought is there all the time that there will be a breakage of gear in the violent sudden motions of the boat, as it is jerked by unseen forces like a horse's head when he exploits a pause, to eat a few blades of grass. And inside, matters are no better. There is that seemingly patternless habit of jerking the kettle when you are about to pour a cup of coffee or tea.

Overhead the sun is dominant. It shines with intense warmth and creates a shimmering jeweled cover over the blue untroubled waters. Beneath, the sea is never still. It asserts its own animate personality. It is volatile even in a calm. For it is the habitat of a thousand creatures in all the many species belonging to the maritime biological world. Around me, creatures of the air and of the sea compete for attention and any food that may be on the menu. A gull swoops to pick up an oatmeal biscuit, which I threw away, the latter having gone soft and soggy. Off to starboard there is quite a commotion, as a dozen porpoises appear to have found a communal meal. They put on a turbulent but entertaining show, even if it is for the one insignificant non paying patron, who cannot leave the theatre but is a prisoner of their art while R*esearch II* idly sits in lifeless immobility in the middle of the ocean.

Voices

I told you before about them. It is hard for anyone on land to imagine all the sounds that can be heard at sea. Especially when these are linked specifically to individual people. I am simply recording what makes a mark on the receptive faculties of my being. We assume these to be biologically fixed and demonstrable as objective sensory and motor systems, producing objective psychological patterns. I would have to add that for my own satisfaction it is reasonable for me to try and account for this auditory visitation, that clearly is out of the usual category of hearing. Briefly these four points come before me as relevant.

Possible explanations

1. Sound fills the atmosphere in the infinite variety of which we hear only a fraction. Sound is energy and as waves, travels continually. These waves are inhabitants of the air. In a primitive illustration, we pick up a shell from the beach, and lo, we hear the sound of the ocean. We do know that the actual sound may be minuscule, but is amplified by the soundbox of the shell so that, to our ear, it seems quite loud.
2. Given the unusual environment of being by oneself on the ocean, there is an elimination of a thousand impedimenta which, normally on land in our busy society, limit the threshold of our hearing. In contrast to land, our hearing receptive faculties are sharpened or made more acute. There is an absence of all the sounds that ration our hearing and cause us to activate the selective principle by which we don't hear what we do not want to hear. What may explain the voices is in part therefore, that the threshold of our hearing is lowered, while at the same time the distracting sounds of our normal environment on land in community living, are to a large extent eliminated. In this situation the sub normal sounds become audible.
3. The third factor that is significant is that of time itself.

Elsewhere I have made the point that time when it is reduced to logical definition, can be construed as a ruler, or a separator, or a divider of our experiences into feasible orderly relationship, so that we do not get our life consciousness scrambled into a tangle of miscomprehension. In normal society, we interact each day with people and their voices, reflecting their many different experiences collectively as groups or individually as persons, impinge upon the receptive faculty of our hearing. It is quite different for me out on the ocean and also for everyone who is in the same category of isolation from other human beings. Now, the barrage of sound from other people wanted and unasked for, is absent. There is no place for a vacuum in our lives. Thus the voices, normally confined to the past - really the present tense of yesterday - intrude their presence on our consciousness.

4. Clearly each of us has a circle of people associated with us today and in all the todays that are now called the yesterdays. These latter are displaced continually by the ongoing experiences of the contemporary, and the immediate to which we relate. But when the occupying influences or sounds of real life communication are withdrawn, as in the case of a loner on the ocean, then those sounds associated with the repertoire of his or her past experiences, become audible. They can be identified as the voices of people whom we know and with persons whom we have heard in the past, but not necessarily listened to.

With these observations, I accept the different situation with regard to sound, on the boat. I do not get agitated as if it were the paranormal. I just take the voices or sounds, as rationally audible in this exclusive situation. Now, to go on. The voices are so real that I am conscious of the people being right here in the cabin. They do not crowd in together in a chaotic cacophony of unintelligible sound. Each is heard as a matter of fact experience. I must say that I cannot really separate my waking hours and my sleeping hours in this respect. The reason for this is the fact that rest is often snatched as catnaps for an hour in the day or the night. And thus sleep and activity have a common bottom line of consciousness dictated to by necessity and the instincts that link us to the will to live and the resolution to survive. I confine myself to one example.

Naturally my life is influenced by my wife Mary with whom I have shared so many experiences since first we met some thirty-five years ago. Whether I was awake or asleep, resting or dozing, she spoke to me in the early hours this morning. I was in the cabin lying down. Suddenly I was aware that she was there in the cabin with me. It seemed quite natural. We were talking to each other. Then I heard her say distinctly,

'Angus wake up, You have to get up at once and go out on deck.'

I answered as if it was quite normal and replied,

'Alright Mary, I'll go, just give me a minute.' I looked for her but there was no sign of her.

I lay back. Again she spoke very emphatically,

'You've got to go at once.'

I jumped up and found myself saying,

'Alright, O.K., I' m going.'

Again I looked round. I felt she was there. But then she was gone.

I jumped out just as there was a loud noise outside. The boat jerked violently, and heeled over the other way, as *Research II* jibed right around, so that she was now speeding on to the southwest. I could not help thinking that *Research II* had some special reason for wanting to go to South America.

Before dealing with the situation, I went back to the cabin. There it hit me, a scent, a perfume I recognized that Mary used often. I looked for her. In a strange uncanny way, I expected her to appear in person. What joy that would be! What joy, even the thought! But no Mary appeared. Yet the scent was there, the pervading perfume that spoke of her presence. How utterly strange that I expected her to be there, to see her dark brown eyes and lovely face. What a perfect remedy to brighten my weary struggle against the damage done to me by the elements. What a sight I was! Did I not bear ugly proof of my solitary battle, in the yellow brown discolored half of my face and the still considerable lump hanging above my right eye, and hands that were a grey white of varying stages of broken and bleeding flesh? Speaking of hands, my fingernails were worn very thin and flush with my fingers. This was a blessing for I did not need to trim them.

I turned away saying in resignation,

'God bless you, Mary *mo ghraidh* and Jane and Agnes too.' For in my heart, I knew that they were probably having supper in Paris.

CHAPTER 13

Mirage

Act I, The Paratroopers

The day was long and hot. The wind was light and the sea was calm. I saw things I would not have believed were possible. In the calm orb of my world out here on the ocean, away from other human beings, time gave me a keen awareness of the sea in all its changing moods, and the continually varied faces of its sister, the ephemeral sky.

Take for instance this evening. The sun heated the clouds until they were puffed up like candy floss. They had broken up throughout the day until now they were individuals. As sky and sea met, these inhabitants of the sky descended to the horizon like a regiment of airborne troops. I watched and studied them, as the little white puffs of candy cloud looked as real as the parachutes of war. How strange, I thought, out here on the ocean, you can watch a war film. You can see a re-enactment of an invasion; you can study the course of a battle and the deployment of troops, using the phenomena of nature itself as the projection of reality. This had the thrills of a battle scene, observed through the lens of the binoculars from the command post. I saw the battle scene from the distance of my boat to the horizon. Action followed and the sight of the parachutes faded as the troops landed and deployed themselves in battle. The image of Arnheim, in the Second World War, that apex of untimely airborne strategy gone askew, was enacted now on the ocean theatre of war. I could see the grim picture of the welcoming party of German shells rocking the ground around the landed Allied troops. And there were the fallen, hundreds of them, the symbol of immortal bravery and at the same time of disaster.

The movies

Thus the eye looks out on the environment of sea and sky. There is nothing passive about this. It is indeed like a movie theatre, where sequences follow one another round the theme of the day. Today, a blue hot sky, a hot sun, and a placid sea dictate the imagery of the play and find in the observer the equivalent imagery of his memory, triggering this into the presence of his consciousness. The result is the projection of his latent thoughts on the screen of nature before him, all animated, like the shuttered sequences of dark and light, which make the films we watch to be indistinguishable from the real.

Act II

The amazing thing about the books of nature that we read in the sky and the sea, is that like the film sequences, one ends, and another begins, comprising the same characters or components. Thus it was the same day but shortly after the first mirage I witnessed, that I came out of the cabin and looked again to the horizon. I had plenty of time and my eyes were now riveted on the scene before me. I thought to myself, 'Am I dreaming?' ' Is this real?' or, 'Is it an illusion?' I can only describe what I saw, and which was recorded so graphically on the computer screen of my mind.

Lord Nelson and the tall ships

The white clouds, which had looked like descending parachutes in the first mirage, now had risen up all along that segment of the horizon. They now took on the appearance of large ballooning white sails, like giant genoas or spinnakers. But the image they presented to me was a re-enactment of one of history's greatest sea battles, the Battle of Trafalgar in 1905, when Horatio Nelson, Admiral of the British fleet, defeated the combined fleet of the French and Spanish.

Now, nearly two hundred years later, I saw the British fleet spread out on the horizon. They were manoeuvring into position and taking the shape of a great big vee. I counted 30 sails.

Now they were coming towards me, the foremost getting bigger and bigger. And there in the centre was the admiral's ship, Nelson's famous *Victory*. In all, the mirage, for surely it was that, extended to an arc of about 30'. What a sight! Across the glassy sea they were advancing, coming nearer and nearer in a silent disciplined flotilla. When I say that this was like Trafalgar, I write retrospectively. First I saw the mirage. It evolved into the similitude of an advancing fleet. They were on a mission. It was natural for me to conclude that it was Trafalgar, the greatest of English sea battles, and the greatest hour of Nelson's glory.

There is no doubt that all perception has its subjective side. Objectively, others could share in seeing the unusual cloud formations that day: of hot sun and calm sea. But the view, for me, took on the characteristics of graphic memories, of studies in history and specifically the bold strategy of Nelson at Trafalgar when he sailed into the French and Spanish line, risking their broadsides, in order to split the fleet in two. These studies under Professor Sir Richard Pares of Edinburgh University, and afterwards of Oxford, were reawakened, to merge with the natural phenomena before my eyes. This synthesis of the subjective and the objective was so apparently authentic that even the number of the white clouds which looked like sails was exactly the same number as the ships in Nelson's fleet, namely 30 ships of the line and 2 lesser sloops or armed pinnaces.

As the mirage had evolved and took shape before me on the horizon, so also it melted and disintegrated before me now. As I looked, there was nothing but rising wisps of cloud merging together in the evening light.

I write an account of these mirages seen on my ocean voyage, to capture them for the record, like the witness to a drama. Now I have climbed right out of the companionway. There is no sign of the fleet and its famous admiral. But there is a noise, a welcome one, the sound of a breeze tuning the shrouds of the mast. Ripples hurry over the sea to change the darkening surface into a corrugated sheet of animation. All this change is part of a continuous sequence, like watching a film. So that even as the breeze rises, it has wiped out the fading imagery of the ships, much as a cloth was used to wipe out the drawings on children's slates in a British classroom before the War.

My mind now is on the breeze. What will it do? Is it a transitory puff reacting to the cooling of sundown? Or is it a message of nature's goodwill, a wind to send us on our way with Godspeed? We will have to wait and see to get the answer. There is something else that must accompany the wind to make it welcome. *Research II* had been helplessly still, becalmed since the early morning, and when the breeze stirred, her bow was, as usual, heading southwest. In other words, my boat is now making for South America. I have to turn her around from her present rebellious course, and start off eastwards towards Britain. Only then can we relish the joy of sailing, whatever the weather may be, or whatever fascinating images of reality blended with glimpses of history, are resurrected by the ocean silence.

Log: Day 24, Sunday, 16th July, 1995

The breeze of yesterday turned into a fair wind from the southwest. When it first blew, *Research II* was heading the wrong way. I have no record written here in my notes, but I must have pulled her around. I do recall being up at midnight and working to get her on an easterly course. This must have been successful. I slept while *Research II* gurgled forward on an easterly course.

My longitude now was well under the West 30' line. This translated into 25 longitudes to reach the Lizard, in the English Channel. Latitude was now a healthy 47' 50', which made me easier in mind, as it was just what I wanted, within easy reach of the 50' parallel.

I woke and got up about 5:30 a.m. Eastern Time - I kept my watch on this.

Clearly the wind was increasing. I trimmed the sheets, checked Stanley and we continued scudding on our way. *Research II* heeled and foamed at her bow, the jib sometimes cracking like a whip as the main spasmodically blocked off the wind. The wind was getting stronger by the minute and the seas were arching under *Research II's* buttocks, as if trying to capsize her. The sky gave no semblance of sympathy, its colour was a liquid grey, a mask of deep, pitiless, unforgiving venom, that brooked no prayer for quarter.

I reefed the main and with the number 2 jib, *Research II* flew along at 6 knots. On all morning she reached, with the Scull-Oar checking her inclination either to go off to the north or to go the other way to the south. What a miracle!, I thought as I watched, without a tiller or a wheel to steer. Here was something I never heard of, yet I myself was part of it. How can I describe my thoughts as I looked on Stanley, that tall crewman who neither ate nor slept, but kept my boat on course and gave me a busman's holiday.

But this was no time for reverie or soliloquy. All hands were needed as the howling wind played its shrill chords in the rigging. The white crests and the flying spume lifting off the waves heralded a full-blown gale. The danger of jibing was real. Though Stanley could keep the boat on course, rogue waves could outmatch him and throw the boat sideways, beyond his power to take corrective action. Then it would be a violent jibe, with control slipping away, conceding it to the elements. I took the main down and lashed the boom inside the rail. We now sailed on more steadily. There was no danger of jibing as the jib pulled the boat along. Amazingly the speed remained the same - 6 knots. All that was required was an adjustment of Stanley every two hours. What a vista to behold, the steel grey sky, and beneath it, the lines of giant coamers marching down on us, with crests that sent a spray in our face, a kind of spiteful signal of frustration that we were escaping from their fury.

Anxiety

The question that occupied my mind as I watched it all, was this, 'Would the jib stand up to all this pounding?' All day *Research II* rolled on, at speed, right into the evening before a strong southwester. Then, by a slim majority vote in my mind, I also left the jib up all night. You can understand that, after blowing all day, the gale force winds whipped up the seas behind us into large walls of water and our track now comprised a sequence of hill climbing and downhill skiing, where the terrain was the volatile heaving mass of ocean water. In the hollows, the jib would go slack and when *Research II* raised her bow to climb the next hill under her keel, the wind could catch the jib and crack it like a whip, so that always, you felt that it might any time be torn to shreds. But we have to live with our decisions. Even though I succeeded in achieving control, there were always the imponderables, chiefly that the wind would change direction, or the jib give out, and of course the ever present hazard of the anonymous rogue waves. These are hunters, scouring the ocean looking for easy victims.

Stanley is given a rest

I slept that night, but fitfully, and often awoke to take readings of the situation. Just before dark, I took Stanley inboard as the clutch of the bracket holding the Scull-Oar vertical was slipping. When out of the vertical, there was no efficiency as the blade skated in the seas. The reason for this was that the stern of the boat was continually being lifted high out of the water on the wave crests, and alternated with a plunging movement when the reverse took place and the stern was practically submerged. I lashed Stanley to the rail and the defunct rudder. I now trimmed both the sheets of the jib, working both, adjusting, and synchronizing their tension, so that even any attempt to yaw or go of course was countered before it got any way on it.

How satisfying this fine tuning was, even in the dark. How long I took before I succeeded, I cannot tell. Time becomes an irrelevance when your mind is locked-in to overcome a problem. How strange, I would feel it like purgatory to spend an hour at many tasks on land that did not demand a fraction of the energy and mental application demanded of me here. The fact is that I was in my element. I knew I had to win. I just would not entertain failure. And there was always the conviction, that just around the corner, after one more try, after two more adjustments, the joy of succeeding would be my prize. Wonderfully, *Research II* plowed on, pulled inexorably forward, finding its own balance.

The rogue waves

These, as adverted to above, are the cause of continual anxiety especially when a gale has had a while to develop. They are the lone marauders of the sea, conceived like shooting stars, visible without warning but unlike the combusting shooting star of the night sky, carry a variety of aquatic punches which a small boat cannot ignore. As I write my journal at this very moment in the cabin, before I sleep, one of these rogue waves has hit us on the weather side. There is a crack like a gun as it strikes the boat, and *Research II* and her total complement together are thrown on their beam-ends. The result is predictable. The bow slews round, so that it is now to the wind. Sail,tackle and boat shudder together in a concert of discontent.

I am tired. Night for me has become early morning as I finally get control of my beloved boat again. I cannot record my efforts in the dark of the night, soaked from the sea and grimly holding on to save being washed overboard. I fell into a fitful sleep. Whenever I reach close to the extremity of my resources, and when I know I can do no more, I ring up heaven's emergency 24 hour service, which our Lord has provided for all who believe and trust in his saving power. He just cannot, by his nature, let you down, even though you are many months overdue with the payments of your vows and the tithes of your givings. No wonder we are clothed with shame as we think of his loving kindness and weep with worshipful praise for his mercy which endureth forever.

Calmly I lift my heart to him as I make my call, and fall asleep with the words of the psalmist silently formed in my heart,

I will both lay me down in peace and sleep: for thou Lord only makest me to dwell in safety.

Log: Day 25, Monday, 17th July, 1995

One assumes that a gale, however bad, will last as a rule for 12 or at most 24 hours. When you wake up after an intermittent rest at a belated matins of 8 a.m., and find the seas a picture of chaotic wildness and sky and sea mingling together in a grey/white mixture of blown spume, it is hard to marshal the needed optimism to face the resultant challenges of this new day. How much can one take? Surely one could say of the week that ended the previous Friday - 'That was the week that was.' There was a full catalogue of negatives, storm and calms, broken tillers, burst rudders, and continual pre-occupation with the experimental sails. All these and the adverse weather conditions together kept *Research II* back, way back.

We were now 25 days out, three to four days over the average of 100 miles a day normally expected in an ocean voyage. Of course that premised a boat with a rudder in full commission. We will just have to see how things develop. There was no respite from the taxing demands upon me. The ship and its gear cried out for attention like an ailing child. At 8 a.m. when I stirred from my sodden bed, after a thunderous crescendo of wind and wave, reinforced by sheets of rain and blown spume, I looked out of the companionway and guardedly surveyed the scene. My eye caught the jib, which now, I studied, noting with uneasiness the second tear on the luff.

Not only was this true, but *Research II* was clearly at the mercy of the seas. Exhaustion had lulled me into a deep sleep for the previous 3 hours. I had a lot of catching up to do on deck. The seas were mountainous walls, coming in long rolling undulations, throwing R*esearch II* about like a cork. The naked challenge was there. And I also was there to grasp it like an unsheathed sword, even though it be with both my hands.

Cat-like, with one hand to my safety, I set to gain some control and bring my bucking boat to heel, as a rider would do with his runaway horse. I loosed the sheets which were as taut as whipcord. Then I crawled forward. Sea and spray clawed at my body, but with my head bent down, I reached the mast and half stood up, clasping it for my life. I then unloosed the halyard, downed the jib and lashed it securely at the pulpit. I write this quickly in a few sentences, but in all, this action took at least 20 minutes on the foredeck. Now there was a decided improvement - a relative silence, with the regret that our speed now went down from 5 knots to 2. But we were in control. Stanley was reset and his stem lowered to the required depth. This countered the tendency to jackknife out of the water. We sailed on eastwards.

Water in the ship

On the ocean, when there is weather, the hatches are usually closed securely. But this is no guarantee that all is well. Waves sweep over the boat in bursts and water somehow penetrates and gets down below. I pumped out about 20 buckets over the last 24 hours. That is about 400 strokes of the pump. The pump is a highly efficient hand type with a corrugated plastic outflow which can be led out over the bridge deck to empty into the self-bailing cockpit. But what if the cockpit is continually filling as it is swept by waves! I chose, for my own satisfaction, to fill the bucket. This is totally necessary where the seas threaten to come in the companionway. In this case I keep the perspex vertical door in place and empty the buckets out over the side through the open hatch above. The pump is vitally necessary as it is nigh impossible to use any other container to empty the bilges as the top of it is closed in such a way that only a pump cylinder can be dropped down to drain it.

Log/Journal note: Looking at the cockpit as a wave on the lee almost flooded the self-bailing cockpit, - a pleasant place to sit in on a fine day but now an alien location to be carefully avoided. I look at the pump, also the sailbags and other gear near the stern. The thought passes through my mind, 'What if a wave washes these all out in a moment?' I would then be in straits.

I grabbed each of them in turn and pulled them to me into the cabin. There is some compensation, in that the sailbags act as cushions against the continual blows, even though they, with all the rest of the furniture, are soaking wet.

Compulsory pause

As I write this, there has just been an enormous crash. A mighty wave has hit *Research II*. She rolled over on her beam-ends so that I fell in a heap on the cupboards. By this time I was used to such compulsory acrobatics and my body was a proof of many hard knocks. The gimbaled stove stuck at its maximum of 45' and would not come back to equilibrium, though it is the only reassuring means of knowing when you are on the level.

But this and the many extraordinary situations are not enough to destroy my basic confidence in my God and in my boat. My mind goes back to the spring and the deadline I set for leaving Nova Scotia, of the middle of June. In spite of the many shortcomings which are traceable to my hurried preparation and especially to my preoccupation with making the self steering gear, I still feel a kind of pride. I ordered all rigging to be doubled, yes, more than doubled in strength. I secured the bottlescrews myself, and each day my eye swept over each in turn, searching out any loosening, slackening or weakness which might by neglect be the cause of my undoing. Ultimately, as this voyage is proof, the sturdiness of the rigging is of primary importance and comes before everything above the waterline, even the rudder itself.

No ships, one plane

No ships have appeared for several days. Visibility has been against this for most of the time. Yesterday morning I heard the drone of an aeroplane. It seemed like the sound of a propeller driven aircraft.

I give continual thought to the sails. Before me there is the continual challenge and each day I have to work out different answers. At this point it is my opinion that my autosails will be a vital requirement, unless there is moderate and favorable weather to use *Research II's* own conventional sails. What a dream to contemplate if I were able to sail up the English Channel with a following southwesterly, filling the conventional main and being pulled along with the big genoa! But we must be thankful and we cannot ask for too much. Meantime we are a long way off from the Lizard, 10' Longitude E. And in any case, survival itself is primary. I am in no hurry.

The dead radio contact

If there is anxiety it is that the weather may be bad when I reach the English Channel. Sadly, with mysterious electrical shorts, water in the electrical wiring and the continuous flooding of the battery compartment on the lee, I just cannot get my transmitter/receiver to operate. It is most frustrating, especially when ships become more plentiful. It means that I cannot communicate with them or send a message through them, to tell Mary how matters are. I've tried every combination. I'll keep trying. I must sign off. God bless you Mary and Jane. Enjoy yourselves in Paris.

Log: Day 26, Tuesday, 18th July, 1995

Log/Journal reads: Looking back to yesterday, by 7 p.m. all sail was set. I tried the conventional main but was stunned to find that the mast winch was missing. It was with great joy that I found it caught in the lifeline netting on the foredeck. This expensive item of gear, a heavy Harken winch, apart from its usefulness would be a serious financial loss, in my reckoning. I then realized that I could, with some difficulty, raise the main myself if I kept the boom held up first. This was not straightforward as I had no topping lift. I raised the main and the jib. Verdict after several hours of trial; no success.

The auto sails to the rescue

I had no option at this point but to take out my own autosails again. You may recall that earlier, they had not proved successful when on a close reach. With them you could not get them to set well. I raised the autosail panel with the mast track fittings. Though much smaller than a full main it drew well with the wind following. The key to its success was that you still could have the jib pulling *Research II* along efficiently without the blanketing effect of the wind, the painful corollary of using the main. I now sat back. A fresh gale force package blew in from the southwest. *Research II* responded with controlled vigor and drove on to the east. With the Scull-Oar keeping its faithful and consistent vigil, I went below. It was long since I had a cooked meal, two full days. I had the 'works': steamed potatoes and onions in equal proportions, Fraser's Irish Stew; tea and biscuits.

What a delight to look out from the companionway and share the universe with the stars. And as the evening gave way to darkness, my friends became visible in the clear sky. Jupiter to the south was bright and welcoming. Then the old favorite constellation, the Plough, to the northwest; always turning through the night so that the pointer led your eye to the Pole star. Yes, Life was good. I sang a verse or two softly to the God and creator of all, for his mercy endureth forever. What mind can linger in the side streets and the mundane aspects of the finite, when we are privileged to explore in thought the realms of truth amid all the riches of wonder in creation, both in the terrestrial and in the nocturnal canopy of the sky! For in the wonder of our own unique consciousness, alone of all creatures fashioned out of the dust of the earth, the finite itself leads our thoughts to extend beyond the parameters of our confirmed knowledge, to dwell upon the infinite.

This is liberation, the highest form of life, reaching to the stars, not in speculative suppositions, nor constructing hypotheses premised on our own era's fashionable developmental interim knowledge, but on the premise of God's omnipotence, where light and sound and all the substance of matter are his servants.

The Psalmist looked up and saw it all, the sparkling carpet of the sky, as a source of great wonder and the artistry of the Maker of it all. Then he composed this song for all mankind to use in worship.

1. O Lord our Lord, how excellent is thy name in all the earth! who hast set thy glory above the heavens.

3. When I consider the heavens, the work of thy fingers, the moon and the stars which thou has ordained;

4. What is man, that thou art mindful of him? and the son of man that thou visitest him?

9. O Lord our Lord, how excellent is thy name in all the earth!

(excerpt from Psalm 8)

Disturbers of the peace

Log/Journal notes: I awoke after a good sleep. *Research II* was journeying on eastwards. In the morning, the wind had freshened, as it often does. The effect is that big seas become disturbers of the peace. They are a continual threat. If one comes along and gets its way, it triggers a long sequence of struggle for me to get *Research II* back in commission and sailing efficiently in the right direction. Every day and every night much of my time is occupied with this corrective effort. Good things do not come alone. For the past few days we have had the following southwester. But that means the following seas, which every so often become unsettling disturbers of the peace.

However, we accept this. It is all in the day's work, alas also often in the night. The day has now passed. The seas have lessened in their fury as the wind has slackened. I always look for this, so that rest can be my portion in the watches of the night. The sky is a dull grey, just like the sea. We look and long for sunshine, so necessary for the solar generator. I depend on this for the masthead navigation lights. To sail at night without the latter is risky, even though I have the radar reflector.

The evening is now near, and I must make a meal. I am also going to take a position check with the GPS. I haven't had one since Saturday, 3 days ago, when we had passed the 30' W Longitude. The question is, 'How much Easting progress have we done in that time? We will find out after a good hot meal.

Log reading:	Waypoint 18	
Speed:	4.7 knots	
Position:	N 47' 26"	W 23' 18"
Time:	3 hours until 1900 hours (exactly three days since last Saturday's reading of W 28' 49")	

Setting goals

That is really quite good progress. Remember, this reading registers pure East progress. Actual distance sailed by *Research II* is much more. During this time she zig-zagged from northeast 30' to southeast 150'. You have to make the best of the wind you get, and extract from it as much easting as you can. If you refused to sail, except in a perfect line of an East course, you could wait on the ocean for many a day. But the idea is to make the best of things. The result is sometimes *Research II* may be sailing on a course for the Shetland Islands to the North of Scotland and at other times, she may be heading for the Azores, but she still is making Easting progress. Hopefully too, we can maintain the required Latitude.

Our lives need goals to keep us going. This is very true of an ocean voyage, especially this one with the major handicap of having no rudder. Not so long ago, I was gratified to pass the 30' West Longitude. That meant putting away the chart for the western half of the North Atlantic and getting out the new one for the central and Eastern half.

Crossing the mountains

I was now in the area of struggle, a period of very agitated seas. There is little doubt that this related, in part, to the geography of the sea floor below our keel. Just as the wind conditions dictate much of the weather and sea conditions we encounter, so also the terrain beneath the waters has a basic influence upon the kind of wave pattern and the kind of animation of the sea.

In studying the new chart, which is also on a much larger scale, you can see that we have been crossing the mountain ridge below. This rises to a height of half a mile or roughly 2000 metres plus. Just imagine the course of *Research II*. Over a week ago it sailed, as it were, driven by the southwest wind, up the slope of a mountain until it had passed the top of the western ridge. It then entered what is known as the Mid European Basin, a wide hollow valley. Here is the area of fissure, the geological divide of the continent of North America and its complement, the continent of Europe. As we noted elsewhere, here is the traditional Rift valley, where the centre area has slipped down to form the valley. All is not passive here. Instead, the temperature is higher through igneous activity and the consequent friction and pressures related to volcanic movement. Add to this the phenomenon of the mountain Pass, which for us was the Faraday Fracture, cutting the Mountain Ridge at right angles. Now you have three identifiable ancillary influences of the physical sea floor acting significantly upon the ocean above and affecting the voyage of *Research II* from Canada to Britain; these are: the raised pattern of the mountain ridge, the right-angled defile created by the Fracture, and the difference in temperature, which oceanographers attest as being very significant in sea and wave formation.

Reaching for the 2000

Having enlarged on this underwater configuration of the sea floor, we now think of our next reasonably attainable goal high up on the surface of the sea above. That is none other than the West Longitude of 2000°, from Greenwich. Notice we are at the 23' W Longitude, a distance of about 180 miles, which means that we have not very many days to go, that is, if we are fortunate. We just cannot sit back and wait and see. This progress demands unremitting effort. In turn, this constant work and pre-occupation with the challenge before one makes time fly, without any sense of tedium.

CHAPTER 14

A Tale of the Unexpected

Log: Day 27, Wednesday, 19th July, 1995

This was a good night. The Scull-Oar has fulfilled all expectations. Who would believe that a few bits of scrap from Hashem's Scrapyard in Sydney could become the efficient crewman that worked on a 24 hour shift without complaint? Stanley, for so is the Christian name which he so rightly deserves, is worthy even of divine benediction. And why not! God uses cars to take people to church, houses to shelter the sick and one could say much more. Does not the Queen and other Ladies -in -waiting, knock off a bottle of champagne as it swings out like a pendulum to break against the bow of warships, at the same time invoking the divine benediction, 'God bless this ship, and all who sail on her!' In Scotland when this ritual is carried out, colored water is wisely used as a substitute, reflecting the traditional virtue of thrift endemic in the thrifty nation's people.

Salute to Stanley

I now look at the tall figure of this invaluable companion with a kind of curious awe. Every time I remember, I realize it is so easy to take him for granted, standing there always on duty. This is more pronounced when I wake up in the morning as I have done a little while ago. There, faithful as ever, my friend Stanley rocks his headgear back and fore, the living proof - can one say that? - that the day of the robot has truly come and is more than justified. Thanks to Stanley, I slept through the night with only the usual breaks to assure me that all was well, and to confirm we were still on course. There was no complaint. *Research II* reached forward, eating up the miles at a good pace, pushed along by a brisk southwesterly.

How can I over-estimate Stanley's prowess! Here we are with no rudder, yet sailing day and night. There is no hand on the tiller nor on a wheel. There cannot be, for there is neither wheel nor tiller on the boat for a hand to turn. But Stanley, the Scull-Oar, is there standing upright at the stern. He seems to know his business and what is expected of him. He has a kind of persistent alertness that makes me marvel at his intuitive reaction. He is not conned into assuming that the wind or waves are suddenly his friends. Like a good opponent in the democratic context, he respects his adversaries, but is always alert to their guile and wily tricks. This is demonstrated even as I watch. The bow is perceptibly pushed off course. Within moments Stanley pauses in his regular pendulum movement, and brings the bow back, so that *Research II* pulls forward to continue across the Atlantic.

The recurring problem

Maybe it should not make me anxious, but I could not help being apprehensive that we would be driven south thereby preventing us from making the entrance to the English Channel. To me, there was a continual need to get up north, a perpetual struggle against what seemed to be unseen forces trying to push me south. Not that I wanted to pass the 50' N Latitude, but to be within striking distance off it when I approach the Scillies at the toe of England. I am caught between two extremities of apprehension. The first is that of getting caught in the path of the Gulf Stream current, coupled with the probability of southwest winds of unknown strength taking me north past the Scillies. The second is that already referred to, the exact opposite, of being carried too far south. Even at present, good as the southwest is that takes me along, I may well have to spend a day or two more, crossing from the Brest area of the French coast of Brittany, to get up to the English side of the Channel. You can see that the southwest has a double meaning for me. On the one hand it is very good as the traditional power source, sailing east. On the other, a storm or gale force winds from that direction, could make it difficult if not impossible to turn south east to avoid the Scillies. I would therefore be pushed up between Ireland and Wales, aided and abetted by the Gulf Stream.

But maybe I should not be so sure that the southwest wind is going to be my enemy. It is not as inevitable as the Law of the Medes and the Persians, that cannot be altered. Didn't the ancient king Darius find a way round it in order to save the devout Daniel who would bow to no earthly potentate, to compromise his faith in the living God! Reflecting on this, I was aware that I already had experienced northerly and easterly winds, - indeed too much of them, in mid ocean. They could well return. I did not know what was before me but they certainly would return, and while being beneficial in some respects, there was a negative aspect which would also cause considerable annoyance. Meanwhile we sailed onward with a good southwesterly behind us.

Hour of Opportunity

The morning was quiet and warm. This was the hour of opportunity for domestic chores, and there was a long list of these. I first checked the out-door needs which always had to have first priority. I reset the jib now on the out-rigger foreboom. This was a flexible system as I had separate sheets from the boom tack. While the boom was kept down by the tension of the vang below it, I could swing it out getting maximum area in the spread of the jib. Also by using the two sheets, the tack was held steady so that the jib did not swing out of position. Then it was spring-cleaning. I stripped myself, the first time for well over a week. All my clothes were soaking wet. It was the same with everything in the cabin, including my bedding. The sun was shining in its strength. Out I put everything, spreading them on deck and cabin, taking precautions to jam them between the lifelines. The subtle danger was that when I put items of clothes out, soaking wet, they were heavy, literally heavy; I think of my big anorak; but after a while if they dried, they then would get light and so easily they could blow overboard. This possibility was always in my mind.

Feeling good

This was a really successful operation. Spring-cleaning, or washing day, call it what you like, all went very well. No wave loped over the cabin or over the gunwale to wet the spread out items of gear. The sun did its work and dried my clothes, so that they were crisp and light. By lunch hour I was able to put all items back down below. For myself, I felt a new man, after a sponge down, and dressed completely in warm dry clothes right down to the socks and shoes on my feet. A complete change of clothes once a week was the average for the whole voyage, and I kept two sets of clothing especially for this alternating process. Now, I drank in the warmth of the sun's rays, enjoying their almost nutritious energy as they filtered through my clothes. There was a sense of freedom without my usual protection of oilskins. What a feeling of sheer well-being! Even the cuts on my hands and fingers were on the way to heeling. And in place of lost skin, nature was replacing this with a new and tougher variety, suitable for the ocean environment. The protrusion on the side of my head continued to make itself felt. But it never gave me any real pain. It became a friend, a curiosity, an appanage of my personality. I didn't resent its presence and wondered indeed if it would go down before I reached my destination. I poked around in the boat lockers, examining the small tins - these I reserved for lunch. I settled on a tin of salmon, and savored the meal thereafter with appreciative relish.

Be prepared

I had finished my mid-day meal, and enjoyed a few reflective moments on the morning's work, when I took a look out of the companionway. Time had passed because of all the chores and setting some kind of order below. It was now 4 o'clock in the afternoon (Eastern Time) and one look at the situation around me told its own story. Clearly we were in for a change. I made another mental note of satisfaction, with its own moralistic lesson. It was this: you must grasp the hour of opportunity when you get it, or it will be lost forever. Was I ever glad that I had redeemed the morning and eliminated that long list of overdue chores! Scanning the horizon to the north and west, clearly I could see a piling up of dark grey clouds. And they certainly didn't look as if they were of the 'user-friendly' variety. I wondered, as I looked at them growing bigger, if they would reach south to our latitude and a wind blow hard.

Last night the rain had come down in a total encasing torrent, dropping out of the sky without any warning. Now, the sun is gone. It vanished behind the grey clouds, long before its bed-time. It's not that I had any apprehension of any threat from a gale or a storm. It's just that change is endemic in this North Atlantic. You have sunshine and favorable winds, but these are, for a season, strictly rationed so that you really appreciate them. For they tend to get squeezed out by a variety of other conditions which are generally tolerable, though not so friendly or comfortable. The dictum to follow was 'to be prepared' and always expect change. Now I prepared in that basic manner and put on my oilskins. One outing on deck can mean a total soaking, for the next few days.

A good indulgence

I weighed up the situation. Here we are slipping along with a force 4 from the southwest, freshening in intermittent gusts. It looks as if it will continue, possibly doubling in strength. I look forward to the foredeck and all seems fair and ship-shape. I like the double sheets on the boom and foresail - this compensates for possibility of trouble as the foresail sheets are damaged on both sides about the area of the shrouds. We'll leave position check till tomorrow. Hopefully by 7 p.m., we'll have good news to tell of our progress. Now for my old habit which I have always been reluctant to give up, even in trying conditions - namely my regular afternoon nap, although it is a bit late for it. I now avail myself of this luxury, this personal lapse into indolence, this dropping into decadence, this concession to the flesh or even an egotistical indulgence, call it what you like, because it is also obedience to the dictum, 'be prepared.' This expedient is not original. Did not Sir Winston Churchhill, during the Second World War, adopt this strategy to compensate for his age and steal a march upon his fitter fellows? Did he not come storming out to top meetings of his War Cabinet, full of zest and vigor, burning up the midnight oil with unabated energy? And he could do so by using this method, thus splitting his day into two, with the sweet repose of that unmatched therapy used in the strongest of nature's champions, the lion, namely 'the afternoon nap.' I now lapsed into blissful oblivion, knowing that before me I had an unknown agenda for the rest of the day and even a lesser known agenda for the coming night. I must sign off; until tomorrow, then. A.M.K.

Log: Day 28, Thursday, 20th July, 1995

Mid-Atlantic Basin

I told you that the immediate goal was for us to break the Longitude of 2000° West. That was a coveted prize and sweet thought. This would mean two-thirds of our total distance made good, or 2400 miles. It gives a tremendous feeling which I have not fully analyzed, to contemplate such progress, in view of the increased challenge of sailing without a rudder which the storm gave us to face. Somehow the challenge is a continuous one, that demands alertness and readiness to meet every subterfuge of wind and weather, and overcome any shortcomings of moveable and running gear that show signs of weakness or failure. There is nothing like an ocean voyage to test your gear. And it is not enough to have the best of gear - the Cal T/4 has Harken fittings which must be classified among the very best. You have to maintain all fittings as well as you can, or even the best can fail. For instance, I doubled the retaining studs on Stanley's adjustable body in the holding bracket, but without the grease packed into the threaded holes, electrolysis between the aluminum alloy and the stainless steel could have rendered the whole apparatus useless. I just noticed this in time to obviate the progressive course towards obsolescence.

A restless night

Sometimes *Research II* demands continuous attention like a little child that is troubled and cannot sleep. This was one of these nights.

The evening before, the wind was changeable, as I adverted to earlier. I was up and down until well after midnight, to some extent fretting myself, trying to find some overall solution to the unsatisfactory situation which had resulted from the vagaries of the uncertain wind and more uncertain sea patterns. *Research II* showed herself capable of what I would call negative behavior. She would veer off to one side or another with unpredictable timing. In some cases, she would pass the point of no return, beyond the capability of Stanley to bring her back on course. Then she would luff and come to a dead stop. It was obvious that the irregular wind was basically responsible. But that did not help to solve the problem. Sometime about midnight the wind settled from the west and almost reluctantly R*esearch II* responded, sailing now due east. I had to compromise so that speed was given second place to direction. For this, the sheets had to be so deployed, through trial and error so that the boat was not given rein. Like a horse she had to be held tightly by its rider. Having cajoled *Research II* into some modicum of steadfastness, after several hours in the cockpit, at last I went below and fell asleep.

Fantasies of the night

I cannot believe that my sleep had much substance. In effect, it was as if I was awake all night. I was taken as in a limousine to a huge ballroom. In it were many people, crowds of men and women, all well dressed. They stood in a row to meet me and one after another, I had to meet them in turn and address them. How many I met I could not count, but the unending process left me exhausted. The amazing thing about it was that I retreated into the cabin of my boat. But they followed me with the resulting problem of overcrowding. I think that accounted for the sweat on my forehead when I woke with a start, shouting at them all to get out fast, or the boat would sink. It was therefore with some relief that I woke to reality. I was still sure that there were some of the people hiding away on board, but as I woke fully, that residual element of my night's fantasies also evaporated. I wonder, was this also linked to my sub-consciousness? It was the regular lot of ministers to shake hands with the congregation in the vestibule of the church, as they left on Sunday morning. This was a happy and fulfilling experience. Nevertheless, it was also demanding.

Here was the minister, having had his mind wholly exercised in the earnest spiritual advocacy of his calling, now he had to go through the whole catalogue of his congregation's homes, very quickly one after an other, each with its file of needs and members, state of health and concerns, problems and deficiencies. Often after this, a knot would form within my head, a variety of blood pressure, which left me worked up and unable to relax for several days. With a kind of relief, I felt the coaming of the hatchway. I was glad to be out here safe in the tranquillity of the sea. I breathed in the crisp air of the morning, thus filling my lungs with its goodness and clearing my mind of imagined ball rooms, and overdressed people. Here was reality; I, on a little boat in mid ocean.

Worn Gear and Breakage

Gear was showing wear and tear, some giving way, like the worn sheets, and the dismantled mast winch. At one stage I had to put great pressure on the main halyard to loose the Autosail and bring it down from the mast, where it was jammed in the track. I had to jerk violently. This developed a weakspot in the halyard which I dealt with by making a loop, thus bypassing the weak spot - as a temporary measure. I am certain that this episode caused the mast winch to be incapacitated thereafter. And of course there was the disabled rudder, saved but impotent, lashed there at the transom, the symbol of the storm's fury and my own forgetfulness.

Research II was on course. The wind had veered to the north and was now consistent. I spent some time trimming the sails until they were fine tuned. Each hand worked the sheets for two hours, independent of the other, yet working together. As one sheet was let out a fraction, the other was pulled in. My eye was riveted to the mast and the tension on the jib. The leech gave me the cue for adjustment and, little by little, an equilibrium and balance was achieved. Then I rested, still holding my hands on each foresheet, waiting to see if this was the last adjustment needed. Almost in one movement, then, I turned to Stanley and, having glanced at the compass, then the Canadian Flag which gave me the wind direction, I swiftly loosed the headgear, raised the quadrant to put Stanley in neutral, and turned the headgear so that the vane swept backwards and showed its leading edge to the wind. I relate this as if it was all a smooth successful operation. It was this, but not always having immediate results of success. It worked this time almost flawlessly. The reason for this was the consistency of the wind and the absence of heavy seas that often would make tuning difficult as the boat's stern would lift and fall, making pressure on the Scull-Oar blade variable and erratic.

The wind freshens

Throughout the day the wind freshened, with whitecaps now meeting us on the weatherside. But *Research II* held on her course, defying all attempts to push her to the south. You cannot know how gratifying this was for me. Or should I say, how thankful I felt for this practical benediction of heaven. All I could think of was that I hoped it would continue. We are on a very close reach, the jib taut as a sheet of steel. There is a definite slot, the nature of it being the secret of self steering and the result of trial and error after many hours of experiment. It appears as if we have the wind almost dead ahead of us, but we are locked on course. The spray flies over the cabin top and the waves fold away like the turned up clod cut by the advancing plow.

Above it is bright, with a blue sky to the north. I knew that there was a change the night before. The wind was now considerably colder, quite different from the southwesterly wind. But *Research II* was going forward and matching the contrary wind in a way that would have made the designer, William Lapworth, very proud. What a relief to relax and get some breakfast below, and while doing so, to glance at the inside compass and see the reassuring consistency eastwards.

When all was right above, time was then on my hands for other tasks, or to seek answers to ongoing problems. Thus I now turned to the radio, that irritating 'thorn in the flesh' which I was permitted to retain, throughout the voyage without remedy. Alas to no avail! However, I will keep trying. Who knows? Maybe I will get some change before I reach the busiest waterway in the world, the English Channel. I dwelt on this stage which I had still a long way to reach. But I could not help wondering what would happen when I reached the Channel. It seemed to me that there could be trouble, big trouble. I had no radio to warn shipping that I had little or no capacity to take avoiding action. Of course, if I am spotted from the air, an aerial photograph would reveal my incapacity as the disabled rudder was pulled inboard high above the stern still holding the remnants of the broken tiller. I surmised that it would be up to the coastguards whether I would be allowed to continue up the Channel. It could well be that *Research II* would be designated officially as a hazard to shipping. I could bring her 2500 miles across the North Atlantic without a rudder, but in the confines of the Channel and the density of its shipping, it would be nonsense to assume the same competence to cope with it. I reflected that I could not know what scenario will unfold. I have no insurance to meet any claims by small boat collision, nor compensation for my own loss. It could well be that I will need a tow. Possibly I shall have to go into Falmouth or if I reach further up the Channel it could be to any other, Plymouth, Dartmouth, Weymouth or even Portsmouth. The Channel weather could well be unfriendly. Then I would have no initiative but be very thankful for any help. Why, making the Longitude of Britain and Land's End marked triumph! Anything beyond that was merely a question of disembarking, and any port on the English side would suit me.

But enough, I cannot pre-empt the unfolding will of Providence, nor do I want to. *Sufficient unto the day is the evil thereof.*' To compensate for lack of radio contact or weather warnings, I do not have the anxiety generated by these warnings, when terrible things are promised which the imagination processes and amplifies. My faculties also are sharpened to read the sky and the sea, as old sea captains once did and for which fishermen developed a special competence. I would be the first to appreciate the value of communication and weather warnings, but let's face it, it had its other side. Possibly, this also applies on land and in many general situations. We could get along quite well without the radio alarms of what is to come. It is hard to have a meal at the top of the hour and listen to the news at the same time, without a catalogue of calamity predicted as imminent, just round the corner, hypothetical and often speculative, from the overzealous and enthusiastic journalists. It seems as if they are on the 'hot seat' continually. They have to bring in hard news every day. If it is soft, they have to doctor it and animate it to make it look real, in order to please the producer who in turn has to please someone else. If only many of them knew how painful and transparent their speculative opinions are, they would stick to facts.

It is a historic fact that events, even those that in retrospect are traced as logical evolutionary sequences, occur without warning. Human beings are full of contradiction. Churchill spent the interim years between the World Wars, in the 'doghouse', the prophet of doom warning the world that 1918 was only a truce, a pause while Germany won time to get its technology together to catch up with the innovative British tank, and harness the genius of its own brilliant scientists to serve their nation, making flying bombs to wipe out cities. You could go on. There was so much to do, perfect the weapon of cowardice, the submarine, to mark the demise of honour and pursue the ever attractive possibility of chemical warfare of which Germany was already the proven champion. Hitler was already preparing. In a bleak political scene he was a rising star. Great nations hurried to do him obeisance. One after another he tricked them. His obvious power drew the Catholic Church into compromise if not collusion. With that and the muzzling of the Protestant Church making the compromising Barmen Declaration, the silencing of the German conscience was completed.

It seems that we are so inured to warnings that there is no logic to explain the contradictions. Some, which are authentic, we ignore as alarmist. Others, with which we are fed every day, are given at least a hearing, and therefore indicate a passive acceptance or credibility, by their continued tolerance.

Now back to reality and the mid-Atlantic. My goal is

approaching fulfillment. I hope to break the 2000°W Longitude barrier by the end of this day. If not I shall have to be philosophical. At any rate, *Research II* will be past it tomorrow.

Merry-go-round

Log/journal notes: A moment ago, just as I put my logbook away, *Research II* was hit by a large coamer. The hull was lifted up so that I felt myself pressing into the floor. Then we were on our beam-ends and I, sitting on the lee berth (the kitchen seat), found myself doubled up and my feet striking the ceiling. Slowly *Research II* returned to a relatively level stance. Fortunately that rogue wave was one of a kind, making its solo prowl across the ocean looking for likely victims. One could say, thankfully, that *Research II,* thanks to the double rigging, was more than a match for it. So it moved on. But there were immediate if not serious consequences and I had work on my hands. *Research II* was thrown off course so far that when I pulled myself together and looked out of the cabin, she had turned 180'.

We were already picking up speed and sailing as usual, pushed by the strong northerly wind, down to South America. This I found was not a casual canter like a horse, which for a moment, has taken a diversionary turn to lope round the farmyard. This was an aggressive challenge to my leadership and it looked as if *Research II* was a willing accessory, if not an active accomplice. I allowed myself to entertain some dark and very negative thoughts about my boat's personality - all boats have personalities - but meantime I had to apply myself to the situation and assert my rightful authority as captain, cook, crew and mate.

Now it was all skills applied to stop her on what was, according to the knotmeter, a 7 knot flight to South America to the southwest. I can only be thankful that three weeks of familiarity and continual practice sailing a boat without a rudder, plus the absolute determination to avoid South America at this juncture in my life, produced a successful return to an eastward course. No one could deny me the pride I felt, as *Research II* turned again to her course.

The wind, now against us, threw the spray in my face, a futile gesture of defiance in compulsively conceding to my authority. There is often a gain in misfortune. Having reset sail sheets, Stanley was left alone, a bit embarrassed by the effects of that rogue wave which was too much for him to handle. Now he is more conscientious than ever. At any rate, he is behaving in a very dignified manner, and the yawing and luffing of *Research II* is hardly noticeable. As I relax, I think of South America and recall Joshua Slocum and his visitors in Tierra del Fuego, not to mention in our modern day, the drug dealers and marginal maritime business people. Well, let's keep away from them meantime.

Log: Day 29, Friday, 21st July, 1995

Winning a goal

GPS Reading:
Position: N 47' 24" W 19' 88"
Speed: 2-4 knots
Time: 13.53

As you see, I took these readings about mid-day. The wind has noticeably slacked and our speed is thus reduced. But that cannot cancel the fact that we have won another goal, 10 longitudes in just over 4 days. That was good going, average of 150 miles a day. My aim now is to get up to Latitude N 49' 50" without having to lose progress eastward. I hope the wind will help. We are on a close reach just now. The jib is outhauled on the boom. Otherwise it would flap to ribbons. The problem is that the wind keeps changing in the 24 hour period. It is steady at night. It ends towards morning. It then freshens in the afternoon, and what follows is unknown and unpredictable, sometimes a half gale, as night falls, or at other times a steady breeze. Always there is need for constant attention. I have to accept at times a speed of 3-4 knots, though I would like it to be 5-6. But at the end of the day what does it matter? Though the main is down, the Autosail gives a steady, if slower, speed. Trying to achieve maximum performance with the attendant wear on gear also means exhaustion of mind and body, that could be interpreted as worse than control in an ordinary situation with a rudder and tiller.

I have to be philosophical, accept every change and adjust to the needs of the hour. For instance, 3 times in the space of two hours, *Research II* happily going east, suddenly whipped around by north and off she sped southwest to South America. Maybe the boat is trying to tell me something. I think that Stanley, the Scull-Oar, is like the Maytag maintenance man on the television advertisement. He gets bored because business is slow and is tempted then to go to sleep. Then a wicked wave comes so that he is caught napping. Stanley is not a replacement for a rudder. He can keep the boat on course, within certain parameters. First, the boat must have a certain level of speed for him to be efficient, and secondly, the cross-waves must also be limited in force. Within these limits, themselves being variables, Stanley is an able and reliable crewman.

Word from outside

I hear from the Short Wave that London has a heat wave - probably imported from the USA, where a hundred people died within a week through heat related causes. Out here, we get it all, especially when the wind is northerly, when it can be very cold. In contrast, it can be really hot in the direct rays of the sun.

Note on last night : There was a half gale. I reduced the jib and we sped on through the darkness in relative peace. What a contrast to the constant banging and tension before then! Indeed I was very exhausted over the last 24 hours. I have still to learn to do what I can and to accept what I cannot help. I still have to get up to near 50' Latitude before we come to the Channel, that means in the next 3-5 days and it may mean a northerly tack and losing easting. We'll see. Meantime I am charging both batteries before the weekend, which usually brings weather.

Climbing maritime mountains

Friday, 7 p.m.
Position: N 47' 18" W 19' 45"
Speed: 2.7 knots.

Research II is becalmed shortly after 7 p.m. I think that the northerly flow is past. It's strange how this coincides with our passing the 2000' Longitude. At this part of the voyage, there is a large mountain range, the eastern part of the mid-Atlantic Basin underneath the keel. It is easy to think that we are struggling to get over this mountain ridge. Even though there are great waters below, there are also these ragged peaks and ridges. Think of the irregular terrain, the precipices, the defiles, the caves, the rocks riddled with fissures. Think of the currents, the eddies, the eroded uneven undulations of igneous basalts.

There is really no flat seabottom at an even depth a mile below. Instead we have a world of variety, of landscape and hills, of plain and elevation. There is no need to look through a telescope to marvel at the surface of the moon or wonder at the 'oceans' and 'icecapped mountains' of Mars. The flooded rift valleys, mountain ridges and passes, give our seaborne voyage a character of its own which only the ocean can provide as a human experience. If only by some means oceanographers could correlate the terrain below and the varied characteristics on the surface of the sea above, many different faces of the ocean, from calm to violent would thus be identified. If the northerly is indeed finished, I look forward to tomorrow, for I am sure the southwest will take over.

Scenes from the night

Two ships appeared, one traveling east and one traveling west about a mile away from us. I was helpless at the time and did not want any ships close to me in the semi-dark of the gloaming. Re*search II* was doing her fancy footwork at the time and intermittently heading for the Caribbean and South America. I spent 3 to 4 hours trying to get her to head east. But could I? Not a bit. Then philosophically I settled for the Pole star. It seemed that there were forces pushing me back from getting right over the eastern ridge of the mountains below. Or was this just imagined? The evening gave place to night. The full carpet of the sky became clear and studded with stars, as we moved forward silently at minimal speed. At least I was getting north, and at the same time I was not going back on my tracks.

A tale of the unexpected

We all are programmed in our minds by what we already know. When we think of a house, we have a mental vision of shape, size and colour with which we are familiar. In a way what I now relate is a tale of the unexpected, a contradiction of what we automatically already know and, in consequence, expect to meet in our ongoing experience of life.

Amidst the clattering racket made by the idle sails and moving gear, I thought I heard an unusual sound. It was very dark outside. The sound was distinctive and as if coming from something living. I hastened out of the companionway and checked the compass. I looked to starboard. *Research II* had done one of her familiar merry-go-rounds and was heading southwest towards the planet Jupiter rising above the horizon. About a hundred metres away there was a commotion, a mingling of animated sounds and the splashing of water. Immediately I assumed that all this was caused by a school of porpoises. Then, still looking into the sea, I saw before me a great flaming phosphorescent light. It resembled the long luminous wake which you would see behind a destroyer or a fast large ship. Or if you think for another analogy, it was like the white vapour trail left in the sky by our modern jetliners on a summer day.

I felt a cold chill on the back of my neck. I swallowed as if my stomach was unhappy and wanted to empty itself. I consciously trembled as the snake of phosphorescent light made a circle. I gripped the cabin top as this unidentified object, not in space - but in the sea, curved round and started coming towards me. The strange phenomenon found nothing familiar in my repertoire of human experience or knowledge, to identify with. I could hear through my body, my heart thumping as this snake of light drew nearer. I felt that I had made a mistake by coming out on deck. I was seen and now this creature was after me. The silence was unbearable. I shouted, releasing the tension with a human sound. I called 'Is anyone out there?' In a way I wanted to confirm my presence, that indeed there was someone 'at home' on old Res*earch II.*

The spectacular lighted phenomenon broadened, and in moments the silvery light appeared split into two. I looked and there beside the boat, not ten feet away, was the dark glistening back of my old friend, the big whale. Again the size of the hot-blooded mammal made me almost breathless as I considered its massive moving back. The silvery phosphorescent light between the whale's body and the boat dissolved into a shimmering froth. It resembled the terminal white foam of a swell as it recedes from an island or coast. My eyes adjusted to the dark and I peered over the side as the animal slowed to the almost minimal speed of the boat. The body stood out of the water close to the height of *Research II*'s cabin, extending forward and backwards beyond my vision. It was like a dark island emerging from the sea, truly a monster of the deep, an ocean traveler with journeys to its credit that would the great submarines of our nuclear age. Was it not here in the north Atlantic just on a seasonal visit for the summer? And in a few months, it would rise among the icebergs in South Georgia, the Antarctic where it made its corresponding summer home in the southern hemisphere.

With realization that a friend had come to visit me, a calm overcame me, like the stillness of the ocean night and the assured equanimity of the leviathan a few feet from the boat.

I called gently, 'Is that you?'

Was I dreaming? Was I just imagining it, a short silence, a pause, and then a kind of whistling sound! I was caught in an experience that words could not describe. I was overwhelmed by a consciousness of kinship with this gentle giant, this visitor in the space of the ocean vastness right beside me. I could not help feeling small, dwarfed by his physical presence. How graphically I, as a human, was cut down to size in physical comparison. And yet it seemed that we both had communion which no language could transcribe. Time is hard to keep track of when our experience is vivid and all-embracing. For me, the experience had a transcendent quality that omitted the very relevance of time. There was no haste, no nervous reaction. How long we communed together, no clock, no monitor could record. Then without fuss, the largest of God's creatures on our planet heaved his mighty body in a kind of swelling motion. The phosphorescent luminous light reappeared, recreated by the motion of his body and streamed towards me, stirring the calm sea, a greenish tinge in it, resembling the composite wave from a ship at speed. Researc*h II* rocked visibly to port. The luminous light reformed into a single broad snake of phosphorescence as the whale submerged beneath. I watched as it passed away from my boat and disappeared into the darkness.

The thoughts of a loner

Here was my friend who came to see me, far out in mid-Atlantic. No human being had spoken to me for a month from this day. But (Patrick) who had met me earlier some two weeks ago, was back to see me. It gave me a tremendous feeling that he had taken me under his care, that he was keeping an eye on me. Moreover my thinking went further. Was he sent as a messenger, a servant of our common Creator, the governor of the universe and maker of all, just to see how I was getting on? Or, to reassure me that I was not alone? Some would dismiss this thinking as imagination. But that could not nullify the good feeling that pervaded my being, the reassurance of belonging and the sense of oversight of a loving God. There is ground for believing that in the lonely vastness of the ocean, where one human being sailed alone out of the 6 billion inhabitants of our crowded planet, that co-existent communion was, in this shared experience, a justifiable interpretation.

What a train of thought this leads to! God has his messengers who do his bidding on land but also on the high seas. And his love to us, as the children of mankind, in spite of our sinful denial of our true happiness, is still the same and endures forever as he himself is eternal.

That love is clothed with mercy, redeeming, forgiving love. It means that we are preserved for the time appointed when God himself ordains that we leave this island planet in space. Then we become united through Christ in the enduring Covenant of Redemption that is sealed with His blood, so that we share forever an inheritance, a spiritual inheritance with the redeemed in glory.

'Goodbye *Padruig*, goodbye.' Maybe I'll see you again, if not in the immediacy of time, maybe in the renewed world and the dimension of the eternal. Goodbye.'

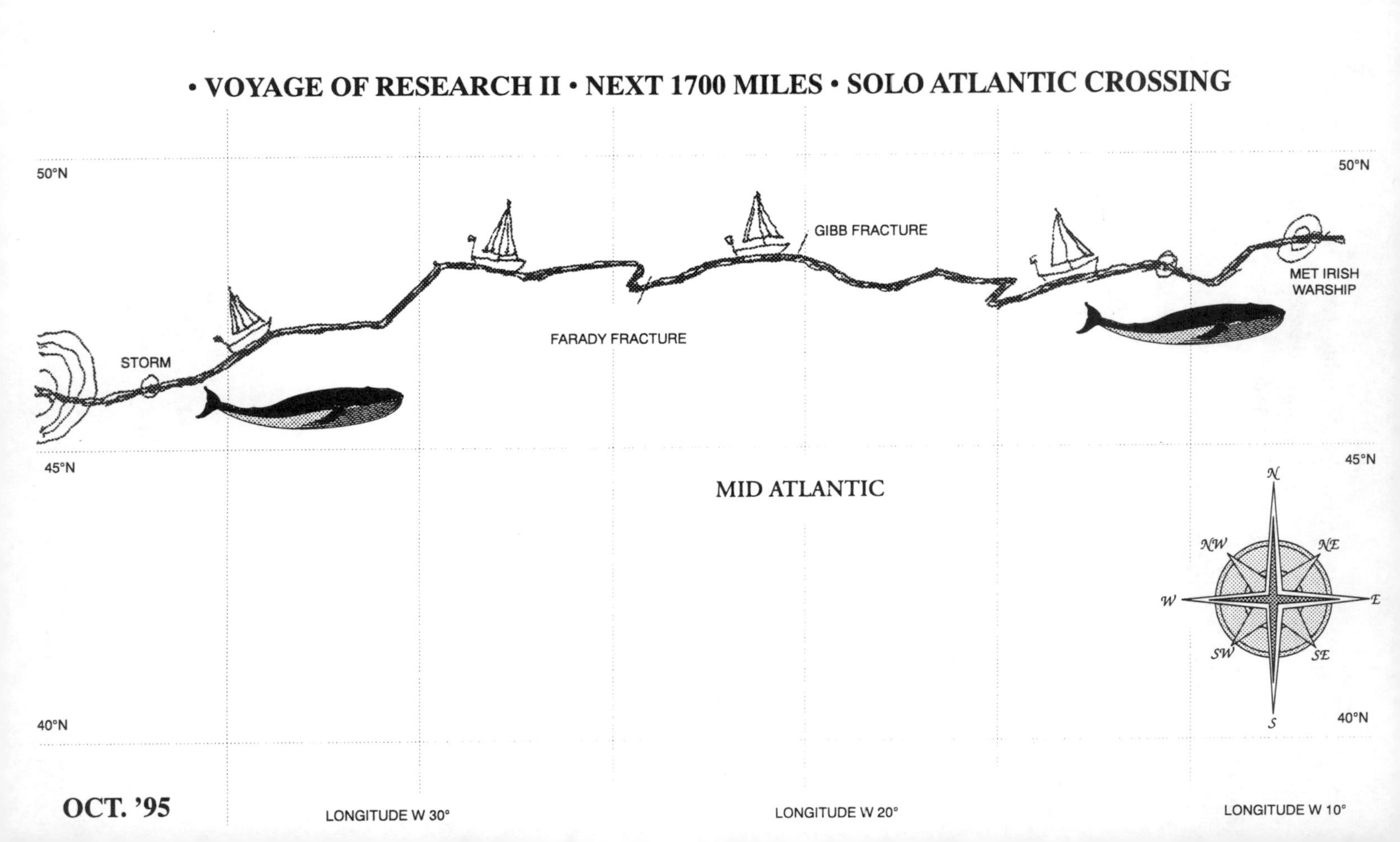
• VOYAGE OF RESEARCH II • NEXT 1700 MILES • SOLO ATLANTIC CROSSING
50°N
50°N
GIBB FRACTURE
MET IRISH
WARSHIP
FARADY FRACTURE
STORM
45°N
45°N
MID ATLANTIC
N
NW
NE
W
E
SW
SE
S
40°N
40°N
OCT. '95
LONGITUDE W 30°
LONGITUDE W 20°
LONGITUDE W 10°

PART IV

North Atlantic - European Side

CHAPTER 15

The "*Cianalas*"

Log: Day 30, Saturday 22nd, July, 1995

I slept fitfully for several hours, after a breeze at last whispered from the southwest. Two ships were visible though not near me. Their lights disappeared before I went below. As a rule I always stayed up when a ship's light was in the vicinity. With the southwest now a working wind, I raised the main, swinging *Research II* around from her maverick course, so that she now ambled along easily at about 4 knots. I slacked the jib and let the mainsheet right out, giving *Research II* her liberty to find a comfortable course northwards, with the Pole star about 10 o'clock on my starboard bow. I watched until there was constancy, standing up at the stern rail, adjusting Stanley and his headgear accordingly. Notice that I had to have some speed on the boat before resetting the Scull-Oar to make it function effectively in keeping us on course.

Morning

About 4 a.m. by my watch, still on Eastern Maritime time, the sun was up in the northeast. I tended the sails. The wind was light but constant. The sky was clear with only a few clouds, to keep us guessing and keep us humble. *Research II* ambled on hopefully for a long time, steadily reaching towards the northeast. I stress that it was essential to achieve the goal of getting up to the 48' W latitude, and indeed even further to the 49' latitude, before I came into the approaches to the English Channel.

Log/Journal note: I've just looked out. The wind has freshened as it does often in the morning. *Research II* registers 3.5 to 4.5 knots on the knotmeter.

GPS Reading:

Position: N 47' 24" W 18' 14"

Time: 18.87 (Eastern US)

Reflections

One fact about this life at sea alone is indisputable. There is plenty time for a person to commune with himself, and explore reflectively, his relation to his environment, and the teleological significance, reason for being, or just plain purpose of his life. I said that there is plenty time for this reflection. But, for me, I did very little thinking of this philosophic structured nature. I was in many ways like an engine that was switched off. Thinking, in the dimension of the spiritual, came to a standstill. Even my Gaelic Bible, I left unopened, its damp pages clinging together, sealed and unopened. My mind was literally taking a vacation.

All construction of premise and perceived truths or insights, and the logical stories of subjective tenets built up in the precarious edifices of our own making, came to a standstill the day I took off from the Canadian shore. You might say that with this passive state, I no longer imposed or projected my thinking, from my own fortified and strongly held positions, outward upon my environment. Rather, I, in turn, was like a blank page or a clean slate so that new impressions were made inwards upon my mind. It is thus that I record what the sea says to me, what the sky says to me, what the life in its varied forms of whale or little bird says to me. I do not impinge upon the ocean. The ocean impinges upon me.

Perfection

What contrasting imagery speaks to us from sea and sky and the varied life forms of nature that make both sky and sea their habitat! I think of the dark sky, the mountainous seas, the angry waves, the foaming crests hitting *Research II*, demanding of every ounce of resolution and endurance. And here at the moment, it is impossible to ignore the glory of this day, a scintillating panorama of sea and sky, matching together in perfect symmetry and coordinates of colour, a masterpiece of aesthetic taste which stirs within me a sense of unsullied perfection.

Couple this with a wind that fills the sails and brings a gurgle of merriment to the forefoot of the bow, that perfection extends beyond our worth to deserve, and humbles us in a sense of God's goodness and his benevolent presence.

I wanted to raise the big genoa which would give greater pulling power, but sadly I cannot do this. The peak of the jib extension has become fouled in the shroud, so that the jib cannot come down fully. It has two positions now, one fully up, and one quarter up. It just will not come down further. I have to be thankful as things are. It could be worse. If the genoa was up, and weather came on, it would bring potential trouble if we were taken unawares. And this was a habit especially in sudden blasts from the north and east. Further, just to gain one or two knots, it would mean putting an extra strain on gear which even now was far short of perfect condition.

Continued Vigilance

Your life depends on continual checking of all fittings on the boat and to do with the propulsion, the mast and its support. Huge pressures are put on bolts, twisting forces demand daily examination of cotter pins and clevis pins. Shackles and rigging screws, forks and eyes have to be continually watched. Strength in metals is linked closely with tempering. The harder the metal is, the stronger it is, but at the same time the forces that act upon it, if out of line, can make the metal part snap. This happened to the second forestay. Gale force winds over two days and nights jerked the luff sideways, causing the stainless steel fork on the turnbuckle to snap. Again, if the metal is soft, it gives scope to bend instead of break. But then it has far less strength. The block on the spreader, to which the radar reflector was attached when I left Canada, simply disintegrated. Again this was only after the constant stresses during one gale. The fitting was made of soft brass. The gudgeon rod, over half an inch in diameter, which I put on as a replacement for the stainless steel original that was worn, was made of copper. Having less strength than brass, it failed in the storm.

Sudden forces jerk sails, shrouds and the very boat itself into violent spasms of stress. In addition, the frequency of this in the darkness of the night with real and imagined terrors - you can understand how eternal vigilance is called for. There is a kind of animal instinct latent in us all, which is triggered off, that is, hopefully, when life depends on ourselves and our own alertness.

This came home to me today. The sun shone since the morning, its rays reaching over the ocean in a wide arc of life-giving energy. The southwest wind blew consistently, and pushed *Research II* along NE by East. Relaxed, I was in the cabin, listening to the news about the sad chronic bleeding of broken-up Yugoslavia and the proposed extended air-raids by the UN on the Bosnian Serb positions. I heard a new sound from above. It sounded like a rattle. In a flash I was out on deck. My eye searched the boom and the gooseneck by which it swiveled on the mast. The boat at the time was heeled to port. No nut, bolt, washer or any other metal part was to be seen, which might have fallen on the deck. I took a closer look at the gooseneck on the starboard side, that vital hinge that carried the boom with the mainsail. Yes, there was the nut as clear as ever still on the three eighth inch throughbolt. I was puzzled. I could not think of any other fitting from which a nut or other metal part could have loosened and fallen on deck to cause the rattle. I concluded that it was a false alarm.

Some three hours later I was on deck and looked forward. The mainboom appeared askew. At the same time I saw that the throughbolt was missing. The strain on the mainsail was tremendous, as the wind tugged, trying to tear it apart. I could see that it was held only by the track slide. That could soon be pulled apart. Had this happened at night, the sail could have been ripped apart and even the mast track bent, before I would have known what was wrong. I was just fortunate to be on deck at this time, having finished turning R*esearch II* back on course from one of her wandering excursions, this time to the north west. When you think of it, I suppose the boat was bored after two days, day and night on the same course. The question is, how did I not notice something wrong three hours earlier when I heard the rattle on the deck above the cabin? There were two reasons.

One, the nut could have bounced overboard to the lee. Second, last time I fitted the gooseneck, I put the bolt in from the starboard side of the boom instead of the usual way from the port. I forgot that I had done this. Therefore, when I looked at the starboard side, expecting to see if the nut was on securely, what I saw was the head of the throughbolt. Had I checked the other side, I would have found that the nut and washer were missing. Fortunately both of these, which had caused the rattle, were trapped at the gunwale. Soon they were back in place and I gave thanks.

Another instance involved risk to my life. As you can well imagine, if one should fall overboard, there is really no chance of getting aboard again in rough seas. I might have had a chance some ten or twenty years earlier, even then only on inland, relatively sheltered waters like the Great Lakes. But it was nil chance of ever getting on board out here in the cold inhospitable North Atlantic - in its pitching unforgiving seas. Moreover I was habitually dressed at night and, for the most part, every day in three sweaters and oilskins. Even though you were wearing a Hayward Safety harness or its equivalent, you would have little or no chance, as you were dragged alongside in protracted futility. One yacht designer attempted to find a solution, especially with the increase in freeboard in recent design in the late 70's. He cut holes or notches in the outer edge of the rudder blade to act as steps for an overboard sailor to climb back up on board. The fact that this has not caught on, in subsequent and the latest yachts designs, nullifies it as a popular remedy. At the same time, it should be considered by solo sailors especially.

Meanwhile, back to the point I was making, the life threatening occasion. Just as I was lowering myself down the companionway, a glance at the lifeline riveted my attention on the turnbuckle. The securing clevis ring was missing. I could hardly believe it but there it was before my eyes, the recipe for disaster. Shame on me, as I looked at its sister turnbuckle on the opposite side. The clevis pin there also was missing. The painful conclusion hit me, that I had traveled a month into the Atlantic without these turnbuckles being secured by a clevis pin or an endless ring. I trembled physically at the possible scenario as I crawled over the wave-washed pitching deck so often in the darkness of the night, my hand always reaching for the feel of the reassuring lifeline, as my last guarantee of safety. I needed no carping critic to condemn me. I was humbled there in self conviction of my negligence. At the same time I lifted my heart to heaven and acknowledged the mercy and forbearance of my Lord and my God. Surely God is good to us all, long-suffering and slow to wrath, patient and forbearing in the face of our weaknesses, and plenteous in his mercies, which he presents to us as new every morning along with his faithfulness every night.

Before the Wind

I was very encouraged by the conduct of Stanley, the Scull-Oar. Here we are rolling onward with a following southwesterly wind. The main boom is fully out on the beam. The jib gets an occasional push back into its place to the wind. This equilibrium is all due to Stanley the Scull-Oar. It is true that the sea is perfect just now for this high performance, presenting a relatively uniform surface and accompanied by a steady breeze. And above, is a cloudless sky. There is no sign of the waiting beasts, the lurking rogue waves, which at other times, sneak in to throw *Research II* off course and cancel out Stanley's efficiency. However, though we cannot help being gratified by Stanley's now proven performance, we cannot be complacent or presumptive. Another day will present a new configuration which, in turn, will require a different answer, searching out the weakness of the handicapped boat, and the limitations of its captain and robot mate. May this day continue with these favorable conditions. May tomorrow, man's own special day for renewal, be a day of rest and peace, that I remember man's Creator and Redeemer and join with folks in churches across the globe, in worship and thanksgiving for all his mercies.

As I reflect upon the catholicity of the church, beyond the local and provincial fences of denomination and historic tradition, I recall a service some thirty-five years ago, held not far from where I sail at this time. It was a combined service on the Canadian Pacific Liner, the Empress of Canada. We were out from Greennock some two days and bound for Montreal. The service was conducted by her captain. That service and the praise we all engaged in, on the morning of the Sabbath, was an assertion both of God's sovereignty over the whole earth, and also an affirmation of our faith as human beings who saw life fulfilled in redemptive communion with him through Christ Jesus, our risen Lord and King of kings.

The "Cianalas"

That is the Gaelic for 'homesickness.' Now waves of this came over me as it would a schoolboy leaving his loving home for the next term, at a school far away. This *Cianalas* is inexorable, a heavy insistent pervasive nostalgia, that stays over the spirit, like a lingering fog on a windless day. All the associations of warmth and love, of kindred and friendship, of places and people, past and present, come before me as on a stage. Yet they are distant from me, and I am separated from them as if by an unbridgeable divide. I think of Mary, my ever beautiful wife, who is the epitome of the Gaelic song,

'Ho, ro, mo nighean donn bhoidheach.
(Ho, ro my dark haired maiden)

I just miss her. I wonder how she, her sister, Agnes, and our daughter, Jane, are getting on in Paris! All kinds of like thoughts come to me. I just cannot shake off this feeling. I recognize it as something I felt at several times in my life before. It is the direct impact upon us, when we are separated from the circle of dear ones and the places that have become home to us.

But I thrust reason into the argument. I project positive data to counter the negatives. I think of God's kindness to me in Providence, his protecting care, and above all his own presence which sweetens my spirit and renews my mind. How thankful I ought to be for all his goodness. Here I am without any need for air-conditioning, now considered a 'must' in most enclosed environments of work and even domestic dwellings. This is confirmed as I listen to Saturday morning's talk by that old and seasoned contributor of talks on radio about America, Alister Cook. On listening to him over the past month on Saturday mornings, when possible, he seems to get better as he gets older, like a good wine.

This morning he spoke of the unprecedented heat wave - well over 100° Centigrade - in the city of Chicago and also in New York, and the resultant deaths, numbered in the hundreds. And on the other side of the Atlantic for which I was heading, the BBC newscaster referred to the inordinately hot weather in London. I noticed that he quickly qualified his comments, by saying that for him and the rest of the BBC staff at Bush House, they had perfect cool air conditioning.

Yes, Mary, my sweetheart, you are probably suffering from the heat there, in Paris, too. For me the heat of the sun when it shines, is tempered by wind and sea. There is no crowding nor stuffiness.

I pause, as the fact sinks in further that there is no one, no human being, to alleviate the already sad feelings that the *Cianalas* has brought to my heart.

Log: Day 31, Sunday, 23rd July, 1995

Just a moment's glance back at last evening. All day the southwesterly wind blew, and we sailed close, or nearly so, before it. As night approached I studied the sky. I had to do so like reading a book to find out the weather, as I had no radio forecasts. Dark clouds patched the northern sky. To the west, banks of precipitation bordered the horizon. I looked and knew instinctively that weather can quickly backtrack in an anti-sun direction, that is west to east - as a rule a bad sign. I should like to have the barometer reading, but the needle just won't budge since the barometer took an airborne trip across the cabin some time previously.

Pause: I returned below a few moments ago to pour myself a big hot cup of morning coffee.

Back to the subject of last evening. My conclusion was that the weather would be settled, despite the threatening look of the north and west. Somehow, even should the wind create problems, I had lost a considerable amount of weight and was a changed man indeed, who now could swiftly brave a stormy night on the wet heaving deck, feeling my way like a cat in the inky darkness. Fortunately the night did remain quiet. I left all the cares of the day and of the night, the continual attendance on the ship and preoccupation with its welfare and performance. Yes, I left them all in the hands of God, our Heavenly Father. After a cup of tea with my favorite blueberry jam, biscuits and cheese spread, I rolled into my sleeping bag under the hatch, and off I dropped into a good night's slumber. Always, as I did so, I checked to make sure that the masthead navigation lights were on. The others on deck at the bow, I regarded as useless on the ocean.

A review of Sundays

I now have been over a month on my journey to Britain. Modern man travels, using the air as the road between the continents. Yet the road of the ocean needs no airfields but brings its users to every corner of the earth, with the sideroads of its river estuaries, already there before sophisticated ports and docks were introduced by the merchants of Venice in the Middle Ages, to service their deep cargo carrying traders. For me, I can stop off at the roadside of the English Channel highway, any where along its length, a decision, which will be made when I pass Land's End, the official goal of my voyage. Sundays are the markers of our time, representing the reasonable pause which the human being needs after a week of exertion.

In an irrational attempt to distance themselves from the Christian Church, the French, after their Revolution in 1790, changed the week from 7 to 10 days. It all sounds reasonable following the metric pattern as in other measurements of time and volume. But it did not work. Just as utilitarian communism didn't work because it did not correspond with the human spirit, so the French experiment failed. Soon they were back on track on the seven day week. It is a marvel how little narrow minds that cannot see with the three-dimensional perspective of the physical, spiritual and social, are so bigoted that they cannot bear to acknowledge the premise of Biblical wisdom. The Creator made all things that relate to our senses in segments of seven periods, where time is specified not in measurable definition, but the division of seven parts. Somehow, as the religious tradition, it has been shown to suit the physiology of man in his personal life and in the community.

It was therefore reasonable for me to treat the Sundays as special. I often did a lot of work, but I did not think God frowned upon me for that. I believe he would look with disfavor upon me if I used that day for idleness and neglect, and made his day an excuse for laziness. In fact, Sunday provided a day when we can review the week that has passed. We can, as it were, take stock. We need to take an inventory of our resources. How much have been expended? We check to see how much stock we still have on the shelves, the spiritual stock that we all must use to cope with life and rely upon for every duty and circumstance. It is good to use Sundays to check our access to our sources in the store house, the warehouses of God's mercies, the many promises of heaven. That is all in the Word of God. I personally have found that the Psalms are the outlet, the shopping plaza where we can walk around and see the varied goods of heaven, displayed in the different psalms, in the working experiences that they reflect.

We all have memory banks. It is good, on Sundays especially, to recall those we cherish as a blessing in our lives and if we cannot read the Word or worship with others in church, we can still bring out one of heaven's blessed treasures. And even in the middle of the ocean, yes in the violence surrounding one in a cramped little cabin, we can open the parcel of God's provision and have a feast for our soul. The Psalmist said that he hid the Word of God in his heart, and that this was sweet to him, sweeter than honey.

1. Thanksgiving

I look back at the notes in the Log at the beginning of my voyage, when I left Canada. That first Sunday comes back to me. I had been two nights out on my voyage, with a gale from the north west. There was a blanket of fog which funneled down from the Cabot Strait between Nova Scotia and Newfoundland. Then came Sunday, my first. I quote:

Tranquil, after the gale. The Lord be praised. He kept me safe and all the gear held as we sailed by day and especially through the dark watches of the night. The Psalmist expressed his confidence in God and the debt he owed to God's loving care.

> *'I laid me down and slept. I waked and the Lord sustained me.'*

2. Reflection

I look back on the next Sunday, the 2nd of July 1995. Fog and sun mingled together in a haze as *Research II* slowed down during the day from 6-7 knots of the previous night in the fresh southwesterly. Sunday brings a welcome respite from the exacting demands of the boat. This made me think of loved ones.

I thought of Mary, my wife now for 33 years. Mary Stewart, the dark Celtic beauty, with traces of Spanish blood, going back to shipwrecked mariners from Spain's Armada that failed to get back home to Spain in 1588. Many hundreds of shipwrecked seamen settled in the Outer and Inner Hebrides - often themselves of Celtic blood from the Basque country. My mind dwelt on her, remembering when I fell in love with her, and in my heart knowing she was mine. I recall during our courtship, being in Prince Edward Island for the church. That separation was a test. It convinced me that she was mine for life - unless of course she left me. But Mary stayed with me for better or for worse and she is still my wife. She is now in Nova Scotia and will soon be going to Paris with my daughter Jane. I recall being in the marina cafeteria during a trip with Norman, my son, on the St. Laurence. Mary was off to Paris at that time too, some six years earlier.

This Frenchman from Quebec with whom I was conversing, on hearing Mary was in Paris, tried to convince me that she would be off with a Frenchman from Paris and that I was unlikely to see her again. But he was mistaken. Mary came back. More thoughts came to me, some happy and some very sad. There are many nostalgic thoughts of regret in the album of memory. The negative ones that are linked to pain and sorrow, failure and spiritual blindness, we leave them at the Mercy Seat where they are met by God's redeeming and forgiving love. We have suffered less than our iniquities deserve. God has chastised us but this is a sign of his love to us. Then we think of Christ in the prophetic words of his redemptive work, 'Surely he have borne *our griefs, and carried our sorrows.'* Therefore we will rejoice in Him.

3. Persistence

Sunday, 9th July, 1995. I look at the chart and trace the path of the storm, Barry, as it left the Caribbean area and made its way northeast into the Atlantic. It has left its aftermath still visibly felt in the sea conditions about me. A storm is a great circle of dynamic energy like a giant whirlwind. The centrifugal forces that give it the corkscrew effect, widen out to an amplified diameter and the forces so generated still act in a great circle, a long way from the storm centre and for many days afterwards. I recall being in a Highland congregation in Kilchoan in Argyll, Scotland. The Hydro power was not then connected to the community. At the manse was a long stroke, water cooled Lister diesel driving the 5 kilowatt generator. The engine was switched off automatically as the last light was switched off at night. I would listen to be assured that the engine stopped. It was in a shed near the house. The engine did not stop immediately. Rather, it continued making revolutions for quite some time, before the stored energy in the massive flywheel eventually was expended.

It's the same with this tropical storm, Barry, which was identified well to the south of me. The outer circle of its power met us from the west and northwest. The seas whipped up by the storm have left a legacy of residual and disturbing motion, driving a boat this way and that. The aftermath still is clearly experienced as we journey east. The whole spectrum of sky and sea are still the theatre of the storm's fury. The wind is not strong now from the northwest, but the seas are a mosaic of mighty hills and valleys, the proof of the monolithic forces that stirred the ocean, as you would stir a pan of soup on the kitchen stove. As I look through the perspex window towards the stern, the broken rudder and tiller stand there, in their idle impotence as testimony to the storm's fury. But we have not given in. We will continue and win. Everything around me is soaking wet. Water still comes aboard and finds its way below. Plenty bailing when I can. There is a continual rocking, so that the portholes plunge under the water on the lee. A sound like a heavy hammer hits the quarter. Peace becomes relative, a redefined relic of land life, only faintly identifiable as having any real meaning. It could be classified as an ephemeral appendix, a distant curio from the landsman's parameters.

But persistence will enable us to prevail. We have survived the might of a storm so far. I had no sleep for 36 hours, and exhaustion and weariness, without eating a meal for two days, erodes the resolution. There is the temptation to give in, to stop bailing and let everything go. As the storm closed in, and the second ship, the big red ore carrier hove to, there was the temptation to light a flare, or just wave a distress sign. The ship lingered there, watching me. And I could not help thinking of its warmth and security, its comfort and human company. I had a natural yearning for human company, craving for the chance to eat a meal and curl up and sleep.

But temptation we all get. Resolution shuts this out so that resolution, persistence and positive thinking win. The second week is over. What is in store for us, we do not know. Only that 2500 miles have yet to be sailed to reach the English Channel. I have yet to grasp fully that there is no rudder to steer. But that is a challenge that we will answer and with God's help we will prevail.

I was encouraged, listening to the service from London on the World Service of the BBC, when the Jazz minister was preaching. I blend the gist of his message with my own thinking. Our life is full of contrasts. Just as peace and calms are not constants, neither are storms and bad experiences. They alternate. The night with its darkness, its sorrow, its pain, its tears, its anguish, its shame, its regrets, does not last. The morning comes and the brightness of the day with its warmth, its joy, its hope, its encouragement, its smile, its opportunities. Hold fast to your faith, hold on to the hem of the coat of Christ. Do not let go whatever you are going through, whatever forces seek to destroy you from within yourself or from without. There is an end to bad things. The morning cometh.

I was refreshed and renewed by this marshalling of my spiritual forces. Persistence reveals that bad things come to an end. They pass if we sit tight and challenge them. This persistence is given substance in a practical way. Even though you were a saint out here and prayed non-stop huddled in the cabin, what good would that do? It would be the same as a bull charging at you in a field and you getting on your knees to pray. I doubt if the bull would be impressed. The virtues of man's spirit, like persistence, must translate into action. If not, they evaporate like forgotten resolutions at the turn of the year.

Thus I pegged it down to a practical positive program.

My energies concentrated on a simple three point formula, which I had worked out and used to sort out work to be done in the course of a day as a minister.

1. **Identify purpose**: Namely to overcome handicap and complete the voyage under my own steam.
2. **Give this definition**: Deploy Autosails; explore capabilities of the Scull-Oar.
3. **Dynamic direction**: This is vital; to get the sustaining power to overcome, I have to be strengthened in mind and body and spirit. I will keep my mind renewed, drinking the living waters that I draw by faith from heaven, to nurture my resolution and give dynamic strength to all my efforts.

Here is a test for the Scull-Oar, the Auto-Sails, and my spiritual faith.

The Jazz minister spoke of HOPE, as persistent in human beings. For me, two days of storm and still today bailing 5 buckets of water already seem little reason to entertain much hope. But hope springs eternal. It is like a weed that keeps coming up between the flagstones in the garden path. Hope, if we nourish it, will not be denied. And when we say it is eternal, we speak of its intrinsic nature as it rests on the redemptive facts of the Finished Work of Christ. For that hope entertained by the 'chief of sinners', as St. Paul designated himself and as is also true of me, converts into life eternal. It is the antidote to all fears and makes us, even now, 'more than conquerors through him that loved us.'

4. Anxiety

Sunday 16th July, 1995: Anxiety rises up in the most optimistic of us, for we can get worn down by adversity. When things go wrong or repeated efforts fail to succeed, we are tempted by that negative visitor with his suitcase full of doubts. If we let this visitor in the door, we are finished. But it is bad enough if we accept a pamphlet from him, for when we read it, it may well undermine our resolution.

I wanted to rest and hoped that I could spend a quiet day. But anxiety kept intruding so that this was not possible. Remember how we are told in the Book of Nehemiah the governor in charge of the returned exiles to Judah, that as the Hebrews worked restoring the house of God in Jerusalem, Tobiah sought to undermine their resolution by a bombardment of verbal propaganda. Nehemiah and Ezra sought to encourage the people in the good work and not to worry, because God was with them. And did not the Lord while on earth tell his disciples not to be anxious for anything, but to rest their confidence in our Heavenly Father and trust in the certainty of His goodwill?

Yet the temptation to be anxious was there and with some practical foundation. Re*search II* was going at a good speed - just think of it, 6 knots. I had left the jib up too long. Now I worried that it would soon fall apart. And I had to face it, the alternative of my own auto-sails was a limited one. They were not ruggedly made with double stitching and reinforced corners. They would stand up to the wear and tear of day and night sailing, for only a limited time. And a succession of gales could well finish them. A second cause for concern was the not infrequent rogue waves that now developed in the increased seas. When hit suddenly by one of these, the boat would heel right over until the gunwale was awash and very heavy stresses would threaten a breakage of gear.

I gave thought to all this and then I said to myself,

'Look, speed isn't everything. Finishing is what counts. Watch and care for your gear so that nothing breaks. Accept when the wind is too strong. Even heave to if you have to. Let her head off course, if it means easing the strain on gear. You have plenty of water and food. This is mid-summer. Give yourself time and enjoy your trip. Do not be the slave of the calendar or the clock. If Mary misses you let her miss you a bit longer, and that goes for yourself as well.'

I listened to this and thought that it made good sense. I pulled down the jib. Remarkably, with only a third of the area, we still romped onwards at a good 4 knots. Thus anxiety was neutralized by Christian philosophy, or plain down to earth common sense. And as a relevant analogy of our life, yours and mine, in the general circumstances which meet us from day to day, we can prove this formula works as well.

There you have it then, in our review of the past few Sundays, Thanksgiving, Reflection, Persistence, Anxiety and the way they fit into our life. And now today Sunday, 23rd July, 1995, after over four weeks at sea, we see it as a day, given to us for a real necessity, but one of enjoyment.

5. Relaxation

Research II is going along fine. For the previous few days there was a continual strain, trying to keep her from going southeast. By

God's grace she sails northeast and all by herself. All she asks is a mindful watch on the compass and every few hours an adjustment on the sheets. Just think of it, I haven't touched Stanley the steersman, for 24 hours. The sheets are slacked or tightened as the sails, however, do require occasional trimming.

This afternoon, while writing below in the cabin, I heard a loud crack. I suspected that it could be an electric short or blown fuse in the radios. Then *Research II* gave a definite list to starboard. I jumped up at once, making sure I left my glasses on the side shelf. Sure enough, we had jibed so that we were now heading NNW. There were two ships in sight and one was heading so that it would pass close to us, something I felt would be a welcome change - they might stop and give us some fresh food. But by the time I had *Research II* back on track, both ships had passed and were now a considerable way off. I felt a pang of disappointment. I surmised that they did not notice or chose to notice that my boat was sailing without the rudder down. Anyway, they sailed on, each in the opposite direction. Good luck to them. We will journey on. We are assured. We'll do it ourselves. This confirmed me that I would not seek any help from a ship, until we reached port with our rudderless boat. Had a ship stopped, it would be a little matter for a half inch steel rod to be cut the 2 feet length required for a substitute gudgeon pin to commission the rudder. I had the wood for a tiller already aboard if the rudder were in service.

Good feeling

I feel as if we have entered on another phase of our voyage, one I had hoped for, namely sailing before a steady southwesterly. How long this will last, I cannot predict, but hope looks for good things. This is a great life, I think. What relaxation, no chores, only airing the linen on deck in the warm rays of the sun. We all need periods of relaxation. Life wears us out. Even as thoughts on this occupied my mind, I felt uplifted at the happy incidence of God's favour repeatedly shown to me so far. I had visions of all the trials and tribulations and losses of sailors over the centuries who often never came back from the sea to their homes and loved ones.

I rested my mind on God's mercies and loving kindnesses so bountifully demonstrated even in the beauty of nature around me. I marveled at the wideness of the ocean, the glory of the cloudless sky, the matchless rays of the sun. What a foundation for peace and relaxation. Well, might I join with the Psalmist and all who have his perspective;

> *'Surely goodness and mercy have followed me, all*
> *the days of my life.*
> *And I will dwell in the house of the Lord forever.'*

Log: Sunday, 23rd July

Position Reading:	East 105'	Track 99'
Speed:	4.2 knots	
	N 47' 57"	W 15' 18"
Time:	18.24 (US Eastern Time)	

CHAPTER 16

A Battle of Wills

Log: Day 32, Monday, 24th July, 1995

Two days of exquisite weather gave *Research II*, its captain and its crew, a steady diet of ocean sailing at its best. But by 11 p.m. last night the outlook had changed. Clouds now filled the skies. The stars in their jeweled splendor disappeared, like the inky blue carpet in which they were set.

Grey and black are the colours of trouble. Wisps of cloud heralded something. I did not look for a storm. But, there just had to be a reaction to all that heat and stable southwesterlies that had blown for the past two days.

Some time before this I had resorted to the cabin to sleep, hoping for the best. Sleep came fitfully, and then I dreamed that all was not well. It all was graphically clear. I heard a voice in the cabin. The words were clearly articulated,

'What's that? You had better go and see.' It was the voice of my wife Mary.

I replied calmly, 'All right Mary, I think I should.'

I got up and as I left the companionway, I glanced down. No, I didn't see Mary in the shadows. But I found it very hard to believe that she was not there. There was a powerful sense of her being there in spirit. It was almost natural for me to feel this. We always were close all these thirty-three years. On deck, I saw at once that *Research II* had jibed.

With a long struggle I got her back on course. To do this, I backed the jib to the wind at the same time slacking the main. Then at the crucial moment, grabbing the boom vang, I swung the main to port. How many times I tried I cannot tell. But at length, I managed it. I just made it. I pressed the boom against the wind and pushed until I was leaning over the life-line, and lo, as the bow turned around, so the pressure on me was released. What a triumph of will. I had gotten her around once more. You see, there was a problem here. If you played it safe you stayed near the mast and pushed the boom around. In that way, you would not be in danger of being thrown overboard, should you slip or a gust force you back. The trouble is, when playing safe like that, you had little leverage as the point to which you applied pressure was too near the fixed point of the gooseneck.

The alternative by which you generated much greater force was to grab the boom near the outside end or tack and run across the deck with all your might. If it worked you ended up hanging right over the side with your feet caught in the lifeline. *Research II* demanded of me that I practice this aquatic acrobatics, sometimes several times a day and in the night, and sometimes trying for two hours or longer until I succeeded. There was no question of giving up. Often I had to take a rest and if I felt weakened by the prolonged effort, and discouraged, I then would go below and make a cup of coffee. I would say to myself, 'I'll get her round yet. Help me God, my heavenly Father.' I then stopped dwelling on the problem and enjoyed my coffee.

After this break, having finished my coffee, I went straight into battle again. This was done with studied thought. Timing was of primary importance, and wave and wind were weighed and considered. Speed was then vital. Hands deftly worked the sheets, my eye fixed on the sails, then every successive movement in the sequence followed. I developed a remarkable agility that continued to surprise myself. There was always the danger accompanying the bolder action, that you might be thrown right back, and over the other side into the sea. The sail where it met the boom made it very difficult to keep a firm grip that would hold you, hanging over the sea. And as I perceived on several abortive occasions, had I not let go in time, the boom would have been near the water with me in the sea, as the wind pushed *Research II* over to the lee. Little wonder that my fingernails were worn smooth and short with this unorthodox manicure.

The sweetness of winning

Having now been at sea for over a month, I was very much used to the different situations that would meet me. Also, though life had often arduous demands that taxed me close to the limits of my strength, they blended in with a sense of rhythm and enjoyment. Enjoyment and exultant buoyancy often were dominant when we rode the white horses and *Research II* heeled, burying her rail, with spray drenching her captain. Joy, peace, and happiness should not be bracketed off as the connotation of lovely, mild, sunny, favorable winds and moderate seas.

Such times were welcome. But often the converse was true, where the human spirit reveled in the brinkmanship of latent danger, and exhilaration made the adrenaline flow, when *Research II* showed her colours and went through her paces, proving what stuff she was made of, with the needle passing 7, 8, and several times 9 knots on the knotmeter.

But I cannot predict the future. I cannot assume that my spirits will be buoyant. I have found that I am kept humble and dependent upon daily spiritual power from heaven. At this present time, the night has fully come, the seas are uneven and very big, the wind surly and inconstant. Heavy gusts heel *Research II* and breaking crests climb aboard to wash the cabin top and decks. No wonder they stay so beautiful and clean.

More than I asked for

Log/Journal notes: (I write next day)

The night was on me. I knew intuitively that there would be no rest. I had closed the hatch, willing the uneasiness to go away. I rebelled against the draining, taxing hours that comprised deck work in the pitching motion of my little boat, all in the darkness of a moonless night.

Suddenly I felt drained. Free for a while as the boat surged onward to the east, my knees became weak. I gasped for breath. But there was to be no respite. I was thrown across the cabin as the boat jibed in the darkness. I hastened into the cockpit, lifting myself out of the cabin with my hands. I fell into the cockpit just as a composite of black, green and white phosphorescent water poured over the cockpit coaming to the lee.

Research II had done it again. She had changed course and was now scudding northwest. With the wind now rising in vicious gusts, instinct told me there was danger latent, like deadly nightshade lurking in the darkness of the night. My teeth met and my jaws clamped together in grim determination and deliberate steely resolution of will as I gathered my resources. My left leg was numb like a wooden stick so that I dragged it after me rather than relied upon it. This would be a battle of wills. I calmed myself, breathing systematically until I felt my body primed for the fight. My muscles had never let me down before and something of my boyhood pride in the explosive strength I used to prove, now came back to me with a kind of wicked reckless defiance. My intuition was right. There would be no sleep for me this night.

Watching for my chance

Deliberately I set about bringing my boat to the course of my will. I sheeted in the jib and main, glancing at the lights of a ship some distance away. How shall I tell you in words the drama of that hour? I watched for my chance. How can one watch in the pitch darkness of a starless night? The answer is found here on the ocean, as it is found and illustrated in many situations on land, namely, teamwork. The fact is that I was one with the boat. We were bonded together by weeks of coping with adversity. I, at times, saved the boat. The boat at times took the knocks and saved me. One could not do without the other. Each was indispensable for the survival of the other. The boat had heard my groans, and my cries to heaven in many a crisis. I, in turn, knew my boat, my beloved boat that kept me afloat. I knew its moods, its eccentricities, its foibles, as a wife knows her husband's and as a husband knows his wife's.

In this relationship, my perceptions were more than sensory. My mind, pushed to ultra-alertness, served as a signal of cognition that brought my motor reflexes to act with dynamic dexterity. The sequence must be smooth, the timing must be perfect. You could not slip or fumble; once you begin, you have to follow through. There can be no faltering, no hesitation. There is always the right moment, like a boxer seeing his chance.

Above, I saw that the blanket of cloud was broken and there I could see the friendly Plough. The wind had now increased and *Research II* was heading northwest for Greenland at 5 knots. I had marshalled my resources, I knew what I had to do. My will now was on automatic. I had left the starting blocks as surely as a sprinter in an Olympic race.

I jerked the mainsheet, and with it in my hand I lay prostrate on the cabin top, almost vertically as *Research II* heeled to port. I pulled in the mainsheet bit by bit, my feet jammed for purchase on the gunwale and rail. Then I turned round the other way, raising myself so that my shoulder caught the boom. I bent double, pushing the boom until I was hanging over the weather rail. The boom stiffened and tried to push me back. I bent further with all my might. Then my breath would not come, my vision blurred, my knees buckled. I was jerked back by a vicious overwhelming force as the wind prevailed. My body dropped as my back arched backwards, and the jibing boom whizzed like a rocket over my head. It had missed me. I found myself drooping in an impotent heap with my arm hanging in the water over the lifeline, right at the double upright stanchion.

Coming to my senses

I lay still. Slowly I recovered myself. I was still alive. I'm still aboard, I said to myself. That's enough. The forces here are unequal. I remembered then, my friend, a marine engineer, Duncan MacPherson of Kyle, Rosshire, the gateway to the Isle of Skye. He would say,

'Angus my friend, you just do not win them all.'

The spirit is willing but the flesh is weak. I had lost the physical fight. *Research II* marched on northwards. Maybe she wanted to try and emulate Sir Humphrey Gilbert and sail through the Northwest passage round the north of Canada. Maybe she thought she could win where he failed! Reluctantly, but of necessity, I had to adopt the one of two other alternatives; reef the main or bring it down. I chose the latter. Within a short time, the main was lashed down and using the jib and Stanley the Scull-Oar, we were back on track going east.

I checked the speed and saw we were doing 4-5 knots, practically as fast as with the main up. The fact is that before the wind, main and jib compete. Now no main blotted out the wind from the jib, hence the speed.

The day has come, the morning has passed to noon of Monday, the 24th of July, and the 32nd day out. We go rolling on at 4-5 knots. I think forward. Our next goal is the Fastnet. Can you believe it? We will soon be in the longitude of Eire, Ireland, the Emerald Isle, the land of kings and fairies, the land of ancient heroes, of saints like Columba and Brendon; the land of gifted minds like that of Burke or Joyce; the land of poets like Yeats and Behan. And the mind turns to the present, and pain saddens us as we think of the contradictions in Ireland today. We think of the lives that have been broken by people's unwillingness to bend and live together in tolerance. Is it not true that this land like others has been exploited by aliens, both of church and state? That is why many of Erin's blood have left to live their lives on distant shores, especially in America.

Thinking of the Fastnet

God-willing, we may reach the Fastnet Longitude by Wednesday evening. That will be a landmark day, 34 days out from Sydney, reaching Ireland, sailing 2000 miles without a rudder. After that it is 5 longitudes to the Lizard. Now I believed that as shipping increases in the Approaches to the English Channel, planes of Coastal Command may be on patrol and visually notice my big rudder conspicuously pulled upright out of the water on deck. We have to wait and see. But that is not unreasonable to assume. There are bound to be aircraft patrolling the perimeter of the British Isles and the extremity of their maritime territory. Meantime, seas are very irregular and *Research II* surges and yaws left and right, but still pulls along before the southwest wind at a brisk pace. The sun comes out. Hopefully the blustery weather of the last 12 hours will moderate or evolve into a steady wind. But just to prove how contrary is the sea, as I stepped back into the cabin a wave hit the ship's side, climbed up the cabin and a bucket or more of salt water followed me below. Do you wonder why I pulled the hatch shut above me although the sun was out?

The Domestic Scene

On any voyage the cabin becomes home. If, as in my case, it is over the Atlantic, you cannot call in somewhere along the route for more supplies or to get repairs for items that won't work.

Some things are vitally necessary aboard. To start with you have to have hot food. *Research II* has a basic two-burner alcohol stove. I made gimbals for it some eight years ago. It has proved itself over that time. I have often marveled as it swung upright with a pan or kettle on it, while we were heeled and rocked by waves and wind. It has never failed me and its simplicity means total reliability without any sophisticated mechanism or electrical controls to go wrong. My son Norman and I had constant hot meals, day and night, in wind and in port, especially on our trip from Hamilton, at the west end of Lake Ontario, down the St. Lawrence, round the Gaspé Peninsula, along past the Magdalens, through the Cabot Strait and home to Sydney, Nova Scotia.

Food

I am a man of simple but eclectic and discriminating taste. I know what I want and do not care for any deviation from my choice. I speak of course with reference to food and in the context of a rather restricted menu. For me breakfast was cereal, with a preference for Scotch oatmeal brose, which I made three or four times a week. My blood pressure condition makes me wary of taking it more often as too rich a food. Brose is not porridge. Brose is made with a little meal, salt and boiling water left to set for two minutes with some lid over the bowl. Then taken with a little sugar and milk, you just can't beat it. You are ready for a full day's work on land or sea. Tea, coffee, Rye Vita in place of bread, Cape Breton cookies, cheese, marmalade, Blueberry jam, Digestive biscuits plus Ginger Snaps provide a good range of pleasant eating. Tins of Frasers, Campbells, Baxters stews, ham, salmon, beans, carrots; soups of beef, vegetable or chicken - these all get opened in turn. Another two basics are potatoes, and onions. I took two 10 lb. bags of potatoes aboard and two satchels of onions of the same weight. About every third day I would steam up a good panful of chopped up potatoes and onions in equal quantities all together. I ate this over three evening meals, with various stews, corned beef, ham and gravy and meat balls. And a few times I ate Vienna sausage, which was quite appetizing, at midday.

As a rule I omitted a cooked meal every 4th day, having instead some cold ham and beans, with fruit cocktail to follow. A bowl of hot tinned soup is to me a perfect lunch, or a tin of sardines which I always relish. Occasionally I might have both. I felt that there was no need of a cup of tea or coffee after this. Food is indispensable, I mean hot tasty meals. You take this regularly, cooking even when you are tired. If I anticipated bad weather or jobs to do on deck, or the likelihood of all night duty, I prepared for this by fueling up my body with energy, to make me feel warm and strong and confident that I could face anything.

I must acknowledge a debt to my wife Mary and daughter Jane who stocked *Research II*'s larder for the voyage. It's true that Mary consulted me so that the content of inventory coincided with my wishes. Otherwise I was relieved of responsibility in this vital respect. And would you believe it, every so often, I would open a plastic container and find a note from Mary to lift up my spirits and reassure me that she did not forget me though she was sunning herself in Paris.

If a soldier is known to march on his stomach, more so a sailor also sails on his stomach, especially if he sails by himself on a wild ocean. The three essentials are there, Faith in God, faith in his boat and faith in himself. God just cannot fail. The boat will not fail if it is nurtured and well found from the beginning. That leaves the loner. The ocean will strip the most confident as the millwright strips the bark of the tree. There is no selection. The person is what he is and what stuff he is made of will soon become apparent, whether softwood or hardwood. There the analogy changes. You may be weak and yet win against the sea, while strong men may fail. The reason is that the virtue that is needed to prevail is more than strength; spiritual, physical, or mental. The secret is resilience, the ability to adjust to the ever changing conditions and alternating tactics of wind and sea. Resilience enables us to let things be for a while. Then to come back, literally to make up the lost miles even if it be fifty in a day. Resilience enables you to bend, but not to be broken. And if you keep coming back, in the end you triumph. You just cannot fail. You win. For he who takes on the elements must have the stamina to stay the distance, as well as use all power of will and resolve to triumph. Only then, as with all endeavors that are undertaken, can he come at last in to port, at peace with the sea. And food is the basic fuel of his power. For without this physical reality, there can be no beginning of dynamic spiritual resourcefulness.

To the Celt, barley or oatmeal brose was the staple food of history, just like rice is the staple food of the Chinese.

James Graham, the 17th century Duke of Montrose, who hammered the Campbells and their chief, the Duke of Argyll at the battle of Inverlochy, on one occasion tells how he relied on brose to keep alive and give him strength. His fortunes had changed when he felt that he could not fight against his king, but for the king - Charles I. When he was a fugitive from justice on the Scottish hills, he woke up one morning beside a Highland burn. He took some meal from his pouch - not the one with the gunpowder - stirred it in his deerskin leather boot (*brog*) with cold water and ate it all. That cold morning his hair was turned grey by the night frost as he slept with a stone for his pillow. Yet he valued that simple staple food as a banquet of a king. When he finished he said in Gaelic verse attributed to him,

Carraig eorna 'na sal mo bhroige,
'S e biodh a's fhearr a thuair mi riamh.

English

Barley brose in the sole of my boot,
Is the best food that I have ever eaten.

Alas, poor deluded Montrose, came to ruin by following the Stewarts and their destructive and distorted belief in the *Divine Right of kings*. Betrayed by one of the Duke of Sutherland's cronies, the young nobleman was hanged in the Grassmarket in Edinburgh. There was a sequel which followed, which is hard to believe was not also a judgment upon the Sutherland informer. The house of the Sutherland MacLeod, who gave Montrose to the authorities, one night burned to the ground when a big social event was in progress. The ruins can be seen by travelers, when you take the road west to the parish of Assynt and the town of Lochinver on the West coast of Sutherland. But to get back to our immediate theme, food should be chosen well, for it is the fuel of fortune.

The Stowaway

It has been said that no one can travel alone in this world without some companions. I have to confirm that assertion. Just before leaving the quay, I spotted a June bug on the deck of *Research II*. It was on its back, shaking its legs, trying desperately to get rightway up and back on its feet. I was not familiar with the creature. My first interpretation of his movements was that he might be practising for deep-sea acrobatics as a prospective companion on our ocean voyage. There is no doubt that the ocean environment is something like space to the traveler. In both, levitation and gravity are not constants and can affect balance and what we call weight. As the astronauts condition themselves for weightlessness, so our little friend could possibly have had similar thoughts in mind which accounted for his vigorous frolics on the deck. Sadly I had to disappoint his hopes if he so entertained them. I closed my eyes, as my fingers flipped him over the side. Earlier I had to refuse a lovely little deer mouse which had come all the way in the car from Arnish, with the apparent hope of coming along with me for the ride, to Britain.

The big surprise

'That's them all,' I said to myself, with a kind of relief. Until this morning, thirty-three days later, I held to that opinion. Just then I got a big surprise. There while I was sitting in the cockpit, a brown-yellow wasp alighted boldly on my hand. I could hardly believe it. I immediately starting trying to find an explanation. Hitherto I was sure I had no companions. Now I was not quite so sure. Then I speculated, 'Could he be from Ireland?' We were possibly about 200 miles from it at that point in time. I rather think not. It came home upon me that here was a genuine real-life stowaway. It was relatively easy for him, he being a wee fellow, to curl up in a corner below in the cabin. Here he was making his presence known to me, knowing it was too late for me to turn back with him. Who knows, he may well have had his antecedents in Britain, even in the Highlands of Scotland and, in the tradition of thrift, seized the opportunity of a free ride to visit the land of his fathers.

I sought to communicate with him. I tried using several names in addressing him. I went down the alphabet, Archie, Bill, Cuthbert, David. I stopped after trying each, waiting in turn for a response. Almost anything would do. I paused. Maybe this was a female. I switched to girls' names, Edna, Fiona, Gertrude, Henrietta. There was no response. This wouldn't do, I thought, the stowaway owes an explanation to the captain. I went back to names of men. George,

Johnny, Henry. Surely this creature had a name. Everyone has a name. Well, I'll try him with a few more. I went back to the alphabet. I had stopped at H. I'll pass a few and start at M. I turned to my uninvited guest and leaned forward. My voice was louder now, almost demanding some answer. Murdoch, Peter, Robert, Stephen, Tommy. I paused. It was no use.

Then I reflected that I still had a few more at the end of the alphabet. I would give him one last try. I looked at him there on my hand and almost shouted in his ear, WILFRED. Amazingly, he stirred and his head came up and then went down, up, down, up, down, up down. He stopped. I then repeated, WILFRED. His head came up, then down, up then down, up, down, up, down. I was thrilled. I got it. That's his name, I've done it. His name is Wilfred. I associated Wilfred with friends, good friends whom I had known well. I knew three Wilfreds and they were all fine men. Now it was easy to assume that we, just Wilfred and myself, were good friends. I gently nudged Wifred until he removed himself from the back of my hand to an alternative sedentary location.

That's it, I thought. If and when I disembark in Britain, I anticipate the Custom officials will ask me, 'Anyone traveling with you?' What will I say? What would you say? What ought I to say? It is a fair question. But I really do not think that the Customs ever had people like Wilfred in mind. Now, if the question was framed, Is there a wasp called Wilfred aboard? Then I would have to answer in the affirmative. If I do say, 'None,' I will have this mental reservation of the stowaway called Wilfred who buzzed out of the cabin, singing a real musical tune, and sat on my hand to warm himself in the morning sun on this the 33rd day of my voyage across the North Atlantic.

Midday is past and I resort to the cabin for lunch. It is simple and expeditious. Within a few minutes the order is ready, Cream of Chicken soup, piping hot straight off the stove, the whole tin of it. I always enjoy it.

Log: Day 33, Tuesday, 25th July, 1995

Time is passing. *Research II* is coming into the pen-ultimate phase of its rudderless voyage across the Atlantic. Here is the critical period, the Approaches to the English Channel. I had no precedent to study in this exercise of yachtsmanship. Certainly it would create a situation of many possible scenarios, far beyond the capability of anyone to calculate or even anticipate. Apart from the unknown character of the weather and the winds that would meet me in the Channel, here was the relatively narrow maritime road used by all world shipping traffic between northern ports of Europe, and ports on every continent across the world.

Continual Danger

I had not worked out in my mind exactly what I would do. But then, how could I know, given that there were so many unknown factors? It was certain that a little yacht with a 'skeleton' crew - no offense to Stanley - could hardly expect an amorous, far less friendly encounter with any ocean giants of today's world commerce. Already, day and night, ships appear within my vision. I must be doing the right thing as they are appearing well to starboard, either going or leaving northern ports in Britain or Eire. Two hours ago on looking out, I studied one of these giants, plodding through the ocean. It may have been five miles away. Its bleak appearance had a species of inexorable menace, as if it said to all challengers, 'Don't mess with me.'

This set me thinking of my navigation lights. I had tried the cabin light this morning just to check that there was electricity in the battery after the night use of the navigation lights. The light had only a dim glow. My source of electrical power was the solar generator. I had first approached Siemens, the big American manufacturers. They directed me to an outlet in Quebec, declining to sponsor me as a test trip. Inevitably my trip is also a test of equipment used, with performance good or bad, reflecting upon the manufacturer. I have been at sea for well over a month now in the north Atlantic. I have reserved electrical power strictly for the navigation lights at the masthead, and using only one cabin light sparingly. The fact is that the 12 volt heavy duty marine battery, fully charged when we left, is now flat. Also, the test of the cabin light has confirmed my fear that the navigation lights were non-existent long before the dawn made my little boat visible for other craft to avoid.

How much the deficiency is due to the limitations of the solar generator or the scarcity of sun power, is an open question. Every day the solar panel was out on the top of the dodger or the cabin top feeding the battery with electricity. The fact is that though New York and London, if not the whole of Europe and all North America, had the hottest summer in history, there was little sun for me in the north Atlantic. Is it not enough that I was able to dry my clothes and bedding only once every week? It seemed that the sun was strictly rationed. The makers made rather strong claims for their product and possibly would qualify these verbal claims made to me over the phone, if they were written on paper. At any rate the battery was flat and I was entering the busiest shipping Channel in the world, a sailing boat with only the captain and no rudder to steer by.

One might well have assumed that nearer the continent of Europe I might share in some of their excess sunshine. But so far there is no indication that this is the case. As I speak, the day, though pleasant, is overcast, and this is typical of most days hitherto, with limited and intermittent periods of sunshine. Fortunately I was frankly skeptical of the claims by the purveyors, and allowed for the fact that they could not possibly be conversant with the grey, bleak, sunless wilderness of the north Atlantic, which is a marked contrast from the ocean in more southern latitudes. Also knowing that I would be entering a danger zone in nearing Europe, I brought along an extra new fully charged heavy duty marine battery. Now was the time to use it. I linked both batteries in parallel, drawing from classes of magnetism and electricity, which I attended nearly fifty years ago. This would keep voltage at the required 12 for the whole needs of the boat. Had I crossed the connecting leads - in series rather than in parallel - I would have an unwanted 24 volts. As I say, I connected the leads in parallel. I also had a tester and this registered 12 volts when I had done the work and connected up the solar generator. On trying on the radio, a fuse immediately blew on the radio. Why, I could not understand. I replaced the fuse, hoping to have some joy in getting the radio in commission now that we needed it so badly, but alas that was not so. I had to resign myself to navigating the Channel Approaches and negotiating through the ship traffic night and day, without any communication on radio. Rather than risk a malfunction or leak, I disconnected the old battery and just used the new one in commission. Over the next few days, I would have this one recharged and held as a spare, given sunshine of course.

Choice of course

Three courses seemed open for me to take, as I approached the Channel. 1. To head straight for the Lizard, and within a few miles distance from the Bishop Rock Light on the Scillies. 2. Keep close to Brest and the French coast, and head up the Channel happily to the Solent with the expected traditional southwesterly behind me. 3. The third was a compromise, head into the centre and take it from there, in an open-minded flexible approach. If I took the first, a hard gale from the southwest might push me past the Scillies north, aided and abetted by the Gulf Stream which twisted left to turn up between Ireland and Wales. Or, indeed my little boat might meet the fate of hundreds of sailing ships which over the centuries had fallen prey to the jagged rocks which comprise the phenomenon called the Scillies. Taking the second would be ideal if the southwest held. If the wind failed or blew from the north or east, then I would be in trouble. I chose the third alternative. I would not commit myself to either British or French coast but go up the middle.

Rain now rattles on the cabin-top and a misty haze, though not a heavy one, gives a grey uniformity to sky and sea. Meantime *Research II* rolls on at 4 knots plus on a close reach to a northerly wind. This comes in the early morning, about 3 a.m., after a night of vacillating wind and calm. I have a feeling of well-being. The feeling is pervasive, a uniform therapy of good flows through 'my body, mind and spirit.' What more could I wish for, rolling along at a leisurely gait, aided by the northeast current? This Gulf stream current will leave us and head off to the left going up north of the Scillies. We will keep on to enter the English Channel to the East.

Mary is here

I cannot but advert to Mary, my wife. I was speaking freely to her again last night. It is totally incredible. The whole experience is so matter of fact. She speaks as if she were lying here beside me. Not only so, but I answer her questions and each contributes to the conversation, much as we would do at home in Arnish. This morning, I heard myself say, after a lengthy conversation, 'Mary, you are there, aren't you?'

There was a silence. But even the absence of her voice did not dispel the sense of her presence. Then I shook off the last vestiges of sleep, and sitting up, said aloud,

'Of course, you can't be. You are in Paris with Jane just now. I am sailing by myself.'

Do we really need to know all the answers to everything in life? I think not. No more than a driver needs to know all the intricacies of the car he or she operates. For me, I accept this experience as something good. The effect upon me is a quiet therapy, a reassuring message to my disposition, a positive invisible force which prevents the intrusion of negative doubts or imagined fears. The defenses of my already strong spiritual confidence are reinforced by this. No one can boast that he or she is impervious to doubt or apprehension, however beautifully his defenses are built on a sound faith and a stable mind. When we are smug, we are vulnerable. We all need one another, especially the support of loved ones and the prayers and good-will of friends. No man is sufficient unto himself. We are members, one of another, so that as we give out, so also we receive, in the reciprocal service that makes our common humanity the community of law and love, projected for us as the kingdom of God. Did not our Lord give us the glorious and matchless words to keep them as our common universal inclusive goal for all our fellow human beings: 'Our Father which art in heaven, ...Thy kingdom come on earth as it is in heaven...?'

Even as God is with us as we walk or sail in his ways, so are loved ones who are part of us; especially a spouse is with us in spirit. It is true of course that Mary and I are ethnically Celts. We are part of that volatile, amorphous, colorful, Celtic pageant of history, the Picots, Irish, Welsh, Manx, Breton Basque, to name the branches, recognized as peoples in Western Europe. Celtic people have a highly developed imagery of reality. This does not coincide with the apparent events in time, but transcends these. The Celtic mind has a powerful psychic faculty that, as it operates, it overrides the accepted and the expected. In a way it takes a short-cut over obstacles or opposition. This highly developed pathological sense, this affinity with the unseen produces a less practical and pragmatic person. Here the spirit is primary, the mind as its executive is dominant and in turn the physical and the tangible are but projections of reality.

I'm sure that since the 34 days since we parted, that Mary's imagination has been operating fully. I do not say that she is worrying, consciously. I told her not to worry. But still she must be burning up energy and is probably subconsciously concerned, so that my trip could be more of a trial for her and take more out of her than it would take out of me. I told her that I could well be a week or more longer than the projected 32 - 35 days. And that is the likely case, remembering that there is the added hindrance or x factor, the absence of a rudder.

Turning my thoughts again to navigation and the continual danger that shipping traffic presents to a small boat, I think it would be a good idea for all passing ships to report at once by radio to a central registry of Maritime Traffic Information - something like the Information Highway. Thus the course of every yacht on passage, its position and progress, anything unusual about it's appearance, like my rudder clearly raised above the deck out of the water, would be recorded. This could be monitored as an ever changing visual chart and requests for information could be answered. Some simple system like this would be of great value and alleviate anxiety on the part of loved ones. All prospective ocean voyagers would be willing to contribute, to make this a viable amenity for all.

Tuesday, 25th July, 1995

GPS Reading:	Waypoint 24	
Track 138'	Speed 3.5 knots	
Position:	N. 49' 11"	W. 12' 18"
Time:	17. 57 (Eastern Time US)	

CHAPTER 17

The Visitors

Log: Day 34, Wednesday, 26th July, 1995

Journal of voyage of sloop *Research II* from Sydney, Nova Scotia, to the UK.

Had a good sleep. I have found that I can go one night without, but I renege at two. Thus I slept the conventional seven hours until 5 a.m., and lazily returned to my bunk as there was nothing to do. This itself is a unique experience.

Note on the night. I passed a well-lighted ship to starboard. At first I assumed that it was on passage. But no. It was a fishing vessel, with a huge electric light on its mast lighting up the deck. R*esearch II* sails on at 4 knots to a moderate northerly. We'll leave well alone. I haven't had to tend the Scull-Oar or sails for 24 hours.

Visitors

This time they were human. I was roused from my stolen hours of dreamy reverie by the loud blast of a ship's horn. And I knew instantly that the ship was very close. Fog and a misty rain had cut visibility quite low the last time I had looked out on the grey dawn. Now it was 10 a.m. GMT. I jumped up and looked out the companionway and adjusted my eyes to the scene before me. I was alert and totally unsure what to expect. Thoughts raced before my mind. Regret that I had not stayed on watch more attentively in this grey, bleak, foggy weather. Was I to pay the ultimate penalty of being run down by an ocean giant that now bore down on me, unable to avoid me in time? Was this the final swansong to herald the premature end of my dream and mark my failure to match the challenge of finishing the crossing, though crippled without a rudder to steer by?

These negatives rushed through my mind, sending uneasy waves of apprehension right to the motor reflexes of my eyes. They swept the horizon, first over the bow, then in a quick arc to port. And there my eyes stopped. Some three hundred yards on my quarter, a grey warship wallowed from side to side in the Atlantic swell. It's curious how this struck me as odd. I, in my little boat, was unaware that the sea beneath me was essentially an undulating plain in the north Atlantic pretty well all the time even when storms or gales were busy elsewhere. The heavy-set ship before me seemed to have a very uncomfortable motion, which at the time, I really did not envy. There was another factor. The motion of a sailing boat is qualified by the lateral pressure of the sails, thus reducing the extremes. The effect is similar to the shock absorbers which take the punch out of the bumps for an automobile.

As I stood in the cockpit, clad from head to foot in my yellow oilskins, the warship gave another loud blast. I waved several times. I knew they saw me. The ship stood at right angles to me. As *Research II* sailed on northeast, the warship picked up some speed and passed my stern away southwest. I foresaw what would follow. Into the cabin I dropped. Excitedly I fumbled in the shelf enclosure for the plastic case with the diary in which Mary had put phone numbers in Scotland where messages could be relayed to her. I wrote a note, with the phone numbers of two of my sisters, Katie and Ina, in Scotland. I was very excited. I could not find the phone number in Paris which I had been given, at the Museum where my daughter Jane worked. Spray was coming over the hatch and threatening to blot my hasty handwriting, so that I worried that no one could read it. I placed the note in a plastic bag and went outside into the cockpit and waited. The warship had now turned in a circle and was making its way back upwind this time. It slowed to a stop as I watched, off my stern. There, I could see a rubber tender being lowered. It soon sped towards me, and came close alongside, but watchful that we did not knock into each other in the uneven seas. Its two big Yamahas kept her going slowly beside me, as if they were horses, being checked from going off at the start of a race.

I could hardly believe all this was happening, as it was exactly as I had envisaged. On Sunday, three days ago, I had estimated that I would not be far from the 1000° Longitude, that is, that of the Fastnet Light at the southwest tip of Ireland. This gives the name of the traditional annual race of yachts from Cowes, a tough race which some years ago brought tragedy and loss to men and boats. And here I was, almost right on the line. A warship meets me. The last vessel I saw in Canada was a squat muscular powerful warship of the Italian navy. I did not know what this one was at this moment. There were two in the tender, young men, a seaman and the coxswain at the tiller.

I heard one speak in English.

I answered, 'I see you're British.'

He replied, 'No, we're from Ireland.'

I replied, 'That's even better.'

We had to raise our voices above the noise of sea and wind and also these smelly outboards at the stern. I did not take kindly to motors after the quiet of sailing and the long absence from their potential pollution. You can understand that to communicate was not easy for me. I had not spoken to any human being for a long time. Apart from singing a verse or two of a Gaelic Psalm, I had not used my vocal chords or voice facilities to articulate the sounds, for close to five weeks. My jaws were stiff, my tongue was lazy, even my lips were reluctant to open to formulate the linguistic shapes of speech. It was with difficulty that I could power the words with air so that they would leave my mouth and get airborne.

Even as he spoke, the soft brogue of the Gaelic came through this young man's speech. He spoke in English, but with a Celtic tongue. I knew also by my reception, that the feelings were mutual. Instead of a stranger, they had met a brother. The Celt, by nature and history, inhabits the mountainous regions on the edge of Europe's continent. For example, in Britain, the Cornish, the Welsh, and the

Scottish Highlander were pushed back to the extremities by more ambitious peoples, Romans or Angles and Saxons. Rome tried but failed to subdue them, but where 'might is right', the organized discipline of its legions kept the Scottish Celt for the most part to the north of the Clyde Forth river line which cuts Scotland in two. The Welsh were driven into their mountain vastness where they were contained to the west of the Mercy/Avon Longitude. In Scotland, the Celts were the last to be contained. They had lost their ancient warlike glory and couldn't see that there were other kinds, more noble and enduring which integration into Britain's nationhood could bring for the deployment of their gifts. Culloden was at the one time the last luminous light from a falling shooting star, and at the same time, with attendant birthpains, the beginning towards a new maturity. History reveals that the Celts in all the various locations, in the mountainous regions of countries were 'contained, but never tamed.' And they never will be.

The Celt, in general, is not linked to one geographic location, though his ties can be very authentic in his attachment to a past inheritance. The definition of a Celt is elusive and his roots are obscure as scholars have found in seeking definition. This gives him a kind of universalism. He is at home in every part of the globe, wherever he is, as much as Jew or Arab. His mind carries with him all the riches of his past. He travels light through the ages, because his nature is not defined by geography, nor his wealth by his possessions. Volatile, prone to fall, yet capable of rising to noble heights, he has a spiritual ancestry that is somehow transmitted through generations, long after he has ceased to use his language. Thus in countries like Canada, and in the US states like Montana and Carolina, where thousands of Scottish Highlanders settled during the 19th century, there is more than a grain of truth in the refrain, 'But yet the blood is strong, the heart is Highland.'

I mention these thoughts as they explain the sentiments of that meeting between Celtic sons of Ireland and a Scottish Celt right there in mid-Atlantic. The special relationship at once came into the picture, the sense of brotherhood, which is valid across the world. To me, a

Scots Canadian Highlander, an Irish Celt is very close. I cannot analyze the bond I feel, except in the umbrella-like parameters of our common Celtic origin and the enduring essence which is retained from one generation to another, as an active consciousness of its characteristics and values.

We exchanged notes. I had asked for their names. They wrote these down and passed them to me. These were Noel Collins and Damien Murphy. I asked for the name of the ship. It was the LE EITHNE. I found it difficult to place the name in a meaningful category. At first I thought it must be French. Then it occurred to me that it was old Irish for the word go or dynamic. Thus the name implied 'with energy' or 'with power'. That seems a plausible possible title for a warship, land of poets, of music and Gaelic. I cannot but admire the alertness of the Irish navy, meeting me here in the grey dawn. We were right on the longitude of Eire where its western border touched the Atlantic. It was as if I crossed an electric fence, and out popped the owner with a shotgun. But there were no shots over my bow. Instead a solicitous offer of help and kindness.

They asked me if I required anything or if there was any way they could help me. Did I need water, food, anything else?

I shook my head. I just could not think of anything that I needed at the time. I did not want for anything. I felt in perfect health, the egg on my face was well down and hidden any way under my bonnet. I did point to the disabled rudder, raised up and lashed to the stern guard rail. But the sailors made no suggestion or comment on this. They left the initiative to me. Furthermore, our meeting was on the 'briny wave', not in the quiet comfort of a drawing room. Seas threatened to make our craft collide. Conversation was a contest with the noise of wind and also those perfidious propulsion units, the huge outboards, which sent their oily odor down wind to my nostrils. I cannot say that I wanted the interview to be protracted. Also, I felt that I was wasting their time. They were service men and the navy had its work to do. Who was I, a lone sailor on my little boat, to interrupt their schedule and interfere with their duties?

It's strange indeed, I thought, that the first people I meet crossing the ocean to Europe, are Celts of a common Gaelic heritage. My mind went back to my first visit to Ottawa some fifteen years earlier, to the Presbyterian Church Assembly. Going for a walk along the Rideau Canal in the early morning, the first person I spoke to was an exiled Highlander from Sutherland. He was Donald Ross, and though over 90 years old, was taking his exercises at 6 a. m. on that frosty morning in June. He was a remarkable man, uncle of Donald MacKay, then an advocate in Edinburgh and afterwards Lord Chief Justice in the Thatcher government, and now in the House of Lords. There on the towpath with no one else in sight that Sunday morning, we sang two verses of Psalm 103, chanting the lines in the traditional manner in a Gaelic service of worship. Each of us chanted a verse in turn,

O m'anam, beannaich thus nis
an Dia Iehobhah mor:
Moladh gach ni an toabh stigh dhiom
'ainm naomha mar is coir.

O m'anam beannaich fein a nis
Iehobhah mor do Dhia:
Na dichuimhnich na todhlacan
a dheonaich dhiut an Triath.

English:

O Thou my soul bless God the Lord;
and all that in me is
Be stirred up his holy name
to magnify and bless.

Bless, O my soul, the Lord thy God,
and not forgetful be
Of all his gracious benefits
he hath bestowed on thee.

(From the Scottish Psalter)

I saw the parallel. In a city of over half a million French and English speakers, the first resident I spoke to was a Gaelic speaking Highlander from the north of Scotland. And here, entering the perimeter of the British Isles (with deference to Eire's political independence), I also meet two sons of Gaeldom who had a fair smattering of their ancestral tongue.

But back to business. The Irish sailors took my message for my wife Mary. I also told them to let the coastguard in the Channel ports know of my presence and that I had no rudder. I asked for a weather report. They spoke on the cellular phone to the ship. The answer was good weather and southwest winds all the way to take me up the English Channel some 400-500 miles away.

I wasn't too happy with this summary information. It sounded rather bland and almost too good to be true.

I said,

'What do you mean southwest wind. The wind is blowing from the north just now!'

The seaman replied,

'Yes, but the wind will change very soon.'

Some how I felt skeptical but left it at that.

We parted with a Celtic Goodbye, that neither of us could hear. I waved; they waved. They returned to their ship and it steamed away, I noticed, north, very likely to Cork. I thought of the warmth and comfort and hot food these fellows would get in the big ship. For me, I turned to face the day, the grey bleak day, interrupted by my morning visitors, and now gone, as suddenly as they had appeared.

I took a GPS Reading to see how close we were to the 1000° W Longitude of the Fastnet Rock.

Reading: Speed 3.4 knots

Position: N 29' 11" W 10' 19"

Time: 12:42 hrs (GMT)

Sudden Change

This is the afternoon. There is a definite deterioration in circumstances, which is a cause for real alarm. All is not well. The Irish told me that there was good weather, with the southwest wind coming shortly, to take me up the English Channel all the way to Lymington, 500 miles away. An hour after their ship left me, a vicious gale bore down on me from the northwest. For the past five hours I battled with its fury. Alas, both mainsail and jib were torn, before I could get them down. I could hardly believe the change in my fortunes. I had been sailing happily along, with not a care. Suddenly I get a visit from a warship. Now my world is troubled, my sails torn and *Research II* is being tossed about like a cork in a very unpleasant kind of sea.

The Continental Shelf

The pattern of the waves was quite different to that which I had been used to a short time ago. Now, there were no longer the Atlantic rollers, coming on in relays of big undulating walls of water. I had got used to them, and strange as it might seem, so did *Research II.* It was as if she adapted to the large scale motion of the ocean. Now, the seas were broken up into short steep curling crests. They looked short-lived, as if they had sprung up suddenly the progeny of a vicious northerly blow. They were not mature, a kind of instant gale, intent on quick trouble, the equivalent of our modern instant cooking, as if time were rationed and all were in a hurry to dish it out whatever was on the menu.

There is an explanation for this change. We were now just after crossing onto the Continental Shelf, that shallow plateau of underwater shore that circumscribes the land mass of the European continent. Within a short time *Research II* had changed from sailing over the ocean floor in thousands of metres below, to sailing over the Continental Shelf, roughly one hundred metres, at the minimum at least one tenth of that ocean depth. It is not difficult to see that the waters would react very differently and in the new situation, that seas would be shorter, less mature and less structured than those of the mid ocean, traversed earlier.

Log/Journal: For the past hour, I am pretty well hove-to, with my own patent mainsail on the mast. But I cannot make any way without the jib, and this has to be on the foreboom as the regular halyard will not come down. All is not well. *Research II* has taken a few real side-bangers. I've come down below for a breather as I write this. Pause. One of these side-bangers has hit us and I am thrown back on the seat. The radio flies from the top of the shelf opposite and I give it a rugby catch as I half-somersault against the cupboards behind me. *Research II* comes back to an even keel and I have the radio on my lap. The wind howls in the rigging. The foredeck rises and falls with a jarring motion so that it is not possible for me to go forward.

We'll sit it out, I thought, and hope that the Irish were not wrong, and that a southwester will indeed come along. Here we are entering the crucial phase, the approaches to the Channel, and making a landfall. My aim is to get past the Scillies unscathed and reach the Lizard. It is possible that I will need help then. I'm alright with searoom and moderate winds and as I proved, *Research II* could handle the storm itself as long as one had searoom, the luxury of the ocean. That was past. Instead you had the tight narrow confines of the Channel with its strong changing tides and currents, and its constant traffic of ocean shipping to contend with now. I had no illusions. My boat was vitally disabled. When I recall the weeks at sea behind me, the days and nights of continuous fighting to control my boat, the times when I was near the end of my resources and even my will to overcome was bent, but not broken, I am humbled and in a way full of wonder that 2000 miles of hostile ocean have passed under my keel, and that with the added factor of predominantly contrary winds.

Add to the equation, tears in the sails, the limitation of my own autosails, the known limits of the Scull-Oar to keep the boat on course, but not able to get her on course. Then remember I had no rudder. Truly all these lead to a negative situation. But we will prevail. I bowed my head in thanksgiving and praised my Lord with this assurance,

'Hitherto the Lord hath helped us.'

Log: Day 35, Thursday, 27th July, 1995

It's morning after the night before. And that was not the most pleasant of nights. There was a perpetual earthquake, it seemed, as *Research II* lay to in the pitching seas. We are now well inside the British-Eire Maritime region. I saw ships' lights to the south and east of me. The gale that sprung up yesterday from the northwest, is pushing us southeast. But the current of the Gulf Stream is pushing us to the northeast. Hopefully we'll get a bit of easting as they compromise their directions.

9 am. The weather has brightened. To my surprise and delight, I examine the main and see that it is not seriously torn. The brass eye for the Cunningham hole for reefing has come out with some canvas torn but there is reinforcing at this point. Hopefully the tear will not run. I set the main and the jib and both do not look too bad. The problem now is to get *Research II* to sail east. She kept veering southeast and that could not continue. I had to hand the main and put up my own smaller autosail. I used my foreboom as a spinnaker for the jib. I spent a fairly long time at this, some three hours. At last I managed to get *Research II* to come up and sail consistently due east. I know that I can get northing and also southing. But here I want due east and I continue like this for the day.

Overhead the sky is a consistent grey. I wonder is this ordinary weather, or the exception? For the past three and a half days, we have not seen a sight of the sun. One negative result of this is that the solar generator has not been able to feed the batteries. I have the two hooked up now. But we hope for sun as the navigation lights are a 'must' in the English Channel at night. Also, I have a searchlight wired up which, if used, consumes a lot of power. It may be necessary in a crisis for identity and also if I lose control in bad weather and need to signal the ultimate lighted call, S.O.S.

Now we journey on, the wind to my joy has switched round as the Irish predicted, to the southwest. I hope this continues for four or five days without gales. I think that four gales and a storm are quite enough for the trip.

The BBC reported a terrorist bombing in Paris on Tuesday. Four people died and twenty were injured, some critically. Naturally this news was of deep concern to me as my daughter Jane was in Paris. Possibly Mary my wife had left by that time. The bombing was in a Metro subway, but radio news comment shed no light on the identity of victims. Though the bombing makes the news in every bulletin since then, there is nothing added to confirm or allay one's anxiety.

I heard the engines of a propeller driven aircraft an hour ago. I conjectured that it was from Coastal Command out on patrol. But on going out and scanning the sky there was no sight of it, and I did not expect any, in the limited visibility of the opaque foggy canopy we call the sky. I should have told the Irish to let the coastguards in the Channel ports know, especially in Falmouth, Plymouth and Brixham. But maybe they will, a part of their surveillance procedures. If I recall rightly, it was indicated before leaving that contact would be made between the Coastguard Service in the Maritimes and that of Britain and specifically the Channel ports. I used Lymington as a general term for my destination of the Channel. Needless to say, any port after Land's End would serve for disembarkation. Now as I reflected on the matter, it would be reassuring if the authorities on patrol kept an eye out for me, a little yacht without a rudder making its way night and day with only one human being to keep watch, in a dense traffic of commercial shipping. No innate pride could muster a false confidence in my own ability to compensate for the crippled state of my boat. I could feel as helpless as anyone in the limited control I have of *Research II,* even in favorable weather, not to mention the aggravated hazards of bad weather. Even with a rudder, most sailing boats have few options in the last resort. The sail driven boat is dependent on the wind, its direction, and its force. How can anyone argue against that? Very few ocean loners believed otherwise; I think of one Peter Tangvald who threw every mechanical and modern gadget into the sea. One of the first to go was his engine, and the last was the lavatory toilet, or *head.* Bobby Sheink, the German lawyer - yachtsman, maintains that in severe weather conditions, no sailing vessel can actually make headway against the wind, but has to bow before the elements, and make the best of it.

I now take readings with the GPS. What a day we live in that we can track our path across land or sea on the surface of the earth, without a sight of the sun or any star, or even terrestrial landmark!

Log: Thursday, 27th July,

This is Waypoint 26

Readings:	Speed 4.5 knots corrected	In surge 7.7 knots
Position:	N. 49' '11" W. 09' 14"	
Time:	12:16 p.m.	

Progress Report

As you see, *Research II*, though it was hove-to for much of the past 30 hours since we had a visit from the warship, still disposed of one more Longitude (60 miles). This takes us well into the Celtic Sea, albeit in its southerly sector. In fact we are keeping parallel to the 50th Latitude, but not much over the 49th as you can see from the above GPS reading. We hope to continue on this course until we pass the Lizard, when we will have to bear northeast, to avoid running through the shipping traffic. As I look ahead, we may well continue past the east corner of the Isle of Wight and then turn northwest into the famous Southampton Roads. This could well be the better option than trying to negotiate the inside of the Isle of Wight through the Needles and the Solent, without a rudder to steer by. But my goal will be achieved if I pass Land's End and I will be only too willing to leave the initiative with the Coastguards, who may judge it wise to tow me in to any port in the Channel.

Marine Massage

Who would believe that this trip provides a free massage? There is no need to pay for expensive health therapy which is purveyed on land. I have a two-fold range of services right here on *Research II*. And the two kinds are obligatory. No one is excused the exercise. You just cannot get out of taking the'free' massage.

The first massage - I speak with some feeling on both literally. You have it when you are sitting down on the hard wooden or fibreglass seats in or out of the cabin. At every opportunity the bedding and other 'software' is put out into the cockpit to dry and air. Therefore often I have to sit on the hard forms beneath. At the beginning of the voyage I rolled up the thick Dunlopillo cushions and stowed them away. To get an idea of what it is like in the cabin I will try and tell you as this is the essential premise upon which the massage is made available. The first kind is a **mild** massage. You generally have this as you lie down in the day or the night. The definitive position is your posture. You are always lying down, or stretched out. The sea may be wild or moderately calm. It does not matter, there is a rhythmic motion, as the boat sails on, that is transmitted to the physical body. You relax in spite of yourself. Your whole body, with the limbs, moves in tune with the ocean. There is a constant difference between the gravity that affects you and the ocean's effect on the position of the boat. In effect you are still, but the boat moves continually under you. This means that your body is being subjected to this rubbing motion. The more the boat yaws and pitches, heels and bucks, the more vigorous is the massage. I call this the **mild** massage. The experience is, as I said, a pleasant one, and lends itself to relaxation and therefore is therapeutic. This mild massage makes one feel an Elvis-like suppleness. Your body seems to have all kinds of movement that you never before suspected. It is all rather pleasant as long as you are not thrown out of your bunk. And more - you certainly lose weight by this involuntary, effortless exercise. Possibly there is a market for a simulated machine to reproduce the same effects. It could be a real winner with men and women, right in the privacy of the home, possibly even as a substitute for the ordinary bed, providing the perfect and most pleasant way to relax and get rid of all kinds of worry and tension. I have no recollection of insomnia. Only the warning instincts of danger, for which we are programmed, interrupts sleep on the ocean.

Alas, like the shoe, the massage comes in pairs. And the companion of the mild massage is the **wild** massage, a very different species to the first and one that has significant negative effects. While you lie down for the first, you sit up for the second. As you sit on the hard seat, you get a **wild** massage. The situation can be deceptive. You think at first that this is like the first, rather pleasant. Your cheeks move back and fore and act like cushions. You feel comfortable and you may begin to wonder what all the fuss is about. This happy impression may also be entertained, quite convincingly, if the weather is good and the motion of the boat is gentle and forgiving.

But wait, we are not playing with facts. You sit down in a boat on the ocean, to try and rest. You cannot lie down or stand up forever. Further, when there is weather, and I mean weather; bad, hostile, vicious weather where waves exhibit all that is wicked as a mirror of all unpleasantness, then you are in for a **wild** massage, without any polite ifs or buts. To ensure you get it, the cabin feels like a bucking horse in the rodeo in Calgary. The boat heaves and jerks. It pitches forward, and heels suddenly sideways. From your perspective, the seat under you moves without warning to right or left, up or down. Your whole weight hangs on the fulcrum of your 'bottom.' The result is that your cheeks wobble. They keep on wobbling, until they are at last not dissimilar to pasta, a kind of flexible jelly-like roll of stinging wet painful flesh. Pain becomes the hallmark of your experience.

You try to stabilize your body by grabbing cupboards, by wedging your feet against corners of the cabin floor, all to no avail. You lean sideways to give one cheek a rest, but pins and needles bring you back to an even keel and more of this shared torture. Alas, there is no let-up. Damp, hard, wood rubbing your clothes bring a salty sting to the bottom that is quite disillusioning. That is phase one. Didn't I warn you that there is another stage, one which is protracted and unavoidable as a continued effect for many days afterward? Phase

Two comes in when your bottom develops a thick pad like that on the sole of your shoe.

The effect of sitting down now in this phase is like the pounding and thudding of dough in the hands of a baker or an American housewife, making bread in the kitchen. Like dough, my cheeks and yours, if you follow me, wobble this way and that. At last it is impossible to continue sitting. Now wet or not, you crawl into your sleeping-bag, hold on to any supports and pretend that you are sleeping in a soft comfortable stable bed in Buckingham Palace. Unfortunately the discomfort develops into a stage of protracted tenderness of the posterior. The result is that for many days afterwards, it is impossible to sit in a normal position. You add this condition to the list of inconveniences related to the sea. At the same time, because you can do little about it, you come to terms with it and put up with it as best you can.

Log: Day 36, Friday, 28th July, 1995

Research II has kept her course since yesterday, moving due east. All night long she sailed at 4.5 knots, trimmed to the southwest wind which is at times gentle and sometimes brisk.

The Opened Canopy

Just like the roof that opens over the sports stadium in Toronto, so the roof of cloud that had closed us in for several days, opened up last evening. What a wonderful transformation! As night came down, I took to the cockpit, or stood sometimes in the companionway. I was exhilarated, just looking round me at the glory of creation. Thoughts came back to me from long ago and days in Keil School, whose Headmaster, James Mason, Fellow of the Royal Astronomical Society, gave us, his pupils, an introduction to the three-dimensional world of space. This course had no certificate or diploma. It was given by the busy Headmaster because of his love for astronomy and because of his dedication to teaching and passing on something of his own love of true knowledge. And he succeeded. One's thinking could never be narrow after that. It could never be restricted to a narrow-minded dogmatism of tunnel-thinking. Mason was a Christian and like Newton, the effect of his knowledge as a teacher of science gave him a sense of humility and a sense of the greatness of the Creator.

And those whom he influenced could no more exercise the mind in one-plane thinking, nor even in two, like the physical and spiritual. There had to be a third. That third may be elusive to define, but as the moral or the mandatory that evokes the motions of conscience and infers the inescapable accountability we all have as individuals to our Maker for our stewardship of life here, it is magnified and intensified by at least a fundamental acquaintance with Newton and his students in the study and observation of space. That is not to conceive of such erudition as justification for elitist views. Instead there is a humbling of you or me, in the face of the vastness of knowledge, just tapped at the edge. And what is seen infers as a reasonable deduction, not chaos and chance, but order; order that no mortal, unless prejudiced, can gainsay. And if there is order, the corollary is that there is a mind which conceived a design, and a power that brought it into realization.

Such thoughts filled my mind with peace, as I looked out on the night sky. There Jupiter rose in the southeast. To the north and west, was the familiar Plough, with the pointer. In line with it was the reassuring presence of the Pole star, the unchanging pivotal point of the Plough. It never ceased to amaze me how the Plough always pointed to the Pole. In the early evening the Plough started out horizontal in the northwest. By the early morning it was standing on its head, in the northeast almost upside down, but always the pointer, signaling the direction of the Pole star.

Then there is the Milky Way, that amorphous mass which comprises millions of separate stars. I see it more vividly at sea than ever it was visible on land, traversing the sky from southwest to northeast. That is one wonder of the sky that I missed in Canada. Rarely does one see the Milky Way, as it was so familiar to us, growing up in northern Scotland.

After drinking in the elixir of the heavens and praising the Creator of all, at last I became aware of the chilly night air. I retired to my cabin, closed myself up in my sleeping bag, and was soon fast asleep. Once in the night alarms bells went off. The sub-conscious registered a change in the pattern of sounds, and the physiology sensed that the boat was heeling to starboard, rather than to port. Within moments I was out on deck. A glance at the compass told the story. We had jibed. *Research II* was heading due north. Maybe she was wanting to get up into the Irish Sea, right up to the Clyde and Scotland, who knows. Then began the effort to get *Research II* turned around and back on course. At last we succeeded and we have stayed there ever since.

Anticipation

It is unwise to make assumptions, but I succumbed to the temptation to speculate on my progress. It was hard not to anticipate the days ahead. Given the continuing favorable southwest wind, I believe that within 24 hours we will have passed the 500° Longitude West of the Greenwich Meridian. Looking at the chart of the approaches to the English Channel which I now use, I see that this is the north/south line of the Lizard point. That is well past the Bishop Rock Light on the Scilly Isles and the Wolf Rock Light on Land's End. That is something to look forward to indeed, tomorrow, Saturday evening. I still hold to the view that I should bear as far east as possible on the 49th parallel of Latitude, between France and England. I have a residual 'chip' on my shoulder in this respect that goes back to my boyhood.

My father instilled a dread in me of being caught on a lee shore. 'Always keep up to the weather,' was his constant advice. 'Never get caught in the open and at the mercy of the wind on a lee shore.' Our boats at that time were the design of a miniature Zulu. There was no deep keel and we carried inside ballast of stones, if the sail, the lug sail, were used at all. Sail was discouraged by older men who knew the sea and the sudden squalls that hit a boat from the hills that surrounded the Highland lochs. Memories lingered of those drowned in front of their homes and the lessons learned made a lasting impression upon young boys like me.

One cogent reason in my judgment for approaching closer to France is the current that is shown on the chart that bends round Brest and turns northeast up the Channel. That seems one good reason to distance myself from the Scillies and the Lizard headland, off Falmouth. In any case one is nervous of being anywhere near the vicinity of Bishop Rock, in a boat without a rudder and without a life raft. As I study the chart I am confirmed in this view. As I look at the chart, the Bishop is sticking his mitred head, right out there on the Scilly Isles, as an ecclesiastical bishop would do in his cathedral. And one cannot dispel the impression on one's mind that he is just waiting to lure some unfortunate mariner, even myself, onto the treacherous rocks behind him, to add one more to history's graveyard of lost ships.

'Friday against the week'

Truly, the sun has come out as it has not done in a week. The sky has brightened to fill the air with optimism and raise my spirits to heights of fulfillment and a sense of achievement. The wind continues brisk, with whitecaps animating the summer sea. And so, east we go, *Research II*, Stanley my faithful Scull-Oar and myself, into the English Channel, where thousands of ships have passed before, from every corner of the world. It is as if *Research II* is reaching for its goal, now impatient to get to the finishing line and be at rest after all its exertions and struggles, its conflicts, its knockdowns, its unwillingness to give in to failure. It pulls us along, pushed by that benign and friendly southwester, like a dog that strains at the leash when its master nears his destination. But its master is equally exhilarated. The weeks of struggle, the days and nights of continual experiment, the incessant effort to counter the forces of the sea to nullify endeavor, and to eclipse us both in a watery oblivion, these all pass through my mind like the rerun of a film, a sombre one. Add to this the absence of one human friend in an ocean highway to stop and greet one, until the battle was over. All these mark the days and weeks, like the rounds of a pugilistic fight at the turn of the century, the hard punitive kind, where no mercy was asked for and no favours given. Yet behind was not a citadel of egotistical pride, the making of oneself, the Babel tower of my own construction. Yes, my will to win, to prevail, was there, and all my commitment to overcome as a sustained repetitive confrontation, in the storm, in the darkness, on the slippery deck, in the dark nothingness of confusion as I bailed the water out of a cabin that if, I succumbed to weakness, would be turned into my coffin.

But my will to win was like the will of Jacob of old at Bethel, when he would not let go of his faith in God, until he had the absolute assurance of God's blessing. My trip was a test of my faith and overcoming the unique challenge that faced me confirmed my will that I, through God's strength would prevail. I marvel as I look up at Stanley the Scull-Oar. Repeatedly, he reins in *Research II* and corrects her, bringing her to heel as a man would do a horse that threatens to go to the right or to the left. It is a miracle, for all this takes place without the touch of the captain's hand. It was said of Jacob as he rose from his triumphant night of prayer, that the sun rose upon him as he passed over Penuel, where he had seen God face to face.

For me this Friday, the sun rose upon me, as I passed over from the ocean to sail past the Scillies and enter the gateway to the Channel.

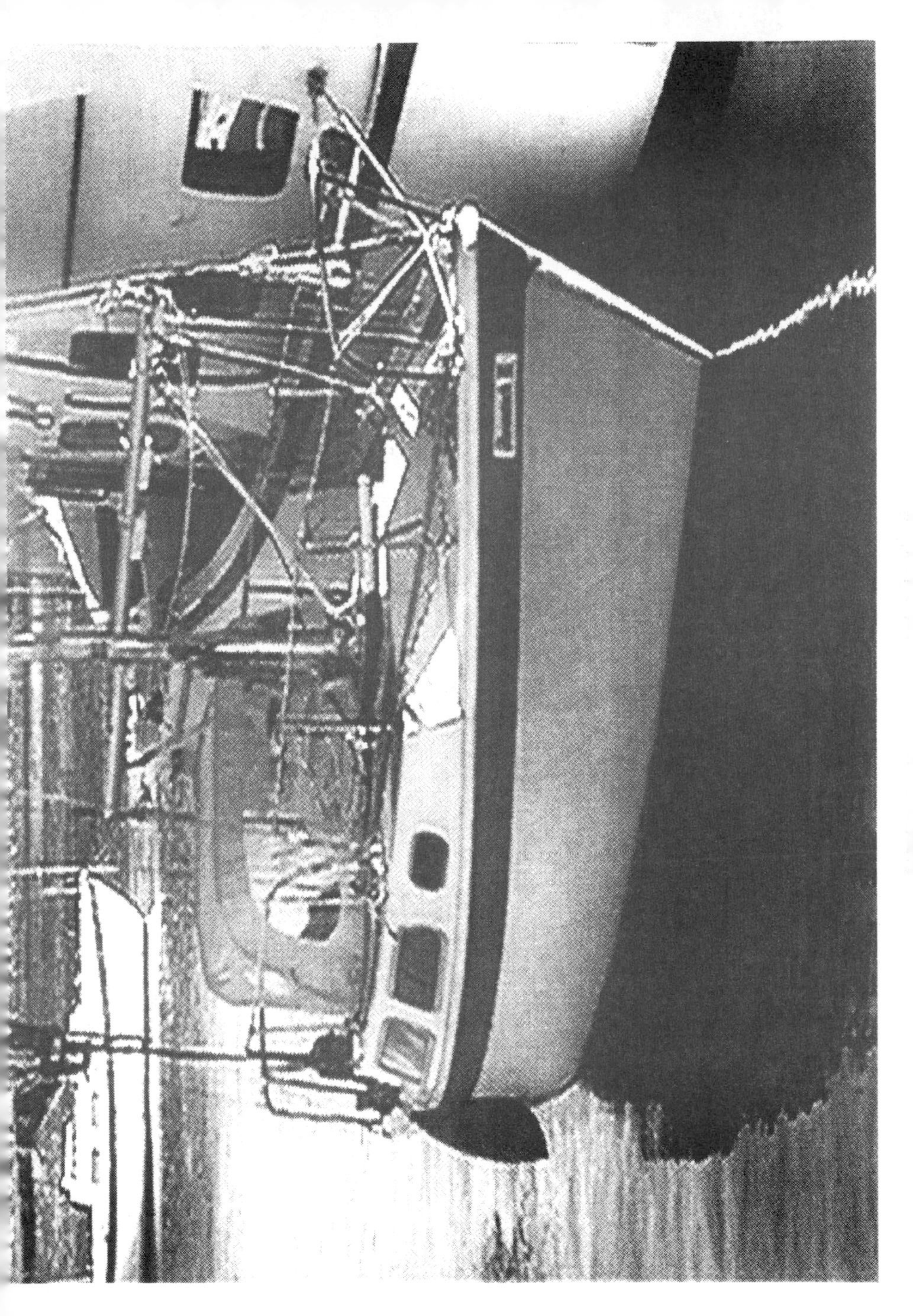

Ready to go - Dick's Marina, Sydney

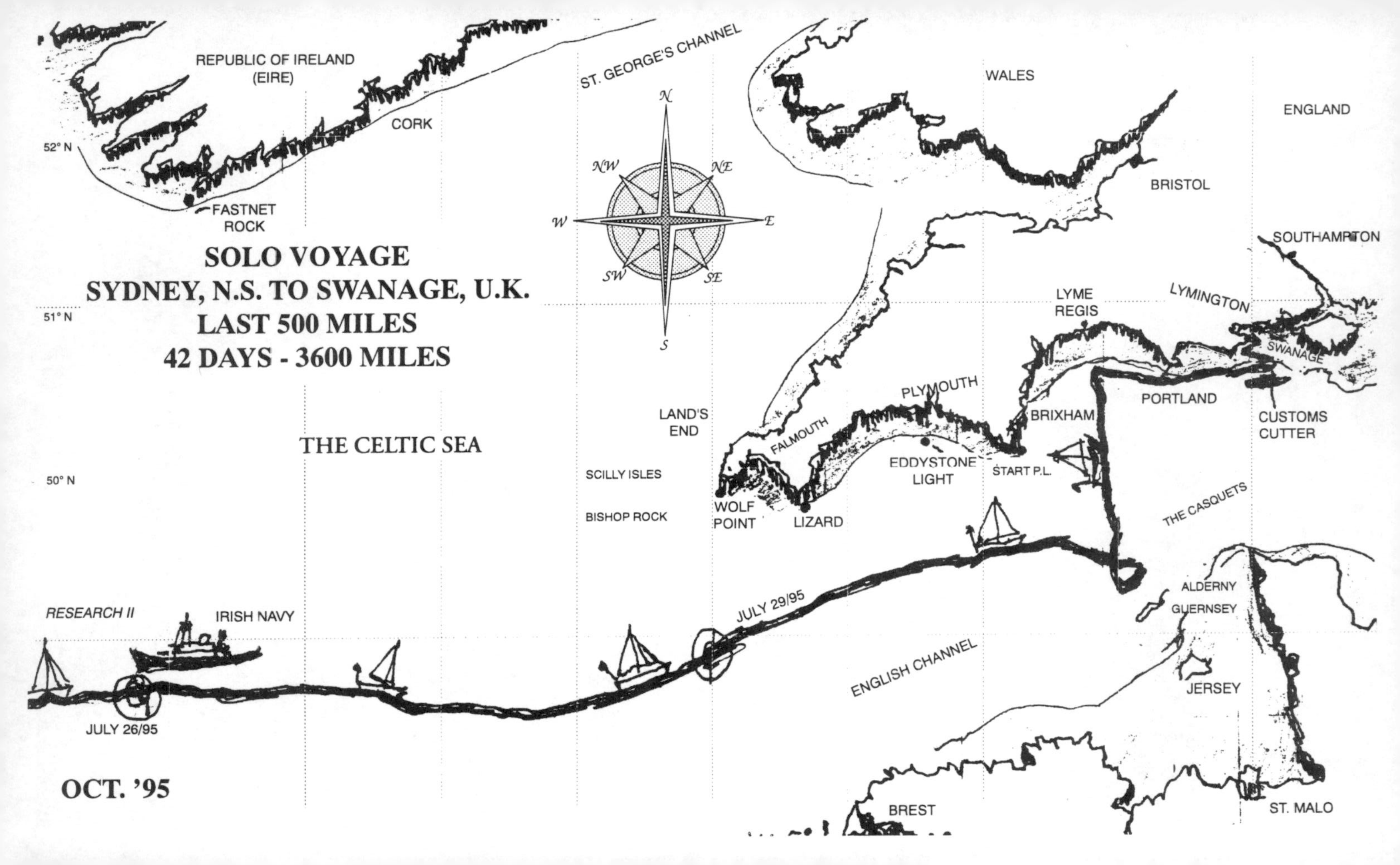
SOLO VOYAGE
SYDNEY, N.S. TO SWANAGE, U.K.
LAST 500 MILES
42 DAYS - 3600 MILES
REPUBLIC OF IRELAND
(EIRE)
CORK
FASTNET
ROCK
52° N
51° N
50° N
ST. GEORGE'S CHANNEL
N
NE
E
SE
S
SW
W
NW
WALES
ENGLAND
BRISTOL
SOUTHAMPTON
LYMINGTON
SWANAGE
LYME
REGIS
PORTLAND
CUSTOMS
CUTTER
BRIXHAM
PLYMOUTH
FALMOUTH
LAND'S
END
EDDYSTONE
LIGHT
START P.L.
THE CELTIC SEA
SCILLY ISLES
BISHOP ROCK
WOLF
POINT
LIZARD
THE CASQUETS
ALDERNY
GUERNSEY
JERSEY
RESEARCH II
IRISH NAVY
JULY 29/95
ENGLISH CHANNEL
JULY 26/95
BREST
ST. MALO
OCT. '95

PART V

The English Channel

CHAPTER 18

Land's End

King Henry's Flagship

For two nights now, fishing-boats are seen lighting up the horizon to the north and to the south of me. They form a kind of carriageway, throwing up their brilliant lights into the darkness of the sky. Each appears stationary in a given area. On each side, about three miles distant, I estimate, they line the route we sail. We are, as it were, in the aisle of a long cathedral, slowly making our way forward up the Channel. How far we will reach we do not yet know, but we sail forward towards the Nab Tower and the Southampton Roads. All along the route are the names of ports, enshrining immortal memories of England's greatness and her famous sons and ships, that over the centuries shaped her course to rise and occupy the throne as a dominant maritime power and one of the great empires of history.

As I write, the radio is switched on. I hear a commentary on the salvaged flagship of King Henry VII, which sank in Portsmouth harbour because the gunports were left open, causing her to fill with water, as she began to get underway. The Mary Rose is now resurrected and slowly by careful preservation techniques, she is being cured and secured as the masterpiece of medieval shipping. Who could begin to describe her real-life image as the symbol of tragedy, the common coffin of hundreds of men, the broken pride of king and country - the greatest warship ever built up to that time, 550 years ago, a warship that never put to sea, and whose guns never fired upon an enemy.

We sail on. No sign of Coastal Command, no plane, no frigate. Where are the ancient walls of England? I hear echoes of history. Here is the entrance to England's castle. A hostile foe who sailed beyond this point in past days, passed the Rubicon. Here the galleons of Spain assembled to make their final push up the Channel, just over 500 years ago. Here King Philip's navy threw down the gauntlet in that historic challenge of England's might. And there in Plymouth, hidden behind its island Eddystone light, the pirate captain Sir Francis Drake waited confidently until he finished his game of bowls. The Channel still echoes with the boom of the ships' cannon, the sound of rushing, oxygen-greedy flames, as English incendiary craft bore down on high-sided galleons, in the engagement of England's little David against Spain's Goliath. Every harbour has its history, every port its record of glory. This extends back long before that memorable victory as keepers of England's driveway, and often since then, in our contemporary day.

My eyes search for the guards of England's skies, but there's no sign. I scan the horizon, but no vessels stand watch at England's gate. Is this, in modern parlance, her Watergate? Has her glory gone? Is it true that at last she is conquered? Why have her maritime walls been dismantled? I look and there is no sign of them. It is hard to rationalize this apathy, and wriggle out of condemnation, claiming England is another Sparta and that her sons are the walls of her defense. Is she already plundered and her riches, the riches of her heritage, of her faith, of her freedom, of her past glory, carried away, like the treasures of Jerusalem to ancient Babylon? Where rivals failed to conquer, has this nation scuttled her pride and might, as the Germans did their fleet, in Scapa Flow in 1918? As I look out on the waters of the English Channel and think of the famous Downs rising to the north, the question is inescapable. Is this like Orkney's waters, the graveyard which marks the death of England's greatness? These and other thoughts race through my mind as I try to focus on the historic seaway before me.

I had suggested to the Irish seamen who met me at the Fastnet Longitude, that the English coastguards be alerted to my presence. If I saw a plane of Coastal Command or a guardian coastguard cutter at the posts, how that would have allayed my concern, and relieved that lurking anxiety as I approached the thickening traffic ahead of me. I swallow my disappointment that there is no proof to the contrary. I am grateful for one thing, that the sun has charged up my batteries and thus I have renewed confidence that *Research II* will be seen at night.

Clouds patch the sky, but blue dominates and their white amorphous appearance is no threat to *Research II*. Nevertheless I cannot feel complacent. We are in God's hands. He loves us with an everlasting love, and I reassure myself that he will not fail me, for again and again, I have witnessed the proof of his favour.

Mary

For me, I heard Mary in the cabin last night. I talk to her quite normally. We venture opinion. We discuss the situation. The conversation goes on like this for some time. It is like a consultation. She has dropped in to see how things were going. I loved the experience of her visit. It seemed to make such sense, in this voiceless wilderness of the sea and absence of any signposts of human identity. There have been several of these visitations, possibly four occasions. And every time it ends, where I hear my own voice, I wake up at this point, audibly speaking. Realization reasons that Mary just cannot be here. After all, I sail by myself. And yet that is not enough. What is our presence? In our modern age, we chat freely with one another, though we are thousands of miles apart. We even see one another though we are equally distant from one another. We think nothing of listening to a conference or discussion, half way across the world. We even watch men or women, traveling in spaceships and instructions are relayed to them from NASA when they are hidden on the other side of the moon. Why should skepticism narrow down our cognition to exclude fields of knowledge that we are simply too uneducated to understand? The fallacy that 'seeing is believing' as a foolproof principle of inductive inquiry, is glaringly obvious to an open mind that is not programmed by pride and conditioned by our pretended prophets.

To get back to the cabin of *Research II*; to me the explanation is simple, like a working formula to calculate the tonnage of my boat, or like an engineer using the slide rule for his calculations. The spiritual transcends the physical, as the whole is greater than the parts. Transfer of the human presence obtains because the spiritual, like the laser beam, cannot be restricted by the physical. If the spiritual is a transitive dynamic force like love, for which another human being is the substantive object, then, there is that ability of transfer of the presence to the location of another. Other spiritual forces, in the full range of good and evil, have this capability as well. But there is a difference. The two spirits must be compatible. Love relates to love, good to good. On the other hand, an opposite or hostile force has to be resisted and regarded as our enemy. Using this thinking, we have a simple formula which we can use to nurture our growth as human beings as members of the human family for the good of all.

As we parted on the quay before I left Sydney, Mary said, 'I feel part of me is going away.' In that sense, she was with me all the time. Her presence was with me, because no barrier, no wall, no divide can separate us from each other's love. Did not the apostle Paul express this thought in defining the characteristics of supreme love, which is the essence of God 's favour and its expression in Christ's forgiving and redeeming work, on our behalf? Hear St. Paul's words. They defy contradiction and the humblest and the most desolate can rest in their integrity.

> *'... I am persuaded, that neither death, nor life, nor angels, nor principalities, nor powers, nor things present, nor things to come,*
>
> *Nor height, nor depth, nor any other creature, shall be able to separate us from the love of God, which is in Christ Jesus our Lord.'*

Foot-note on the Wild Massage

Journal: Having had firsthand experience over the last week, especially I would pass on this advice. You have to stand up rather than sit. Or you have to lie down. You may do both, in order to allow time for your posterior to get back to normal. If you must sit, you do so , using a soft cushion. This helps to rectify the situation so that within a few days, sitting conditions are at least tolerable.

Log: Friday, 28th July, 1995

Waypoint 27

GPS Readings at 12.22 p.m.:

Speed: 5.5 knots

Position: N 48' 58" W 7' 3"

GPS Readings at 8.30 p.m.:

Speed: 4.3 knots

Position: N 48' 59" W 6' 37"

Tonight I would only catnap. Indeed from now on there would be no night's sleep. As lights flickered on the horizon to north and south, as monster ships churned the seas like a multi-furrow plough on the wheatfields of Canada's Prairies, sending shockwaves to rock my little boat, I knew that entering this phase, the last stage of my journey, was a free ticket to potential disaster. If good fortune held and the southwesterly continued, I would be very soon in port. But then, the northwest would also do, or the southwest or the south. All these would fill the bill. I could not know that the exception would be my lot, and the next six days and nights would have all the uneasiness of a waking nightmare.

Log: Day 37, Saturday, 29th July, 1995

8:15 a.m. GMT: Track 87' E

Speed: 3.6 knots

Position: N 49' 23" W 5' 47"

Reaching Land's End, England

I have just taken a sight and we have at this moment literally passed the toe of England, the **Wolf Rock Light at Land's End**. In the early hours we saw the light of the Bishop Rock lighthouse on the Scillies. It shone amid the bobbing lights of the fishing boats as I already pointed out, that were working to north and south of my course. Now it was full daylight and a haze covered the sky and sea. With this, visibility was strictly curtailed and nothing of land could be seen even if we were in proximity to it. What did it matter, we had made the Channel. We are closer to England than to France, our track cuts the longitude between Land's End and Brest, a bit north of the 49th Latitude.

From now on, as I study the chart, we will endeavor to sail up northeast. By God's grace and a steady southwesterly, we should soon be past the Lizard, the sentinel of Falmouth, associated with Sir Francis Chichester, the iron man and solo world voyager, and another minister's son at that. My thoughts stop in the next port, Plymouth, sheltered by the dominating Eddystone Light. One cannot help thinking of the professional pirates associated with the port in Elizabethan times. They were government approved, men like Sir Francis Drake and that ilk. Didn't Drake receive his knighthood from the first Queen called Elizabeth, and why? Yes, for his crimes of piracy, and all the gold and silver he brought home to his queen from plundered Spanish galleons.

There was really no breach of morality in this, but a kind of justice, for the Spanish had robbed the Peruvians as a perennial pseudo-commercial venture, in order to fill the coffers of Philip, King of Spain. And the Pope, Sixtus V, like his predecessor Gregory XIII, had his cut of the loot too. It was Drake's success in redirecting the plunder to England's vaults that spurred Spain to send her Armada. And the Spanish King Philip had the moral sanction of the Church. For, each Spaniard had a written indulgence, waiving normal requirements for heaven itself. Drake and his cohorts were the root of the trouble. But the irony of it lay in the fact that Queen Elizabeth gave piracy on the high seas her approval, and the citation read at

Drake's knighthood was candid. He received his honour for 'singeing the King of Spain's Beard'. The publicity or the 'Press' of the day, stung the pride of Spain's monarch to retaliate with the abortive invasion of his Armada. England's self-confidence and defiance was a blatant challenge. For Spain's ambassador was invited to the ceremony.

There is a curious coincidence in the present time, even this year. Canada's minister of Fisheries Brian Tobin, of ancient English sea-stock, is now charged along with his country, with *piracy on the high seas*, in the international court. And who is the complainant but Spain, which had been systematically robbing the riches of the international seas for the past two decades! Curious, isn't it, how history repeats itself? Maybe, old England no longer has the 'guts' of her Drakes or the 'stomach' of her Raleighs? Or is England compromised and her national character reshaped by her new corporate directorship in Europe's boardroom in Brussels? Silk suits, long dinner menus, polished political prowess on the podium of a fabricated parliament, are proven arguments for compromise.

When an English Government Cabinet minister, Leon Britton, has the insolence to condemn his cousins in Canada, right in Ottawa, and at the same time claim immunity because he is a *Briton*, then history of the English Peoples has come a long way, from that which raised England's stature to a place of honour among nations.

It is laudable that Canada has a Prime minister, John Chretien, and a Fisheries minister Brian Tobin, who are more than a match for the giant consortium of Europe; stirring the stabbing conscience of their assailants is as effective as the expedient of Drake's fireships against the Spanish Armada in 1588. And beyond the skirmishing on the high seas and the fencing on the political platform, legally, jurisdiction over Canada is in question as all their members reflect the interests of Europe and the immediate interests of the European Common Market countries, surrounding the court's locus of The Hague.

The difference is that Canada's Tobin had moral righteousness clearly on his side. That never did cut much ice with the cynical government of the disparate European Union and its 'hired hands' in England. Ask the fishermen of England! See the Canadian flag on their masts. Think on these things.

Comparisons

Now that we are in the Channel, we can see definite differences. The weather, for one, is suddenly warm. It is also more than coincidence that the whole aspect of sea and sky has changed. The sea has lost its long billows and its deep swell. In the sky above, there are lazy white clouds to north and south. They cling nonchalantly to the land masses, which give rise to their formation on the coastline where ocean is abruptly stopped.

The war scene has turned to one of peacetime. The sword of the Atlantic has been blunted and there is now no sign of its menace. Of course that is a simple comparison, which holds good only for the present. But there is a definite difference between the ocean and this corridor, albeit a waterway, carved out of the continent to make England history's northern nursery of democracy, and the elusive and unattained goal of modern demagogues, Napoleon Bonaparte and Adolph Hitler.

Birdlife

This morning I had visitors, little dark colored birds - maybe some kind of tern or sea swallow or cousin of the *tirrick*, a lighter colored species, almost synonymous with Out-Skerries, to the north of Scotland. There were not a few gulls of various kinds. They were all welcome. And we ourselves seemed welcome to them. I greeted them vocally in behalf of *Research II* and my faithful crew, Stanley the Scull-Oar. Birds, especially gulls, have been traditionally the heralds that indicate a ship is nearing land. The presence of gulls is also the signal that a fishing vessel has been successful in a the harvest of the sea.

Round me there is the visual and auditory evidence of human activity. The throb of diesels break the silence of the sea. Half an hour ago, the sound deepened into a throaty pulsating powerful hum. It came from a powerful cargo ship as it passed down channel and westward. I tried to read the name, but the motion of *Research II* prevented me from doing so. She was light grey, with white superstructure, red and black funnel, and well groomed.

Ten minutes ago there was a loud resonating boom. I looked out of the cabin but there was nothing untoward in my view to be seen. The time was 10:05 GMT I believe it could be only one thing, with which we all are familiar. I hear it in Nova Scotia regularly, the sonic boom of the British/French Concorde on its regular run from London or Paris to New York.

How long will it last?

That is the vital question. How long will this fresh southwesterly continue to push me, effortlessly, up the Channel? Thirty-six hours, I estimate, would bring me to the Nab Tower. On the negative side, I've had the favorable wind for four days, quite a long run without a change. But then, this is the traditional direction of wind, as a rule blowing from the southwest across the Atlantic for ninety percent of the time during the summer. Also, I already have had north and easterly winds to face for the greater part of my voyage. It's only that *Research II* liked a close reach and Stanley had the knack of keeping her on course, that enabled me to overcome that extra side to the challenge of continuing without a rudder. One lesson among the many which I have learned over the past five weeks, is that **bad things do not last forever.** This gave me reason for persistence in times of great trouble that demanded all my will and strength to cope with. The storm did not last forever; the need for bailing did not last forever; being becalmed did not last forever. Realizing the import of this proven rule, inevitably one had also to bow to its corollary, namely that even good things can and do come to an end - that is, in the physical terms of weather and our environment.

I cannot help being very thankful that the southwesterly has kept pushing us eastward. But just as I reflect upon my good fortune, the wind has fallen light and our speed is reduced to three knots. I am tempted to replace my small main with the big mainsail. But the question is whether it is worth it for at most one other knot. You see there are negatives as I explained elsewhere. I have to compromise in order to have *Research II* keep on course. Put the main up and I lose the most effective effort, which relates to the boomed jib. The main simply blankets out the wind from the jib, rendering the latter ineffective. Secondly, because of the increased effort behind the mast, the approximate fulcrum affecting the 'moment,' or centre of effort, *Research II* would not be able to keep her northeasterly course. Already this became an issue in which the boat continually sought to head southeast, giving me great anxiety. That would be disastrous at this point, and could not even be contemplated.

Decision

I think we'll opt for lazily carrying on and hope that the wind will increase to a brisk moderate Beaufort 4-5, which *Research II* really likes. My! Look at the time. It doesn't seem any time since breakfast, and now it is time for coffee, a big cup of steaming black coffee. I now have synchronized my watch to GMT, so that I would be used to the adjustment before I disembark, God-willing, by Monday at the latest, or sooner, if I pull in to Brixham or Weymouth before then and call it a day. I wonder if I will get word by ship or coastguard cutter to Mary before then? I've tried but failed to get any joy from my radio. I'm totally non-plussed. There must be a hoodoo on it. And to think how easy and efficient it used to be. The fact is that haste prevented me from testing its performance before I left, and I have to face the fact that this is a substitute for *Research II*'s own radio which was still at the radio shop for a check-up. I really would like to link up with the Coastguards at this stage. I am increasingly aware of imminent danger of being cut down by an ocean monster, should fog roll in or even sudden calm bring me to a state of helplessness. I cannot even think of the situation, finding myself out here in the middle of the channel and heading into the narrowing funnel between Brixham to my left and the notorious Casquets, the rocks off Alderney in the Channel Islands to my right, in the coming night.

Vulnerable

Realistically, should the weather deteriorate or even the wind disappear or blow from the east, my situation would be beyond my ability to control. The skills learned the hard way on the long ocean path of well over 2000 miles, could not produce the same dividends in the narrow confines of the English Channel and the constant traffic of ocean giants passing my little craft on my starboard, going up channel and to port speeding down westwards to their various destinations. How I would love to see a plane of Coastal Command dip its wings to acknowledge my wave, and note the disabled rudder conspicuously pulled up on the guardrail! Or what a relief if a cutter pulled up nearby.

Just think of it, if I heard a familiar English voice, like those of my mates in the Royal Air Force long ago:

'Hey mate, welcome to ol' England. Relax, you're all set now.'

And my reply,

'I'm sorry to trouble you. It's just that I'm at the end of my resources. I came all this way, and now I'm helpless, becalmed in the middle of all these ships.'

'Forget it, Canuck. Leave it to us. This is our job. This is what we're paid for. We're glad to get out of port in this heat.'

I answer, 'You'll never know how happy I am to see you. It's just great. Thanks. I'll let you chaps decide and I'll go along with your decision. Take me in to any port. That will just be great. I can get repairs and hire an outboard to get up to Lymington if I wish. We'll see.'

Regrettably, its all wishful thinking, conjecture, a mirage. But who knows, it might still come true!

I almost succumb to emotion as I think of my possible predicament, but I pull myself together. So far all is well. Why should I harass myself with imagined negative scenarios which erode my confidence and belong to the area of hypothesis! But I just can't help it. I told the Irish navy ship to pass word to the coastguards in ports along the Channel, that I was approaching, the victim of a storm, crippled without a rudder and without an engine or radio. I just cannot understand. I know that I would not be ashamed to be towed into any English port. I've bypassed Falmouth and Plymouth, both of which I felt would be hazardous to approach.

I marshal my resources and as I look at the chart, confidence returns and I renew my resolve to head for Lymington or a port in its vicinity. I could still turn and head for Plymouth for repairs or hire an outboard. My eye still looks at Start point, the next headland after the Eddystone Light. Just past it is Brixham and Dartmouth. I relax. What am I worrying for!? It's time for a cup of coffee.

Journal note: It is afternoon. The southwest wind has gone, vanished silently and left *Research II* wallowing in the calm sea. A zephyr ruffles the surface and repeatedly I will it to grow into a fair wind. But alas! we are stuck, and more than that, there are ominous signs that tide and current are taking over control of speed and direction. What can I do? We'll just have to take it as it comes. Even readings on the knotmeter are now not to be taken at face value. Speed registered on the dial is not distance made good eastwards. Besides the direction of current sideways at this stage, bending round towards the Channel Islands to my starboard practically negates all progress northeastwards.

The day is hot and hazy. I have much time on my hands to muse and reflect. A big ocean carrier comes up astern to starboard. To the north a yacht appears, well ahead of me, I believe coming from Plymouth, likely heading for St. Malo or another French port.

I try with the Citizen's Radio to get reception from any channel and try transmitting. All to no avail. Something chronic is wrong with the wiring. Could it be that putting in all these extra circuits for the trip has jammed the radio works? I just cannot think how there is no joy, whatever I try, after hours of every experiment and checking of circuits, often for whole days at a time throughout the voyage. Could it be that ultimate virtue is indeed to scrap all these modern cons and opt for simplicity! There is no doubt that my senses are sharpened and fine-tuned by reading the sky and sea for coming weather. Repeatedly this served me well. And humbly I am thankful, that rarely was I caught napping in the face of change at the crucial point of time, in the darkness of the night.

I was just listening to a discussion on the subject of cars and their increased numbers in our modern day, on the BBC. The theme was hotly debated, and resolved into the either/or proposition, whether or not cars have reached the stage of their own obsolescence. They are currently responsible for 10 percent of world atmospheric pollution. I must put in here my own two cents worth. For the past several years, across the industrial world, the hydrogen-powered vehicle is being developed. In Canada's British Columbia, a progressive outfit is breaking new ground, teaming up with Mercedes, to introduce a hydrogen-gas powered bus. Introducing this could be a lifesaver for cities, and cushion the ban on private cars in urban areas. I predict that before the year 2000 A.D. Canada, along with Germany, will emulate Henry Ford's success. If you are around, you can correct me if I'm mistaken.

Taking Inventory

It was always essential to know how much of everything was aboard; how much of and what items did I use each day. It is not a simple matter to estimate beforehand what you require. Besides, you may use more of some items than others, by sheer preference or ease of preparation. I thought one and a half dozen tins of sardines was quite sufficient. In fact I could have done with double that amount. On the other hand, though I love my marmalade, I have emptied only one jar and the second is still half full, and there are four more jars on board.

To change to another but fairly essential category, toilet-rolls. By the way, I call this 'fairly' essential, because they all got very soggy and therefore almost unusable in the damp conditions of the Atlantic. When I look at the boxes of unused rolls, I marvel at the surplus. There is enough to cater for the whole Brussels bureaucracy at their annual dinner party. I, being a canny Scot, am still not finished of my first roll and it also serves the ancillary requirement of cleaning my glasses.

Saturday evening

Waypoint 30

Position: N. 49'29" W. 5' 26"

Speed: 3.1 knots.

Note two observations. One, we have not covered much ground over the last 8 hours. Two, the speed recorded is doubly deceptive, in that a slight zephyr breeze at that point in time could generate speed as *Research II* is very responsive to the least wind. Further, current and tide practically cancel out the knotmeter's relevance. I am now taking readings, at least twice a day, far more frequent than on the ocean. These are referred to as Waypoints when using the GPS. I notice we are right on the Longitude of the Lizard. *Research II* yaws from side to side in the hot calm; the sails and idle gear rattle continually. And I am a bit weary. A hazy sheen glitters over the sea, from the sun filtered through the heavy polluted atmosphere. What a contrast to the ocean!

Log: Day 39, Sunday, 30th July, 1995

Waypoint 31

7:30 am. GMT

The night ended for me early as I was on deck often, and long before dawn. With the hazard of ships and the fitful wind, sleep in any extended form was out of the question. How the Channel strikes me in contrast to the ocean. I think of the positive side, especially in the beauty of the morning when the calm has an unmatched beauty as it bathes in the newness of the summer sun. Time is not at a premium.

The joy of boyhood

My mind goes back to my boyhood, rowing out before school in the early morning to check the trammel net. What a reason for getting up, to row out on a glorious morning in Aultbea, to bring in some cod, plaice, haddock, gurnet or even a ling and that pleasant accident to happen, to release a big scaly salmon that God led into the net.

How effortless to row back to my home shore, even though the morning wind should rise against me, when the mind was fed with this fulfillment and the choice food of kings would grace our table in the manse.

But more, there was a special satisfaction that never left me, that the more fish we caught, the more we could give to neighbors. In my mind's eye, I relive these happy days. I see the mountains, 'the tops', with the road bending along the escarpments and hidden between intervening rises, as it snakes along the coastline from away, to wend its way down past the *Tigh h-ailliadh* along the straight below Drumchork (*Druim-a-Choirc*) farm into the village, the hub of my childhood world.

The wonder of an unspoiled coastline

What a marvelous environment, the sharp contrasts of sea and land that form an unspoiled coastline wherever you are! The land does something to the sea. I think it fights back against the continual battering, and only reluctantly concedes the inevitable victory of the sea. On the other hand, the land lets the sea into its geological valleys, and irregular flooded folded mountains that create long undulations. Raised beaches, like those along the estuary of the St. Lawrence river, especially obvious on the south side as the road passes northeast through the 'Eastern townships' of Quebec, or in the sedimentary screes north of Cheticamp, as the road twists its way round the western rim of the Cape Breton Highlands, with its matchless beauty for the traveler.

The English Channel is only in part illustrative of this, but there is great variety if you consider the coast on both the English and the French side. There are unparalleled craggy rocks - look at the Brittany coast - as well as soft forgiving bays. I think there is a softness too, as if the lion of the sea is cajoled in from the ocean, and to some degree, at any rate, its wild personality is tamed.

Reading Garmin GPS.45

Speed: 1.6 knots

Position at 9:19 a.m.:

N. 49' 41" W. 4' 52"

Sadly, the calm yesterday and the fitful wind, which now comes from the northeast, directly ahead, has cut progress drastically. Here we are, scarcely past the Longitude of the Lizard, which threw out its light all through the night. It is hard to get *Research II* to bear northeast, even with the full main. We have to settle for east. The trouble is, we do not have enough way on us to counter the current that is pulling us to the French coast and the notorious Casquet rocks. There is the added hazard of the ocean ships which have to close up as they pass the Casquet Lighthouse, because as you can see from the chart, the Channel narrows considerably at this point. This also causes the down stream current from the North Sea to accelerate at this point and threatens to make it impossible for me to get any further east.

All night, large ships passed to the west on my port and east coming up at my stern. These monsters, laden with containers, plow on through the night, one after another, so that *Research II* rocks as their displacement waves reach us. There is no let-up, from big ocean carriers to fishing-boats and pleasure boats. I saw a beautiful William Garden designed yacht with the envious stern cabin, reminiscent of stern castles on old sailing ships. She was crossing to France well astern. She was motoring, but could easily have sailed with these masts. I seem to be the only craft that uses the wind. And the wind has let me down. My confidence in it has been shattered.

A large dragger has been fishing all night and right on throughout the day. The noise is incessant and it has worked steadily in the vicinity of *Research II*. I must admit that the irritating noise has 'got to me' and I am in a crabbit mood. If only we could get away from here! The pull of the ground nets puts a mighty strain on the diesels. The result is that there is a tremendous deep-throated noise from the engine and only every so often when the drag net is brought to the surface, is there a respite. The men on these boats put up with this for days and nights at a time. They really earn their wages, as few on land could ever do.

As I write, *Research II* bobs on. The wind is northerly and light. For the time being, our speed is reasonable. Stanley the Scull-Oar is in charge and seems to want me not to interfere.

As I look out the companion-way, a large container ship, fully loaded, thunders up the Channel. I check its course coming up astern, a formidable sight, a wall of white water and a massive bow of steel. There is no sign of a human being and how can one not feel a cold chill at the thought of this monster coming down on our little boat? If I stopped to think through all these possibilities every time a brute appeared to head for me, either over my bow or stern, I doubt if I would wait aboard, but jump for it in sheer panic. When they come up at me in the dark, I do not think at all. If they come over the bow, I rely on their radar and the navigation lights which shine forward at the mast-top. If they come up astern or on my quarter, I give a flash of my powerful searchlight on my sails and straight at them. I know that twice, at least, I saw a ship bear off and the engines slowed. My searchlight caught the bulbous foot of the bow in its light, showing the monster had slowed down. Several times they've slowed down and then picked up revolutions which I could clearly hear, just as they passed me to starboard. I somehow have got into the middle of the traffic.

The southwest wind has abandoned me

The southwest wind let me go. It has forsaken me. I am abandoned, and I am at the mercy of the northeast and the cross currents of the Channel. I came out in a sweat as I traced a current on the chart, showing how it bent in towards Alderney and Guernsey. You can see how the current from the North Sea counters the current from the Atlantic and causes the latter to bend in towards the French coast. You ask, where is the famous Gulf Stream current? A good question. The Gulf Stream leaves only a residual water force to go into the Channel. The main stream turns northeast between Wales and Ireland.

Meanwhile, I try and figure out what is best to do. In actual fact, options are limited if not eliminated. The rocks all around these Channel islands, and especially close to St. Peter's Port, make me dismiss the idea of going in there for an outboard. I wouldn't have a chance of making port but would be driven among the rocks and sunk. One effect of huge ships passing all the time is that the triple displacement wave from the ship continues to travel to the shore, creating a recurring hazard for small boats. *Research II* could drift in close to rocks even in a calm. Then a sequence of deep big waves from the big ships traveling miles away could cause my boat to be holed on the rocks. It takes only a foot of movement of a wave to lift my boat and bring it down on a rock, in order to destroy the hull.

We are truly strange creatures, that is, we human beings, or do I just speak for myself? I said that ships sail past, westwards down Channel on my port side and others sail up the Channel on my starboard and there *Research II* sails on in the middle. Do you know, I like it this way. It somehow suits me. It's my thing. Call it what you like. Maybe it is my way of having fun. If it was gambling, you would say that the dice were heavily loaded against me. And I know that few, if any, would put their money on me. Yet I feel great. I haven't slept except in short catnaps since Thursday night, yet I somehow do not feel the worse for it. The fact is that I put little energy out. Even Stanley the Scull-Oar discourages me from touching him.

Boyhood fears

Dare I say it, but I like sea-roaming in this new style, without a rudder. Nevertheless, rocks and high coastlines make me uneasy. I think it is a kick-back from my boyhood. Swell and waves and tide made the height of rocks under the keel of our small boat change so that they were never constant. Yet every day we would row in close to the rocks and tense with apprehension, as we looked over the side at the rocks underwater. The clear water prevented one from knowing how close the rocks were beneath the surface. Further, one moment you would have six feet clearance and next the grey wilk and mussel covered iron hard gneiss hit the oar blade, as you backed water.

Fifty years later the same uneasiness grips me as I contemplate the Casquets and their growling hungry teeth, and all the rest of the cliffs and broken headlands, which willing currents may pull me onto, in forced calms, or sudden gales. This explains to some extent the fact that I have kept away from either side of the Channel. It may seem strange but we are long past Land's End, and yet I have not seen a sight of land, and at this point have not the least desire to do so. In fact, should I see it on the right, the island of Guernsey, it would add to my apprehension.

Now I turn to my Heavenly Father who has given me this day to share with people everywhere in worship and thanksgiving for His great love to us all and His providential care. It will be at least Tuesday or Wednesday before I make port. As time wears on and my progress is sabotaged by that fitful northeast wind dead ahead, it is more than probable that I'll pull in at Brixham or Portland. Who knows? We'll see. Two knots on a close reach and strong currents against me are not the recipe for progress. The net result, is that we are being carried south and off course.

As I speak, another monster thuds up astern, heading at an angle to me to starboard. She will have to swerve to port again to clear the Casquets. I just got out the centre chart for the Channel, a much larger scale - when I looked out and another container giant was thundering past as well, to starboard, again, as if she has just swerved round *Research II*.

The wind has picked up a little and we are clipping along at a fair pace. Going to windward and especially close to the wind on a flat sea is deceptive and the sound of the ripples at the bow overstate the score.

CHAPTER 19

The New Immigrants

GPS Readings:

Waypoint: 32

Track: 84'

Position: N. 49' 42" W. 4' 39"

A Day of Reaction

It is still Sunday and we wander slowly up the Channel, sailing northeast. Probably we will have the famous sentinel of Plymouth on our beam. I hope so. There is something special having the great light of the Eddystone Lighthouse shining on us out of the darkness.

Journal Note: I'm going to relax and listen to a service of worship on the radio. It comes from a Pentecostal church in Cardiff, Wales. The message of the preacher is simple, yet profound. We all have a spiritual side to our lives which must be cultivated. Neglect it and we get weeds.

This Sunday, 30th July, was different to all the previous five. These were spent on the ocean. Today we have a reaction for we are close to land. I felt today as if time had caught up on me. It is like an outboard-speedboat, which is suddenly stopped. There is a feeling that the wave at the stern is going to overwhelm the boat. In a similar way, I feel a bit overwhelmed. Here I am in the English Channel, having sailed 3600 miles across the Atlantic, more than 2000 miles so far, of which I struggled without a rudder. I came through storm and calamity and here I am safe and sound. Even the huge bruise of brown and yellow on the side of my face, along with the egg-sized lump above my right eye, are scarcely visible. There is the remnant of the 'egg'. Just think of it, after 4 weeks! But I am none the worse for it. That is, as far as I know.

Different thoughts come to mind, especially the prospect of seeing Mary again. But even the thoughts cause me to be a bit 'down.' That is, unless and until a good following wind from the southwest will bring us quickly to port. One reaction that keeps coming back, is that the trip is essentially over. Now it is only the formalities that cause me frustration. There is also the reaction of thanksgiving to the Most High for His goodness and kindness to me, for granting my life-long wish before I die.

Log: Day 39, Monday, 31st July, 1995

GPS Readings: Waypoint 33

Track: 87'

Speed: 5.3 (Not mean speed)

Position: N. 49' 45"

W. 3' 2"

We have had a wonderful sail over the past 24 hours. The night was studded with stars on a background of deep dark velvet. Ships passed to right and left. Somehow I felt they were no threat to us. At midnight, surely enough, the famous Eddystone Light came into view, pulsating out its enormous flash, really a revolving light, two flashes one after another.

This morning I trimmed the sails about 6 a.m., and lay down until 0800 hours. I have reason for lying down at every opportunity, to give my sore posterior a chance to heal. One wonders how John Ridgeway and Jay Bligh were able to row the Atlantic with bottoms which must have been inflamed like a hot apple pie that has a broken crust. I take my time making breakfast. There's tea, Rye Vita and a bit of ham, plus my marmalade. The last pound of butter which I came across two days ago, was getting stronger in taste by the hour, and had to go overboard for the gulls. Indeed, only one took a taste of it. I suspect it was too rancid even for the birds, and especially the English ones, who tend to be overly fastidious.

The huge oil tankers and container ships ply endlessly up and down the Channel. Even as I write, a big one is astern of me, thundering on at an angle to my course. The reason is that I am running nearly parallel to the Casquets Light off Alderney, and the ocean monster has to bear to the left of the Light. As I go forward east, the gap between me and the Casquets Light is narrowing. I just may have to tack back north towards Brixham or Lyme Regis in Lyme Bay. Eventually I have to get north as well as east, to disembark at some port in England.

The afternoon has come and with it a great calm. The whole dome from horizon to horizon is an azure blue. The sea around has sultry wavelets rippling the waters as if there were imaginary wind. I look at the chart and see Lymington and the Solent about 90 miles away to the northeast - a comfortable 24 hours or less. But in this situation, a pipe-dream, it seems for me.

Log/Journal notes: It is not uncommon to see three or four large commercial ships at one time coming up and down the Channel. Several sailing yachts can be seen on their way to or from the Brittany coast, probably St. Malo or the Channel Islands, of Alderney and Guernsey. All the yachts are motoring. The Channel Islands are just southeast of me at this point about forty miles. Indeed I had contemplated going into St. Malo and picking up Mary there before sailing on northeast to Lymington. But we are late and Mary will have left Paris by now any way. We have a new situation to face, where the initiative has been taken from me and wind and current dictate their terms which I have to accept, whether I like it or not.

On the positive side, it is not unpleasant to laze away in the cabin or the cockpit while *Research II* ambles on at barely 2 knots. We have to be philosophical, and wait for a wind. If a good southwester or northwester would only come along, I say, we could be in Lymington easily by tomorrow at this time. But there is no sign of such good fortune.

Stowaways

There has been an exciting development on the subject of passengers aboard *Research II*. While I was taking GPS Readings, a wasp was quite calmly sitting on the cabin top beside my hand. A little while later after I had finished my supper, I was about to pick up my plate when there he was again sitting on the edge of the plate, licking the surrounds. I felt a bit guilty as I had cleaned it. Obviously my kitchen skills could be improved upon. But it is good to see that someone else is benefiting from my remissness. As if that was not enough, I thought that I had double vision a few moments ago, when I checked the cabin top and found another fellow was still ensconced there, resting quietly.

The conclusion was clear and inescapable. Things have happened on this trip that I hadn't the faintest clue about. Things were going on almost under my nose, which I did not suspect. Looking at these two wasps, they appeared undersized and weak and underfed. The implication was that they were Wilfred's progeny and that he therefore had a spouse aboard as well. Often when I was lying down during the day for a nap, my eye would see a dark cluster of something stuck to the ceiling in a lazerette at the stern below. It apparently was a live nest that Wilfred occupied as a stowaway. I surmised now that during the voyage it was easy for him to pick up some scraps and also to feed his good wife as well.

The new immigrants

The picture seemed clear to me now. The two of them, Wilfred and his spouse Wilena, had decided to immigrate to Britain, and Wilena being pregnant produced her family aboard *Research II*, much as some mothers bring excitement to a jetliner by producing a little baby on flight or for that matter in a taxi on its way to hospital. Could it be that the newfound couple expected *Research II* to have left a week earlier, as anticipated, and that they expected to be ashore a week ago before Wilena's time had come? And now here we had this unforeseen complication. I just mention these developments in a casual way by default. The results of delay and a broken rudder go far beyond my immediate interests. It only goes to show how interdependent we all are in this world.

Personally I do not mind the odd buzz round my ears, though it is not so acceptable when I try and sleep. I hope we will get a wind to take us to port before more eggs hatch and *Research II* is taken over by a new crew. Isn't that what happens often when new immigrants claim a prescriptive right to take over old settled communities and use their large numbers to change all the laws in the name of democracy and freedom? Remember Captain Bligh of the Bounty? The crew voted him overboard and he with a few others were deported from his own ship, and he had the humiliating experience of changing command of a warship for a lifeboat. By the way, the wee fellow has gone and two adults, one a shapely strapping long-legged thing, as wasps go, are there on my plate and appear to be getting a meal out of it. Have a care; Wilfred and Wilena are having their supper. It reminds one of the Canadian Pacific liners like the Empress of Canada, in the early 1960s, when there were two or three sittings for dinner in the evening.

Monday evening, 31st July

GPS Readings: Waypoint 34

Note: Becalmed for 10 hours till now 6:30 p.m.

Track:	152'
Speed:	1.1 knots
Position :	N. 49' 37" W. 3' 02"
Time:	18.32

Log: Day 40, Tuesday, 1st August, 1995

This is not by any measure the most satisfying part of my trip over the Atlantic. The calm yesterday was bad enough. But it reverted to a wind from northeast by east, a refined attempt to give me the worst direction. The result was that it was impossible to steer a course for Lymington and indeed the Nab Tower at the gate to the Southampton Roads. Further, the wind is so unreliable, gusting at times to force 6, especially in the morning and dying down to nil, that it is almost impossible to maintain headway to any definitive coordinates. I want to put it on record that the hot hazy weather, predominantly calm, has an easterly essence in it which persists day after day now since Saturday. And here we are still struggling in the Channel on Tuesday, threatening to be shipwrecked on the rocky shores of Brittany or the equally treacherous shoals of the Channel Islands.

In the reasonable expectation that a westerly was bound to come along, I kept on heading east. But my reading has put me so close to Guernsey that it will be now impossible to pass north of the Casquets - my avowed intention. Last night the Guernsey Light was boldly flashing to my starboard. This morning I took stock and came to a decision. I must backtrack, north to northwest, as close to the wind as possible and get back as fast as I can to the English coast. After several abortive attempts to get *Research II* around, I finally managed to trim the sails and set Stanley as we changed course and sailed off across the Channel again to a north/northeast morning breeze.

Log/Journal notes: It looks as if I'll have to slog this, all of 50 miles across to Dartmouth or Brixham. If the wind does not change and I get into one of these ports, I might hire an outboard and with this I could be in Lymington by tomorrow. Strictly speaking, I regret that arrangements were made to disembark at Lymington. I have no reason to go there. Only that the arrangement was made, is there any purpose for still thinking of it? And even then there is no information for my wife Mary or sisters and nephews to make arrangements to travel there to meet me.

There are two items on life here. My water supply is quite low. I have at the most, three days' rations and I mean rations, a very minimal supply. If I went in to Brixham I could get extra water there. Second, with very little work I could also get a new tiller and gudgeon pin, to activate the rudder right up to Lymington. Also, the stuck halyard could be unloosed to change the jib and get the genoa up, and the mast winch could be repaired. But then I reflect, that really my voyage is over. I have reached the UK. All I need to do is simply turn in to any port as an automobile would pull in at a town on the motorway.

It is nearly mid-day. A well appointed yacht is just passing on its way across to France. She sports a large blue and white spinnaker. Talking of sails, the trip proved that my auto-sails, while having merit, are not the way of the future. That is for furling, jib and main as is presently well developed. I feel good that I have given the Auto-sail its day in the field. I can now retire the idea, also knowing that it served me well in my trip across the ocean without a rudder. The two-panel foresail on the foreboom and the one on the mast served me well in combination with the Scull-Oar. It is a relief to put the whole project on file for the archives, after thirty-five years of dreaming and scheming. This was Mark III, the third proto-type that I had made and sailed with. For the first I had built a boat, the beautiful Heron Sailing dinghy, still very popular in Britain. Mine was built in plywood, the standard medium in postwar years. Now it is built in fibreglass and continues as a proven and beloved small boat either for sailing or as a tender for yachts.

Tuesday morning 6.30 a.m.

Waypoint 35

Log/Journal: Exasperated. Becalmed all night northeast wind. Speed 1 knot.

Reading: 6:30 a.m. Tuesday:

North 49' 35" West 02' 53"

Time: 6:40 a.m.

Stopping to think

There is something timeless about this kind of life. Day follows day and night follows night in an endless sequence of undisturbed order. I keep informed about the outside world from continuous news programs on the radio. Inside the boat, my senses are heightened so that I am aware of little things which normally would engage very little of my thinking. Maybe that is a cost factor of our fast pace of modern life. We travel through life too fast, so that we miss much that would enrich us. Isn't that true! Think of your journey in your automobile; even round the Cape Breton Highlands or along the *Fleur-de-Lys* trail. Speed has impoverished our lives and deprived us of tranquillity and the myriad forms of interesting life, and wonders of nature that actually provide the blessings of our habitat. Isn't it true that we regard insects as enemies? There is no discrimination between good and bad. They are all lumped together as evil, something hostile to be got rid of with ex-World War surplus poison gas renamed Insecticides.

There is no discrimination, no differentiating, no eclectic choosing. You see *discrimination*, once a word denoting wisdom and enlightenment, the synonym for discernment and good taste, is now to be carefully avoided. The new holy prophets of our do-it-yourself righteousness, who have supplanted the Christian message of trusting in God's mercy and living in His world in harmony with His creatures of whom we humans are but a species - I say this new crowd of holy prophets and priests of the new age have issued their decree. *'Thou shalt have no discrimination.'*

We all are guilty of being hypocrites as we try and get around any situation which might suggest that we practice discrimination. Next time you listen to reporters firing questions at a politician, watch how he carefully avoids any hint that he discriminates in his answers. It is the same with teachers. They have to self-censor every history lesson, or they may be ruined by being called racist.

Preachers have a different problem. The prevailing fashion dictates that they see mankind as one amorphous mass, where they dare not differentiate between man and woman, good or bad, righteous or wicked, sin and sinner. The result is that the message of redeeming love is unread. It remains stacked up in the warehouses of heaven, unused in all its plenitude for spiritually starved people. It is just like the warehouses full of thousands of tons of food lying unused on the quay at Mogadiscio, because evil, in one form or an other, kept it from reaching a desperately hungry Somali people.

A word that expresses wisdom is in effect condemned to the waste basket. Impoverish and pervert the English language much more and we will be left with garbage, the garbled mealy-mouthed gibberish that is purveyed by starved and bankrupt minds, which have filled up with the sewage of alternative knowledge, the powerful kind that rots the human fabric like acidic rain on our homes.

When we stop to think of some of the trash that comes over on the television especially, and the subtle slant that shapes discussion on news programs, we see this trend that is continually edging out the living truth of the Christian revelation as the Way of Life. And what is there in its place but the empty barrels of despair, from which our generation are asked to drink their illusory fill. The fruit of all this is the residual echo of hopelessness that haunts the new generation of young people and provides them with nothing to live for and no forgiving love of a redeeming Saviour to believe in.

An update on Wilfred

I now turn to the lighter side of life. And why shouldn't I? I have to find my own entertainment and there are all kinds of entertainment right here and all around me! Yesterday, I told you about Wilfred the wasp and the discovery that he was not traveling alone. I dubbed his spouse, or partner, Wilena. And besides the two of them, I mentioned that there were now at least two little ones which were born in the nest hidden in the stern. Today I must confirm my fears. It looks as if I have a full family of immigrants to the UK. I just cannot tell how many there are. They fly out of the cabin in turn and fly back again like fighter planes on an airfield, during the Second World War. I think they have a food problem. Naturally the menu is rather limited on *Research II*, not only because much of the food is in tins, but to a large extent most commodities of biscuits and butter and cereal are pretty well exhausted. Sadly for this new batch of travelers there is little to eat. Further, though I cannot claim to be a distinguished domestic, there are few crumbs or left-overs for a second sitting when my regular meals are over. I do not do too much household work. That can be done in a total clean-up when we get in to port. Then *Research II* will be unloaded of all goods, and that includes the new immigrants.

I had a conversation with Wilfred. He was sitting on the table and a wee fellow was perched innocently on my arm. The conversation went something like this.

'Hello Wilfred. So you tricked me!' I said.

'What do you mean, Tricked you?' he replied, giving me a hurt look.

'Well,' I said, 'I understood that you were traveling by yourself and not with a pregnant wife.'

'I didn't know,' he said,' putting his head down, 'I really didn't.'

I took him at his word. After all it was probably true. These matters are not always cut and dried.

But it seemed to me that we had a problem on our hands, and I was in some way drawn into a situation in which I could well be compromised and unwittingly get into trouble.

I put it to Wilfred.

'The question is how are you and Wilena and that large family of yours going to get through Immigration?' I said.

'Now, that is something I was going to speak to you about,' he replied. His voice, I noticed was not in the least apologetic. He had turned away and was looking up. My eyes followed to see a flight of nine tiny wasps, circling beautifully in formation as the old R.A.F. Hurricanes used to do.

'My, aren't they just beautiful?' Wilfred exclaimed, forgetting me completely and lost in paternal admiration for his new progeny.

He went on, 'They are just about ready.'

I couldn't believe it. I was non-plussed.

'What do you mean, They are almost ready?' I asked.

There was a pause. He turned to me, rather hesitantly, with a mix of tolerance and condescension, in his voice and replied,

'Oh, Look. I think it would be better for you, if you did not know any of my plans. You could get into trouble, especially with all that alarm about animals and all that, in Britain, this last year - you know, the 'calves being cruelly trucked from England to Europe!'

'I see, Wilfred, I thank you for being so considerate. That is very decent of you, keeping me out of it,' I responded, with some ambivalence in my voice.

'Oh, there's one thing,' he piped up with renewed self-assurance, 'But then you are doing it already, if I'm not mistaken.'

'And what is that?' I asked, rather exasperated. One never knew where one was with this smart smooth-talking stowaway. He seemed to be one jump ahead of me, all the time.

'Alright, what is it,' I said with resignation.

He appeared to cough, then continued,

'I should like you to do me one last favour. It looks as if it will not mean any change in your plans.'

He paused again, and for the life of me it looked as if he was examining his fingernails-that is if he had any. By this time I would have believed anything. This fellow had taken over. He's a riot, as Ralph Cramdon would say to Alice. It was easy to visualize himself and his bunch of little blighters hijacking *Research II*, in an act of piratical nepotism which could hit the headlines of the Times and bring me to humiliation like Captain Bligh himself. He gave the impression that he was doing me a favour, being so tolerant and forbearing.

'Get on with it, what do you want?' I said, a bit abruptly.

'Yes, just this one last favour,' Wilfred continued, 'I hope it is not too much to ask. I want you to pass near to land, Brixham, Portland, Weymouth, Swanage, Bournemouth, or anywhere in between, before you go in to a port. Then I will take Wilena and my family with me ashore. I am certain that they will have their wings stretched and be fully fledged by tomorrow. Then it's Bye-bye to *Research II*, and to you, Rev Angus.'

Here he paused again, and blurted out,

'And it's goodbye to that dumb tall fellow at the stern, you keep calling Stanley who keeps nodding that Vane on his headgear non-stop day and night so that any self-respecting stowaway is nearly a nervous wreck.'

I was aghast, at the nerve of this little vermin. At the same time it was hard not to admire him, his sheer boldness, his self-assurance, his skilled diplomacy. I was about to say something, but he beat me to it and added, with a hint that I was actually to blame for this overcrowding on a little boat, and scarcity of food for this swarm of newborn little wasps.

'Remember,' he went on, pointing a finger in my direction, almost accusingly,

'If you had left a week earlier as you said you would, and if you had gone into a port, either Falmouth or Plymouth as any sensible person would do, when you reached the Channel, instead of messing around here in the middle of nowhere, making everyone nervous with all this traffic, there would be no little ones hatched out, and Wilena and I would have made a discreet exit, without all this anxiety long ago. You understand.'

I turned away, shaking my head. Who would believe that little wasps were so clever. Obviously we humans are being watched by animals of all kinds every day and being manipulated for their purposes too. In my mind, I remember Sammy Squirrel and Bertie Blue Jay, perched in the birch tree opposite the parlour window back home at Arnish in Cape Breton. So that's it. They are watching us, a kind of Big brother surveillance, monitoring our movements and sending reports in to Central Intelligence. Do I hear echoes of George Orwell's 1984?

Probably they use the Information Highway. Why worry about all that surveillance by police cameras on the highways, and on city streets and in restaurants, and in banks - maybe even in bathrooms, as I was told recently. No wonder people have lost their bearings. They've lost the spiritual station of God's message, the three-fold message of His law, His mercy, and His grace. It all makes sense. Who would believe that so many wise people who know so much and who are in so many pulpits and power positions are actually 'being had', and all their calculations are a load of mischief and rubbish?

I am suddenly interrupted. Wifred has coughed again. He starts speaking, breaking into the train of my thoughts,

'I want to thank you for being kind to me and mine. I am very well aware that you could easily have followed the usual mindless way that we are treated by many humans, who are highly esteemed and praised for their tolerance.'

Here he paused, then went on,

'No, I'm not going to name any, but they're there, and in high places too. A long list of them is circulated to all wasps, and I believe to friends of other species, to be very wary of these ruthless, unthinking people, that give all humans a bad reputation.'

Wilfred turned to me at this point, saying,

'Rev Angus, there's no doubt you have let the side down many a time. You know that inside you. All you humans, have a long list of misdemeanours to your credit. If you reflect on them, you are ashamed, just like ourselves, and hope only that you are forgiven. I must confess I too was a bit waspish a few times when I reacted a bit hastily.'

'Well Wilfred, I sure am glad to hear that you have some imperfections. I was beginning to feel a bit lonely out here, big sinner that I am. Tell us about your crimes.'

'Alright, just one,' said Wilfred, 'and only because you are a clergyman. Maybe I'll feel the better of getting it off my chest, so to speak.'

I nodded, encouragingly,

'Go on, I'm listening.'

'It was like this. I had a bad day. Wilena was in a crabbit mood for the past week. Food was not up to scratch and the weather was not all that one would desire. I took a turn round Sydney about lunchtime and flew into Wentworth Park. You know, at the west end of the city. The day had brightened up and the sun was doing its best to dry everything up. Naturally I was also looking for a free lunch. Usually I get a fair selection from the regular lunchers who sit on the park seats. Well, I was sitting on this bench, taking in the warmth of the sun while it would last, when a young girl with high heels and an attractive outfit on, sat down beside me. I felt rather flattered, and was nearly bowled over by the perfume she sported. I thought to myself, 'That stuff would attract an elephant.'

'Anyway, I'm lucky to be here to tell the tale. I saw her looking into her handbag, and out she pulled a mirror and a powder puff, at least that is what I thought, as Wilena had something like it at home in our bedroom, - sorry your bedroom.' He paused and then went on.

'Next moment she raised the powder puff to her face and dropped the heavy mirror right down on top of me. It was like a ton of bricks. I passed out for a moment, or moments, or minutes, I just don't know how long. But I woke up on the grass beside her high-heeled shoe with a splitting headache to boot. And when I looked up, there was her ladyship, this bright young thing, admiring herself in the mirror and adding some more paint to her lips.'

'So what,' I asked, 'You didn't do anything wrong.'

'Hold it, replied Wilfred, impatient to continue.

'I was real mad. Why should I get treated like this, as if I didn't count? I actually was hopping mad, if you know what I mean.'

'I think I understand,' I said, 'We all feel like that at some time or other.'

Encouraged by my sympathetic comment, Wilfred went on,

'She was wearing that new fangled pantihose, and had her legs crossed. As I said, I was hopping mad. I looked at her shoe and without a second thought I hopped on to it and next minute I jabbed her in the ankle, the soft fleshly bit just below the bone.'

Here Wilfred paused and I do believe I heard him laughing or did I imagine it. Then he went on,

'She let out a fearful scream. I never heard the like of it. I felt her foot moving under me as if it was an earthquake. I just managed to get enough speed for a power takeoff and buzzed off as fast as I could.'

Here Wilfred went into some athletic contortions. He was rolling around the table, doubled up with laughing.

'Look, Wilfred,' I said, when he was quiet again, 'You don't sound very penitent.'

'Right, that is the last time I'll make a confession,' he said, obviously offended.

'No Wilfred, It's alright. I accept it. And I understand. A lot of things we do which are not very good are still very funny, especially when we stop to think about them later. We thank the Lord for that. He does freely forgive us as long as we mend our ways.'

'That's great, then I'm forgiven. That's a load of my mind.' He bounced back to good humour and went on,

'Now back to the present. I want to thank you because you could have swept the lot of us overboard in the last day or two. You knew my nest was there in the cabin but you left it alone although it must have occurred to you that it was fully occupied. But you didn't harm us. I want it on record, that I and my family are deeply grateful to you. For we must all abide by the Creator's universal law as all God's creatures, that we love one another and do unto others as we would have them do unto us.'

I was impressed. What a great chap this wasp was! I had learned so much from him, not only about him, but about myself. Then his voice, his rasping little voice, as all wasps have, spoke up again,

'Just one last favour.'

'What is that?' I said.

He replied, 'Please leave a little of that spreading cheese on the plate after your supper. Also some of that Fraser's Irish Stew. I've had a taste of it already, when you weren't looking. It's real good. Also smear some marmalade on the knife, and sprinkle a little dried milk powder on the table - I'm partial to both and it is all good for the kids, you know what I mean, easy for them to eat.'

'Enough, enough, enough, Wilfred. So be it. You made your point. I'll do as you wish. And good luck in England. From what I hear, you'll need it all.'

A Formula for thrills

There is a navigation note which urges boats crossing the English Channel to do so as close to right angles as possible, rather than cross obliquely. This is understandable as there is less complication for big ships, calculating the course for small vessels. Not only so a course at right angles is the shortest route, but that is the best so that you get out of the way of the big ones and run less risk of getting obliterated. Meanwhile, *Research II* is hopping along to the north, making the best of it on a close reach, the tentative wind hovering between north and northeast. It will be tomorrow at least before we make landfall. On the other hand, if the wind would switch to southwest, we could head straight up towards Lymington.

I just looked out and there are two container ships, which have just passed up Channel about a mile from me. I am now entering the busiest part. To get an idea of what it is like, imagine if you were starting to cross a broad highway, with big trucks thundering along it, and you in a little car with a sail instead of an engine. If you had an engine, you would scoot over as fast as you could and even then it would be a hair-raising experience. Try it without the engine, and remember each huge ship that passes is 500 times bigger than the usual road tractor trailer unit, with 8 to 10 massive diesels turning giant propellers, so that the ships are doing about 30 miles per hour, with stopping distances of a mile.

Come aboard with me on my little boat *Research II*. We will be in the thick of it for an hour if we log 3 knots - that is, if the wind holds. If it stops, we will be left becalmed right in the middle of the traffic. Already the thundering noise is continuous, a steady deep rumbling from the line of monsters, going each way. What a sight! I have been writing this, from the companionway, as *Research II* crabs her way at right angles. Moments ago I looked out and again three ocean container ships - they are all pretty well standard at 25,000 tons, appeared. They are passing now, right now. I think one has swerved. Her bow wave has stopped and she lists as she passes me to port. She must have cut her engines as the big bulbous forefoot can clearly be seen rising up as she drops speed. As she passes me, and her wave hits me, the engines pick up revolutions and she roars on. Another is coming at me right at my bow to starboard. What a size! She's pushing a wall of white water that is ten times higher than my little boat. I scan the ship from stem to stern but there is no sight of a human being.

I feel the adrenaline. Blood is pumping through my body. I didn't believe it but now I do. My hair is rising up or trying to under my bonnet. They keep coming like walls shutting me in. I read the huge lettering. There at my stern is a well kept grey monster. Written on its side I see *Cool Carriers*. And right after it a long monster - it must be the length of a football pitch - seems to split the Channel into two with her massive bow. She is loaded with oil to her scuppers so that it looks almost like two ships, bow and stern. I read the name on the superstructure, *Stolt Tankers*.

There is a hazy shimmering light over the sea so that visibility is very restricted. It takes only six minutes from the time I see a ship approaching, for it to reach me. My boat is continually being rocked by displacement waves and this slows *Research II* down even more, making this passage an even more hair-raising experience. I simply shut out the possible and even probable catastrophe that at any moment may happen. What good would it do for me to dwell on that, anyway? The ships must see my radar and take avoiding action long before they can see me visually. Otherwise, you would not be reading this. And I cannot guarantee that I'll make it to the other side.

There's a monster passing my stern right now, coming up. There are others similar to it. But this has such a load of containers from bow to stern, right aft of the bridge and funnel, that it looks like an aircraft carrier. I calculate that the time between seeing a ship coming towards me and it vanishing is 15 minutes. The reason they thunder on is that they are in line on each side like traffic on a highway and all the ships are very alike and going at the same speed, more or less.

One way or another, this is no place to relax, and could not be recommended for a Sunday School picnic, though it is the middle of summer and the weather is probably idyllic in the estimation of a landlubber.

Remember, *Research II* has no engine. It's like a driver pushing his go-cart across a motorway, just hoping the big tractor-ships of the road don't blow him to smithereens. But even worse, there is no rudder to steer with. Big waves hit my boat and threaten to stop her. I work like lightening, then pulling and slacking sheets to keep her under way. My eyes look only to the sails to see them catch the little wind there is, my hands work, each doing its work expertly and yet synchronized together. Weeks of practice night and day has made this automatic. I win, the boat takes on a steady heel, the sails curve steadily, we move forward. As I watch the pantomime round about me in which I appear to be at the centre of the stage, little gnomes shout in my ears on both sides of my head, making their rasping irritating voices heard whenever there's a lull in the traffic.

'That's it, you should have taken your outboard and two cans of gas. Look at you now, the mess you're in. You know, you just might not make it. You were plain stupid. You never listen to anyone. You just go on your own way. You just love *doing it the hard way*. Who on earth would try and cross the English Channel on a hazy day that is almost calm, in a little boat with only a sail, and no engine and no rudder! You must be round the bend. Look out. There's another one to starboard. One of them's bound to hit you. You're right in the middle.'

Unfortunately, in spite of my considerable ego, which was almost under water at this stage, I knew in my heart that there was more than a grain of truth in what was said to me. If I had stowed the outboard instead of leaving it in Sydney and with two cans of gas- for all the room this would have taken up, I would be in Lymington this evening, without any of this hair-raising exercise. Meanwhile, heavy vibrations from the engines of the ocean giants fill the air, making everything shake, even the air itself. Excuse my writing, we must have got caught in two sets of waves from two ships as *Research II* is rocking and my writing is going awry.

As another giant passes my stern at an angle, I look up at its flared bow. It is just picking up speed again, and I can hear the multiple diesels kicking in one after another to push her through the water. What a silhouette as I see her profile against the background of the hazy light from the midday sun! The old familiar shapes of ships, with masts and derricks, whaleback, a wheelhouse, long ventilators and high funnels are but a memory. The new shape of maritime commercial traffic is as different from the past as the latest model of automobile from Ford, GM or Chrysler in 1995, is removed from Henry Ford's first Model T Ford. I feel a hankering for the old, with the quiet of her steam engines and her long thin bow, instead of the giant bathtub that passes for beauty today. But that's the way of it in our utilitarian world. And let's face it, these are really some ships and the captains must be proud to be in the driving seat.

The big one not far from me must have swerved to pass me. I have food for thought. The deep rumbling noise of many engines continues and now increases. There's no end to it. Ships are coming and going, filling the air and making everything shake and vibrate as the noise from both lines of ships hits me in the middle. It is kind of reassuring that the impersonal monsters round about me, actually see me on their screens. I must believe this. If not, I wouldn't be still afloat. I must appear to them like a little mouse crossing the room and they are to be commended that they bother to miss me instead of crushing me into oblivion. And they cannot know that I have no engine and not even the basic necessity of a rudder.

Although I am on full alert, there is really nothing I can do about it should one head straight for me. There is a sensational thrill that makes my whole body tingle, as the bows keep coming up from east and west. This is a one-off experience that I do not expect I will have again in my life. It is almost impossible that I'll come through. One of them is bound to miscalculate.

Hold it, hold it. The one coming down channel is now passing to my stern. Do you realize what that means? I'm reaching the other side; I'm out of the mainstream. I can hardly believe it. We've made it. I slump into the cockpit and shake my head. That's over. I still cannot get over it. It was like a wartime convoy sailing into Lochewe, my home base, and my brother Ian and I, rowing there in our little clinker fishing boat. The difference was that here two convoys were passing each other and barging along at 20 or more knots.

I go down below, feeling the crisis was over. There are many ships in the Channel coming and going from different directions. These pass, local coasters, small cargo ships, small oil tankers, specialist ships with odd derricks and cranes. But who cares for them or any other odd travelers in the country lanes of the sea. The main point is that I got over the maritime motor-way, the busiest in the world in the English Channel. It is impossible for me to give a figure of how many ships passed me, as there was continuous traffic and my mind just shut out the function of counting, because of the extraordinary immediacy of the experience. Time itself was irrelevant with the intensity of expectation as monsters appeared to port and to starboard. I recall just as I entered the mainstream, the picture of six ships going and coming on each side of me within my vision at one time. That has stuck in my memory. How long did I take to get through to the other side?

I have told you that there were times of crisis on my voyage when I prayed, when I was completely at the end of my resources, and God delivered me. But the strange thing is that here over the past two hours, I didn't ask God to do anything. I think I felt possibly that even God thought that I had gone too far this time and that He couldn't be responsible for me. It is also true that I actually did not feel that there was any real danger to my life.

A small boat, and especially a yacht like *Research II* would never touch the steel hull of the huge ships. Why not? Simply because the massive bow wave would act like a cushion, throwing her away from the ship. Also because of the yacht's shape and ballast keel, even though she were thrown on her beam ends with her mast horizontal in the water, she would soon right herself and we would be none the worse for the experience. I was absolutely convinced of this as it happened several times in the mid Atlantic in the storm that hit me, and more than once by rogue waves in a gale. So that prayer did not come into it, nor even faith. In fact I am sure that God left me to my own devices. If you think through it, this was an experience of thrills, one after another, outmatching anything you'll ever see on television and in my view equal to any hockey, football, rugby game or boxing match that you will ever see. And the time frame of one and a half to two hours, was common to both.

Excuse me, I am going below to put on a tin of cream of chicken soup, if there is any left. All the tins have lost their paper wraps and are a rusty brown. I now go by shape, but I cannot really be sure what is on the menu until the lid is off.

GPS Readings: Waypoint 36

Tuesday evening, 6:30 p.m.

Track:	14'	
Speed:	2.5 knots	
Position:	N. 49' 59"	W. 3' 5"
Time:	18:49	

Log/Journal:

Forty miles to Portland Bill, 30' northeast. But regret, I cannot sail eastwards to get there because of the east and north wind. Still I made good progress during the day. *Research II* first sailed northwest across the Channel. In the late afternoon, the north wind followed the sun to northeast, allowing me to sail due north. Now from 6:30 p.m., no change. Could do with a westerly or south. But we have to be thankful. Cannot expect to disembark till Thursday unless I go straight in to Brixham or Dartmouth, or possibly Weymouth on the other side of the Portland Bill. We'll see.

CHAPTER 20

Swanage

Log: Day 41, Wednesday, 2nd August, 1995

GPS Readings

Position: N. 50' 26" W. 3' 10"

Time: 5:28

Sailed north approximately 3° longitude all night. Slept very little, just catnaps. Have not had more than an hour or two at a time since last Thursday. At dawn, reached into Lyme Bay, a huge indentation into the southern coast of England. It is bordered by Start Point off Dartmouth and close to Brixham to the west, and Portland Bill to the East, sheltering Portland itself and Weymouth. Lyme Bay has a number of rivers running into it. Thus you have the towns and villages at the estuary of each, namely, the Dart, the Teign, the Exe, the Sid, the Char and the Wey. Add 'mouth' to each and you have the names of these towns or cities.

At the head of the bay is Lyme Regis, which as its name suggests was the lodging place of kings. When William the Conqueror defeated King Harold at Hastings in 1066, he ordered the great inventory of the ancient Anglo Saxon shire network of administration that covered all England. This detailed study, completed in two years, became known as the famous Domesday Book. All tax dodgers were caught, and for many who had got off for years this was like the Day of Judgment, when they had to face a reckoning. Most of the places along the coast of Lyme Bay, and indeed of the whole of Dorset, are mentioned in the Domesday Book. But they are identified mostly by the rivers, as we pointed out above. Lyme Regis at the head of the bay has a curved jetty which goes back to the Roman Occupation.

In 1685 the Duke of Monmouth landed here to lead a Protestant Revolt against the Catholic James II. Monmouth was defeated and brought to London where he was beheaded as a traitor. That signalled the end of Stewart royal doctrines of Divine Rights and their pretensions to the throne of Scotland or England. The Stuart dynasty made three further abortive attempts to reestablish themselves on the throne of England and Scotland, the last being romanticised round the Bonnie Prince Charlie.

At Monmouth's execution, the executioner, with 20 years experience, took five swings of his axe before the poor duke's head was severed. Lyme Regis paid a heavy price for supporting him. Three hundred men were taken away and many of them hanged. King James promoted Judge Jeffries to be chief judge of the Assizes. The judge who traveled from county to county dealing out justice had no scruples, and hangings and beheadings were the order of the day. The court became the dread of everyone who lived near the edge of the law, and became known as the Bloody Assizes. Lyme Regis, like other coastal towns along the southern coast, is also reputed to have had a palace to the east of the town which King John, of *Magna Carta* fame, used for his vacation. Also, its ancient medieval church has a striking row of carved figures representing the twelve apostles, dressed up in English Medieval dress. Like the rest of England, the whole south coast is a feast of centuries of historical interest.

The coast around Lyme Bay is an endless treasure of geological interest, from the rocky limestone to the sedimentary deposits. It is called the bay of a thousand square miles. Looking out over the bay you get the impression that there is no shelter here for ships or boats. That is indeed true, and even when I was in the huge bay, there was the usual morning blast of wind. I was taken aback by its force, and was afraid my sails would rip to pieces. The fierce wind lasted for about an hour. Then it left us in a calm for the rest of the day with an apologetic zephyr that hardly filled the canvas, and always from dead ahead, the east.

At this point I was right in the middle between Dartmouth and Portland

Bill, each about 30 miles distant. In the dim morning light, thoughts flashed back four hundred years to 1588. I was right on t spot where Drake's Golden Hind fired the first broadside into one o Spain's invading Armada. But to the present. You realize that I had not as yet seen England's shore and this was four full days since I had passed Land's End on Saturday morning. I was sailing by calculation from each waypoint or position check, and speak of the places which I passed from the chart, but which I did not actually see from my boat.

I now turned on an east tack but the wind kept coming around in front of me, traveling with the sun. That is a sign of good weather but it was the last thing I needed as it kept me going southeast. Tide and current were often a match for the wind and I was at the mercy of both. I kept trying to get to Portland Bill, intending to round it and head along the coast to the Solent. The day was very hot and *Research II* was stuck in the middle of the Bay with very little progress. I wanted to get a phone message to Mary, but I had no luck. Two fishing boats passed, but deliberately avoided me and ignored my wave. Possibly they were on automatic pilot and also were hurrying with their catch to market.

Express Post

Soon after the fishing boats let me down, a big power yacht came up astern from Dartmouth or Torquay. I waved, and the boat slowed down and came alongside. The skipper came out to speak to me, and was very obliging. I had a note inside a plastic bag and a discarded iron bolt for weight, which I threw into his large cockpit. I asked if they would be so kind as to phone Mary so that she would know I was alright. Several people were aboard and were studying me. I do not think they really took it all in, but the Canadian flag was there, regrettably with a kind of hang-dog look because of the calm. I must have presented a sorry sight to the ladies aboard. They were looking down from the upper steering station. One of them called to me.

‘Are you alright; can we do anything for you?’

I assured her that all was well and that I felt fine. But she was ›t convinced and asked again,

‘Are you sure that you are alright?’

I answered a bit gruffly, so that she said no more.

The fact is that this is an imperfect world, and feeling fine is relative. I suppose that a woman would see a great deal of negatives in my appearance and situation. If I relented and even began to think of all the comforts and commodities that we regard as essential on land or in a big well appointed boat with a crew, I might actually break down under a load of emotion. After all I was six weeks, less a day, in the north Atlantic which at best has little mercy or concession to human comfort. Further I had not heard the voice of a woman speaking to me with concern, anxious for my condition, in a long time. And her voice reminded me of Mary and the hint, despite herself, in her voice before I left, that she might be worried about me. That was an emotional onslaught that could quickly disarm my stoicism, for I would not claim to be immune to the soft soothing solicitude of the fair sex.

There were several of my family who made the sea their profession, uncles and cousins, captains and bo’suns (or boatswains.) One of them, in retirement, spoke of the combination of a sea life and married life in the first half of this century, as no life at all. He discouraged me from thinking of the sea as a career. In short, men sail away in ships and spouses sit at home and suffer. That of course was the seaman’s life of yesteryear, the days of no rights when ships came to port and captain and crew were ready when the ship had her holds full with another cargo. If they were not there, a new crew were signed on right there.

The skipper of the power yacht gave a bearing for Lymington,

'Sail 080,’ he shouted twice.

But sadly the wind, or lack of it, prevented me from sailing on that course at the time, as you can see from the chart of my course. I was very grateful for this yacht stopping by. It was the *Princess*

Amarant, number 0853, registered in London. I want to record h my thanks to the skipper and the ladies who were so concerned fc me. It was only the second ship that spoke to me since I left Canada six weeks earlier. Joshua Slocum, 100 years ago, bemoaned the passing of the days when ships hailed each other as they met on the wide ocean. News was exchanged and it was common to send over on a line a bottle of good cheer and victuals, especially to a small boat. If he did this 100 years ago, little wonder that there is anything more in the hurry of life today. It is a truism that the faster we live the less time we have to spare.

Log/Journal note: A bad day; 2 p.m. Stuck in the middle of Lyme Bay.

GPS Reading

Waypoint 38

Position: N 50' 30" W 2' 42"

Time: 13:39

Wednesday evening

Lyme Bay will long be remembered. That was the day that started at 5:30 a.m. I turned *Research II* to a starboard tack, hoping to clear Portland Bill some 30 miles from that point. Now I am still in the huge bay in almost a flat calm at 10 p.m. The dark has come and the whole spectrum of the headland and island which forms Portland Bill is lighted up so that it is clearly visible, like the lighted shape of illuminated buildings in Madison Square, New York or Atlanta. Coming across the bay all day with fitful winds, including nearly an hour of a thunderstorm, or at any rate a gale, which laid *Research II's* gunwale under the water, and all in a very hazy summer heat, left me rather spent. This Channel is almost getting me down. And yet I do not do the obvious thing, just get in to one of these ports, and finish up or alternatively, hire an outboard to motor to Lymington. Without a motor, I can hardly make any headway. Tide and currents plus the east wind are stacked against my progress any further along the coast. The idea of disembarking in Lymington is problematic and for me is ow really on hold. A coastguard cutter will have to tow me in anyway. told the yacht owner to inform the coastguards that I was crawling forward without a rudder.

Hope springs eternal and I long for a favorable breeze to blow from the west. It is hard to believe that for most of my trip, I've had to struggle against easterly or northeasterly winds. What has happened to the traditional weather and winds that synchronize with the Atlantic Drift currents that we usually take for granted to push us effortlessly to Britain and to Europe?

It really is a glorious evening and I almost literally drink in the unique beauty of this experience. Envisage me about a couple of miles from the huge headland that sticks out to the east of the bay. There is a long row of street lights that runs out to the island over what must be a causeway. The whole headland is lighted up with thousands of lights. I see some lights moving which must be cars on the roads. I look at the chart and in my mind, I mull over the idea of just rounding the clanging bell light at the extremity of Portland Bill, and then trying to turn in to Portland or to Weymouth. The idea of Weymouth appeals to me. It brings back memories of my school days in Keil School Dumbarton, where the esteemed headmaster James Mason conducted the evening service in the assembly hall. He used different translations of the New testament - this was before the discovery of the ancient parchments of Scripture including parts of the prophecy of Isaiah, called the Dead Sea Scrolls. The latter brought an explosion of new translations of the whole of Scripture. It specifically brought into being the New English Bible - the most authoritative of modern scholarship, and most of those published since then, that are used so commonly today. Two earlier ones Mr. Mason used in Keil were Dr. Moffat's and the Weymouth Translation of the New Testament. There was a further connotation that came to me. Alexander Selkirk, the Scot who was the central character of Defoe's *Robinson Crusoe* later became a lieutenant in *HMS Weymouth*.

And here I am fifty years later, passing Weymouth in the darkness of the night in my little yacht *Research II*, the first contact with land for six weeks since I left Canada. You see how experiences are not dependent on what we observe with our vision. I cannot see wi. eyes in the dark. Yet in my mind's eye, I see Weymouth and it trig off sublime thoughts of God's Word, and of people to whom God Word was precious and Scots from my homeland whose names are household words around the globe. Just as I write, I looked out.

The tide and/or some strong current has been pushing us away to the southwest. I have had to man the sheets and struggle to get the boat around to sail east. This reminds me of weeks ago when *Research II* kept wanting to sail off to South America. Now we have come out far enough to set a course past that clanging bell light which will take us away from this treacherous area round the famous Portland Bill, along the coast eastwards. A slight breeze is stirring from the northeast. I work the sheets and reset Stanley. This takes time but I succeed. I watch the lights on the headland and slowly we are passing the famous Portland Bill. As I see the silhouette drawn in the dark by the myriad lights, there is a peculiar shape, unless it is my imagination, a shape that resembles the head and bill of a large duck or goose.

Hours pass as we make our way along the coast. There is anxiety and tension as we clear the headland. Think of it, here I was without a rudder in the dark, off one of the most tidal parts of the English Channel. Eddies and currents continually try to turn *Research II* off course. I work the main sheet and the two jib sheets, slacking one, tightening another. Chart reading is continuous; different navigation buoys have to be identified; every so often a ship or a fishing boat barges along in the dark, all ablaze with lights which cast an eerie glow over the sea. There is little room for mistakes. All I have is the pair of little lights on the masthead. My course is a struggle to keep constant, as rip tides and currents try to pull the bow to right or left. If I lose way, then I am at the mercy of these and the boat is turned helplessly out of control. It is something like a bicycle. If it goes too slow, the rider loses control. But I do not entertain the idea of failure. I impose my will upon the contrary conditions. Wind and tide are against me and you could add a half dozen other factors. But I will never give up. I get a kick out of the odds being so completely against me. Days and weeks of this have made me able to do it with each

, almost automatically. I never look at a rope; I never use two ds to make fast a rope; my eye is always on the sails or glancing the compass. Even if I get all steady and set the Self-Steering Vane, the latter cannot respond if the wind is too light. Hour after hour, I hold my breath, creeping east.

There is the continual clatter of that warning bell light. The light flashes as it circles in an arc, lighting up the sails. There is a steady hum from the land where human society revolves around itself in its many component wheels of activity. The sea is lumpy and irregular. Strong tidal currents change their direction and come out from nowhere to be reckoned with. We move along past what looks like a nasty shoal that would finish our trip abruptly. It is called the Shambles. That is enough for anyone to give it a wide berth. Sadly I have to give up going in to Weymouth, or Portland just beside me. I cannot rely on my ability to get into a port under my own steam, even in the daytime but definitely not in the dark.

Coming in to the finish

Gradually the tension eased. The wind steadied and we held a course east to clear several lights and especially St. Alban's Head. I stayed in the cockpit until 3 a.m. I am amazed how I have managed with rarely more than two hours sleep or at the most three hours each day for the past week. I was now set on a course, the last but one which would take me to the Isle of Wight. I estimated I would reach it within four hours. Before I went below for a short sleep, I was almost past St. Alban's Head and ahead of me to starboard was a faint light which could be none other than St. Catherine's Light on the southwest corner of the Isle of Wight. I resolved that when I reached near the Isle of Wight on this compass course of 95° East, there would be the option to turn in to the Needles and the Solent, or go on the outside of the Isle of Wight up to the Nab Tower with a final tack northwest into the Southampton Roads, down into the Solent past Cowes and in to Lymington. The two options would depend on the wind conditions being the more favorable for one or the other.

Rude Awakening

A shrill blast from a ship's horn gave me a rude awakening. T dawn had come. It was about 5 a.m. GMT. In a moment I wa looking out of the open hatch. There was a grey cutter some hundred yards off to port. My compass read 95° which assured me I was on course. A rubber tender was already alongside and a lone official called curtly,

'Customs. This is Customs. We're boarding your vessel.'

I pointed to the rudder and the broken tiller pulled up and lashed in the stern, saying,

'I'm a disabled vessel. I was hit by a storm. I have no rudder.'

He made no comment. Then said,

'Where are you sailing from; what was your last port?'

I pointed to the Canadian flag which was waving proudly at the stern, and said,

'I just came from Canada. I left Sydney and am heading for Lymington.'

He said, making a painter fast to a stanchion,

'I am coming aboard. We have to. I'm sorry. We're customs. How many of a crew have you?'

I almost said, thinking of Stanley in the stern, 'There's just the two of us.' But I didn't. This was not the right time for jokes. I also felt something was wrong, there ought to be two men in the boat.

'Sure, come aboard,' I said, 'You're welcome. I'm glad to see anyone to talk to. It makes a change from talking to myself.'

He sat down in the cockpit and fired some questions at me, name of boat; what I had aboard, why was I coming to Britain? He assured me all this was a formality but he had to do this.

I could well understand and told him that he was free to search the ship. He peered into the cabin and lowered himself through the companionway. He was maybe about five minutes having a look d, pushing and poking and looking into cupboards and under ...es. He was not over enthusiastic, but could not show this. He ...nfully went through the motions. If there was any contraband it was a hard task locating it, and he knew it. Even to begin to try, especially in the fore cabin area piled up with wet clothes, gear, tool boxes and supplies. At length he gave up and emerged.

'I'm sorry about this,' he said, ' but we have to do it. It's our job.'

I told him that I didn't mind. I pointed out again that I was disabled and could not steer the boat into a port without risk to other boats and my own. I said that I made the self judgment that I was a hazard to shipping and could cause an accident. Would he be good enough to tell this to the authorities so that they would tow me in. I could not get through the Needles into the Solent.

While I spoke, he apologized for tripping the sheets when he came aboard which caused the boat to jibe to port. He climbed out into his tender and made off to the cutter. I called after him,

'I've lost my course. Give me a position and course for Lymington. How far is the distance.'

By this time *Research II* was close to the cutter, though parallel, because the cutter had positioned herself parallel to *Research II* on her now changed tack. I got an answer back,

'You are 18 miles from Lymington. Steer 035.'

'Why don't you tow me in?'

There was some ambivalent answer about the little rubber dinghy. The officer didn't look at me. He couldn't wait to get back to the warm cozy comfort of the cutter, and out of the chill damp of the morning air.

With that the cutter took off and disappeared. Perhaps this was a busy day. I do not know. But one thing is sure. I did not get a welcome from this representative of England. Indeed one would have to characterize my reception as curt and certainly in no way could it be interpreted as constructive. Maybe it is the nature of their job, but the English Customs had no time to help a lone Cana yachtsman who had managed to carry on 2500 miles to England w a crippled boat.

Disillusioned

I must say that the whole episode was a shock to me. I was quite prepared to meet the Customs in port, but this meeting at sea at 6 a.m. British Summertime was a shambles. My boat could have been filled with contraband but it would be undiscovered for all the search of it meant. I pointed out to the officer that I was disabled, having sailed well over 4000 miles actual sailing to make the 3600 mile journey from Canada. The Canadian flag was there on the mast. Furthermore, the coastguards had been alerted to look out for me from the Coastguard in Halifax, over two weeks previously. Also at that time Halifax spoke to coastguards in the Channel at Falmouth. The latter mentioned that I would have headwinds on the European side most of the way. So the Coastguard Service knew that I was overdue. Yet there was no reconnaissance ship or plane to be seen over the past week since reaching British Waters. A friend in Sydney, Bernie Seward, who sails an Acadia 23, anxious for word, put out a message on the Internet saying I was overdue and seeking information. A university lecturer in the U.K. read it and faxed a message to the Coastguards. The latter, after some some considerable delay, let him know that the Coastguards could not help as they were not yet on the Internet. Can you believe it? When we are almost into the third millenium and not on the Internet! That is hard to believe, the Guardians of the once great Maritime nation of Great Britain, where no one's home is more than a hundred miles from the sea, is in effect still in the Stone Age of Communications. I should have known it. Stonehenge is not far away in Wiltshire. Some of this I did not know at the time, but part of it I did know, and that was enough to make me uncertain as to what was before me.

at a contradiction of Thomas Campbell's poem:

> *Ye mariners of England*
> *That guard our native seas,*
> *whose flag has braved a thousand years,*
> *The battle and the breeze.*

Visibility was, I estimated from the disappearing Customs cutter, about two miles at best. The sun, though well up in the sky, was blanketed by a mixture of cloud and haze. I am convinced that this haze which has characterized the sky for the past week is a synonym for atmospheric pollution. No landmarks could be seen for a bearing. The St. Alban's Light nor the St. Catherine's Light nor the Anvil Point light could be seen. My position, I calculated by DR and the information from the cutter, was Latitude N. 50' 32"; Longitude W. 1' 48".

The yacht, thanks to the Customs fiasco, was now making 4-5 knots on a course back west. The wind had been picking up steadily and was now freshening with short, steep, little whitecapped waves. With difficulty I trimmed her as close to the northeast wind as I could, hoping to get up to the coast and then to tack towards the Needles. At one point I thought that I could just squeeze in past Anvil point into the Bournemouth, Christchurch area, maybe even make land there.

I was full of misgivings. Suddenly the orderly pattern of my trip, so essential to peace of mind, was interrupted for the second time. It's not that I resented the Customs visit. Indeed I welcomed them just as I did the Irish warship over a week before. Maybe I was somehow too independent in the case of my meeting with the Irish warship. But I did not wish our rendezvous to be protracted in the unpleasant conditions. I was in their debt for their courtesy in phoning to let Mary know all was well and relaying a message to the Channel Coastguards that I was disabled, without a rudder. After the warship parted from me, a near gale sprang up that ripped my mainsail. In the case of my meeting with the English Customs cutter, there seemed no positive outcome of the visit.

Now after the Customs cutter left, the wind was freshen again in a similar manner. And their visit was directly respon for my boat being put off course. Was this to be my undoing? T thought was very much in the forefront of my thinking. Sadly, anothe thought crept onto the stage of my reflections. Could it be that Canada's defiant stand against the European Union over the Fishing question, by the so-called pirate captain, Fisheries minister Brian Tobin, meant that the halcyon days of the Commonwealth family were now over? Further on that premise, my presence under the Canadian Flag could well be an opportunity to air official resentment. Away unworthy thoughts, Angus. Surely these things could not be! But then, I am not sure.

I am very tired. I think Stanley at the stern is very tired. The sails are tired, and look as if they want to curl up. My beloved boat is tired. She just wants to get into port and take a rest. What was the point of going on, if there was no one on the look out for me? I had been listening to the BBC radio with comment on Cowes Week. It was said that up to 5000 yachts great and small were crowded into the Solent. Just think of *Research II,* a foreign boat from Canada, barging into one of these expensive toys - and without any insurance cover to meet any claims against it! Remember Joshua Slocum, the Father of all lone sailors, even he scraped the paint of a shiny yacht as he left for his world voyage. And as he took off, there were shouts of, 'You'll pay, you'll pay.'

A yacht passed at right angles, motor sailing with main up. She was a slick beauty and I judged that she was making for Cowes the long way around, by the outside route around the Isle of Wight and the Nab Tower. I did think of turning and following her, but in a close decision I decided against it. The Customs visit, and the apparent indifference to my plight by the Coastguard service gave me a double psychological blow. Probably my feelings were not fully warranted. I did realize that the guardians of the British coast would have their hands full giving tender loving care to the vast London bureaucracy, now afloat in their shiny yachts during the Cowes Week. And there was the traditional scrambling for a place, the royal presence of Her majesty at Cowes. Add to that Prince ..ip being as usual at the helm of the latest of the Asher owned ..ulti-million dollar Yeoman yacht. Being realistic, there was no way that a Scots-Canadian in a rudderless American yacht could fit in to the busy Coast Guard schedule. My reasoning was that I dreaded being pushed out from the English coast again after the tricky experience close to the Channel Islands and the hair-raising crossing through the big shipping Channel.

Also, humanly speaking, it was time for me to give myself a break. It was out of the question to think of going below and having a sleep, in the restricted waters of the Channel, especially in the vicinity of the Solent and the Isle of Wight. I had been on duty almost constantly over the past six days, with only catnaps for recharging my physical batteries. I was well and fit, but tiredness was definitely there.

Thoughts of Mary

I cannot deny that thoughts of Mary were now coming to my mind. I had not seen her since leaving Canada six weeks earlier. My mind was weary of continual exertion; continual contriving to keep the boat going. Furthermore, the bewildering complexity of currents and tide in the Channel, coupled with the perpetually contrary or non-existent wind since reaching Land's End five days ago had taken their toll of my energy. And for what? It did not seem worthwhile to go further up the channel. I had already achieved my goal. We had sailed 2500 miles, distance made good, without a rudder. I let my mind spell out my heart's desire in Gaelic verse. Roughly it went like this,

Is leamsa smuaintean milis blasd',
Air cuspair graidh mo nighean donn.
Oir cha neil aon am measg nam mnàthan,
Cho toileach breagh ri Maìri dhönn.

English

How sweet and warm to me the thoughts,
That linger on the one I love.
For there is none among all women,
So pleasing beautiful as Mary.

That itself was reason to get into port as fast as I could.

A yearning to see land

There was something else. I wanted to see land, the historic bluffs of the Channel. Remember, I had reached England the previous Saturday morning, but had as yet observed the land only in a hazy outline of night and the imagery of electric lights.

I looked up at the mainsail. *Research II* was heeling far as I had all sheets tight as whipcord. The leech was gone on the main and threatening with every gust to split right down to the boom. The Cunningham hole brass grommet was torn out, and hanging rather grotesquely down towards the foot of the mainsail. It would be impossible to reef the main as it could not set with the strain on the torn leech. My eye took in the jib. Two feet of the luff was torn and it would not take much longer for the whole luff to come off the forestay. Then there was the foresheet. It was worn almost halfway through where it rubbed against the shroud.

Before me for the first time since leaving Canada were the cliffs of England. What thoughts passed through my mind. Here is a history book, whose pages are full of vivid scenes of plunder and piracy, of men whose hearts were made of oak like the timbers of their ships. Here immortal names of ships that passed up the Channel came before my mind, like successive scenes on a stage, Drake's Golden Hind, Nelson's Victory. Here England waited with drawn sword for invaders, the Normans, the Spanish, the Dutch, the French, the Germans. After the Normans, no enemy was suffered to set foot on English soil. Here kings and captains returned in triumph after battle on land and sea. I think of Henry V returning from the battle of Agincourt when England recaptured Normandy in the 15th century.

. of Captain Moody making land in the famous Scottish built y's *Sark* after her rudder was smashed in the China Sea just over entury ago. You can see her yet preserved on land at Greenwich, n the Thames. The whole southern coast of England represents a catalogue of human exploits that gives depths and meaning to the island's history and to a large extent explains Britain's contribution to world political order and the enrichment of all peoples through the nation's literature.

I made a move to try and bring *Research II* around to a starboard tack, but she would not budge. She was locked in to this port tack. It seemed that my boat had some port of her own in mind, that I had not considered. Anyway, I knew now that I had missed Anvil Point by half a mile. I could now see it like a hook to starboard as I closed in to the cliffs. Tide and wind were driving me back. I checked the depthmeter and there was plenty water below. The sight of a fishing boat working lobster pots brought me to a final decision. I waved. He saw me and at once came around to stand off at my stern. The boat's name was the *Catherine.* I spoke to the crew of two young men and the skipper. The latter, who had sailed a schooner to Africa some years earlier, advised me to call it a day. I hauled down the sails for the last time. The skipper spoke on the radio to the coastguards. I was on the point of asking him to tow me in with his boat. But just at that moment, he told me the Swanage Lifeboat, the *Robert Charles Brown* would come out to tow me in. And this it did.

After a while the Lifeboat arrived. Two men came aboard and took control. A drogue was put out the stern and *Research II* headed for Anvil point, now being towed at a good pace against tide and wind. We sailed past the famous cliffs. We were close in so that we could see dozens of tourists sitting on the hills. Others were climbing up the cliffs with ropes and mountain-climbing gear. In the face of the cliffs you could see the quarries, like caves indenting the coast. All along this Dorset coast building stone is found, making Portland renowned as its source.

The famous Purbeck Marble

Near Swanage, the cliffs that I am looking at are the source of the famous Purbeck Marble. Geologically, marble is metamorphosed limestone or chalk, which accounts for the white cliffs like those of Dover. The marble of Purbeck is of special value and beauty because it has some other elements, which give it its special colour in three different shades. Throughout history miners worked in the caves clearly seen as we pass along the coast, and barges were brought alongside to take the marble away. If you want to see Purbeck marble, you can do so by walking over London Bridge. It is there on the bridge parapets. It was also used in the making of St. Paul's Cathedral, with spectacular effect. It is now found elsewhere with easier accessibility and the mines here are no longer worked. But Purbeck marble, or its equivalent, is still used for dressed stonework in many buildings where luxury and aesthetic appearance are primary considerations.

It is easy to visualize ships being loaded with ballast from the blocks of sandstone, essentially composites of compressed gravel from the numerous sedimentary deposits that complement the limestone. Such stone could be identified at Louisbourg in Cape Breton, Nova Scotia. This stone in large blocks are thought to have been quarried here and near Bristol after the Treaty of Utrecht which marked the end of the Seven Years' War with France in 1763. Is it not remarkable that some of these same stones comprise the foundation walls of the old Free Church, now Union Presbyterian Church at Mira Ferry, Nova Scotia, on the other side of the Atlantic?

And that speaks a message for our spiritual thinking, that the foundations of Britain's history, the basic strength of its Christian heritage, sealed with the blood of martyrs is to be found across the Atlantic, in the witness to the Christian Faith and in lives and communities - built upon the foundation of the apostles and the prophets, Jesus Christ, being the chief corner stone.

But we are now not far from port. I have got to know the two Swanage men, one by the name of Martin, a cockney from London, married to a Swanage girl and a plumber by trade. The other, Nick, is a carpenter. Martin is intrigued by looking at my last book, Spiritual Shopping for the Soul - 2. He sees a sub-heading in the introduction, called 'For Sinners only',

'That's for me,' he says, 'I'm a bloody sinner.'

'That's right: that makes two us.' I said.

'Crickey, I thought this church stuff was for saints,' he added, peering at the pages.

'Not likely,' I said, 'Saints have their own righteousness. This is for sinners like you and me. We haven't the money. Christ is the captain of our salvation. We get it for free. He's bought us. We're His and He is ours, and His righteousness is ours. It's just great. It's all of grace. The church has tens of thousands of sinners. You can ask them. The point is that they also are 'forgiven sinners.' If you know that you are a sinner, you are on another tack. It makes sense. You are saved by faith, the shed blood of Christ.

Martin and Nick were listening. Martin says,

"Could be. Could be. There's something in it. I never thought of it like that."

The lifeboat eases her powerful engines as the tide makes *Research II* buck like a horse. A 30 foot yacht makes a fascinating sight as she motors between us and the rocks.

Martin flips through the pages and read about my Make and Break gas engine in my old boat, the *Arnish Light I*, which I sailed out of Glace Bay where I was minister. He stopped at a page and read:

'He put a new song in my mouth
our God to magnify
Many shall see it and shall fear
and on the Lord rely.'

(Psalm 40:3)

Then he exclaims, in that unself-conscious inimicable Cockney manner,

'Hey, I like that. I play the guitar; I'm going to a big music festival soon. Some chaps sing that kind of stuff.'

'Alright, you do the same,' I said, 'You go there this year and sing the psalms. Change the word if you like but keep the message.'

He replied, 'I might just try that.'

Martin was so keen that I told him to keep the book. When I told him that I wrote it and that it was my photo on the back cover, he thought I was kidding him. I must say that my appearance, still with the bump discernible above my right eye, a white beard and a very nondescript outfit, bore little or no resemblance to the photo on the book cover. I suppose I resembled Coleridge's Ancient Mariner.

Rounding the Anvil Light

But now, we are rounding the Light. Swanage is coming into view. Swanage goes back to settlements in the time of the Druidic period some four to five thousand years ago. At that time England was largely covered in dense forests. Today the population of Swanage rises to forty thousand in the summer time. At the time of the Domesday Book, this was the whole population of the county of Dorset. It is tenable that the name of Swanage is Norse in origin. The Norsemen or Vikings were regular if unwelcome visitors round the whole coast of Britain and indeed occupied many coastal locations, stamping them with the Norse character including its nomenclature. *Sven* is Norse for peasant, or youth or servant. In AngloSaxon the word is *swain. Age* is really *ich* as in Sandwich. In the Hebrides this is represented by Sandwick, or Wick in Caithness. All these variations traceable to the Norse word *vik*, meaning a bay. Thus Swanage is likely to represent the bay of swains or peasants, or young men. Compare this with old English *swayne* meaning servant, and the word *coxswain* for the steersman of an English *cockboat.*

Meanwhile our eyes take in the scene before us. The houses, perched on the cliffs are packed in rows, some of them threatening to topple over or slide down the screes to the shore. There is a sense that we are approaching a medieval town. Time has stood still here. That is the impression of a 20th century visitor as he draws near this cove, coming in from the sea, this ancient inlet where the inhabitants trace their lineage through the centuries of history into the grey unknown of the distant past.

Stone Age hunters once lived in the caves in the rocks. Here communities settled and prospered in Roman times. Here Anglo-Saxons fished a living from the sea. Here fearsome Norsemen raided and plundered the hamlet, kidnapping its women, to renew their Viking stock. Here professional pirates left in longboats to join Raleigh and Frobisher in their profitable trade, plundering the gold and silver laden galleons of Spain in the 16th century, with the royal benediction. And in recent history, this was the setting specifically for the books of Thomas Hardy, whose great grand nephew Captain Neil Hardy is honorary secretary of the Swanage branch of the R.L.N.I.

History continues to unfold. Swanage, little humble Swanage lives on. It is true that it is small, but it survives. It has honourable mention in the great Domesday Book, William the Conqueror's first census of England. Its landlord at the time, we are told in the thousand year old record, was *Walter Thundor*. He held the land from the Countess of Boulogne, across in France. She was a remarkable woman, a bit unconventional and married to an *avante guard* pirate called Hugh Fitzgrip. Tradition has it that the landlord was habitually shouting at his tenants. His voice would echo from the rocks so that this was amplified. Hence they called him Walter Thundor. Most surnames in Britain derive from personal eccentricities or vocational employment, in the forbears of the distant past.

Manãna

The fascinating point that gives Swanage uniqueness is that 11th century people learned to take no notice of the shouting of the landlord, Walter Thundor. And to my great surprise the tradition is retained to this day. Time has indeed stood still. This is a holiday resort where people find a real rest from the business of life. The town motto, unofficially of course, is *Mañana,* the Spanish word for 'tomorrow' and the equivalent of *Do not do today what you can do tomorrow.* Many people in Swanage hold the view that this motto dates from the 16th century and was introduced by survivors from the Spanish Armada who stayed in Swanage and married local girls there. If you study the people there you can easily believe that there is Spanish blood mixed in with the Anglo Saxon, just as it is also found in the Celtic peoples in the Scottish Hebrides Today Swanage is no longer isolated. Yet it retains a certain timelessness, which is surely the very therapy people need, in an age of the new slavery to the clock, in our supposed emancipated modern life. It boasts a population of 9000 people. This is augmented in the summer to over 40,000. For Swanage on the seaward frontage, is one of the most desirable unspoilt holiday resorts, among the many, on the Dorset coast.

Ode to Swanage

Little Swanage by the sea,
Is full of blessed company.
It nestles in the rocky nook,
A veritable history book.

For here the walls of England's past,
Still stand on guard while ages last.
For ships that come within their sight,
That fail to see the Anvil Light.

It cannot be an idle boast,
Of all the towns along the coast,
That Swanage earns immortal fame,
And Domesday Book records its name.

Little Swanage by the sea,
You make the best of company.
For all who chose your town to see,
Receive both rest and therapy.

Guardians of England

The lifeboat like all those in the Royal National Lifeboat Institution whose patron is the current monarch,is manned by volunteers, with only one maintenance engineer, a very efficient and obliging man called Michael. Round the inside walls of the Station lists of ships and seamen rescued over the centuries can be read. At one time the lifeboat was just like a whaler or double-ended longboat with men, 'strong men and true' at the oars and their coxswain at the helm. Now the modern boat is self-righting and has a cabin like a bus. It is powered by twin supercharged diesels which drive four-bladed props in tunnels at each side of the keel.

The skipper today was a dentist. There are ex-sea captains, and marine engineers and men from all kinds of trades and professions. There is a pool of these to draw from. Today eleven were aboard to tow me in. This was treated as an outing, a chance to get away from the heat and humdrum monotony of the land on a summer day. It also acted as a fitness training role for boat and crew. In this way they would not be 'rusty' when demanding duty needed their response. Real duty came in the calls that took the men out in stormy seas and often in the darkness of the night. Then their virtues as real men of England, the walls of her history's greatness are put to the test and have so far never failed.

Coming into port

Suddenly the Lifeboat station is near us. The lifeboat p
and *Research II* is moored to a buoy. Photos are taken. I climb
the lifeboat as it pulls in to the quay where it will shortly be winch
up the steep ramp into the covered station. I adjust my eyes to th
scene before me.

Crowds, hundreds of people are parked before us on buildings and the jetty. Interest is always high as a boat with a mariner comes in. The flag of Canada waves in the wind to signify my identity. I step onto the quay, but I cannot stand without falling. A big Englishman holds me on each side as I make my way slowly up the sloping pier towards the Station Lookout room.

People greet me with good will. I feel I have come among friends. History has opened a door through which I have entered and round me are the proofs of England's enduring strength. Here, not in the instant cities, the prefrabricated towers of modern glass and the choking motorways of polluted travel, I say, here is England and the heart of its greatness, that produced the Nelsons and the Drakes, the Hoods and the Howes. And in the continued readiness of these volunteers in the Lifeboat Service to go out in the hour of need, the tradition of England's history is continued.

I climbed up the stairs to the Lookout room and sat down. I met two charming ladies, Liz and Lucy, who kindly ministered to me and all my needs. I drank in the peace, the stillness. I thanked them all. I sat back and savoured a deep satisfaction.

Last Duty

There was one thing left for me to do before I would take my leave and join up with my Mary, my own, *nighean donn bhoidheach*, (my beautiful dark-haired maiden) in Scotland. It was a sacred duty, a vicarious act of acknowledgement of a winning team, that 'had fought a good fight, had finished the course, had won the crown.'

I rose up, steadying myself against the windowsill and turned

.owards the little harbour, where the fresh east wind kicked .e whitehorses on the incoming seas. There *Research II* which me over the north Atlantic, lay to a buoy. My heart filled with overwhelming justifiable pride and thankfulness as a kaleidoscope .f experiences of our trip together over the past six weeks since leaving Canada, raced like a film through my mind. I looked at my faithful partner, now at anchor in this little port in the English Channel. She swung round at her mooring, so that the sun glinted on her white top-side. It was as if she became aware that I was looking at her. I could almost hear her thinking,

So there you are. I thought you had forgotten me, you old rascal, Reverend Angus. And to think what we've being through together. I know of course that you could never forget me for long. We will live forever.'

A smile creased my bearded face, as I whispered through the glass,

'We made it; we made it; you and I, and Stanley; we made it, together.'

I watched. Her bow dipped in agreement. The Vane of Stanley, the Self-Steering Scull-Oar nodded in acquiescence; the flag of Canada, the Maple Leaf, waved triumphantly, in confirming approval.

Until the next time.

I must down to the seas again, to the lonely sea and the sky,
And all I ask is a tall ship and a star to steer her by.

I must down to the seas again, for the call of the running tide
Is a wild call and a clear call that may not be denied.

I must down to the seas again, to the vagrant gypsy life,
To the gull's way and the whale's way where the wind's like a whetted knife;
And all I ask is a merry yarn from a laughing fellow-rover,
And a quiet sleep and a sweet dream when the long trick's over.

(John Masefield's Sea-Fever)

Finis

With Martin at Swanage

View of stern and raised rudder

Research II at anchor in Swanage

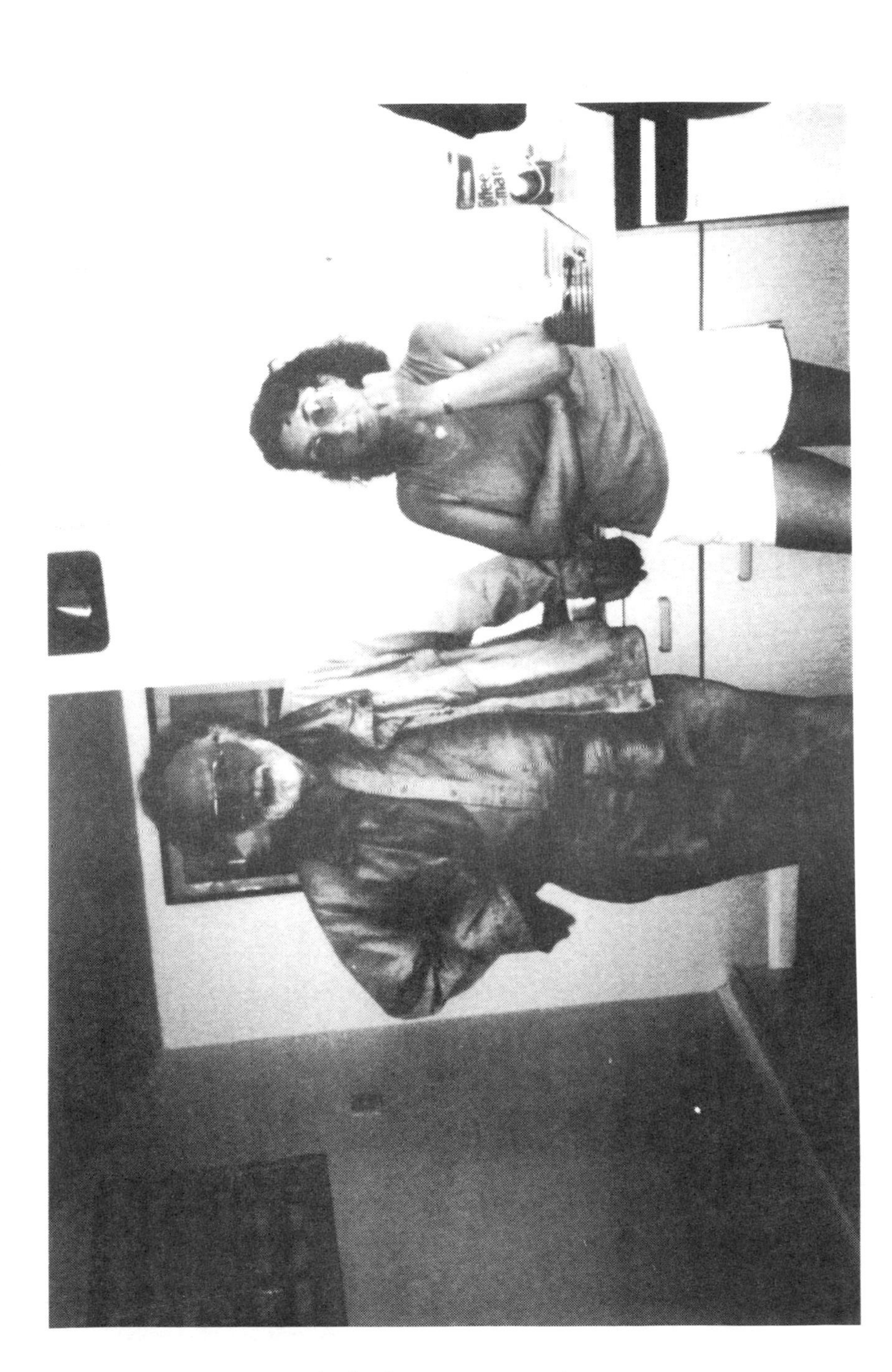

In the look-out room with Lucy

Standing in Aultbea with my father's church in the background